WWE LEGENDS

SUPERSTAR
BILLY
GRAHAM

WWE LEGENDS

SUPERSTAR BILLY GRAHAM

Tangled Ropes

Superstar Billy Graham

with Keith Elliot Greenberg

POCKET BOOKS

World Wrestling Entertainment® BOOKS

New York London Toronto Sydney

POCKET BOOKS, a division of Simon & Schuster, Inc.
1230 Avenue of the Americas, New York, NY 10020

Photos on pages ii–iii, 2, 88, 124, 157, 177, 183, 200, 208, 215, 237, 278, 338 Courtesy of *Pro Wrestling Illustrated* Photographs. Photos on pages 4–41, 52, 62, 126, 136, 146, 160, 163, 187, 227, 242, 254, 265, 303, 309, 314, 323 Courtesy of Wayne Coleman. Illustration on page 44 Courtesy of Jerry Lawler. Photos on pages 105–115 Courtesy of Viktor Berry. Photo on page 191 Courtesy of George Napolitano. Photo on page 282 Courtesy of Mariana M. Rogers. Photo on page 319 Courtesy of the Gillroy family.

Library of Congress Cataloging-in-Publication Data

Graham, Billy, 1943—
   WWE legends : Superstar Billy Graham : tangled ropes / Superstar Billy Graham with Keith Elliot Greenberg.
   p. cm.
   1. Graham, Billy, 1943– 2. Wrestlers—United States—Biography. 3. Doping in sports. 4. World Wrestling Federation—History. I. Greenberg, Keith Elliot, 1959– II. World Wrestling Entertainment, Inc.

GV1196.G73A3 2006
796.812'092—dc22
[B]
                                                         2005049170

ISBN-13: 978-1-4165-0753-6
ISBN-10:   1-4165-0753-1

This Pocket Books hardcover edition January 2006

10 9 8 7 6 5 4 3 2 1

POCKET and colophon are registered trademarks of Simon & Schuster, Inc.

Design by Charles Kreloff

Visit us on the World Wide Web
http://www.simonsays.com
http://www.wwe.com

Manufactured in the United States of America

For information regarding special discounts for bulk purchases, please contact Simon & Schuster Special Sales at 1-800-456-6798 or business@simonandschuster.com.

FOR VALERIE

Who sometimes I believe was doomed to love me. She was an innocent young girl and my sweet virgin angel. Valerie knows about loss, has seen pools of tears beneath her feet along with shattered dreams. But through it all she remains by my side, and I know if the flesh fell off of my face she would still be here to care. She is my soul mate and true companion, my covenant woman. Not only do I dedicate this book to her, but my life as well. It was destiny that brought us together.

FOREWORD

It was August 24, 2003, a normal Sunday afternoon in Phoenix, where it was about 100 degrees and I was sweating Crisco (dry heat, my Oklahoma backside!). It was WWE's annual summertime extravaganza known as *SummerSlam,* headlined by an Elimination Chamber match for the paying customers. But behind the scenes a very different kind of main event was going down that scorching day in Arizona. After years of exile, years filled with controversy and near-death experiences, that was the day that former WWE Champion and future WWE Hall of Famer Superstar Billy Graham physically returned "home" to rejoin his WWE brethren and to slowly begin to mend fences and establish new relationships within the company he helped build.

But not everyone was overjoyed to see Superstar.

Some people have long memories, and to "old school" wrestling people, forgiveness, in their eyes, has to be earned. Right or wrong, that's just the way it is.

This was the first time I ever personally met Superstar, even though I had heard a truckload of stories about this colorful character from many of our mutual friends and acquaintances from my over thirty-plus-year career in "the business." I had no issues with Billy, no grudges, no bad experiences or memories. He didn't owe me money, he had not no-showed an event I was involved with, and while I did not know him personally I felt badly for him that day. While many of the WWE Superstars embraced Billy like a returning brother who had been absent from the family for years, others gave the former WWE Champion the cold shoulder. I felt uncomfortable for Billy because of how some were snubbing him, but I don't know if Billy was even aware of it that day. Superstar Billy Graham was back as the center of attention and receiving accolades from wrestlers, many of whom he had never met, and loving every minute of it!

You see, Superstar Billy Graham isn't Switzerland—he's not neutral—on any subject. Superstar is a guy who has always been a lightning rod of controversy, and as a peer or coworker you either liked him or you did not. There was no gray area when it came to Superstar and how people felt about this man, who could arguably be considered the first sports entertainer . . . EVER. (In all due respect to Gorgeous George.)

But, cutting to the chase, Superstar Billy Graham is simply lucky to be alive today.

He should have died several times, but he was always able to get a foot on the rope before the fatal three count went down. It's funny how that works. Billy won the WWE title from the legendary Bruno Sammartino in 1977 in Baltimore by using both feet on the ropes to "rob" the Living Legend of the coveted championship. Ironically, when Billy lost the WWE title to Bob Backlund, a little less than a year later, once again Billy had his foot on the bottom rope as he was pinned by Backlund. It almost seems like God has put Billy's feet not only to the fire a few times but near the ropes, as well.

I respect Superstar for many things, but especially for the innovative stylings he brought to "the business." Superstar's physique was "freak of nature" material, but he has paid dearly for how he attained his "twenty-two-inch pythons." Superstar was one of the very first wrestlers to fully grasp the psychology and importance of how to verbally communicate with the paying customers and with wrestlers, who to this very day utilize this art form Billy perfected. He influenced the careers and in-ring personas of Hulk Hogan, Jesse "The Body" Ventura, Dusty Rhodes, Austin Idol, Big Papa Pump Scott Steiner, and another lifelong fan of Superstar's, Triple H, to name a few. That's a helluva legacy.

Billy Graham has been many things in his life, albeit none of them were of the low-key, Ward Cleaver variety. He has been, among other things, a competitive bodybuilder, a contestant in strong-man contests, a bouncer, a pro football player, an evangelist, a motivational speaker, and a pro wrestler of worldwide stature. He has run afoul of the law, has been physically abused by legendary wrestler and trainer of wrestlers Stu Hart, has clashed with the business's biggest and most powerful promoters, went on *Donahue* to rant on Vince McMahon, and probably attempted a thousand times to "get rich quick." He has had issues with exes, his children, and, as I have mentioned, has almost died more than once.

What a life. What a story. This book details in brutal honesty the life of one of the most colorful, controversial, and candid individuals I have encountered in my almost four decades in "the business."

I am happy that I can call Superstar Billy Graham my friend. I have also had the privilege of meeting and getting to know his wife, a saint who without a doubt heaven sent to be the Superstar's soul mate. Valerie has gone through more hell with Billy than any woman should have to endure in nine lifetimes. This is really their story. It's a story of living . . . dying . . . and surviving.

Drugs, sex, rock'n'roll, wrestling, preaching, beautiful people, famous friends and more are all a part of this incredible story. This is one book you will not soon forget.

—Jim "J.R." Ross

THE NUMBER ONE CREATION

Ravage away, demons of sorrow
Unleash your armies, devils of pain
Your dark magic can't dim the memories
Of Superstar Billy Graham's golden reign

—poem by Jeff Marshall,
literature professor and wrestling fan

I wasn't supposed to be here.

By October 2002, I'd become a literal shell of the man who'd sold out Madison Square Garden nineteen times, when the world knew me not by my birth name of Eldridge Wayne Coleman, but as Superstar Billy Graham, perhaps the first modern "sports entertainer" in the pro wrestling fraternity. Now, when I stepped out of the shower, I'd shift my back to the mirror and turn out the light to avoid glancing at my reflection, knowing that my withered body could never measure up to what it was in my glory years—

charismatic, bronzed and blond, a spectacle with bulging veins, twenty-two-inch "pythons," and a rap that was more responsible for my drawing power than my actual wrestling ability.

"I am the sensation of the nation. The number-one creation."

Twenty-five years had passed since 1977, the year I became heavyweight champion of the World Wide Wrestling Federation (WWWF), the company now known as World Wrestling Entertainment (WWE). Our business was divided into dozens of regional promotions, but the WWWF was the biggest, stretching from Bangor, Maine, down to the nation's capital. Of all the towns around the horn, New York was the focal point of the territory, and—in my opinion—the criterion for everything.

It was a city that was both terrible and wonderful. In the places where my fans came from—Queens, Brooklyn, and the Bronx—the Son of Sam, a man later exposed as a pudgy postal worker, slaughtered innocent lovers passing time in their cars, then sent taunting letters to the press, convinced that his neighbor's dog had commanded him to kill. In midtown Manhattan, people were bathing in coke-induced disco decadence at Studio 54, while downtown on the Bowery, others were rebelling against it, as punk rock went through its toddler stage at CBGB's. The Bronx was burning—with landlords torching tenements that were no longer worth the bother—but nowhere as brightly as in Yankee Stadium, where Reggie Jackson fought the team's owner, manager, and the rest of the American League, slamming baseballs in the direction of the number 4 train that rumbled on the tracks behind the bleachers.

The city crackled with kinetic energy, and I was part of it. From the corporate towers of Wall Street to the heroin dens off Times Square, New York venerated Superstar Billy Graham, getting down on one knee in the middle of the ring at the Garden and flexing, while my manager, the Grand Wizard, stood behind me—in wraparound shades and a red, white, and blue sequined turban with a feather sticking out of the top—grooming my glowing locks with a comb he reserved for just such occasions. I wrestled Bruno Sammartino, symbol of immigrant pride, and took his title away by pinning him with my feet on the ropes. I fought Andre the Giant, the "Eighth Wonder of the World." I dragged the "American Dream" Dusty Rhodes around the ring with a bullrope. And I'd stroll out of the Garden and hail a cab as cops, pretzel men, and street walkers looked on in wonder. Because I was the Superstar, and I had that patter I learned as a teenage evangelist to lift up a struggling city and fill its soul.

"I'm the man of the hour, the man with the power. Too sweet to be sour."

Back then, I thought that I was indestructible, a concept enhanced by my gluttonous consumption of anabolic steroids. But thirty years later, I was paying the devil his due in large, painful doses. Nearly three decades of ingesting reckless amounts of Delatestryl, Winstrol, and Deca Durabolin had eroded away my joints—my ankle was fused with bone from my pelvic area, both of my hips had been replaced, and my spine was collapsing. Hepatitis C had decayed my liver to the point of failure. My mind was confused because of the release of ammonia into my brain. My urine was as brown as Coca-Cola.

I was going to die.

Then, on October 18, Katie Gillroy, a beautiful woman I'd never met, was riding in the passenger seat of a pickup truck on Interstate 17, near Cactus Road, just a few miles from my apartment in Phoenix, Arizona. Police

That's Vance, Annette, Joyce, and me in the middle.

think the driver might have been cut off by another car and hit the brakes too hard, skidding into the median and flipping over. Katie was ejected from the vehicle and hit the guardrail. At 3:00 A.M., she was declared brain-dead.

Katie was only twenty-six years old—vibrant, healthy, funny, and caring. She volunteered at the Humane Society, raised a small son as a single mother, and—when she was just a teenager—showed maturity and compassion far beyond her years. She signed her donor card. With that simple, selfless act, Katie saved my life.

I don't think it's fair that Katie Gillroy died at such a promising age, and left me on this earth with her liver transplanted in my body. I never imagined that God would *literally* give me a second chance at life. I've asked him about this, but I haven't heard back. Yet, here I am, still alive after all my mistakes, able to bask in the sun of the Arizona desert, hear the voices of my wife and grandchildren, and tell you the unvarnished story of Superstar Billy Graham.

There weren't any pyrotechnics or entrance music when I made my debut in this world on June 7, 1943. But I never needed those kinds of gimmicks to get a pop. Even in the delivery room, there was a lot of screaming.

I was a breech baby, coming out of my mother feetfirst. As I was being delivered, my umbilical cord wrapped around my neck. I was wiggling around a lot, and the doctor was scared that I'd strangle myself. So he drenched me in ether. Then he sent me home, still doused in the flammable liquid. Everybody smoked in my family—my mother, my dad, my uncles—and it's incredible that the house didn't blow up.

That was the *first* miracle in my life.

My mom, Juanita Bingaman, came from Paris, Arkansas. She had black hair and strong features and, somewhere in her past, was descended from Arkansas Cherokee. Throughout my life, I always felt an affinity toward Native Americans. I wore turquoise on wrestling interviews and incorporated it into the oil paintings I did at home—aged Native American hands polishing blue stone; a warrior standing in front of his horse, his spear and shield held together with strips of leather. Part of me empathized with the outsider status forced onto the Native Americans on their own soil.

Nonetheless, I'm convinced that my interest in Native American culture has less to do with my own ancestry than the fact that my parents chose to raise me in Arizona, among the Hopi, Navajo, and Apache, as well as the cacti, Painted Desert, and Joshua trees.

I was the last of Juanita's four children. I shared a father—Eldridge John Coleman—with my sisters Annette, six years older than me, and Joyce, two years my senior. My brother, Vance, was born in Arkansas in 1933, the product of a romance between my mother and some boy down there. I was very proud of Vance—

he fought in the Korean War, and became a police captain in Phoenix—and have a framed photo of him in uniform next to my writing desk at home. But his presence in our household nearly split my family apart.

> **Joyce Coleman Sampson (Superstar Billy Graham's sister):** *My older brother was born out of wedlock. My grandfather chased the happy couple down before they could get married, and told my mother, "You're coming home with us." My grandfather said, "This boy will be raised in our home." He never gave the father a chance.*
>
> *I have no idea what happened to that young man. But when Vance was about six years old, my mother met my father, Eldridge John Coleman. My father had bad feelings toward Vance. He never adopted our brother. So Vance's name was Bingaman, and the rest of us were Colemans.*
>
> *When my mother's parents moved to Arizona, she moved, too. And she told my dad, "I don't care if you come to Arizona or not. I'm going, and I'm taking my son." She was going to divorce my dad because he wouldn't accept my older brother. But my father eventually followed her to Arizona.*

I never knew that my first name was Eldridge until I wrestled in Japan and had to show my birth certificate to get a passport. Everybody called me Wayne. In fact, many of my close friends and family members still do. When you play a character for as many years as I played Superstar Billy Graham, there's going to be some overlap. But—while other guys lose themselves in their personas—I never stopped being Wayne Coleman.

My father came from Mississippi, raising chickens and turkeys on the family farm, while my grandfather, Tom Coleman, plowed the fields by mule. As a young man, my dad had wavy brown hair, a strong, chiseled face, and deep-set eyes. According to some relatives, at six-foot-four and more than two hundred pounds, he bore a striking resemblance to Superstar Billy Graham. As the city of Phoenix expanded, my dad drove telephone poles into the ground for the local power company, Arizona Public Service (APS). He used to wear shoes with metal hooks and clasps on the front and a belt that looked like a six-shooter, so he could climb up and wrap himself around the poles.

But I never saw *that* Eldridge John Coleman. By the time I was born, my father was no longer tanned or vigorous. Multiple sclerosis had driven him out of the sunlight and into a job as a shop foreman. In time, his face became puffy. The muscle between his thumb and index finger started to concave. Our backyard became overgrown, and my mother had to push him

My dad is the second guy from the right.

around in his wheelchair and pick him up to put him on the commode. I remember her having hernia surgery from lifting him so much.

My dad tried medicating himself with alcohol, but the intoxicants never soothed him. He gambled and always came up short. And because I was the youngest one in the house, he took out his frustrations on me.

According to my mother, I didn't walk until I was nearly three years old. There was nothing physically wrong with me. I was just afraid. Beset with his own insecurities over his body's limitations, my father expected perfection from his offspring. If I hesitated or stumbled, he beat me down. So I stayed down. The one time my mother stepped forward to protect me, she also became a victim; my father broke her arm.

> ***Joyce Sampson:*** *Wayne* was *a slow learner. He didn't learn to walk fast, he didn't learn to speak fast, and he was uncoordinated. And my father tried to shake that out of him. It was like he was saying, "Vance is not my son. You're my son. And you'll be strong and healthy!"*

Arizona had been a state for only thirty-one years when I was born. The city of Phoenix was sprinkled with lettuce, cotton, and cantaloupe fields, but changing fast. Between 1940 and 1950, the city's population increased sixty-

A man among boys. I'm the shirtless one in the top row.

three percent—between 1950 and 1960, three hundred percent. Today, there are nearly 1,400,000 people in Phoenix; in the 1990s, it trailed just New York City in U.S. population growth. It's incredible. The orange and grapefruit groves have been leveled and turned into strip malls and gated housing developments. The desert sand we couldn't give away is worth hundreds of thousands of dollars per acre.

I grew up in a squat, stucco house, smaller than some of the hotel rooms I occupied while working for the WWWF, with a parched driveway along the side leading to a detached garage. At one point, my father had some guys from work pour cement in the backyard to create a square above-ground pool for physical therapy. Then he became really sick and never finished the project. But the empty shell remained, a symbol of frustrated hopes, for years and years.

One of the problems with my dad was that his mind never slowed down, even as his body wasted away. He was always a creative guy, using car batteries to craft an electric wheelchair for himself, with a specially designed joystick. He invented a tool for guys working for the power company—a long rod for stringing wire from below—and wanted to patent it. But like the pool for physical therapy, it just didn't happen.

His brother, Herb, also had a disability, but a completely different outlook. When he was a furniture builder back in Mississippi, Herb was pushing a hunk of wood through a huge saw and sliced off his arm, just below the elbow.

"If somebody ever tells you he cut his arm off and it didn't hurt," he used to joke, "don't believe him."

After the accident, Herb moved to California and built a competition hydroplane. He did all the complicated welding and repair with one arm, and went through life with a smile on his face and the attitude of a winner. But Herb's problems had ended the day he unwrapped the gauze around the stump of his arm. When my father looked into the future, there was nothing waiting for him but more hardship.

There was a little strip of sidewalk in front of our house, then a patch of grass where the city had built an irrigation culvert—a circular concrete block with a metal handle on top. Sometimes it would overflow and flood the lawn. On summer nights, though, I remember sitting on top of the culvert with a kid from the block, looking at the stars and talking about whether or not God was up there.

In Sunday school—my mother was Church of Christ, my father a nonobservant Baptist—I developed a lifelong fascination with the story of Noah's Ark. As a child, my mind danced with images of the animals walking into the ark, two by two, while Noah's neighbors laughed and scorned him. As I grew older, I read about ancient rocks being found in places like the Grand Canyon—layered on top of newer rock. I heard about fossilized fish discovered at the peaks of very high mountains. Could the glaciers have come through and created these phenomena? Or is this proof of a worldwide flood?

Today, scientists are exploring the possibility of a global deluge that would have covered the highest mountaintops. Some experts believe that this natural disaster would have required more than five times the volume of all the oceans on earth. But where would the water come from, and recede to?

How did the penguins from the South Pole and polar bears from the Arctic Circle get onto the ark? Were they even there? In the natural world, these animals would never have made it. But with divine intervention, they could have been transported.

What happened *after* the ark came to rest on Mount Ararat in eastern Turkey? How did the alligators and hippos make it down? Could the delicate gazelles have traveled over the cracks and crevices? It's not even close to being logical. Again, that's before you take the hand of God into account.

My interest in Noah's Ark led to other fixations. To this day, I wonder

My dad and me.
I'm eight here.

how the earth spins on its axis. What triggered that? Was there a divine plan to rotate and tilt the planet, and have seasons? There's too much mathematical complexity in the universe for *everything* to have started by accident—in a primordial soup of mud.

When I wasn't pondering such mysteries, I'd occasionally engage in more pedestrian activities. Phoenix was not a significant wrestling town when I was a kid, but we did receive broadcasts on the old Dumont Network from the Marigold Arena in Chicago. Sky Hi Lee was a mammoth wrestler from Canada, afflicted with acromegaly—or "giantism"—the same disease that infiltrated Andre the Giant's body. When he appeared on the screen, I was awestruck. He took bites out of lightbulbs and chewed on razor blades. But the thing that intrigued me the most was when he pierced his pecs with a sharp steel pin, underneath the nipple, drawing no blood. There had to be bleeding—right?! Unless Sky Hi Lee was satanic.

I don't remember a lot of adult supervision. In third or fourth grade, I was playing army with a little pal, and we decided to dig a foxhole on the side of his house. He had a real shovel, and I had a real pick—a pick a miner would use if he wanted to smash through rocks and hunt for gold. We were turned in opposite directions from each other, and—as my friend was bending over—I accidentally cocked back the pick and caught the poor kid just near the spine.

He let out these ungodly screams. Then his mother came out of the house and began yelling, "My son! Oh, my God! My son!"

The pick was still in the kid's back.

I ran home, and he was rushed into surgery. Because I missed his spine, thank God, there wasn't any kind of paralysis. But my parents were from backwood country, raised to discipline their kids by beating them with switches from weeping willow trees. Unfortunately for me, somebody had transplanted weeping willows into Phoenix. Now I was told to go out to our tree, break off my own branch, peel the leaves off the switch, and bring it back in.

Needless to say, I got a pretty good lashing.

Phoenix looks a lot different today than it did when I was growing up there in the forties and fifties, so I often forget about this period of my life. But on those occasions when I pass a weeping willow tree, it all comes right back.

Once we moved to a different part of town, into a house without a weeping willow tree out front, my father found a different way to punish me—taking off his belt, backing me into a corner, and whaling away. Sometimes I asked for trouble. Sometimes I didn't. Once, when I was walking home from school, I saw an old, abandoned house that was going to be gutted and renovated. So I picked up a rock and threw it through the window. One of my sisters told on me, and when I got home, off came the belt. I didn't really think this was fair because the windows were going to be taken out anyway. It's not like I vandalized Senator Goldwater's home, or anything like that.

My mother would be right in the middle of these beatings, screaming for my father to stop—until one day, I didn't go into the corner. I just stood there and faced my dad as he sat in his wheelchair, looking ever more gaunt, with the strap clutched in his nicotine-stained fingers. When he swung, I caught the belt and pulled it out of his hands. Here he was, getting weaker, and I was growing stronger, right in front of his eyes. There was nothing that he could do. As relieved as I was to be putting an end to the beatings, I felt sad for my father. He was wasting away.

> *Joyce Sampson: Wayne was a big boy his whole life. The last time I hit him, I was eleven years old, and I hit him in the head with a brick because he was too big to hit with anything else. That could have caused some of his problems later on.*
>
> *He was nine.*

Even in elementary school, I was able to play football with high school kids. In one game, I got hit so hard that I broke my collarbone. It was sticking up through my skin as I pedaled home on my bicycle. The doctors put me in a wraparound cast, with a big, jagged piece on the inside, digging into my back. The pain and itching were excruciating. I'd rub against a spot in the house where two walls joined together, and stick a coat hanger down the plaster and scratch. Everybody said I was just experiencing normal cast itch and complaining too much. It wasn't until the cast was removed and my parents saw the three-inch indentation in my back that I was vindicated.

It was around this time that I started to become an artist, drawing and painting. I built a mobile for my fifth-grade class at the Whittier School—a mobile that kind of looked like a globe, with a few abstract items hanging from it—and received an A on my report card as a result. I suspended my project from the ceiling with fishing wire, and made the frame with copper wire from my dad's job; they had rolls and rolls of the stuff for telephone lines. The experience exemplifies the complexity of our relationship—my dad had been giving me all these beatings, yet he offered to take me down to work to help me with my art.

I also began challenging my physical abilities. We used to play softball

Mom and Dad. You can feel the heaviness of spirit.

next to a basketball court outside our school. The cafeteria was just to the side of the third baseline. I knew there were teachers in that room, taking their breaks, and I wanted to pull a foul ball so it would crash through the cafeteria window. Utilizing both athletic skill and mental strength, I stood at home plate until I accomplished that goal. As warped as this sounds, when I drove that ball through the glass and teachers went scattering everywhere, I became a hero.

At the Boys Club near my house, I started to get involved in track and field events; at that age, the broad jump was my forte. During a visit to one of the coach's offices, I spotted a can of Bob Hoffman's Protein Pills. Bob Hoffman had a bodybuilding magazine, in which he editorialized about the fortifying powers of the supplements he just happened to market. I believed every word, and when no one was around, I stole the entire can.

But as I was walking home, I became frightened that I was going to get caught. There was only one choice—hiding the evidence. There's a fight-or-flight response in everyone. And with a huge release of adrenaline, I began eating the pills by the handful. They were carob, and by the time I arrived at my house, I'd finished all 150.

I threw up as soon as I stepped through the door—but my long, dark journey into the clandestine acquisition of performance-enhancing supplements was under way.

For reasons I'll never really fathom, the neighborhood bully seemed preoccupied with me. Because of my size, most of the kids my age left me alone. But this guy was in eighth grade when I was in fifth. I remember him having a lot of pimples on his face; I guess his hormones were making him aggressive. Whenever he saw me, he'd promise to "pants" me—remove my Levi's and string them on the flagpole.

I didn't know what to do. So I told my brother, Vance. Vance was one of the toughest guys I ever met, but he was twenty years old at the time, ready to go over and fight in the Korean War. He wasn't about to swagger into the playground and beat up an eighth-grader.

"Look," Vance said, "you're gonna have to fight this kid on your own. It's the only way you're gonna learn to take care of yourself."

I avoided the bully for as long as I could. Then, on a scorching hot day in May, as I was shooting baskets, he saw me.

"Hey, Coleman, are you ready to get *pants*ed?"

He came up to me, sweating, with the pimples bursting on his face. I bounced the ball to him. "Would you like to shoot some baskets?" I asked, ignoring his previous comment.

I was trying to work him. And he went for it. We shot baskets for a while, then he moved on. He didn't exactly become my friend, but I never had to fight him. Along with my physical gifts, God had blessed me with charisma and a sharp mind—and this wouldn't be the last time I used them to escape an uncomfortable encounter.

Before Vance left for the service, though, he wanted me to start working out—it didn't matter to him that I was only in the fifth grade. When I came out of school one day, Vance was waiting in his car, and drove me to his gym on Washington Street in downtown Phoenix. The place was on the second floor, across the street from the historic police building where my brother would later work. The vision of these weightlifters, walking around in their black muscle shirts with their arms bulging out, just captured my imagination. I wanted to be a bodybuilder, too.

It wasn't going to be easy. Almost instantly, I got stuck with 80 pounds of weight on my chest at the bench press. I couldn't budge the bar, and someone had to come over and take the weights off me. Then I went over to the squat rack. But I didn't understand physics, and wasn't sure how to balance the weights on the bar. When I unloaded 200 or so pounds from one side, the loaded end crashed to the ground and the bar flew up out of my hands, smashing through the window like a javelin, raining shattered glass on all those people on the sidewalk below.

When the day was over, though, I asked Vance to bring me back. The seed had definitely been planted. Soon, my room was covered with magazine photos of John Grimek, Steve Reeves, and other bodybuilders.

I think I needed bodybuilding because my treatment at home caused some major self-esteem problems. As soon as I hit adolescence, I had acne. So when the whole family made ice cream together in the summertime— and I did the churning for a solid hour—I couldn't eat any. "You don't need any more pimples, Wayne," everyone would say. No one had a clue that my *hormones* had caused my acne, not sugar.

Once, we were in the family car, driving out to Los Angeles to see some of my mother's relatives, and my father looked at me in the backseat through the rearview mirror.

"Why can't you get rid of those damn pimples?" he grunted condemningly. How do you think that makes a kid feel when he's already so insecure?

While Vance was in Korea, I made my own weights—screwing together metal bands from my dad's job, twisting them into a circular shape, and pouring concrete down the middle. I'd place a pipe in the center of the cement and turn it around until the concrete dried. Then I had a hole for the bar. I used this method to make six big plates, about 40 pounds apiece. I made smaller plates, too. When I wanted dumbbells, I had a similar system, filling Folger's coffee cans with cement.

At fourteen, I was playing Pony League baseball—just above Little League level—generally walking the two miles or so between the diamond and my home. One afternoon I was taking a shortcut, and happened to glance into some guy's front yard. He had an entire gym there: a bench press, chin-up bar, lat machine, and dumbbells all set up on the lawn. I went right up to the front door and knocked. A fairly attractive woman named Sandy answered.

"Whose gym is this?" I asked.

"My husband, Roy's. He and his friend Chester like working out."

Training with my concrete weights.

"Even in the summer, here in Arizona?"

"Yeah. They just wait until the sun goes down and work out under the porch light."

This is cool, I thought. "I'd like to work out with these guys," I offered.

"You can come over any time you want."

I took her up on her offer. Chester worked in a welding shop, and Roy drilled water wells. He was a bodybuilder and was getting ready for a physique contest. Once he came home from work every day, Sandy cooked him a huge dinner, and he'd start pumping iron.

"How can you work out after such a big meal?" I asked him one day.

"It doesn't bother me," he said. "Let's hit it."

After a few weeks, I began to feel like part of the family. Roy would hook a little lightbulb at the top of the doorway, and we'd pose under it, like we were in some competition. One night, everyone was sitting around when

Sandy mentioned, "You know, it gets so hot during the daytime that I walk around the house nude." She smiled. "No air conditioner."

I don't think I did a very good job of containing my surprise. "Really? *Nude?*"

"Yeah, when Roy's at work and Chester's busy in the welding shop, I just walk around nude. I can't stand the heat."

"Really?" I replied, trying to play it casual. Then, "What time of the day do you usually do this?"

She was giving me all this information in front of her husband, but he seemed oblivious. Chester was sitting there, squinting through his glasses and grinning. I'd had the impression that Chester lusted for Sandy. But she wasn't talking to Chester. She was talking to me.

"Where does Roy work, by the way?" I inquired.

"About thirty miles from here."

"Does he ever come home early?"

"Never."

This seemed too good to be true, but it wasn't. When I stopped by a few days later, Sandy was more than happy to treat an inexperienced teenager to some afternoon delight—a craving I indulged in for the remainder of that long, hot summer.

Soon, though, I didn't have to visit the house anymore. When I was fifteen, my father made me an offer. If I would massage his feet once a day, he'd buy me a membership at a place like the one where Vance worked out. It was heartbreaking. His circulation problems were so severe that he needed his fifteen-year-old son—the kid he'd been smacking around since birth—to *massage his feet.* Money was tight in our family, and a gym membership was a luxury. But I took it and, in the process, managed to create even more distance between myself and my dad's moods—turning the garage into my bedroom.

Joe Ehlers, North High track team captain, 1957–58: No one felt comfortable visiting Wayne's home. You could tell there was a lot of disharmony. His father was in the wheelchair. There was just an eerie feeling that things weren't right. You'd come in, say hello, and just want to get away.

Our school had quite a reputation for sport. We had all these multiple athletes on the track team. When Wayne was in eighth grade, he was at the meet where Jim Brewer set a national record, clearing 15 feet in the pole vault. During Wayne's freshman year, Dallas Long set a national high school record for the shot put—

69 feet and 3¾ inches. Dallas would compete for our coach, Vern Wolfe, at USC (University of Southern California) and win a bronze at the Rome Olympics in 1960 and a gold at the Tokyo Games in '64.

In 1959, Karl Johnstone threw the discus almost 200 feet.

Wayne was a pretty good-sized boy for his age, slender but very muscular. Outstandingly so. His specialty was the decathlon. At North High, if he'd continued at the pace he was going, he had the potential to be the greatest athlete of all of them.

From a distance, North High—with its earth-tone walls and simulated adobe roof—looked like any other school in the Southwest. But I'm still amazed by the quality of some of the people I met there.

It was exciting to be on the same team as guys like Joe Ehlers and Dallas Long. Joe ran the half-mile in 1:58.5 but treated me as a peer, even as a freshman. It's a lesson I never forgot. After becoming a wrestling headliner, I always remembered to make the lesser-known talent feel welcome.

After Coach Wolfe got to USC, twenty-four of his athletes set world records, and six became Olympic gold medalists. Anyone who met him knows why. When I first started at North High, we were throwing the shot put on the grass. Then I helped Coach Wolfe build a cement platform on the side of the football stadium. This was a coach who understood that the small touches meant a lot. A cement shot put ring was just one way of raising our standards.

I loved Coach Wolfe. One day he challenged me to a contest: who could walk the farthest upside down on their hands. I made it about ten yards, while my beloved coach walked the entire length of the football field—one hundred yards. I congratulated him and said, "I bet you can't do that in handcuffs."

"Go get them," he replied.

I wanted to perform well—for myself and our coach. And at fifteen, I was told that I was a few feet ahead of Dallas Long's freshman records in shot put and discus. I had unlimited potential.

My friends called me "Abs." I'd ask my friend Bob Calvan to hold my feet, while I did three sets of 500 sit-ups. But I believe the pronounced formation of my abdominal wall had as much to do with genetics as exercise. My calves looked better than at any other time of my life from running track. I developed my lats by doing bent-over rows—curving my body forward as I pulled weights up to my chest. I was very conscious of my appearance, and enhanced it by mixing iodine with baby oil when I tanned.

Many times on the way to school, I'd pass an apartment complex and duck into it, lying out on the lounge chairs by the pool. Sometimes I'd miss

the first couple of classes. But I definitely had the look. Even then, I was all about the look.

I had friends take pictures of me posing, like in the bodybuilding magazines, showing off the cuts and separation in my lat shots, turning my back to the camera to display the thickness of my delts, folding my arms behind me to emphasize my triceps. One of my ideas was having an amateur photographer I knew shoot me in my posing trunks, imitating the classic discus thrower pose with a ten-pound plate.

I was still a pimply-faced freshman, but I was running around with seniors—chiseled, handsome guys. These were the Casanovas of the school, and I wasn't in their league. But they let me hang around with them and pick up their leftovers.

When my sister Joyce was studying to be a beautician, I asked her to practice her budding trade on me. She was supposed to bleach my hair blond, but it turned out orange. I went to school anyway, walking into the cafeteria with my fiery mane. Every head turned. The students let out a collective gasp. Being an exhibitionist, I didn't mind the attention. But the principal sent me home.

A generation or so later, Vince McMahon put this incident in context for me: "Superstar, you were always years ahead of your time."

Joyce Sampson: As my father got sicker, the kids had to take on more work in our family—the yard, the housekeeping, the cooking. My father had been a big, muscular man, and a bit of a womanizer. He liked to have a good time. If there was a party going on, he was at the party. Now he couldn't take care of himself, and Wayne was growing bigger and bigger. And my father became even more angry and jealous.

When you come from an abusive home, you carry a lot of rage inside of you. And most likely, it isn't directed in the most intelligent way. As a pimpled-out, high-testosteroned teenager, I went out with trouble on my shoulder, always looking for a fight. So did my friends. We'd cruise up and down Central Avenue and get into fights with guys from other high schools. These fights created a pecking order that everyone knew about.

My friend Fred Hinkle was four years older than me, and loved to box; he once hit a speed bag so hard that it broke loose from its mooring. It was Fred who gave me these words of wisdom: "Wear work gloves when you fight." The thin leather would keep your hand compact, so you wouldn't break any knuckles and fingers when you were striking someone in the jaw.

It was also Fred who encouraged me to enter the 1959 Golden Gloves. I had a good right hook, and usually knocked people out in the first round. Taking note of my 210-pound frame, the newspapers described me as "The Giant"—a high school shot-putting star with professional boxing potential. My father came to some of my fights, and seemed really proud of me. Ironically, I lost in the finals to one of his coworkers—a really nice kid who loved my dad. I'd trained with this guy, and destroyed him in the gym. But this time, I held back a little bit because I liked him, and lost on a split decision.

Unfortunately, with all my other activities, I stopped caring about my grades. And to the disappointment of Coach Wolfe, Joe Ehlers, and some others who'd personally invested in me, I dropped out during my junior year.

Joe Ehlers: I didn't understand that at all. Wayne was surrounded by these great athletes. It was an incredible time, and he was in it. But he had so many things going on. There were the problems with his father. And he'd gotten himself involved with some young men who I felt were leading him astray. He lost his way.

I wasn't worried about making money. The city was getting bigger, and I'd already started digging ditches for an underground sprinkler system. When the workday was over, the fun started. At one point, I grew a goatee like my idol Steve Reeves, the actor who played Hercules in the movies. Every now and then, my bodybuilder friends and I amused ourselves by going to this lesbian nightclub on Van Buren Street and having fun with the clientele.

"Hey," I'd challenge, shirtless and tan and hitting a bicep pose, "don't you want some of this?"

Some of the women were appalled. Others laughed with us. And some, I was positive, thought about switching.

Yet I was extremely serious about my bodybuilding. I was now regularly entering contests, shaving my legs, chest, and arms for a better look. I still had pimples on my back. But, believe it or not, the acne scars on my face actually gave me a mature look when I competed.

Because airfare was not readily available to a lot of kids in the early sixties, Mr. Teenage America awarded East and West Coast championships. In 1961, I won the overall title for my part of the country; Frank Zane took the honors on the East Coast. Seven years after I stole that can of Bob Hoffman's Protein Pills, my photo was featured in Bob Hoffman's bodybuilding magazine *Strength & Fitness*. I thought that the award was tiny, so—like a wrestling heel—I stole the heat from the prize and made myself the focus of the picture, holding a magnifying glass to the trophy.

UNCTION OF THE HOLY GHOST

Peter replied, "Repent and be baptized, every one of you, in the name of Jesus Christ for the forgiveness of your sins. And you will receive the gift of the Holy Spirit."

—Acts 2:38

While I was still attending North High, Robert Allen Zimmerman was completing his senior year of high school in Hibbing, Minnesota. Then, like me, he'd pick up a gimmick name and embark on his road to glory through Minneapolis—ultimately hitting the big stage in New York City. For more than forty years, I'd find myself fascinated by Bob Dylan's nasal twang and sharp, poetic lyrics. But, also like Dylan at different stages of his career, I was about to find a deeper, spiritual influence in my life.

Beverly Swink Welch: *My late husband, James, and I were living in Phoenix with our two children, and had received a phone call from a*

Both Phoenix and me in the sixties.

couple we met at a Full Gospel Businessmen's convention. This was a group of born-again Christian businessmen with chapters in different cities and states, mostly in the South and Southwest, who helped fund fellowship activities around the country. This couple told us that their daughter and their son—an amateur weightlifter—had seen a picture of a boy from Phoenix in a bodybuilding magazine. God had put a burden on their heart that we contact this boy, Wayne Coleman, and lay the gospel on him. They prayed on it, and felt that, if we found him, he would become a Christian.

I believe in God, but this was freaking me out, the concept of contacting someone I didn't know and possibly interfering with his personal belief system.

I said, "Well, do you have a phone number and address?"

They told me, "No, but God will point you to the right person."

I'm saying, "Well, okay." This couple had been very nice to us, and I couldn't tell these people, I can't do this. So I opened the phone book and began calling Colemans.

When I finally found Wayne's family, a male voice answered the phone, "Well, what's this regarding?"

That's when I really got scared. I said, "I have some friends in Houston who want to meet Wayne Coleman."

Wayne wasn't home, but I left a number.

The Full Gospel Businessmen would get together, hold workshops, and bring in flamboyant evangelists like Katherine Khulman, the traveling healer, and Brother William Branham. They called themselves "Full Gospel" because they took the gospel literally. It says, "Lay hands on the sick, and they shall recover." They would literally lay hands on the sick, hoping to cure them with prayers of faith. They didn't believe that this power had ended in the days of the Apostles. All Christians had it through the ages, they contended, from day one. Their creed was, "God has never stopped performing miracles."

Bev and her husband knocked on my door and asked if I was Wayne Coleman. They were nice-looking people with a soothing manner. "We have a friend of ours in Houston, Texas," Bev told me, "with a daughter who has a burden to pray for you."

My mother was standing behind me, with my dad in his wheelchair, listening to the conversation.

"Would you like to come to church with our family?" Bev boldly requested.

"We're not church people," I answered.

"Well, can I give this girl your address, so she and her brother can write to you?"

Imagine that, I thought. *Write to me about* God?! I was just a kid. What was this woman talking about?

Bev left me her address and phone number, too, and I handed it to my mom and dad. "Good Lord, boy," my mother said, as soon as Bev was out of earshot. "These damn people are crazy. *God's* telling them to write to you? How stupid!"

A few days later, I received my first letter from the girl in Houston, Jenny, and her brother, Andy:

Dear Wayne,

We saw your photo in a bodybuilding magazine, and we want to pray that you'll accept Jesus Christ as your personal savior.

I'd never encountered anything like this before in my life. This was strange behavior.

At the time, I was driving my father to work in the mornings, and sometimes picking him up in the afternoons—loading him in and out of the car. One afternoon, I passed a dirt lot at Sixteenth and Roosevelt, where a tent was being erected. There was a billboard on the property, too, with big red letters over a white background:

YE MUST BE BORN AGAIN

I caught a glimpse of the sign, picked up my father, then looked at it again on the way home. Day after day, I continued to see this billboard, and all this activity. They were having a revival. After about a week, I decided that I was going to stop by the site, and see what all of this was about. I felt I was being drawn there.

The tent was packed with benches situated on sawdust—and people, shouting and swaying and singing.

Walking up the highway to heaven
Walking up the King's highway

The pastor was a legendary Baptist evangelist, Dr. John R. Rice, preaching about hellfire and brimstone, and how by simply dedicating yourself to Jesus—becoming born again—you could receive everlasting life. "Once saved, always saved," he promised. "Even if you're in the arms of a harlot with heroin in your veins, you will still make the Rapture."

At the end of the service, they had the "altar call," summoning people forward to be "born again." The preacher looked me dead in the eye and pointed. "Come on, son," he stated authoritatively. "It's your turn to be saved."

Man, I thought, *he's talking to me.*

And so I walked the "sawdust trail," as we say when a person becomes born again in a tent revival, past women with eyes shut tight and hands and fingers extended above their heads, and rosy-cheeked men with tears streaming down their faces, all feeling the power of the Holy Ghost. When I got to the altar, though, I realized that I didn't know how to pray.

Dr. Rice had "counselors" posted around the tent, and a man and woman—wonderful people exuding kindness and compassion—came over to me. "What you have to do," the man began, "is get down on your knees, confess your sins, and accept Christ as your savior because he died on the cross for all sinners."

"Confess my *sins?*" I hesitated. Here I was, getting into fights on Saturday nights with total strangers and messing around with girls. Those were a lot of sins. "Do I have to go through this one by one?"

The man replied that I just had to utter a blanket prayer: "God, I am sorry for all of my sins, and I accept Jesus Christ as my personal savior because he was nailed to a tree [inside terminology for the wooden cross at Calvary] for my transgressions."

I repeated these words, and added, "I receive you into my life as my Savior."

Looking over at the counselors, I questioned, "What else do I do?"

The woman responded, "Well, you need to tell God that you will serve him for the rest of your life, and thank Jesus for dying for you, and shedding his blood for the remission of your sins."

I followed her instructions. It was a blanket deal. I turned to the counselors. "So now I'm saved?"

"Yes. You are saved."

There had to be more to it than that, I thought, but the important thing was that I had truly repented. To be saved, you have to believe it in your heart, not just your mind. I had to keep my hands off the high school girls, and stop busting my knuckles on guys from other parts of Phoenix. That would be the hard part. The drinking ban imposed on a lot of born-again Christians didn't affect me because—thanks to the example my father set at home—I already abhorred alcohol.

> **Beverly Swink Welch:** *The phone rang, and it was Wayne. He said, "I'd like to go to church with you now."*
>
> *When we went to pick him up, and he came out of his house, I really got to see him from far away. He looked like a monster. He was so big that one of my little boys started to cry. But I said, "No, he's our friend, and he's going to church with us."*
>
> *I know his parents weren't happy about that at all.*

When I came back from that revival meeting, I felt great. I bounded through the door and told my parents, "Guess what? I've been saved." Well, I might as well have told them that I was bringing Jesus over as a house guest.

"What the hell do you mean, *saved?*" my mother asked. "Saved from what and by who?"

Joyce was incredulous. "If there's a God," she said, "can you tell me who made God? Who was there before?"

Right away, I was at war with my whole family.

My friends, at least, attempted to be understanding. Walking out of the gym one day, I was trying to explain my beliefs to one of the local Casanovas. "It's okay to serve God," he said, "and do what you want to do with God. But don't stop"—he pumped his arm—"the girls."

I invited one of my buddies to the Pentecostal church I attended with Beverly and her family. Unlike the Baptists, the Pentecostals shouted spontaneous praises to God, spoke in tongues, prophesized, and had healing ceremonies. My friend would go only if I agreed to attend a mass at his family's Catholic church. That seemed fair enough. At my church, people were joyfully shaking tambourines, banging drums, dancing, clapping, and praying for the sick. At his, people were quiet, kneeling and lighting candles. The priest was in his robe, and everything appeared holy, especially the stained-glass windows.

"This is better," my friend insisted. "More reverent."

One of the best things about becoming a born-again Christian was that I felt motivated to return to high school. My grades shot up; suddenly, I was pulling A's in subjects I'd been failing. I attributed everything to my conversion. I was a new person.

I'd lost my eligibility for the track team, but still hung around the field, working out with the guys. When they took their team picture, I jumped into the shot, standing in the top row of the bleachers, towering over everybody else. Compared to the other kids, I looked like a grown man—shirtless while my teammates were in their uniforms, bronzed, and smiling like a matinee idol.

> **Joe Ehlers, track team captain:** *Before one meet, Wayne asked Coach Wolfe if he could compete. He wasn't eligible, but the coach went against the grain and said yes. Wayne competed in bare feet that day—I still don't know why. His shot put was in the mid-60s, and the discus throw around 180. He could have been in the Olympics if he'd continued his training. There's no question in my mind.*

There are people who become born-again Christians because they yearn for stability in their lives. When *I* observed the whole Pentecostal scene, I saw adventure. Instead of getting my diploma from North High when I had a second chance, I left school, beginning my journey into evangelism.

Standing six-foot-five with his jet-black pompadour and movie-star countenance, Jerry Russell became my hero and role model. Jerry had been

Jerry Russell.

a maniac before he was saved, a violent youth and regular guest at the state prison in Florence, Arizona. Even after he began preaching, he signed all his correspondence with his prison ID number: 18139. I still have it memorized because Jerry used it in his testimonials: "I wasn't Jerry Russell. I was prisoner number 18139."

An outsider would say that Jerry had charisma. Christians called it anointing—he was anointed by the Holy Ghost to deliver a high message. The man could drain the emotions out of a church when he told his life story, yelling at God for his cursed earlier life, "Why did you do this to me? I hate your guts, God!" Then, he'd start weeping, as he told of his repentance. "I love you, Jesus!" he'd sob.

To me, Jerry was the embodiment of the term "on fire for God."

"Jesus of Nazareth!" he'd howl, sliding across the front of the church like Chuck Berry playing "Sweet Little Sixteen." "The Nazarene Carpenter! The Mighty Sea Walker!"

I wanted to meet him the first time I saw him preach, and soon he took me under his wing the way guys like Dr. Jerry Graham, Abdullah the

Butcher, Ray Stevens, and Pat Patterson would in my wrestling career. The connection between us was electric, and Jerry began calling me up to the pulpit to give my testimony, too.

"Hello, my name is Wayne Coleman. I'm a Mr. Teenage America, and I just got saved. Praise God. I love you guys."

Jerry would listen and critique: "You give revivals to *revive* the spirit of the folks who are serving God," he'd coach, "and to bring in new people to get saved."

On Central Avenue, we'd sit together in McDonald's as he schooled me on the impediments I might encounter on the revival circuit. "This is what you have to watch out for. You have to watch out for the Jehovah's Witnesses. You've got to get a book and learn their doctrine, so you can go against them. You have to learn about the Christian Scientists. You have to learn about the Mormons. These are cults, and you have to be ready to defend yourself. It's going to be spiritual warfare."

I also had to be wary of "lukewarm" churches, he argued. Lutheran, Episcopal, Presbyterian, even some Pentecostal churches, might be lukewarm if they were lax in their intensity for God. "You can't be on the fence," Jerry insisted. "There is no middle ground. Because God will spew all the lukewarm Christians out of his mouth."

He urged me to shave my underarms. When you preach, he explained, you sweat, and retain the moisture and odor. The first time I followed this advice, I didn't use any lather and ended up with a horrible rash. But I continued hanging on to every pearl of wisdom Jerry had to offer.

In his words, he was *discipling* me.

Like Vince McMahon, Jerry knew how to keep an audience primed and hungry. Vince does it with entrance music, pyrotechnics, and backstage vignettes. Jerry read a congregation's moods, and never gave away too much too soon.

Before a service, he'd duck into a side office and wait for the church to fill up. "If you're the guest preacher and people see you just sitting there in the front row," he told me, "you lose your impact."

With Jerry out of sight, a feeling of anticipation would saturate the room. Was he in the building yet? Was he even in the town? As the band played and the choir sang, the congregants rose, singing, swaying, throwing back their arms and heads, eyes tightly shut, communing with the Lord.

I'll fly away, Old Glory
I'll fly away in the morning
When I die, hallelujah, by and by, I'll fly away

Just as the last song was playing—with the people all primed and at a fever pitch—Jerry would materialize, sending chills through the room. The dark, tall, and handsome stranger had arrived.

It was no different than the feeling at a WWE show when the arena darkens, an eerie gong reverberates, organ music seeps through the public address system—and then, as the lights go on, there's Undertaker, a dramatic, solitary icon casting a shadow on the canvas. Pure show business.

Jerry's congregants never had a chance to come down. He'd bombard them with lightning oratory about Jesus Christ—the Prince of Peace, Lion of Judah, First and Last, Alpha and Omega.

There was always a definite cadence to his preaching: "Oh, *God-uh! Jeee-sus-uh!*" Each breath would be drawn out, each *"Praise God-uh"* delivered in a deep, resolute voice. It was a rhythmic tempo that seemed to emphasize the end of the world. That was the message at the time: the Second Coming of Christ was around the corner. All the things we were reading about in the press—evil on the march, advances in scientific knowledge—had been foretold.

"And suddenly came a sound from heaven, as if a mighty rushing wind."

Christ would return like a thief in the night. And if you weren't seeking forgiveness, he was leaving without you.

I sometimes wonder about the origin of the cadence that I heard in those churches. I imagine that the tone, the emphasis, the inflections, came from Africa. I *know* that the pulse of these sermons ended up in my wrestling promos—and most likely contributed to the special connection I had with my black brothers in the crowd.

Another parallel to the wrestling universe was the "us versus them" mentality. Society—"the world," as we called it—was judgmental, condescending, malevolent. Our attitude was no different than the paranoia members of the wrestling fraternity felt toward those interlopers everyone believed would "expose the business."

As my involvement in the world of evangelism grew, I drove a wedge between myself and "the world." I smashed my trophies with a hammer, justifying the desecration by quoting Matthew 6:19–20: "Do not store up for yourselves treasures on earth where moths and rust destroy. . . . Store up for yourselves treasures in heaven."

Jerry told me that street preaching was a rite of passage, a sign of boldness, an affirmation of your commitment to the Word. So I held court on the corner of Central and Washington in downtown Phoenix, bringing my hand down on top of a trash can or newspaper box the way Jerry slammed his palm on the pulpit.

"*You must be born again! Repent your sins and be filled with the Holy Ghost! Plant yourself at the foot of the cross, and grow into Jeees-us-uh! The Second Coming of Christ is at hand! Get ready for the Rapture, all you sinners!*" Standing on a street corner and screaming took a lot of nerve—or a lack of brains.

> *Joyce Sampson: Wayne had never been religious in his life. He had done all of these other things, hanging out with the bad guys in school—whether he admits it or not, they were bad guys—and then, all of the sudden, he's a preacher! Give me a break! My parents did not consider this a job. They felt that a job was when you worked eight to five, and came home at the end of the week with a paycheck. My mother had taught Sunday school at one time, and didn't believe the whole thing with Wayne. I thought he was nuts already, but this was a whole different thing. This was not normal.*

In the mornings, before the family woke up, I'd pace back and forth by the clothesline in our backyard, mimicking the affectations of Jerry Russell when he was entranced and talking to God. My father figured out that something was going on when he noticed that I'd worn out a path on the grass. One morning, he looked out the kitchen window and caught me, with my head down and my arms behind my back—an old biblical posture—spouting out, "*God-uh! Jeee-sus-uh! Praise your holy name!*"

In the past, when I'd clashed with my father, I had the rest of the family to defend me. Now, I was catching heat from everybody at home. They thought I was nuts, and I believed that they were all in desperate need of salvation. The situation just wasn't working; I wanted to be among Christians who understood and appreciated me. So I accepted an offer from Bev Swink to move in with her family.

> *Beverly Swink Welch: Wayne shared a room with one of my sons. One night at about ten o'clock, a Methodist minister I knew showed up at the door with a group of young people who'd just come back from a Christian retreat. There was a girl with them who looked like she was eight or nine years old. I thought, "This must be the minister's daughter. She looks so little."*

All of a sudden, she looked up at Wayne and spoke in this voice—I'm telling you the God's honest truth, I've never heard anything like it: "You can't frighten me. I'm stronger than you."

She started foaming at the mouth. The minister looked like he was going to faint. "That's not her voice," *he said. She fell on the floor, and kept talking in this horrible man's voice. I mean, it was gravelly. And Wayne's face turned white as snow.*

Back then, we used to pray for people who we thought were possessed. We'd lay hands on them, and try to cast out the demons in the name of Jesus—everything was done in the name of Jesus.

Beverly Swink Welch: The minister told us that when this girl was eight years old, her parents had done something that made her mad. So she said, "I'm gonna punish you. I'm not gonna grow anymore." *She was really about seventeen years old. I don't remember all the things she said, but they were scary. It was nasty.*

We all just knelt around her, and I was thinking, "Oh, my God. She's in my house. What am I going to do?" *I don't think anyone there had ever witnessed anything like this before.*

Everybody started praying that Jesus would help her, praying in Jesus' name. After about an hour, she just went limp with exhaustion. Evidently, she came out of it.

As I matured in the ministry, I lost my fear of demon-possessed people. Interestingly, in the born-again Christian circles where I travel today, I rarely encounter this situation anymore. Unless you're really at a church in the backwoods somewhere, you don't hear much about demon possession. It's too old-school. I now believe that a person who claims to be demon-possessed is probably schizophrenic, or has some other mental illness.

I was going on the road with Jerry Russell. The Full Gospel Businessmen had given him a powder blue Cadillac with a white roof; they could use it as a tax deduction, and he needed reliable transportation. Here I was, man. I felt the calling. I was going to be a Holy Ghost preacher. Jerry showed me how to write a sermon, taking one piece of scripture and building around it. This was big stuff, traveling the highways and byways and preaching the Word of God. I was on my way.

A year after I became Mr. Teenage America, Jerry and I camped out in this beat-up church in Gilbert, Arizona, for a revival. The place was filthy,

Proving to kids you don't have to be a "wimp" to serve God.

but we cleaned it up, scraping human feces out of the bathtub. There was only one room with a bed in the building. Jerry got the bed, of course. I slept on a blanket in front of the pulpit.

Sleeping at the foot of the pulpit, I thought. I'm liking this.

The revival was exhilarating. Jerry spoke about crossing the river Jordan, into his next life. "I'll be passing over the river someday!" he'd shout, breaking into unknown tongues with the people singing:

If you see my Savior, tell him that you saw me.
Tell him I am coming home someday.

There were "evil-doers" in the world, he said (that's a biblical term, by the way, not one invented by President George W. Bush), and for them, condemnation was certain. They would be cast into the flaming pit, tormented in the lake of eternal fire, their eardrums pierced by the sounds of wailing and gnashing teeth.

With Jerry's recommendation, and the help of some of the Full Gospel Businessmen, I was soon accepting solo invitations to small churches, doing altar calls, reciting the Sinner's Prayer with converts, laying hands on people. I was "Brother Coleman," and thought I was a healer. Deafness, blindness, I could make them all disappear, then show the sinners how to repent and save them from the fiery lake.

You didn't have to be a bookworm or a wimp to serve God, I'd preach, standing at the pulpit in shiny shoes, a white shirt, black pants, and a thin matching tie. With the elders of the church holding clasped hands over crossed legs on folding chairs behind me, I'd rip phone books in half and bend steel bars behind my neck.

I was embedded into the community of Holy Rollers. Girls could wear braided or bunned hair, flat powder, and natural lip gloss—no other makeup or gold earrings. These could entice men—or even women, I was told—to lust after them. When they played softball, they had to wear dresses; pants were strictly forbidden. Before a sermon in Page, Arizona, on the Utah border, I caught the female pianist goofing around, playing rock'n'roll. I immediately tracked down the pastor.

"Oh, God, pastor, she's playing worldly music in the sanctuary." This was contrary to our overriding message: Come out and be separate from the world. No dancing. No movies. No drinking. And, most important, no rock'n'roll.

She was just a kid—sixteen or seventeen years old. And I stooged on her for having a good time.

The next step for me was speaking in tongues, a euphoric type of jabber that's supposed to occur when the Holy Ghost comes into your body and fills it up. But first, I had to be baptized in the Holy Spirit. A group of Full Gospel Businessmen flew me, by private plane, up to a chapter meeting at a Flagstaff hotel. After prayer and testimonials, one of the speakers requested that all those who wished to be baptized in the Holy Ghost raise their hands and come forward.

I walked up to the speaker's podium and was immediately surrounded. The speaker spread his fingers, placed his hands on my head, and intoned,

"Please God, baptize this brother in the Holy Ghost and fire. Let him speak in other tongues."

The coaching began: "Come on, brother, start speaking, start speaking. Just start saying, 'Shan-da-da-la, shan-da-da-la,' and it will come." One man actually wrapped his hand around my jaw, to manipulate my mouth into chanting this heavenly language.

I didn't disappoint anybody. I'd heard others speaking in tongues before, so I imitated what I'd memorized. But I was faking. I was elated, ecstatic, and—in my opinion—overcome by the Holy Ghost. My hands were raised, my arms extended toward heaven, my head was lifted, and I couldn't stop.

The businessmen saw that I was having this experience and decided to drag/carry me to a private room so the rest of the service could resume. I remember being pulled through the hotel lobby, flailing my arms and wailing. For a brief moment, I opened an eye and caught a peek of the front desk, where the clerk was looking on in amazement. My sponsors positioned themselves under me, so I felt like I was levitating, and carried me onto the elevator.

In the hotel room, they placed me on the carpet, where the episode continued. I was kicking my feet, as they prayed over me, and accidentally knocked off one of my shoes. There were holes in my socks, and someone cried, "Oh, my God, somebody go and get this kid some socks!"

I flushed with embarrassment, yet kept going until finally—after an hour and a half—my exultation subsided.

"Wow," one of the businessmen noted, "you got a double portion of the Holy Ghost. Congratulations."

Another talent that I was trying to nurture was decoding the sounds of other people speaking in tongues. I figured that if I had the nerve to speak in tongues in front of a group of people, I could also interpret. So I began repeating translations I heard in the past: "I, the Lord, your God, will bless this church. I will increase this church in numbers because of your faithfulness. This revival will be a blessing to all, and many souls will be added to the Kingdom. Thus saith the Lord."

This was a very generic translation; I did not have the guts to do a doomsday interpretation.

It always ended with "thus saith the Lord" because the utterances were supposed to be coming directly from God. This took a lot of gall—and a lack of reverence—on my part. Where was the dignity?

In retrospect, I know that I was duping everybody. But I just wanted to be a part of things, speaking in tongues, interpreting tongues, healing the sick. After all, by that point I was an official minister, ordained by the Assemblies of God denomination. I had the papers to prove it.

In 1963, I traveled through Louisiana, preaching in the Bayou in simple little wood-framed churches, set back from the road. At the most, we could jam thirty-five people into these buildings, and it was always oppressively hot. Jack Moore was a successful builder and contractor who'd become a lay preacher, but was more interested in subsidizing evangelists who he believed could do a better job. When he invited me to preach at a Christian summer camp that he ran, I was thrilled.

> **Anna Jean Price, Jack Moore's daughter:** *We'd found out about Wayne through the Full Gospel Businessmen. His fame had spread pretty rapidly, and the Houston chapter president routed him to us.*
>
> *We had a tent, and swimming in the afternoon, classes in the morning, and by nighttime we'd end the day with music and prayer and little skits.*
>
> *The kids would follow Wayne all over the campgrounds. We'd do illustrated sermons—or plays—based on scripture, and Wayne played Samson. That was an easy one for him because Samson was so strong that he pulled down a whole building. Wayne understood the story well enough from a scriptural point of view that he could make it really serious at points. He could connect supernatural strength with the fear of God.*
>
> *We loved him and still love him. His influence on the young people had a permanent effect. They were convinced and convicted by the messages he gave to them, even though he dropped out of the church later on. If he came back today, those kids—who are in their fifties now—would just flock around him again.*

Regardless of how righteous I pretended to be, I was still a flesh-and-blood male, and felt the same stirrings as other guys my age. After one sermon in a small church in Tyler, Texas, I sat down in the front row to pray with a shapely Filipino woman in her thirties. She moved as close to me as she could, crossed her legs, and put her elbow on the back of the pew. Her large breasts were rubbing against me, and she was breathing on my neck, whispering in my ear, "Brother Coleman, can you help me? I am so distraught."

Then, after a pause, "I'm so lonely. My husband doesn't want me anymore."

I resisted this temptation, but I was weakening. Soon, I *was* getting intimate with young women I met at the services. I justified this by telling myself that everything was okay because these were "church girls." And we *were* still trying to serve God, after all.

The Full Gospel Businessmen realized that having a muscular, twenty-year-old evangelist on the revival circuit was a formula for scandal. So they found me a wife. Shirley was a nice little Christian girl who worked at a Dairy Queen and attended a church in Houston where I'd preached. There wasn't any love there. It was pretty much an arranged marriage to prevent me from fornicating with the rest of the flock.

The Full Gospel Businessmen set everything up. They bought my wedding suit. I didn't have a vehicle at the time, so they located a Christian with a used-car lot, and got me a dilapidated auto. There was an offering taken to pay for the wedding at the Ramada Inn in Phoenix—coinciding with a Christian convention there—as well as our honeymoon.

I was so immersed in this world that I didn't bother telling my parents about the wedding. I told my sister, Joyce, who let Shirley stay at her house before the ceremony.

> *Joyce Sampson: It was an outdoor ceremony at the Ramada Inn. I looked around, and I hardly knew anyone there. Who were these people? Who was this girl? Where was the money coming from? It was like I left one culture and walked into another. It was very strange.*

They'd built a platform for the ceremony by the swimming pool. My high school buddy Bob Calvan and some other guys were sitting on an overhang by the water, their feet dangling over the ledge. Before the actual wedding—when Shirley was in the back with Joyce—I decided to give a sermon. I said that the swimming pool reminded me of the story of Jesus turning water into wine at a wedding party—his first recorded miracle. I just got into it, so I just went on and on.

> *Joyce Sampson: I was more or less the bridesmaid. I was supposed to walk this girl down the aisle, and deliver her to my brother. And I'm listening to this lecture about God. I'm going, "If he would just shut up, we could get this thing under way. There is something definitely wrong."*

When the ceremony was over, everyone came up to kiss the bride. I'll never forget that when it was Jerry Russell's turn, he laid one right on her lips—with a little tongue penetrating her mouth. I froze in disbelief—my mentor, hitting on my new bride.

We spent the first night at the Ramada, and didn't consummate the marriage. I was exhausted. Shirley told me that I fell into a deep sleep and started praising God and shouting out, *"Jees-us-uh."*

"You were talking about the Lord in your sleep," she said.

We drove down to Mexico for our honeymoon. I was warned not to drink the water, but did anyway. I ended up getting diarrhea. And the room reeked.

When we finally consummated the marriage, she told me, "Wow. No wonder girls turn bad."

Joyce told my parents about the marriage, and my father died a few weeks later. He'd been totally bedridden for a year. Now, all his kids were married. As cruel as he'd been, he did feel responsible for us. It was finally time to let go.

My marriage was over within months. We barely knew each other, and didn't have a romantic spark. Still, I felt guilty. I believed that by breaking the sacred bonds of matrimony, I'd sinned. The possibility of an afterlife in that lake of fire terrified me.

I remained committed to my faith, and had the privilege to appear at the same service as Brother William Branham—aka "The Man Sent by God." Slight of build and bald of head, Branham claimed to have the gift of prophesy, and saw himself as a throwback to Old Testament times—when crowds would stone so-called prophets whose prognostications did not come to pass. He always seemed to be in a trance, a glazed expression on his face, like he was looking into eternity. His son would lead him out at the beginning of a service, then lead him back when it was over. Branham's followers circulated a photo of what they asserted was a "halo of fire" appearing over the preacher's head. Branham said that an angel of the Lord had bestowed him with special endowments, including the abilities to cure polio and raise the dead.

I believed in Branham, and he didn't let me down. At this particular revival, I was seated behind him when I spotted a young couple near the front of the church. The man was in a wheelchair.

"Brother Coleman, could you come here?" the woman asked, motioning me forward. "Would you be able to get Brother Branham to pray for my husband? He was in a car wreck, and now he's paralyzed."

"You know what?" I replied. "I don't even know Brother Branham. I can't just go up to him. But while he's speaking, I'll pray that *God* will tell Brother Branham about your husband's wreck."

I went back to my seat on the stage and began praying, staring directly at Branham. His sermon progressed. He faced the congregation, then turned around to look at the choir. He was demonstrating his "word of knowledge" skills—pointing to a choir member and declaring, "Young woman. I know you have a malignant cyst on your kidney. It has been healed." As he glanced away from the singers, moving toward the congregation again, his eyes crossed mine. For a very brief moment, they continued sweeping toward the center of the room, then suddenly spun back my way. Brother Branham was staring straight at me.

I froze, sweating and clutching my chair in a death grip. Time stood still as I took in the prophet's words: *"Your marriage has been forgiven because it wasn't ordained by God."*

A huge feeling of relief washed over me. I wasn't going to the fiery pit.

A miracle had occurred. The prophet had spoken, and I was set free. I no longer felt bound by guilt and fear.

CHAPTER THREE

IN THE SNAKE DEN

A serpent is a serpent, and none less a viper because it is nestled in the bosom of an honest hearted man.

—Martin Delany,
the Malcolm X of the nineteenth century

I'm not exactly sure how I got involved with Terry Gee. His father had been a man of some wealth in Dallas, who ran in the same social circles as the Full Gospel Businessmen. When the old man died and left Terry $250,000, the kid remained on the fringes of the Christian scene. Terry was curly-haired and handsome, with a bodybuilder's physique, and loved throwing around the money his dad had worked so hard to earn. He was also something of a ladies' man. I imagine that our initial conversations centered around weightlifting. But pretty soon he was leading me down the devil's path.

And I wasn't doing anything to stop it.

Terry and I both liked exotic cats. So we bought a South African lion and kept it tethered on a nylon rope in Terry's apartment, where the animal chewed on the furniture. Terry also purchased a gym—not like the places where I banged iron back in Phoenix, but a sleek health club—and I was going to run it. We wanted the grand opening to be spectacular, and incorporated the lion into the angle.

We had the lion tied up in front of the building, so people would stop and gape. Then, we herded it into the backseat of Terry's Cadillac convertible and drove around Dallas with the top down. Of course, people were freaking out. We stopped by a radio station, and the deejay put us on the air.

After that, we got back on the Stemmons Freeway. Suddenly, this cat started growling like it was hungry. That prompted us to pull over on the side of the road and walk down an embankment with the lion. We went into a market, purchased a hunk of raw meat, and tossed it on the sidewalk.

As the lion began eating, we noticed a pool hall. "Let's take the lion inside," Terry suggested.

The people in the billiards parlor were petrified. The lion leaped up on one pool table, then jumped to another and jumped to the next. It was complete chaos—billiard balls were spilling to the floor, bouncing and clanging everywhere, people were screaming, and we were laughing.

The health club folded pretty quickly. Neither of us wanted to be there. We just wanted to goof around.

Terry had a friend named Tom who was always taking downers—Quaaludes especially. We'd be out partying somewhere, pick up some girls, rent a hotel room, and open a bag of drugs. Then Tom would pass out. We'd turn off the lights and leave. We knew that he'd be there for at least a day.

One afternoon, we came back to the room—on the ninth floor of an upscale Holiday Inn, packed with guests—to check on Tom, and he was still sleeping. But now, he was nude.

"Let's do it," Terry suggested.

Each of us grabbed an arm and dragged him down the hallway. Tom was basically unconscious, but, occasionally, he'd moan, *"Teeeerrrry, nooooo."* We pushed the elevator button and pulled him onto it. Then, we let him go, pressed "L" for lobby, and stepped out.

There were a lot of things going on in the building that day; the hotel had a ballroom. We watched the doors close, jumped on another elevator, and got downstairs before Tom.

Terry and I checked out the elevator lights. First, it stopped on the seventh floor, then on the sixth. Every time the elevator doors opened, it was bedlam. Finally, the car came down to the lobby, where a ton of people were waiting. We stood there and watched Tom's arrival.

Imagine stepping onto an elevator with your family, and seeing a nude man asleep—not a derelict, but a handsome, six-foot-four, collegiate-looking guy?

And he was groaning, *"Teeerrrry!"*

Another time in Houston, we showed up at a hotel room, and Tom couldn't be revived. It was the dead of summer, and broiling outside. So Terry turned the heat as high as it could go, and put the Do Not Disturb sign on the door.

I knew I was doing things that weren't right, things that were inconsistent with the life I'd been trying to lead for the past several years. But if you don't remain "prayed up"—staying on top of your Bible reading, and seeking the fellowship of other pious Christians—you lose your burden for lost souls. It became like some tug-of-war.

I was still preaching here and there. But in between, I took a job as a bouncer at a nightclub called the Blue Room. It happened to be directly across the street from the "world famous" Dallas Sportatorium. And it was there that Wayne Coleman unknowingly looked into the future, and caught a peek of the world where Superstar Billy Graham would reside.

The guy who owned the Blue Room was a wrestling fan, and attended the matches at the Sportatorium. One night, he told me that the promotion needed some guys to help put up a steel cage for the main event. I volunteered, made a few extra dollars, then stuck around to watch the show.

I have absolutely no recollection of the guys who squared off in the cage. Earlier in the night, though, "Killer" Karl Kox, a balding, trash-talking wrestling heel, was trying to leave the ring when the fans surrounded it. There wasn't much security around, so Kox attempted to barrel through the crowd. In the process, he knocked over a pregnant woman. That's when I intervened, rushing toward Kox and actually placing my hands on him. "You can't do that to a pregnant girl!" I yelled. Kox shoved me back before the cops broke everything up.

They handcuffed me and marched me to the rear of the building, not sure about whether they really wanted to take me downtown and fill out paperwork for such a trivial altercation. At one stage, they walked me past an open door, and I looked inside. It was the heel dressing room. And there was "Killer" Karl Kox, relaxing and combing what hair he had left. He gave me a bemused look and turned back to the mirror. This had been a big deal to me, but to "Killer" Karl Kox, it was just another night, and I was just another wrestling mark—or fanatic—who got carried away.

"We're gonna let you go," the cops told me, "as long as you promise to never do this again."

I agreed and left the building, still tensed up, breathing in the thick Texas air, as I shambled back to the Blue Room. By then, I'm sure, Kox had forgotten that the incident had even occurred.

I still wanted to hold on to the Lord. Through the connections of the Full Gospel Businessmen, I went up to Washington, D.C., preaching in this church where the worshippers were black and the minister was white and rich. African Americans were known for really giving financially, and the congregation was housed in a mega building.

The associate pastor was a friendly guy who also played the organ at church, and he invited me to stay in his home with his wife and small child.

The two of us were alone one night, driving through downtown D.C., when he suddenly confessed to me, "I can't stop going to bed with guys."

To this day, I don't believe that this was a come-on. The man was engaging in acts that went against all his teachings, and he was desperate to talk about it with someone who wouldn't expose his secret.

If you asked me now, I'd tell you that—in my opinion—gay people are gay, and can't force themselves straight. Back then, I viewed things differently. I counseled the man that with the help of Jesus he could beat this thing. "You've got to turn this over to the Lord, brother. You need to be delivered and set free from this demonic sin."

Maybe it was my own homophobia, maybe it was the man's wrenching conflict within himself—but the conversation left me with a creepy feeling. That night, I woke up from a deep sleep, looked around the bedroom, and saw snakes everywhere. Anyone familiar with the story of Adam and Eve knows that the snake represents Satan. There were thousands of serpents three feet deep on the floor, on the dresser, wrapped around the bedpost, hissing and slithering. This was an attack straight from hell.

I stood up on the bed and screamed as loudly as I could. The minister and his wife came rushing into the room, and I broke out of my spell.

I believe that, on a spiritual level, the man's anxiety seeped into a room in my soul and manifested itself in the form of snakes. But for the next twenty years, I had tremendous anxiety about these reptiles. If I saw one on TV, I changed the channel.

I listened to some great evangelists in Washington, particularly African-American ones. No one can sermonize like a black preacher. I remember one guy captivating me with his prayer beseeching God to keep the hijack-ers away from the church—the hijackers, the thieves, the criminals. But his entreaties could not protect me. I could no longer control my carnal desires. Christians say that when you let the devil get a foothold, the door opens wider and wider. I felt dirty, and began my sojourn away from the Lord.

I took a bus up to New York City, rented a small studio apartment at the Henry Hudson Hotel, and started bouncing at the old Metropole Café. It wasn't a strip club, but they had girls go-go dancing on platforms behind the bar. There were these bright lights shining down from the marquee in front of the building, and—from my spot near the bar—I could see the face of every person who passed by on the sidewalk.

One night, I noticed the familiar pear shape of a minister who'd invited me to preach at his church down South. He'd been walking by, with his hands in his pockets, turned to see the go-go dancers, and stayed there for thirty minutes, without moving. He was engrossed.

There were so many girls working at the Metropole that the club had a cafeteria upstairs for workers to take breaks. I was walking up the steps one night when I saw a guy coming down with a saxophone shoved under his coat. The horn was sticking out through the buttons. The tip of the reed was protruding through the collar. When we passed each other, I nailed him with a clothesline. As he stumbled, I slipped behind him and shoved my forearm under his throat, cranking upward and sitting on the stairs until two other bouncers arrived to recover the instrument. Then we dragged the guy to the front door and gave him a few shots on the way out.

I'd sometimes get out of the Metropole at four-thirty in the morning and walk back to the Henry Hudson through the darkness. During the winter, it seemed like the streets were overrun with hookers, shrouded in freezing drizzle, frantically trying to solicit business.

"You want a date?"

I never acknowledged them. But I'd think about them, wretchedly lurking in stairwells, and recall how, just a few months earlier, I was preaching about the redeeming power of God.

"How have I sunk so low so fast?" I'd ask myself.

I enjoyed fighting in the Golden Gloves, and decided to give professional boxing a try. I asked around Manhattan and found the best trainer I could, Gil Clancy, who was coaching Emile Griffith, a welterweight and middleweight champion. Griffith was known for foot and hand speed, combinations, and very short, quick punches. Unfortunately, whenever his name is mentioned today, fans remember his tragic bout with Benny "Kid" Paret in 1962, an encounter that ultimately led to Paret's death.

Clancy agreed to train me and—lo and behold—got me a three-round fight one month later, on October 21, 1966, at the old Madison Square Garden. Another Clancy protégé, Johnny Persol, fought Amos "Freight Train" Lincoln in the main event. My opponent was a fellow unknown named Willis Miles.

When I arrived at the Garden and began getting taped up, the backstage denizens were curious. "Gil, who's this big guy you got?" They thought that I might be a new great white hope. I really had a buzz going.

I came to the ring with just a towel around my neck—there was no money for a robe—and felt pretty confident in the first round. I dropped my opponent twice. The bell rang for the second round, and I dropped him again. In the third round, I went for the kill, but missed and left myself wide open. Miles took advantage, smashing my face with a giant straight right. I went down, completely delirious, but managed to climb up at the count of eight. I advanced toward my foe, but the referee held on to me.

"Are you all right?" he asked.

"I'm okay," I responded, but the ref knew better. I'd been knocked silly, and there was no way that I could continue the bout. Even though I'd been ahead on points, I lost via TKO.

In the locker room, I was so dazed that when I went into the shower, I didn't come out for thirty minutes. People lost track of me. "Where's Coleman?" I heard someone say, as the water beat down on my pummeled features.

After paying off my second, I slipped my $150 purse into my pocket and began making my way back to the Henry Hudson. I was totally disoriented, walking through red lights while cars honked at me. As soon as I made it to the room, I undressed and passed out on the bed.

At 3:00 A.M. I woke up frantic. "My God," I said out loud. "I have to get to Madison Square Garden. I'm late for my fight."

I looked over at the dresser and saw my $150 payoff, rolled up next to my room key. Could I have boxed already? I went over to the mirror and gazed at my reflection. My nose was swollen. My eyes were puffy, and one was practically sealed shut.

Obviously, I'd been to the Garden.

New York was not for me. Not yet, anyway. A few days later, I left town on a Greyhound for Phoenix.

Back on familiar ground, I hit the gym. I wanted muscle mass, and was willing to do whatever it took to get big. While pursuing this endeavor, I became friends with Ron Pritchard, a linebacker at Arizona State University (ASU). Ron would become the Sun Devils' team captain, and play in the NFL for the Houston Oilers and Cincinnati Bengals.

Around the same time, I began using Dianabol, an ingestible steroid. Steroids were legal in those days, and most of my bodybuilder friends said that was the way to go. Were there any side effects? Not that I saw. My hairline was beginning to recede, but my mother told me that all the men in her family suffered from male-pattern baldness.

As my relationship with God faltered, my compulsion for anabolic steroids took over. Some of the drug manufacturers—in an attempt to cover themselves in the event of future lawsuits, I guess—included labeling alleging that their products did not enhance physical ability. But people were becoming huge from steroids, and setting world records. The drug companies were lying—the same way they'd lie about the consequences of steroid abuse once people like me began losing our health.

I became a regular at the Oasis Apartments in Tempe, near ASU, hanging out with Ron Pritchard and his friends on the team. When the players were hungry, they could go to an off-campus Kentucky Fried Chicken and eat for free. Ron would take me with him a lot, and I never had to pay for anything. It was such a good deal that I decided to go to Kentucky Fried Chicken by myself from time to time.

This posed a bit of a problem: I was twenty-six years old, and didn't really look like a college student. So I came up with a solution. When the folks at Kentucky Fried Chicken asked me to sign for my meals, like the other players, I scribbled out the name of Frank Kush, the school's head coach.

After a couple of weeks, I'd run up a tab of about forty dollars, and the people at the restaurant were getting wise to me. I was sitting in my mother's house one afternoon when the doorbell rang. It was the police, and I was under arrest for forgery—charged with seven counts, each one a felony, for seven separate meals.

I made my first phone call to my brother Vance, the police captain. He wasn't too happy about getting pulled out of a meeting because his younger brother was ripping off chicken breasts and drumsticks. But he was a stand-up guy who couldn't turn away a family member in trouble.

Vance arranged bail and found me an attorney associated with the Fraternal Order of Police. But this was going to be a battle. Frank Kush was mad, and wanted the case to go to court.

Before the trial, Pritchard put me in touch with his teammate, Rick Shaw. Shaw was a crazy man, but a great tight end. I came up with the idea of having Shaw write a note for the court: "I, Rick Shaw, give Wayne Coleman permission to sign the name of Frank Kush for all meals at Kentucky Fried Chicken."

Shaw, who was on the verge of leaving for the Canadian Football League (CFL) and wasn't concerned about repercussions, signed the document and had it notarized by my lawyer.

When the trial started, my lawyer called Frank Kush to the stand and handed him the note. "Could you please read this for the court?" my attorney asked.

Kush contemplated the piece of paper. "I, Rick Shaw," he began, and started shaking his head and laughing. "This idiot gave you permission to sign my name?" Kush asked me from the witness box.

The judge, who was a big ASU fan himself, and thus familiar with Rick Shaw's antics, laughed, too. The case was dismissed.

I should have learned from my mistakes. But now I didn't know how to stay out of trouble. A short time later, I needed Vance's help again.

I was in a parking lot outside of a restaurant called Hobo Joe's when some unsavory associate looked through the open window of an auto and spotted a wallet on the front seat. We took it, and I used one of the credit cards to get a nice stereo for my car.

While I was paying for the purchase, the clerk examined the card and said, "You know, it says 'DDS' after your name."

I was smart enough to realize that I didn't look like a dentist. "I know," I answered. "My dad is a dentist."

I felt uneasy now, but I was stuck. As I returned to the area where the stereo was being installed, a squad car pulled up. The cops quickly ran the card and put me in handcuffs. This time, the charge was possession of a stolen credit card and forgery.

Vance went nuts when, again, I interrupted a conference with a plead-ing phone call. Stomping into the jailhouse, he demanded to know what I'd gotten myself into now.

"I don't know," I responded. "I was with a bunch of buddies outside Hobo Joe's. We found a wallet in the bushes. It looked like it was dis-carded—all the money was gone. I just used the credit card."

Vance glared at me: "You better straighten up." It was pretty clear that I was running out of favors.

Still, he contacted the same lawyer, who knew his way around the courthouse—from defending cops and screwups in their families—and arranged a plea deal. I'd pay for the stereo and the installation out of my own pocket, and that was about it. But I hardly felt victorious. I'd preached, loved God, and been treated as a family member by upstanding people like Bev Swink, Anna Jean Price, and many pastors around the country. Now I was *stealing*. How different was I from the guy I caught lifting the saxo-phone in New York? What was wrong with my brain?

I found a job bouncing at a huge club called J.D.'s, next to ASU. The top floor was country and western. The bottom level was rock'n'roll. In the 1960s, hippies and cowboys were an extremely potent mixture—particularly when you factored in alcohol. My buddy Brick Darrow was CEO of the bouncing committee, and went for quality over quantity. He only hired power lifters, football players, and in my case, a former pro boxer. It was a wise choice. We were constantly breaking up fights.

> **Steve Cepello, aka Steve Strong:** *People have asked me why so many big, muscular guys came out of Arizona. And I think it's be-cause, 80 percent of the year, we're in 115-degree temperatures with-out shirts. You end up with guys who are physically conscious all the time, guys interested in strength training and weightlifting.*
>
> *Even before I ever met Wayne—years before we wrestled to-gether and became Tag Team partners—I knew of him. Phoenix was one of those towns where you could meet the same person twice in one day. Everyone remembered Wayne from North High. Everyone knew he was a teenage phenomenon. When I was too young to even get into J.D.'s, I'd see Wayne out front, checking IDs. He held a very prestigious spot in the pecking order of tough guys and monsters.*

Guys would line up to arm-wrestle me at J.D.'s, and I'd put them down and take their money. If someone became disruptive, we dispensed with the friendly warnings. One night, this big cowboy—he was probably six-foot-six—came into the club drunk, wild-eyed, and obnoxious. He tossed over a few tables and knocked down a woman—then had the audacity to take a seat at the bar. I couldn't allow him to stay there.

From my days of street fighting, I still had an aversion to hurting my knuckles. So I grabbed a glass ashtray off a table, palmed it, and *boom!* The idiot's hat flew off, and he dropped from the bar stool, out cold. He was a bloody mess when the other bouncers dragged him out.

Well, the guy filed assault charges against a bouncer at J.D.'s. He was so drunk, though, that he didn't know *which* bouncer. Brick corralled a bunch of the staffers—all power lifters—and a few of our friends from the weight room to come down for a lineup. There were about twenty of us there, and I was hidden in the middle. The cowboy looked and looked, but couldn't make a positive ID.

> *Steve Strong: J.D.'s was the most notorious club in the area, and Wayne was the most ridiculous specimen. I think he was six-four, and weighed 285. You had people coming from far and wide just to observe him. People would drive in and say, "We came from Flagstaff, and just wanted to see this guy. We're going home now."*

Another night, I was downstairs, keeping an eye on the rockers, when I heard a burst of shouting—then my name. This giant Samoan who played for ASU was bolting through the front door, screaming, "Coleman! I want Wayne Coleman!"

I'd never met this guy before in my life. Now, he was drunk—out of his mind—and wanted to fight me.

The two of us went outside, with hordes of patrons milling behind us, excitedly waiting for the altercation. As I'd later learn in wrestling, the Samoans are a very tough people. The advantage I had, of course, was that I was completely sober. My antagonist never had a chance. As soon as we got under the front marquee, I kneed him in the groin. When he bent forward, I gave him a hard right hook to the side of the head. He hit the ground and tried staggering to his feet. But I got behind him and clamped my forearm across his throat.

Unfortunately, I had on a new pair of silk pants with no underwear. As I bent over my adversary, the pants tore right up the butt—in front of all those spectators. It was not a pretty sight.

Two cops showed up, each wielding a can of pepper spray. They weren't taking any chances. People told the officers what had transpired, and they aimed at the big Samoan. I was still choking the guy, and he was gagging. Then, suddenly, he snapped to his senses. As the mist spewed forward, he ducked—just like in a pro wrestling high spot—and I got blasted with the stinging fluid instead.

Of course, women were everywhere. There were many girls I liked at J.D.'s, and I found one who wanted to marry me. On a whim, Leslie and I went to a justice of the peace and had a little ceremony. It was an immature thing to do. This time, I didn't even tell my sisters about it.

We returned to my apartment, and—once again—the marriage was not consummated on our wedding night. Nor the next night, or the night after that. We'd had sex many times before—I'd picked her up in a nightclub, after all—but once that paper was signed, Leslie froze. It seemed that this dramatic life choice had forced her to admit a tormenting secret.

"The truth of the matter," she told me, "is, I like girls."

I smiled back at her. "I like girls, too."

"No," she emphasized. "I *really* like girls."

"Ooooh."

My friends joke that I was so bad in bed that I had turned Leslie into a lesbian.

My third wife *seemed* like a normal girl. But I believe that she was a legitimate kleptomaniac. In her defense, I barely made a living as a bouncer. Nonetheless, if we were walking through the supermarket, she'd open up her coat and slip in a couple of steaks. She also stole clothes and, like me, had a fondness for speed. I can't tell you exactly how long this marriage lasted—to be honest, I have enough trouble just remembering her *name*—but I know that it ended pretty fast.

One of our bouncers, Bob Lueck, was also a starter for the Calgary Stampeders in the CFL. The 1967 season was starting, and he suggested that I try to make the team.

I hadn't been on a football field since my freshman year of high school, but I was a natural athlete, and ended up playing defensive end in the preseason. I had one good game, and struggled the rest of the time. Still, just before preseason ended, I was traded to the Montreal Alouettes.

Even though the coaches made sure that I got into games, I didn't feel comfortable on the gridiron. I was a mediocre player at best, and toward the end of the year, I was let go.

I returned to Phoenix, where another friend, George Flint, encouraged me to try out for *his* team, the NFL's Oakland Raiders. I did, made the 1968 preseason squad, and was offered a contract for $9,000, the league's minimum salary. Then, before the official season began, I tore my Achilles tendon.

On my first trip to the great white north, playing for the Montreal Alouettes.

The Raiders gave me a week off, to see if I would heal on my own. When I didn't, they released me.

On the way home, I had to change planes in Los Angeles. I had my football gear in my bag, and as a stewardess was shoving my belongings into the overhead compartment, she asked, "What do you have in here? This bag is heavy."

"I've got a bomb," I replied, raising my eyebrows and smiling flirtatiously.

I sat down and buckled my seat belt. A few minutes later, a half dozen law enforcement officers came rushing onto the aircraft. "Mr. Coleman," the lead cop said, "we'd like to talk to you outside the plane."

"Regarding what?"

"The comment you made to the stewardess before."

I stepped into the interrogation room, replaying the conversation in my mind, wondering if the flight attendant was offended because I'd flirted with her.

"Did you tell the stewardess that you had a bomb in your bag?"

"Yeah," I shot back. "I was just joking. It was off-the-cuff. Look"—I motioned at my bag—"open it up."

I showed the officers my cleats and NFL contract. "I'm not a bomber," I insisted. They believed me, but were not amused. Still, this was thirty-three years before 9/11, and there didn't seem to be any penalty for making terroristic threats. One of the officers even called another airline, like a travel agent, and arranged for me to leave on the next flight to Phoenix. I boarded and flew home, my Achilles tendon still aching.

I was planning to try football again and attend the Houston Oilers' training camp as a walk-on the next season. (I wouldn't make that team, either; pro football just was not for me.) In the interim, I landed a job working as a debt collector for some Las Vegas casinos. My territory was mainly Arizona. The way it worked was that I'd show up at some gambler's door and inform him that he owed money. I never had one physical altercation, and my size was not as much of a factor as you'd think. Most people assumed that if a Las Vegas casino sent you to find them, you were probably a hit man for the mob.

In late 1968, I was getting bored with Phoenix, so I went to Los Angeles to hang out. I was still training hard and getting really strong. One night in Gold's Gym, I bumped into the "Blond Bomber" Dave Draper, and an Austrian immigrant with an incredible physique. Arnold Schwarzenegger had recently moved to the United States, with just a gym bag containing his clothes, but he seemed perpetually wide-eyed and happy. I remember him laughing and always telling jokes—he was the one who liked to tell the jokes.

We became workout partners, and Arnold motivated me to push myself harder in the gym than ever before. He was there, along with Franco Colombo, spotting me when I bench-pressed 605 pounds. The world record at the time was 616, held by my friend Pat Casey.

Arnold was different from me in that he had definite goals. "I'm going to be a movie star," he forecast in barely understandable English. I looked on in bemusement and said, "You could make it in foreign movies. That way they could use captions for you."

I asked him what he was going to do about his last name. It was long, and hard to pronounce.

"I'm going to use it in my favor. They won't forget my name because it's so different."

We'd walk on the beach together, and Arnold would spot a couple of pretty girls and—just like that—strike a pose and begin flexing. I'd watch him in wonder, like a little kid. The girls loved his look until Arnold opened his mouth and started talking.

Unable to decipher his English, they'd walk away, shaking their heads and laughing.

THE MENTOR OF MAYHEM

The first thing you're taught in the wrestling business is believe nothing that you hear, and only half of what you see.

—Former Extreme Championship
Wrestling (ECW) head Paul Heyman

Around Christmas, 1969, I received the phone call that changed my life forever.

It was Bob Lueck, the same guy who recommended that I play football in the CFL. Now Bob had an even better idea: professional wrestling. It was something that he was already doing in the off-season in Calgary. Bob's goal wasn't working main events or winning championships. He just wanted to make some extra cash and have fun.

"We're having a great time up here," he told me. "It's easy money."

"Easy money? I could always use easy money."

He claimed to have told Stu Hart, the wrestling promoter in Calgary, all about me—my twenty-two-inch biceps, the 605-pound bench press—and the man was very intrigued.

"But don't I have to know how to *wrestle?*"

Well, what Stu didn't know wouldn't hurt him. Bob had taken it upon himself to assure the promoter that I already *was* a wrestler. It was a lie—but, then again, we were talking about the business of pro wrestling.

I hadn't really watched the diversion later known as "sports entertainment" since I'd been a kid, and Sky Hi Lee was chewing lightbulbs and piercing his pecs. But what were my other options—battering drunks for five dollars an hour, with all the secondhand smoke I could breathe as a bonus? Therefore, I didn't even bother telling Bob that I needed time to "think about" his proposition. I'd already been an evangelist, boxer, and professional football player. Why not make one more critical life decision on an impulse?

Just after New Year's Day 1970, I pulled out of my driveway and began the trek north, following Bob into a frozen world—and an industry dictated by brawn, flamboyance, and backwards logic. It was that simple. Unlike so many who spend their childhoods sitting in front of the television and dreaming about life in the squared circle, I had never once thought about a wrestling career. My entrance into a universe where I'd gain my greatest fame was born on a whim and nothing more.

There was nothing monumental about the excursion out of the desert; I'd seen those sights hundreds of times before. However, as we traversed our way into the mountains, the temperature started to drop, and—when I contemplated the peaks of the Great Rockies—I began to understand what awaited me in the Great White North.

As I reached the end of my sixteen-hour journey, I finally detected Calgary's nighttime glow. The roads were packed with snow, and the line dividing the highway was nowhere to be seen. At a certain point, Bob turned off the road and headed toward his local residence. I continued on ahead, frequently braking, trying to adjust to driving conditions I'd never encountered. Then it happened. I spun out until my car came to a stop sideways, in the middle of the highway. In the distance, the headlights of another vehicle approached. Was this some sort of omen? Trying not to panic, I carefully maneuvered my car back into what I assumed was my lane, and continued the last leg of the trip, having lost track of those city lights I'd seen beckoning me minutes earlier.

I stopped at the first motel. It was agonizingly cold as I checked into my room and huddled under the blankets. The next morning, when I woke up, I phoned the front desk to ask about the temperature. A calm voice delivered an answer that I found hard to grasp: 65 below zero in the shade.

"You mean Fahrenheit—right?"

"No, Celsius."

My intention was eating breakfast at a restaurant a short distance from the motel. But when I opened the door to my room, I was blinded by the reflection of the sun off a frigid sea of pure white. Why would anyone choose to live in this merciless climate? I attempted to take refuge in my vehicle, but was stunned to discover that the door handle was frozen shut. So I began walking to breakfast, and as I did, I experienced another virgin sensation: the sound of crunching snow penetrating my ears with each step. Even when I tried breathing through my nose, my nostrils froze shut.

Bob Lueck was amused by my unease when I phoned him later in the morning. But he told me exactly what I wanted to hear: "I'll be there at six o'clock to pick you up."

We were going to Stu's for my first workout.

Stu Hart was the "Mentor of Mayhem," the patriarch of Canadian wrestling—and the father of twelve children. All the boys worked in wrestling at one point, all the girls married wrestlers. When the Harts shopped, they each grabbed a cart and paraded in a caravan through the supermarket. Their home, situated on top of a hill overlooking the rest of Calgary, housed not only Stu's large brood but his training facility and any number of itinerant wrestlers. His most famous son, future World Wrestling Federation champion Bret "Hit Man" Hart, once said that he wasn't sure if Stu and Helen even made house keys. With so many people always in motion on the grounds, no one locked the door anyway.

Stu's yard was littered with the hulks of old Cadillacs, their hoods up, and engines packed with snow. From outside at twilight, the Hart mansion was pitch-black, with the glow of faded light coming through random windows. No one ever told me this, but I'm sure that the kids at school teased the Hart children about living in the Munsters' house. And I'm even more certain that Stu's kids made their classmates pay dearly for those remarks.

As I shivered on the porch, Bob raised his hand to knock on Stu's front door. But before he could, the door burst open. Three of the Hart children came scurrying outside, chasing each other down the porch steps and through the snow—*in bare feet.* We now could look directly into the dining room, where Stu, big-jawed and barrel-chested, sat eating.

"Hey, Stu, we're here," Bob shouted into the house, and Stu rose to greet us.

Stu was an imposing figure of a man, with impressive bone structure. He is one of the best storytellers I have ever met. There are probably a hundred past and present wrestlers out there still doing Stu Hart imitations. He had a unique way of talking that's a little hard to explain. But he was a real charming man who took time to think before he spoke. Stu had a deceptive gentleness that drew you in and gave you confidence. But in reality, he was the one with all the confidence.

Before he had even introduced himself, Stu's eyes immediately locked on my arms—and he began squeezing the triceps. "God ... um ... uh ... those are the biggest arms I've ... uh ... ever seen," he muttered. The man was just salivating. How could I not love this guy?

Bret later told me that his dad called me "the biggest fish I ever caught."

The three of us walked through the hallway, toward the basement stairway and the "workout area" of the house. I imagined that this wasn't going to be much of a workout. Stu was still in his street clothes.

I'd visualized a wrestling ring with a Canadian maple leaf sewn in the middle, sitting in the basement like a glowing gem. Instead I saw four grimy walls, stained with blood, sweat, saliva, and other body fluids I choose not to name. Above us was a low ceiling crisscrossed with exposed pipes and wires. Below us were paper-thin gymnastic mats, soiled with the same discoloring as the walls.

Yet, as I breathed in the musty, loathsome air, I was standing on hallowed ground, the place where "Rowdy" Roddy Piper, the Junkyard Dog, Chris Benoit, Chris Jericho, the British Bulldogs, and untold others were indoctrinated into the pro wrestling fraternity.

I was in "The Dungeon."

The Mentor of Mayhem didn't ask me about my background in the squared circle. The uncertain look on my face told him everything that he needed to know: I'd never wrestled a day in my life. And he didn't seem to care. In a casual manner, Stu asked if he could show me one of his favorite holds. He wasn't dressed in wrestling gear, I reasoned, so what harm would it do?

"Could you ... uh ... bend over ... um ... uh ... a little bit, and ... uh ... just put your ... uh ... head here?"

I think that this could be called entrapment, but I willingly placed my head in the waiting arms of a man who knew how to inflict pain, and loved doing it. Stu turned his body slightly, and my neck snapped. I saw stars. Stu drove me down to the mat and applied even more pressure. My size and strength notwithstanding, there was nothing I could do, and no place I could go. I don't know which number I was on the list, but I was now a member of a rare fraternity of men who'd been "stretched" by Stu Hart.

I'd later learn that Stu was a notorious "shooter," a guy who could take care of business if a staged wrestling match degenerated into an actual brawl, and a "hooker," or master at crippling torture holds. Once a fan called the Hart mansion, declaring that he was as mean as any of the wrestlers Stu featured in his Stampede Wrestling promotion. "Drive up to the . . . uh . . . house," Stu offered.

"I'm so tough I'll *run* there."

When the guy made it up the hill, Stu immediately got behind his guest and placed him in the "sugar hold," one of the Mentor of Mayhem's most excruciating favorites. The man struggled so much that he swallowed part of his long beard, and passed out.

"Dad, I think you killed him," one of the Hart sons ventured.

"No, I didn't," Stu countered, chopping the man hard across the chest and waking him up.

I know how the guy felt. As I was grasping for the staircase after my first training session, Stu trailed after me, clutching my triceps again. "Look at these . . . um, uh . . . they're like . . . uh . . . horse shoes."

"Thanks, Stu. A lot of good they did me."

One of Stampede Wrestling's official program sponsors, the Safeway food chain, was always giving Stu huge boxes of overripened fruit. He'd leave them around the house for his kids if they wanted to snack, and I'd help myself to some apples and bananas to bring back to the hotel. *Rotting fruit,* I'd tell myself, *a perfect banquet from The Dungeon.*

One lasting image that I have of my time in the basement is of the half-open door just off our training area. Inside a dark, cold room was an old man, covered by layers of blankets, with a wool hat over his ears, frost coming out of his mouth, as he napped in the daytime. He looked like he hadn't shaved for weeks. Next to the bed was a basement window, revealing a snow-packed field. I only saw the man rise from the bed once, walking past the mats and up the stairs without even a fleeting look at us. I remember peeking out his window and seeing him come into view, trudging off through the thick snow, his hands in his coat pockets, shoulders slumped, and head down. He passed the hulks of the old Cadillacs and went wandering away, disappearing into the frozen abyss.

Just like at home, Stu created an intimate atmosphere at the Stampede Victoria Pavilion in Calgary. The same fans showed up every week, and some were given second chances when they got carried away and went after the wrestlers. The talent could only enter the building by walking right past the people waiting at the box office. Once inside the arena, the boys had to jostle their way through the crowd to reach the dressing room.

After a total of five days of training, Stu decided that I was ready to start making my living as a pro wrestler. At the time, I'd yet to set foot in an actual ring, but Stu was confident that I could learn on the job.

Before I had a *match,* though, Stu came up with an idea for me to familiarize myself to the fans. I'd travel around the loop of the Calgary-based territory—wrestling was split into regional promotions then, and this one stretched to places like Red Deer, Regina, Edmonton, and Moose Jaw—and arm-wrestle all challengers from the crowd.

"It'll get you over," Stu said.

Get me over? I thought I knew what that meant, but I wasn't sure. No one had enlightened me to wrestling's esoteric terminology yet.

"We'll offer $500 to anyone who can . . . uh . . . beat you."

"You might as well offer $5,000, because no one can do it. It's humanly impossible."

I was a very strong guy who'd beaten back every arm-wrestling challenge I'd ever had at J.D.'s. Plus, I was a 600-pound bench presser, extremely aggressive, and pumped full of steroids. I was ready to tear someone's arm off.

Stu was moved by my bravado, but since it was his money, he was more at ease with a $500 windfall.

On the night of the first contest, I made my way out of the dressing room in dress pants and a T-shirt. Stu was by my side as we went, drooling every step of the way. When we rounded the corner—there it was. A real ring! The bright lights over the top were in sharp contrast to the gloomy ambiance of The Dungeon.

I climbed through the ropes and paced back and forth. A sturdy wooden table and two chairs had been placed on the canvas a few moments earlier. Stu took the microphone, projecting himself in a voice far clearer than the one we heard at his home: "Wayne Coleman claims to be the arm-wrestling champion of the world. He is offering $500 to anyone who can beat him!"

I was surprised at how quickly a challenger stepped forward. But within seconds a stocky guy who looked like a farmer was swaggering down the aisle, smiling back at his cheering family, and joining us in the ring.

Stu was going to be the official referee for this test of strength. I knew all the advantages when it came to gripping, pulling, and getting the best leverage. As we clasped hands, Stu asked if we were ready. Then he shouted, *"Go!"*

If you were blinking, you would have missed it—I slammed my victim's hand down on the table, rattling the whole ring. On impulse, I continued to slam his knuckles onto the hard wooden surface five or six more times in rapid succession. As my opponent stood up, he made some type of snide comment, and I dumped the table on him. He fell to the mat, while security crawled under the bottom rope and separated us.

"Handcuff this worm and take him to jail!" I screamed. On instinct, I turned to the camera and began flexing. I was hearing my first boos. It was empowering.

Stu had been right. By arm-wrestling—and humiliating a physically inferior human being—I'd gotten over, just like that.

At least with the fans. When I got back to the dressing room, none of the "boys" said a word to me. They'd seen the performance, and I'd guess that a few actually enjoyed it. But wrestlers are very jealous people. Whenever someone enters a promotion who can threaten people's positions, the pettiness begins. Only my friend Bob Lueck greeted me with a grin.

There was never any question that I was over as an arm-wrestler. But now, it was time to actually start wrestling. I was unprepared in a number of ways. For one thing, I didn't own any wrestling gear. I'd been so excited when Bob invited me to join him in Calgary that I never got around to asking where I could purchase some boots and trunks.

Fortunately, "Wild" Bill Dromo, a top heel—wrestling villain—broke ranks with his begrudging colleagues and told me about a place that made ring attire. The drawback was that it would take three weeks for the company to deliver. Dromo was kind enough to lend me some of his gear in the interim. I was lucky the man wore Size 15 boots. His hospitality saved me some embarrassment and humbled me at the same time; wrestling in borrowed equipment was not the way I envisioned my career beginning.

My debut took place on January 16, 1970, against Dan Kroffat. I'd twisted my knee in training, and had to tape it up. I also had no idea what I was supposed to do in the ring. When fans realized how lost and clumsy I was, it dissolved all the heat I'd generated with my arm-wrestling gimmick. I was seen for what I was—a very recognizable rookie who had a lot to learn. It was a disappointment and a revelation.

Another sobering moment came while sitting in the passenger seat, as "Wild" Bill Dromo drove us to one of the towns in the Stampede territory. I noticed that he'd pinned photos of his wife and children to the sun visor, as close to his face as possible. Because of the profession he'd chosen, his kids were growing up without him. I never mentioned the pictures because they obviously meant so much to him. But I'd study them as we traveled those monotonously endless miles on the snow-covered prairies. Would this be my lot in life, too?

Stu hadn't found it necessary to smarten me up to wrestling's true

Struggling to break out of Dan Kroffat's hold.

nature during training. Now, he was paying the price. One Friday night, he asked me to hit the ring while Bob Lueck was wrestling fellow CFL vet Angelo Mosca. I was supposed to jump Bob and help Mosca, the heel in the match, get more heat.

"Could you repeat that?" I asked Stu.

"Go to the ring *now!*" he demanded, fuming.

"I can't," I explained. "The bell has already rung."

I was so green that I believed that I couldn't violate this basic rule of sportsmanship—never intervene once the timekeeper has signaled for the match to begin. Stu didn't tell me that, in wrestling, pandemonium was the paramount rule. Nor did he emphasize that it wasn't right to hurt people.

And I hurt a lot of people, usually after I belted them with "potatoes," or real shots, to the head. Before one Tag Team match, we all went out to the center of the ring to listen to the referee's instructions—we did that back then, just like in boxing. The ref would also go through the motions of checking our boots for foreign objects and so forth. Suddenly, I turned to one of my opponents and kicked him in the stomach. The guy clutched his midsection, as if to say, "Why did you do this to me?" I'd knocked the wind out of him.

I heard the referee mumble to my tag team partner, "Somebody needs to smarten this guy up."

I would soon learn that pro wrestling was a work—predetermined, in the most polite terms. Our profession owed much of its development to the carnivals of Great Britain and North America. It was at these fairs that "worked" matches were first staged—usually in tents—for entertainment. And it was because of this connection that wrestlers still spoke carny—a form of pig-Latin punctuated by Zs—and used insider terms like *babyface* for good guy, *mark* for fan, and *juice* for blood.

The idea of pro wrestling, I discovered, was making your matches look real without injuring anybody. "They can see it," the boys would say about the fans, "but they can't feel it."

It was your responsibility to "sell" your opponent's moves and make them look real. When someone hit you, you weren't just supposed to fall, you were expected to act hurt by making facial expressions, flapping your arms, flopping forward, or wilting against the ropes.

Because I was a rookie, though, some of my opponents didn't want to cooperate. For instance, Jesse Ortega, who wrestled as the Mighty Ursus, was a behemoth whose weight didn't have to be padded in the wrestling program to impress spectators—he was at least 400 pounds. Before a televised match, Stu told me to beat Ursus with a backbreaker over one shoulder. This would really make me look like a powerhouse, since the guy was so huge.

Ursus didn't seem to have a problem while we were discussing the finish in the dressing room. But in the ring, he changed his mind. When I went to grab him, he wriggled around—he was so big that I could barely get a grip on him to begin with. I was ready to just force the guy up with pure power. So he dropped to his knees and weighed himself down. The referee rang the bell, and the television announcer covered for me by saying that I'd beaten my opponent with some type of reverse piledriver—and a very sloppy one at that.

> **Greg "The Hammer" Valentine:** *When I was learning to become a professional wrestler, my dad [wrestling legend Johnny Valentine] sent me up to Calgary to train with Stu Hart. On the night Wayne wrestled Mighty Ursus, I had my first match in the Stampede territory against Angelo Mosca.*
>
> *I remember Ursus didn't want to do the job, and Stu was screaming at him backstage, "We're trying to get this young guy over, and you—you fat slob—you wouldn't even help him. You wouldn't even get up."*
>
> *Stu was also yelling at Wayne—well, not at Wayne, but he was .yelling about what happened: "You should have just beat that old tub up."*

This was not an isolated occurrence. Because of my size—and the fact that I was getting a "push" before I even knew that wrestling was worked—guys were testing me constantly, hoping to expose some dents in the armor. Billy Robinson was an expert shooter who exploited his nefarious knowledge to physically harm his opponents. I was a green musclehead who barely knew how to apply a half nelson. Yet I was savvy enough to avoid the sadistic Englishman.

Somewhere between Calgary and Edmonton, there was a farmer's field with a giant boulder in the middle. Often a group of us made the long jaunt to and from Edmonton in the same car. And every time, Dave Ruhl, one of the other talents, would start babbling about his favorite topic.

"There's a rock in that field," Dave would insist, pointing into an ocean of blackness. *"I've* picked up that rock. If I bet you to go out into that field, Coleman, and lift that rock, you couldn't do it."

I ignored the dare. Besides being a sloppy drunk, Dave Ruhl wasn't my physical peer. I'd bench-pressed more than 600 pounds. If he lifted 200, I would have been shocked.

Still, consorting with Dave Ruhl in a car was better than the alternative. On one of the few occasions that I drove alone, I nearly died. That was the night that I received an education in "black ice," a sheet of water frozen over on the road. When I hit one of those spots, my car slid sideways for about fifty yards.

One of my most shocking revelations about the wrestling business was the fact that the talent was expected to bleed on purpose. If you got hit with a chair or were slammed into a ring post, you were supposed to "get color." That's what would occur in a real fight. Occasionally, a guy juiced the "hard way"—meaning that, intentionally or not, he actually got busted open. Most frequently, the wrestlers taped the sharpened edges of razor blades to their fingers and cut open their foreheads at the appropriate moments during the match.

I'll say it right now—I thought that juicing was barbaric. But everybody did it. Still, certain people were gun-shy, especially Dave Ruhl. I'd call him a minimalist blader. What he'd do was run the razor across his forehead a little bit, stop, wipe the cut with his other hand, and—standing there in the center of the ring—rub his fingers together to see if he bled sufficiently. If there wasn't enough blood, he'd gig himself again, and repeat the routine.

I was once standing next to Stu as he watched this display from a crack in the dressing room curtain. The Mentor of Mayhem's veins were bursting in his head, and it looked like he might hyperventilate. "Um . . . ah . . . um . . . ah, stupid," he mumbled in reference to Ruhl's technique. "Everyone can see."

I'd later learn that there was a much easier way to determine how much you were bleeding: ask the referee.

Up until now, I thought that I was a pretty spiffy dresser, prancing into the dressing room in my rust-colored pants and alpaca sweaters.

Then I met Abdullah the Butcher.

The first time I saw "Abby," as the boys liked to call him, he was seated backstage, wearing a silk suit, shimmering shoes, and big silver dollar rings, an unlit cigar in his mouth. At 360 pounds, he looked like a big, black Buddha. A smile beamed from his dark skin. Despite the hour of the day, and the fact that we were inside, he was sporting even darker shades.

This may have been the coolest guy I ever saw in my life. And what a great wrestling name—right up there with Gorilla Monsoon! Even though Abdullah was really Canadian, he was billed as "the Sudanese Giant"— ironic, since I've yet to see a native of the Sudan even half of Abdullah's size. When the bell rang, he'd simply pounce on a foe and slice him open.

Yes, Abdullah was one of those rare guys who didn't mind helping out an opponent who was nervous about blading. Abby did all the work himself. When he was in the mood, he'd also gig a ringside photographer.

I had to meet him, but felt a little intimidated. When I finally offered my hand, he introduced me to another wrestling oddity, the "working handshake," his wrist going limp as soon as we touched. The lighter the grip, it was implied, the lighter a worker a man was in the ring. If a guy worked light, he was unlikely to hurt you.

Of course, Abdullah hurt people; it went along with his lawless style. But unlike Billy Robinson, it was never his intention.

In future years, whenever we met, I'd refer to Abdullah as "Butcher." It seemed to have more zip to it than Abby. And Abdullah would forever call me "Wayne." Even after I became Superstar Billy Graham, it was always "Coleman" or "Wayne."

Before a trip to Winnipeg, Abdullah and I were invited into Stu's limo. Like everything Stu owned, it was big and a little worn. So a few hours prior to the start of the show, Abdullah offered to bring it to the car wash. Abdullah was about a block away from the arena when Stu realized that all the programs were in the trunk. It was quite a sight when he went tearing through the doors and up the streets of downtown Winnipeg, screaming after this big beast in a limousine.

Abdullah got more heat than anyone in Calgary because the stuff he did was never really fake. One dreadful episode I witnessed took place in the small Alberta city of Lethbridge. A local Indian was hired to be a jobber—a wrestler whose sole mission it was to get squashed by more prominent performers. The man accomplished his task. Abdullah attacked his opponent as he was stepping through the ropes. Instead of taping his blade to his fingers, Abdullah wielded one on a Popsicle stick, and used it on his foe with reckless abandon. I felt queasy watching this exchange. The Indian was cut so badly that he was barely recognizable—all for a payoff of 15 dollars, Canadian. Today, the image of the gore-caked victim staring blankly through the dimness of that grimy dressing room—possibly in shock—remains with me. In another time and place, Abdullah would have been charged with assault and battery.

Abdullah didn't confine this treatment to his opponents. I also watched him use his stick on himself night after bloody night. He had a fetish for the blade. It's just a shame that he was so dark-skinned—all that self-mutilation was occasionally difficult to see. Today, you can slip quarters into the grooves on Abdullah's forehead, and they nearly disappear.

Outside the ring, Abdullah was verbose and philosophical. But because he depicted himself as barely human, he never spoke on television. In Calgary, while I learned how to work in the ring, I was assigned as Abby's manager and spokesperson. Evidently I'd learned Sudanese somewhere, and had become quite a translator.

Larry Shreeve, aka Abdullah the Butcher: *I liked Wayne. He was a nice guy, and he entertained me. He had the gift of gab. I knew it was just a matter of time until he'd make money. And that's the key in this business, making lots of gelt.*

But, man, when Wayne came in, he was so green. He didn't have trunks. He didn't have boots. He didn't have nothing. It was freezing, and he'd only brought a sweater and windbreaker to Calgary. We'd drive together, and he'd say, "Butcher, I didn't know it was this cold up here."

He'd potato people all the time because he didn't know how to work. Then, Stu would take him down to The Dungeon and stretch him, just to let him know who was boss.

I watched every match Abdullah had, and tried to imitate him. One night, I had my opponent throw me onto the announcer's table next to the ring and broke it—just like Abby. I went backstage after the match, feeling satisfied, when Abdullah confronted me. "Coleman, don't ever do that again," he threatened. "That's *my* table."

Yet no one smartened me up to the wrestling business more than Abdullah. The Butcher taught me carny, sermonized about money, and warned me about the perfidious habits of my brothers in the dressing room.

Angelo Mosca liked to work the boys about his payoffs. I guess he believed that if we thought that he was earning more than us, he'd maintain a higher position in the pecking order. "Mosca says he's making two-fifty, three hundred dollars a night," I said to Abdullah once in the dressing room. "Do you think that's true?"

"I know how to find out," Abby responded, rising from his stool, and wobbling over to Stu.

"Stu," Abby demanded, "let me see Mosca's pay stub."

Stu nonchalantly produced it, and Abdullah waddled back to me, grinning.

Mosca was making $250 a *week*, like the rest of us.

"You see, Coleman," Abby proclaimed, like Moses coming down from Mount Sinai. "You can't trust anybody in this business."

Sometimes I couldn't even trust myself. I endeared myself to Stu because I liked his kids. I'd tickle them, and pick them up and toss them around. When Stu mentioned that he needed a TV, I told him that I no longer had any interest in mine. Stu wanted to help me out, so he took it off my hands for about $200. But there were reception problems, and the Mentor of Mayhem had to call a repairman out to the house. The guy went behind the console, and noticed the following engraving: PROPERTY OF THE SUN DEVIL HOTEL, TEMPE, AZ.

Stu forgave me, and was even considering turning me babyface—the result of an angle conceived by Abdullah. To prove that I was the strongest man in the world, I'd do a bench-pressing exhibition in the middle of the ring. Abdullah would be standing there, as my spotter. But as the weight increased, he'd become jealous and snap, jumping on top of me and sending 600 pounds of *real iron* down on my chest. Next, Abdullah would lift up a 45-pound barbell plate and slam me in the head. After that, his stick would come out so I could get juice.

The attack would establish me as a sympathetic character, and I could go for revenge against Abdullah all over the loop.

Abdullah and I were tight, but we weren't *that* tight. Along with visions of my chest caving in from the weights, there was still that indelible memory of Abdullah almost scalping the poor Indian.

I was green. I wasn't stupid.

With no winter coat, it was inevitable that I'd catch pneumonia. When I did, though, Stu still expected me to work for my fifty-dollar payoff. Before a trip to Edmonton, I walked out of my apartment with a blanket wrapped around me, stepped into Stu's limo, and—as the rest of the boys clowned and argued—shivered and slept in the fetal position on the floorboards. I was so weak that I could barely totter from the vehicle into the rickety, cold building where the matches were scheduled.

"I'm not letting you in the ring," the doctor in attendance at the arena insisted.

Shaking and burning up with fever, I convinced him that I needed the money.

"Don't worry," Stu assured the physician. "He's . . . uh . . . only gonna be there . . . um . . . uh . . . a minute or two."

In Stu's defense, he would have made Bret, Owen, or any of his other sons do the same thing under similar circumstances. I don't remember if I squashed somebody, or if I got squashed myself. I did the right thing for the business, even if it wasn't the best thing for me.

Shortly before I left Phoenix, I'd purchased a beautiful red Cadillac. For reasons known to God, I qualified for a loan. Once I arrived in Calgary, though, I stopped making payments. I was in no-man's-land. The finance company would never find me there.

Then, one night, I came out of the arena with Abdullah and Mosca. In the parking lot, my glistening Caddy had been replaced by a gap of icy pavement.

"They got me," I said. I was shocked that, in the frozen white north, someone had repossessed my vehicle.

The boys had a great laugh over this calamity. But I was devastated. Losing my car made me detest the cold even more. The winter was also deplorable because of the lack of good food. Greasy truck stops made "dining" on the road nauseating. And there were no gyms for a workout— unless I wanted to go to The Dungeon. And you know what always happened there.

My friend, the Butcher, had taught me much. Wayne Coleman alone wouldn't make it in this business. I needed a gimmick. My twenty-two-inch arms were just that. While Abdullah just had to eat to maintain his persona, my gimmicks were shrinking by the week. If you subscribe to the theory of paying dues in pro wrestling, mine were paid in full.

I left for Phoenix.

Abdullah the Butcher: *Wayne was a funny guy, and I was sorry to see him go. The women loved him. He should have been in real estate, like Donald Trump and those guys. He could convince you of anything.*

After his car was repossessed, I lent him $300. When he left Calgary, he said he'd pay me back the next time we saw each other. I didn't see him again for about ten years.

THE GOOD DOCTOR

Now take me to where there is luck! Now take me!

—D. H. Lawrence,
"The Rocking Horse Winner"

I had a layover in Denver on the way back from Calgary, and decided to hook up with an old friend. Jerry Russell was ministering in Colorado, and met me at the airport with his new wife and daughter. I told him that I was now a professional wrestler.

"Praise God," he responded. "I know the Lord will watch over you, and keep you safe."

I flew on to Phoenix, where another Jerry was waiting to transform my life.

It was May now, and the searing heat was still a few weeks away. After a winter in Canada, I was actually looking forward to a hot but dry 115-

degree day. The first dust storm of summer seemed equally inviting. I was back in my natural environment, and thrilled to be there.

My first priority was buying a car. With the five hundred dollars I'd salvaged from Stu's bountiful payoffs, I settled for an older Pontiac with no air-conditioning. I also needed a job. I'd been so preoccupied with leaving Calgary that I hadn't bothered inquiring about contacts in another wrestling territory. So I called J.D.'s. My buddy Brick Darrow welcomed me back like the prodigal son.

Not long afterward, I was checking IDs when a well-known local desperado entered the club, filling up most of the space while passing through the front door. "The Good Doctor" Jerry Graham had been pro wrestling royalty in the late 1950s and early 1960s, along with his "brother," Eddie Graham—the real-life Eddie Gossett. The Golden Grahams headlined New York, Boston, Washington, D.C., and other northeastern cities for promoters Vincent James McMahon—better known as Vince Sr., the father of current WWE owner Vincent Kennedy McMahon, or Vince Jr.—and Toots Mondt, battling celebrated tandems like the Bastien Brothers, Antonino Rocca and Miguel Perez, and the Fabulous Kangaroos. Jerry's weight had a tendency to balloon up and down, and he was prone to alcoholic binges and bouts of mental illness—which is why the bouncers in Phoenix knew him so well.

On at least one occasion, Brick and I ejected the Good Doctor from J.D.'s, each slipping under an arm and running him out the back door. And that was Jerry Graham on a good night. On November 18, 1957, he incited a Madison Square Garden riot, slugging and bloodying Rocca after the barefooted Argentine and his partner Edouard Carpentier defeated Graham and Dick "The Bruiser" Afflis. The fans went berserk and stormed the ring, where Bruiser proceeded to hurl several of them back into the stands. In the chaos, several cops were injured, hundreds of chairs were damaged, and someone snatched Graham's ring robe. Bruiser was banned from wrestling in New York State for the rest of his life.

An even more unusual incident occurred in Phoenix on the day Jerry's beloved mother, Mary, died in 1969. Shortly after she was admitted to the hospital, Graham phoned her doctor and pledged that harm would befall him should she expire under his care. When she died later that day, Graham showed up at the hospital with his twelve-year-old son. Wielding a hunting knife and sawed-off shotgun, a tearful Graham shoved down a nurse and tossed a security guard across a hallway, hoisting his dead mother's body off a gurney and draping it over his shoulder. Another security guard rushed forward, and Graham knocked him down and dragged him across the floor, while still holding the corpse with the other arm. My brother, Vance, vividly recalled how squad cars were called to the hospital, surrounding it and blocking off the streets nearby. It was almost like a terrorist situation. Eventually cops stormed the hospital and arrested Graham, who screamed incoherently and pounded on the patrol car doors as he was taken into custody.

Graham was destitute at the time, and dismayed to discover that after all that effort, his mother had left her entire life savings—$500,000—to the Baptist church. For years, Jerry had sent his mother money from the road, and she stashed it in the bank, along with proceeds the family earned when oil was found on their property. Now it was all in the church coffers, leaving Jerry with a lifelong hatred of religion and a feeling of betrayal by the person he loved most.

But in 1970 the sight of "the Good Doctor" enlivened me. "Hey, Jerry," I said, introducing myself. "I'm in the business now."

The famous Jerry Graham looked up at me and smiled.

"I just got back from Calgary, working for Stu Hart."

Apparently, this was my lucky day, because Jerry was not just a wrestler anymore. He was becoming a promoter as well. And he had some big plans for Wayne Coleman.

> **Vince McMahon:** *I was once asked what kind of doctor Jerry Graham was. And I responded, "A doctor of psychology," which was right when it came to the way he could communicate to people.*
>
> *My favorite Dr. Jerry Graham story involves me. The year is 1959. I'm riding shotgun in his blood-red Cadillac. I'm fourteen years old, and my hair is dyed peroxide blond, just like his. I had my stepmother do it for me.*
>
> *I thought Jerry Graham could walk on water. I'm wearing red pants, a red shirt, and red shoes, believe it or not, just like Jerry. And he's riding through every red light that gets in his way in Washington, D.C. He just blows his horn at the intersection and keeps going straight.*
>
> *The cops won't even look at him, generally speaking. When they do, he gives them the finger. Everybody knew who he was. And it wasn't worth pulling over his car for all the grief that was going to go with it.*

I was amazed by the spiel that came out of Jerry Graham's mouth that night at J.D.'s. He had contacts all over the state of Arizona, he bragged, and ran wrestling shows on Indian reservations. "The Indians love wrestling," he claimed. "It's easy money."

Easy money. I'd only been in the business a few months, and this was already the second time I heard that proclamation.

"This is all we need," Graham told me, "me and you, a referee, and two other guys who can wrestle—at least a little."

Jerry laid out his formula. I'd wrestle in a singles match. Then, he'd wrestle in a singles match. After an intermission, all four wrestlers on the show would wrestle a Tag Team match. Jerry and I would be the heels, and lose—putting the babyfaces over, in wrestling terms.

"The Indians don't need much," he emphasized.

I guess not, I thought.

Immediately, Brick volunteered to be the referee. When did *he* ever referee a wrestling match? Then we began putting the rest of the crew together: Rick Cahill, a bouncer, and former amateur wrestler at the University of Pittsburgh—pro wrestling experience, zero—and my friend Ron Pritchard, who by now had been a top draft pick for the Houston Oilers, but worked at J.D.'s in the off-season for something to do.

A promotion had been formed. Only in pro wrestling could a bizarre idea like this become a reality. I gave Jerry Graham a ride home that night. With the windows rolled down and the night wind blowing back his hair, he sounded like he was ready to make another run for Vince McMahon Sr.

To get to Jerry's place, I had to turn onto a dirt road that led to a vacant field. I heard the squeaking noise of an old swamp box cooler. Jerry's home reminded me of the barracks in those internment camps where Japanese Americans were housed during World War II. It was an abandoned boxing gym, almost in ruins.

Inside, one bare lightbulb illuminated a room containing a moldy ring and a few boxing posters peeling off the wall. The building reeked from years of splattered sweat and mildew. Jerry seemed oblivious to his dismal circumstances and ambled jauntily to his bedroom. Words fail me in trying to describe the slum-like conditions of the forlorn dressing room where he slept each night.

The next day, I brought him to my apartment to make the necessary phone calls. And by midday, we had our first venue—the Navajo Indian reservation. "All we have to do is send them some posters," Jerry said.

Posters? Who had money for posters? I suggested the traditional "word of mouth" advertising method instead.

All participants in the upcoming show also had a training session at Jerry's place. Right there, I decided to wrestle Ron Pritchard; as an amateur wrestler, Rick Cahill would probably hurt me. Without a taskmaster like Stu Hart around, it seemed like we were having too much fun. We bounced off ropes instead of walls. But the ring had been made for boxers and was as hard as Stu's mats. They also had the same stained look—and lots of dust.

Still, the place was so depressing that I invited Jerry to stay at my small two-bedroom apartment. When we arrived, he had his newspaper tucked under his arm. He immediately went into my room, took off his clothes, plopped onto *my* bed, and began reading the sports section. Since there was only one bed in the place, I grabbed a bunch of blankets, went into the other bedroom, and slept on the floor.

I also persuaded Brick to give the Good Doctor a job as a bouncer at J.D.'s. The irony was lost on no one—Jerry Graham throwing drunks out of a club instead of being expelled himself.

One night, Jerry and I picked up a couple of women and invited them back to our place. This was pretty cool—going out and scoring women with Dr. Jerry Graham. But the novelty faded as soon as we got back to the apartment. The moment he stepped out of the car, Jerry unzipped his fly and urinated on the gravel—when he was thirty seconds away from the bathroom.

"Oh, my God, what do you think you're doing?" shrieked Jerry's "date."

With this crude gesture, the Good Doctor killed the moment for our female guests—at least temporarily.

Jerry was a magnet for fights. In a nightclub, he'd barge over to a table, grab a woman by the wrist, and pull her away from her date. He'd walk into a biker bar, get in some stranger's face, and announce, "Hi, my name is Balls. Got any?"

The guy was so strange that I found him kind of fascinating. He made you wonder how he was still alive, and I'd sometimes look forward to whatever weird thing he was going to do next.

With 28,000 square miles, the Navajo Indian reservation is the largest in the United States. Window Rock, Arizona—on the New Mexico border—is the home of the group's tribal government, and has the reservation's densest population. The town had its own civic center, seating about 1,000 people, and more importantly, its own ring—a boxing ring, of course. The Navajos would sell tickets at two dollars apiece and promote the card all over the reservation. They even had their own ring announcer. This was going to be a "professional" show, and I anticipated a fairly large house.

Jerry and I made the trip to Window Rock together. Brick, Ron Pritchard, and Rick Cahill followed us in another car. From Phoenix, we drove approximately 330 miles northeast, turning off Interstate 40 and bobbing 20 miles over ruts and rocks on a winding dirt road. The dust was overwhelming, but the civic center was easy to find—it was on the main road going through the "city." It was actually the only road going through the city.

We arrived early to a pleasant surprise: the ring had already been set up. I climbed into it, and noted that the surface was about as hard as the concrete floor on which it had been erected.

Backstage, we went over the match we had rehearsed in Phoenix. Could this really be happening? It most certainly was. There were even separate dressing rooms for the babyfaces and the heels—connected by a hallway. In order to give the impression that we were legitimate opponents, Jerry instructed us to enter the ring from different entrances.

He didn't want to give away the magic, and "kill" the town.

I was sitting on a bench, lacing up my boots, when Dr. Jerry made this startling announcement: "We need to get color. The Indians like color." Jerry noticed a puzzled look on my face. I hadn't heard this term before. And despite my association with Abdullah, I'd never actually juiced in a match.

"I didn't bring a blade," I said truthfully.

As disorganized as he was in every other aspect of his life, Jerry was prepared for this. I felt sickened when he handed me the extra razor blade he kept at the bottom of his bag. There I was, about to disfigure my forehead with a blade that Jerry had probably been using since 1957. "Are the Indians really going to appreciate this?" I questioned.

I began nervously wrapping the blade to my finger, using so much tape that it resembled a lightbulb. It was so tight that my finger began to throb thirty minutes before the match.

The show started quickly enough. I was the first to leave the dressing room, walking to the ring and scrutinizing the crowd. There were about 250 fans in the building, and they were absolutely silent.

Ron Pritchard and I were introduced in the crowd's native tongue. Still more silence.

I don't remember much about this encounter. There was an adrenaline rush when I juiced for the first time. I followed Jerry's advice about blading, and found that it served me well throughout my career. In essence, he recommended going slowly, and slicing along the natural lines of your forehead. That way, your skin wouldn't have those vertical cuts that scarred the features of otherwise handsome wrestlers like Pat Patterson and Rocky Johnson. Words of wisdom from a guy who you'd never think would care.

Still, the match was a disaster. Pritchard pinned me, and I left the ring to no reaction at all. I was sure that I was leaving a trail of blood behind me, like that Indian Abdullah had carved up in Canada. But when I got to the dressing room and looked in the mirror, I was stunned to see it had been nothing more than a trickle.

In the next match, Jerry mercifully laid down for Rick Cahill, and then it was time for intermission. I have no idea why. There was nothing to sell, not even a Coke.

Our Tag Team match followed, and again, I'm hazy on details. Jerry and I were the heels, one of us got pinned, and that was it. The total time of the show: twenty-five minutes.

The crowd was quiet, but they actually seemed kind of happy. Maybe the Indians really *didn't* need much after all.

One of the tribal elders appeared in the dressing room and handed us the payoff. Two hundred and fifty fans at $2 a head meant $500. The Navajos removed $50 for expenses, and we were left with $450 to split five ways—$90 apiece. Compared to some of my payoffs in Calgary, this wasn't bad at all.

Jerry had told the babyfaces that we would split up our money at the all-night gas station at the end of the dirt road that connected with Interstate 40. He wanted to kayfabe the whole way. I'm not sure of the origin of the term *kayfabe,* but it means keeping the marks in the dark about pro wrestling's true nature. When two wrestlers are discussing privileged information and an outsider appears on the scene, they often shut each other up by blubbering, "Kayfabe. Kayfabe. Kayfabe." The sight of two babyfaces and two heels dividing up money at the Indian reservation would have been the most extreme violation of kayfabe and killed the town for good.

Jerry was as happy as if we had sold out Madison Square Garden. I was feeling pretty good myself, maneuvering the car through the pitch-black night. Then, no more than one hundred yards from Interstate 40, I ran over a small boulder, hitting the rock dead center and tearing a gaping hole in the oil pan. The red emergency light flashed as I shut the engine down. We pushed the car into the gas station and stood there helplessly as oil poured all over the ground.

There was only one thing to do: call for a tow truck to haul us some thirty miles away to Gallup, New Mexico, to get the car fixed. Everyone agreed to let Jerry hold on to the $450. We'd all rendezvous in Phoenix the next day and split up what was left—after we paid for a tow, repairs, and a motel room.

The Good Doctor took it all in stride: "It's part of the business."

I was at the garage at 7:00 the next morning. The mechanic said that he'd change the oil pan and would be done in an hour. I decided to wait around, and fifteen minutes later he tracked me down and broke the bad news. The mishap had caused "obstructions," and he would have to pull the engine to replace the oil pan—a job that would take all day. I went back to the motel and took a nap. Checkout time was at noon, so Jerry and I went out to lunch, then sat through a horrible Elvis movie.

It was closing time when the mechanic finally dropped the hood. The bill: just over $400. After towing, lodging, and food, we were in the red. I had just enough of my own money to pay for the gas to take us back to Phoenix. There I learned that Ron, Brick, and Rick had run out of gas in the desert, and had to walk five miles to a station. None of this was the Good Doctor's fault, of course. But was this an indication of things to come?

On our ride home, Jerry had mentioned that the Apache reservation was one of several other "hotbeds" of professional wrestling. But the promotion should probably have its own ring. Then, we could run shows in places like Ajo, Bisbee, Claypool, Eloy, and other abandoned mining towns. And guess what? He knew a guy who had a ring for just $250. I imagined myself in a real money-making business, working out of my home state, where I could train and tan. I could always be a part-time bouncer. And maybe I'd actually become a full-time wrestler, too. By the time we pulled up in front of the apartment, I was sold.

The very next day, Jerry took me to a gas station in Mesa, just outside of Phoenix. I was a little confused. "A wrestling ring at a gas station?" I asked.

I was led toward a storage room just past the pumps. I don't know why, but I was expecting to see a ring with the parts stacked up, perfectly folded mats, and padding. Instead, I found a pile of steel poles, plywood, a tangle of frayed cables, and something that looked like a mat—outside, *next* to the storage room. "Yeah," Jerry said assuredly, "it looks like it's all here."

I told the gas station owner to "hold" the ring for us, in case anyone was thinking of starting a rival promotion in Chandler or Paradise Valley.

At this point in my life, $250 might as well have been $250,000. But I had a plan. My sister, Joyce, had always wanted to see me "make something" of myself, and owning a wrestling promotion was something that might take me in that direction. Not only did she give me a loan, but her husband, Buddy, happened to own a U-Haul rental business. That enabled me to borrow a hitch and trailer, pick up the ring, and transport it back to my apartment.

With Jerry acting as foreman, reclining in the shade of a tree, I started assembling the ring right in front of my place, burning my hands on the metal frame. I was amazed that we had all of the parts. Well, almost. There were no turnbuckles.

When the job was completed, I walked across the canvas. The ring felt awfully small. From rope to rope, it was no more than twelve feet square—

more a toy than a place where 250-pound men could lock up and toss each other around.

But Jerry was unconcerned. "It looks good," he said of my construction work. "Let's get some Mexican food."

Brick, Rick, and Ron had all gotten over the fact that they'd driven more than 600 miles round-trip to Window Rock, earned nothing, and ran out of gas. In fact, they had a good laugh over it. Ron Pritchard didn't need the money anyway—he was in the NFL! He was just doing this for fun.

The next card that Jerry booked was in Prescott, 100 miles from Phoenix. Because we had to work the weekends at J.D.'s, this would be a weekday show. Jerry assured me that the arena had its own ring announcer, timekeeper, and ticket takers.

Once again, our advertising looked like it was going to be "word of mouth." That might have worked on Navajo land, but Prescott was not an Indian reservation. We needed to do something to get people interested in the event.

On the day of the show, Jerry and I drove up early. "We'll stop by the radio station, and do some promos for tonight," he said.

"Do they know we're coming?"

"Don't worry about it."

"I mean, what are we gonna do, man? Just show up and say, 'Here we are. Put us on the radio'?"

The Good Doctor professed to have visited the only radio station in town in the past, and done just that.

Incredibly, when we stopped at the station, the few people who comprised the staff seemed genuinely excited to see us. They ushered Jerry into the studio, where he sat directly in front of a microphone and began to deliver the kind of promo I hadn't heard since I was a kid, watching the Dumont network. "We will throw our opponents from pillar to post," he ranted, "and the blood will flow like water."

Did he say "blood"? At least I brought my own blade this time.

The disc jockey was delighted. He told us that he would replay the promo throughout the remainder of the day, right until showtime.

"I'm impressed," I told the Good Doctor. "You think we might have a sellout?"

"I think it's a very real possibility."

We ate, then headed over to the building, where I expected to see hundreds of fans waiting outside the box office. But that wasn't quite the picture that I encountered. The building was less of a coliseum and more of a hall, where the Elks or American Legion would meet. Still, the people who worked there had set up several hundred chairs and provided plenty of standing room space, in case we had an overflow crowd. We didn't have to bring along our new ring because the building supplied one of their own—a boxing ring, as hard as the one from the Navajo reservation.

Jerry and I settled into our tiny dressing room and changed into our ring gear, waiting for the fans to start pouring in. And we waited some more. Just before showtime, I left the dressing room to gauge the house. Peeking around the corner, I saw that all the chairs were still empty.

"Must be a late-arriving crowd," I said to myself.

Strangely, our opponents were missing, as well.

The show's starting time came and went. Thirty minutes later, not one spectator had entered the building.

With neither fans nor opponents, we decided to call it a night. As we were leaving the building, the rest of our crew pulled up. They'd missed a turn off the freeway and had ended up in Flagstaff, 95 miles away. "Kayfabe," Jerry told them conspiratorially. "We had a sellout, but had to cancel the show because you guys weren't here."

Brick's face dropped, and he drove off. When I told him the real story the next day, he roared with laughter. Once again, no one had made a penny. Through the promotional acumen of the Good Doctor, we were 0 for 2. The handwriting was on the wall.

Jerry's attitude never wavered. The Apache reservation show was coming up. We'd be using the new ring. It would be our charm.

It was now late June, and the temperatures were scorching. I was wondering how long my old Pontiac would last, and the upcoming trip—we'd be climbing 4,000 feet up from the desert floor, with the ring in a trailer hitched to the vehicle—would be a test.

There was a sense of optimism on the day of the card as we left the penetrating heat behind us and passed the copper-mining towns of Globe and Miami. The temperature dropped 30 degrees, and the road leveled off. The Pontiac had made it. We headed down another dirt road into Apache territory. Brick and his crew were following, but Jerry told them to enter the community hall through a separate entrance. "We don't want to smarten up the Indians," he stated.

As it would turn out, these Apaches were smarter than us.

Our dressing rooms contained nothing but a collection of old, rolled-up wrestling mats—no chairs and, of course, no showers. Speaking of chairs, I hadn't noticed any when I'd entered the building. All I'd seen was a large room, with a kitchen off to one side. A half-dozen Apache elders were lounging there, unmoved by our arrival.

It was time to get down to business. I'd spotted some kids strolling into the building, but wasn't sure if anyone was selling tickets. I asked one of the elders where he wanted the ring set up.

"Anywhere you like," he answered indifferently. I detected that these Apaches were not as friendly as the Navajos.

I went out to the trailer and started unloading the ring one piece of plywood at a time. Jerry had forbidden the babyfaces to assist me because that would be a breach of kayfabe. Brick couldn't help because the Indians might think that the referee was going to favor the heels. For a half hour, I tried assembling the ring alone, as some thirty Apaches milled about, ignoring me. This wasn't working, so I stomped back to the dressing room to solicit the support of the Good Doctor.

Jerry was sprawled out on the mats, seemingly in a trance, a small smile curling his lips. I wondered if he was thinking about his long-ago rumbles with Chief Big Heart, Argentina Apollo, and Gene Kiniski. If Tony Bennett left his heart in San Francisco, the Good Doctor's was still in New York. Obviously, he was in no mood to assist.

I went over to Brick. "Hey, man, I need your help," I told him. Once he joined me, we put up the ring relatively quickly.

Pritchard and I were in the first match. No one announced our entry, nor hired a timekeeper. The spectators were a handful of bored, listless Native Americans, some with their backs to the ring. Jerry hadn't said a word tonight about the Indians liking color, and that was fine with me. Why blade when it meant nothing to the crowd?

The ring was so ridiculously tiny. It also moved every time I bounced off the ropes. I "did the job" for Ron—in other words, I lost. Then Jerry went out and worked his match. After that, we had our Tag Team bout. The audience would have been more excited watching leaves blow across a backyard in the suburbs. What was wrong with these people? They acted like we didn't exist.

Two minutes into the match, I heard a loud snapping sound. A second or two later, the ring broke.

"Oooooh."

Finally, a small pop from the crowd. I was standing on the apron, and grabbed the ropes. In the ring, Jerry took an unexpected bump. The ring was leaning to one side, and tilting. It was going to collapse even more.

"Let's go home," Jerry said. Normally, that meant, "Let's end the match with our prearranged finish." This time, he was being literal.

Everyone bailed out. The show was over.

Needless to say, we weren't plagued by autograph seekers.

I went back to the dressing room and pulled my pants on over my boots and trunks. Shirtless, I went looking for someone in charge. My instincts told me not to wait for anybody to come to me. I wanted our payoff before I dismantled the ring.

"Where's my money?" I asked one of the elders.

"There's no money," he replied, annoyed by the discourtesy. "This is a charity event for the Apache Nation."

"What?" I began. But I didn't bother arguing. Was this a little payback for the white man? I'd known all along that the Apaches were smarter than us.

I motioned to the other guys: "Forget about kayfabe. Let's get this ring down."

Everyone except Jerry pitched in. By the time we finished loading up the trailer, there was only one Apache in the building. He was waiting to turn out the lights.

On the way down the mountain, the weight of the trailer began to "push" my car. The brakes grinded, and started overheating. It took me six hours to drive the next 100 miles; I crawled along the road, frequently pulling over.

Back on the desert floor, I asked Jerry, "What do we do now?"

"What do you mean?"

"Look at this. Three shows, and we've made nothing. We can't fix the ring—it's a total death trap. Pritchard's going back to the Oilers in a few weeks. Who do we get to replace him? And you can't work with Rick Cahill. He's hitting you with those amateur leg dives, and you're limping all over the place."

Jerry kind of shrugged.

"I want to be a wrestler, Jerry, but not like this. My days of working in the Wild West are over."

Jerry was quiet for a long time. But as we were pulling into Phoenix, he lit up. "I know what I can do. I'll call Vince McMahon in New York, or Mike LeBell in L.A. We'll go in as a Tag Team."

"You still talk to those guys?"

"Yeah, they're personal friends of mine."

That sounded fine to me. But first, I needed to do something symbolic. I pulled up to the city dump and unloaded the trailer—tossing out the plywood, the ropes, and the frame of that wretched ring, piece by piece. Then I turned and drove away. I didn't look back. That's the mistake Lot's wife had made when she took a final glimpse at the burning cities of Sodom and Gomorrah. She was turned into a pillar of salt, frozen in place, never going forward.

I wasn't going to let that happen to me.

CHAPTER SIX

MY BROTHER'S KEEPER

And the Lord said unto Cain, "Where is Abel, thy brother?"
And he said, "I know not."

—Genesis 4:9

There had already been two incarnations of wrestling's Golden Grahams. After Eddie Graham left the team to settle in Tampa—where he became promoter of the Florida territory, and one of the most influential men in the business—Jerry joined forces with James Grady Johnson, rechristening him Luke Graham. Johnson was a soft-spoken, even-tempered guy in real life, but at the arena—with his Colonel Sanders goatee and long, wild hair—he was "Crazy Luke." On interviews, he'd roll his eyes and point at the ceiling. In the ring, he'd cover his ears and shake his head while fans chanted, "Crazy Luke! Crazy Luke! Crazy Luke!"

I'm not sure if either of them realized that mental illness seemed to run in the family.

Now I suggested that Jerry needed another Graham brother, a six-foot-four-inch Graham brother with twenty-two-inch biceps. "Any idea what you wanna call yourself?" he asked, as we hung out in the apartment, strategizing our next move.

My days on the evangelical circuit left me with no other choice: *"Billy Graham."* The reverend was one of my heroes—a confidant of presidents, prime ministers, and kings, whose goodness and sincerity enabled him to ignite the faith of the common man. I can't count the number of times later on when I'd introduce myself, and the person replied, "You mean, like the *real* Billy Graham?"

Jerry pulled out his address book and called Mike LeBell in Los Angeles. There was a buoyancy in Jerry's voice as he greeted the promoter and informed him about the youngest and largest sibling in the Graham clan. The Good Doctor's sell job was superb—along the lines of the promo I had heard at the Prescott radio station. I knew we were in. But as the conversation was ending, Jerry's facial expression and vocal inflection changed.

"I'll think about it," LeBell was saying on the other end of the line. Then, believe it or not, he actually uttered, "Don't call me. I'll call you."

Waiting for Mike LeBell to call Jerry would be like waiting for the Apaches to mail us a payoff. I took control of the situation. The only way that we had a chance of working in L.A. was by driving over there, walking into the man's office, and saying, "Here we are." That would take nerves of steel, something Jerry had in ample supply. If he could swagger up to strangers and say, "My name is Balls. Got any?" he could certainly do this.

We went to a local photo studio and had some publicity shots taken. Both of us were dark-haired, in shades and terrycloth robes—we couldn't afford anything else. The entire session cost $25, if that.

My real brother, Vance, wasn't happy at all. The Phoenix police hated Jerry Graham. I'd already been arrested for forging signatures at Kentucky Fried Chicken and scamming a stereo with a stolen credit card. Now I was calling myself Jerry Graham's brother.

"Why would you want to do something like that?" Vance snapped, as I stood across from him in his office. "Why can't you use your real name?"

"It's a gimmick. Do you know what a gimmick is?"

Vance had had it with me: "At this point, Wayne, I don't really care what a gimmick is." He was going ballistic. I left, hoping that—given his track record—the power brokers in the wrestling business had a more tempered reaction to the Good Doctor.

Jerry and I drove to California at night to avoid the incinerating heat of the desert. Arriving in Santa Monica at midmorning, we found a motel and took care of the next order of business, purchasing two kits of Lady Clairol Ultra Blue. It was what we needed to turn into blonds.

Back at the room, Jerry prepared the bleach, resembling a mad chemist. He had obviously done this many times before. With the blue mixture smeared into my hair, I caught my reflection in the mirror. It looked like someone had poured a bowl of cake frosting on my head. Jerry said that it would take about an hour for the concoction to "cook," so we headed to the pool.

Laying back on my deck chair, inhaling the salt water air and taking in the sun, I glanced over at my new "brother," with blue cake frosting in his hair, a cigar in his mouth, and the *L.A. Times* spread across his huge belly. In the pool, some parents and kids tried not to gawk too much. We were only a few miles from Hollywood, so I could imagine the kinds of things that floated through their minds. Turning my attention back to Jerry, I studied his features and tried to read his thoughts. This was likely his last chance to recapture the splendor of years gone by.

The Olympic Auditorium stood at the corner of Eighteenth Street and Grand Avenue in a predominantly Mexican section of Los Angeles. The building had been constructed for bicycle races at the 1932 Los Angeles Olympics, but now was utilized mainly for boxing and wrestling, as well as the Roller Games—an outlaw version of the Roller Derby. On a good night, more than 5,000 fans filled the arena to watch performers like "Classy" Freddie Blassie, Mil Mascaras, John Tolos, Black Gordman, and Great Goliath and Mr. Moto. Moto's real name was Charlie Iwamoto. He played the stereotypical World War II–era Japanese heel in the ring, but during the week he worked in the second-floor wrestling office with LeBell and Blassie, the gravelly-voiced originator of the term "pencil-neck geek." Both were involved in "booking" the cards—conceptualizing story lines and determining the creative fates of the various wrestlers.

With our hair freshly bleached, Jerry and I entered the building un-announced and clambered up the stairs. The moment of truth had arrived. Jerry was 350 pounds and out of shape. I had the deep tan, tank top, and bodybuilder's physique—the overall look that would take me far in the business.

At first, LeBell, Blassie, and Moto greeted our brazen visit with faces that reminded me of those statues carved out of stone on Easter Island. LeBell shot Jerry a piercing glare, radiating disgust. "I thought I said I'd call you," the promoter said.

I jumped into the conversation: "I figured it would be better if we came in person, in case you wanted to use us." I flexed as the words left my lips, hoping that the body oil I'd smeared on myself at the hotel enhanced my magnetism.

I blurted out that I was the legitimate arm-wrestling champion of the world. "We can offer $1,000 to anyone who can beat me, to get heat. Then I can shoot an arm-wrestling angle with the top babyface." Between Jerry and Abdullah, I was beginning to talk wrestling lingo like a native.

Right on cue, Jerry followed up. "You can bring us in every week on TV for a month, just to get us over. The way Vince does. We'll drive back and forth from Phoenix, and pay for our gas."

We were giving them the hard sell. The air sparkled with tension. Freddie Blassie looked chillingly into Jerry's eyes with an expression of complete disdain. To this day, I've never seen that much contempt on a person's face. What had the Good Doctor done to Freddie Blassie? Could one man really hate another person that much?

Jeff Walton: I was the publicity director for the territory, and promoted shows for Mike LeBell at very small arenas around the southland. I knew that Fred hated drunks. He looked at Jerry Graham as someone who was really talented, but wasting his life. Fred couldn't stand guys like that. It just turned him off. Fred never drank at all. He chased women.

I walked into the meeting while Wayne and Jerry were talking. And Jerry was a great talker. When he was sober, there was no one who could beat him. He was just a sensational talker.

Suddenly, the room went quiet. For thirty seconds, there was silence—*thunderous* silence. Mike LeBell looked stunned. The only sound to be heard was the rhythmic thumping of his pencil on the desk. Then he spoke, directing his words and his glower at me. "I'm going to let you work under one condition. You have to take full responsibility for him. If he screws up once, he's gone, and you're gone with him."

Take responsibility for Jerry Graham? Babysitting the Good Doctor would be a harsh and unreasonable condition, to my mind. But I agreed to it anyway.

Our official starting date would be in August. But we'd begin making TV appearances the following Wednesday night. There were no handshakes offered to welcome us aboard. So I simply said, "Thank you." I would have loved to have heard what they said about us after we left.

Jeff Walton: Charlie Moto wasn't really buying this Billy Graham character. He didn't like bodybuilder types or football players. He didn't think they could work. They didn't have the coordination.

"What do you think of this guy?" Charlie asked me.

"He's kind of different." I'd never seen another bodybuilder of that caliber with his kind of look, tall with blond hair. And of course, Jerry Graham was with him.

"You like him?" Charlie asked.

"Yeah, he's okay."

"You'll take him in your town?"

One of the places where I ran small shows was El Monte. "Yeah, sure. If he wants to wrestle in El Monte, sure."

You see, every week, we'd run El Monte and Bakersfield on the same night. Jules Strongbow was the promoter who had Bakersfield. He'd been around a long time, and got first choice. We'd sit down and split up the wrestlers, and he'd say, "Okay, I'll take Freddie Blassie and Mil Mascaras. You can have the Oregon Lumberjack and Art 'Boom Boom' Mihalic."

I thought, Wow, I could take this guy, Billy Graham, and do something really colorful with him.

In August we started with the territory full-time, moving into the Figueroa Hotel in downtown L.A. Although the Figueroa was a local landmark, the building was going through a decrepit phase at the time, enabling the Good Doctor to feel very much at home. He was back in the business again, and kayfabing to the extreme. One afternoon we were coming down in the elevator with a businessman, whose company was cutting corners by sticking the poor guy in lodging alongside the most recent amalgamation of the Golden Grahams. Jerry and I were talking about nothing—the weather, and maybe what we were having for lunch. But in the presence of an outsider, the Good Doctor began prattling away in Z-talk—the form of carny where *weather* became "wee-iz-eather" and *tuna* was "tee-iz-una." The businessman had no idea what we were saying, but—with this absurd attempt to "protect the business"—Jerry had the stranger's undivided attention.

In Jerry's defense, many of the other boys were as radical. I remember how captivated I was in 1977, watching my friend, Gorilla Monsoon, do a television interview about the validity of our profession. Staring unblinkingly into the camera, Gorilla defiantly told the reporter, "There is no such monster in pro wrestling as a predetermined winner." He conveyed the statement so convincingly that I almost believed him myself.

In some ways, L.A. was a dream promotion, with short trips, sunny beaches, and good gyms. Every day, Jerry and I would drive over to Venice Beach, where I worked out on an open-air platform while—fifty yards away—Jerry slept in the sand like a beached whale. It was a great lifestyle. Now all we had to do was make some money. That would be the hard part.

For all the hostility we encountered on the day we barnstormed the wrestling office, Mike LeBell bought my arm-wrestling pitch, and pushed it from the start. This was apparent on the first day I turned up at the Olympic to work television. Several hours before showtime, after getting myself in the mood by walking the ring—a work of art, by the way, compared to that knickknack we used on the Apache reservation—I sat down in the dressing room and leafed through a large stack of programs. Big bold letters declared, "Billy Graham holds the title of Arm-Wrestling Champion of the World, and offers $1,000 to anyone who can beat him."

Like in Calgary, these contests were shoots. But I should mention that my arm-wrestling opponents were initially wrestling photographers and guys who did odd jobs in the company's office. All these adversaries were half my size, which greatly increased my heat with our fan base.

The promotion had two television programs, one in English and one in Spanish. You could get a real sense of the socioeconomic background of our audience by looking through our program. One prominent ad featured an illustration of a man from ancient Baghdad, floating on a rug toward an ornate palace. The slogan above it read: "Aladdin Bail Bonds. Ride the Magic Carpet Home."

Of course, to all the wrestlers back then, the fans were marks. It was a degrading term. Marks were suckers, fanatics, overbearing, and gullible. Socializing with them was taboo. Why would you anyway, when they believed all this stupid stuff? It was a regrettable mentality. Today, I look at our fans as just that—fans. Many are my friends—people who appreciated the way I entertained them, particularly during periods when they wanted to escape complications in their lives. In turn, they stayed in touch with me when I needed their camaraderie. Yes, you will see the word *mark* throughout this book—because that's how we spoke—but only when necessary.

Before my first arm-wrestling matchup, I recommended that Jerry Graham accompany me to the ring. LeBell consented, of course. He understood how gifted Jerry was at antagonizing the fans. The man had an aura that made spectators loathe his presence.

Professional wrestling was still a few years behind the times in 1970. Despite the fact that we were three years past the Summer of Love—and

That's my "brother," the "Good Doctor" Jerry Graham, on the left.

just down the coast from San Francisco—wrestlers in L.A. had yet to adopt the hippie look. Until I came on the scene. I liked the hippie lifestyle—at least the part about freedom, rebellion, and independence—and the wardrobe that went along with it. In L.A., there were no velour or sequin jackets for me. Instead, the fans got pork-chop sideburns, medallions, and knee-high Indian moccasin boots with peace signs sewn on the side. I personally cut the leather for my fringed vests, slipping silver adornments through the rawhide, and strung my beaded headbands.

I even got the Good Doctor to dress like a hippie. You'd think that a guy from his era would show some resistance. But Jerry was oblivious. If I said the gimmick would get over, he was okay with it.

Meanwhile, the arm-wrestling gimmick was going so well that the promotion—without ever consulting me—began issuing open challenges to anyone in the arena. That worked fine in Calgary. But this was California, where the city of Petaluma was home to the world arm-wrestling championships. I was chilled by the thought that one of the contestants might show up at a taping, waiting for the chance to beat me on television.

Most legitimate arm wrestlers are psychological animals. Before matches, their buddies fire them up by slapping them in the face. When they compete, they look each other in the eye, hissing, grunting, and yelling. There was no way to screen out these shooters, and, yes, they did arrive. Aware of this, I came up with a technique that would give me an advantage. When my opponent and I linked hands, the referee—Mike LeBell's brother, Gene—placed his palm on top of our knuckles and asked my opponent if he was ready. When he answered affirmatively, Gene would turn to me and repeat the question. But as soon as I said yes, he'd lift his hand prematurely, allowing me to get the jump by sliding my right elbow forward and leaning down with my right shoulder for more leverage. Once this happened, I felt like it was impossible for anybody to defeat me.

The shooters were incensed. One guy I beat actually grabbed the table and threw it at me. I snatched a metal chair and whacked him with it as hard as I could. The cops hit the ring and pulled my opponent away. "You cheated!" he was screaming. "You cheated! You got the jump on me!"

"Welcome to the world of pro wrestling," I said under my breath.

The shooters started stalking me away from the arena. I remember fixing a tire in front of my hotel and being surprised to see one of these guys cruising by slowly.

"Hey, Graham," the man said. "You wanna arm-wrestle?"

"Are you kidding?" I answered. "I have to change my flat and leave." What was wrong with these shooters? I was out in the middle of the street, and this nut wanted to me to stop, go into the hotel, sit down at a table, and arm-wrestle! These guys were obsessed.

One Saturday evening, I had my biggest scare. A guy from the office told me that my arm-wrestling opponent wanted to talk to me in the hallway before our match. I went out to meet him and was astonished by what I saw—an individual built more like a gorilla than a human being. His fingers practically touched his knees! His forearms were huge, and had giant veins running all over them like a road map. Three or four friends stood behind him as he proposed that we make a $10,000 bet. He owned a steel mill, he added, and had the cash. To accentuate his point, he unzipped a bag to show me the money.

Did he really expect me to have ten grand in *my* wrestling bag? "It was nice meeting you," I replied. "See you in the ring."

I walked away, but the man had done an incredible psych job. What if this guy actually beat me? The big arm-wrestling angle we were planning would come crashing to an end.

I refused to be intimidated, though. I paced back and forth in the dressing room, building up my adrenaline. No one else had beaten me, and he wouldn't, either. There was no turning back.

I went out to the ring. We sat, hooked hands, and maneuvered for the best grip. Gene LeBell did the quick-start thing, and once again, I had the jump. The man's arm went down. I'd survived.

My opponent rose and smiled at me. "Let's do it again sometime," he said. "But next time, bring some money."

He knew he'd been had on television, but chose to part company like a gentleman. Not your average arm-wrestler's attitude, for sure.

We milked the arm-wrestling gimmick to the max. Now it was time to move on and shoot the big angle. The week after my defeat of the steel mill owner, I swaggered up to the ring, tables and chairs in place. As always, I antagonized the crowd, reminding them that there was no one who could beat me. I went through my posing ritual to get as much heat as possible, then sat down. That was the cue for Freddie Blassie to storm the ring. This, unfortunately, is one place where the word *mark* really applies. Blassie was L.A.'s hottest commodity, but he was in his fifties, and reminded me of a cranky grandfather. Although he was broad-chested, he was hardly a gym rat. But the fans were in a complete frenzy, on their feet, deliriously chanting, "Blassie! Blassie! Blassie!" The man was their savior.

We hooked hands together and started pulling. It was a stalemate. Then, slowly, Blassie's arm began to go down. When his hand was about three inches from the table, he started making his comeback, using supernatural strength to pull my arm back and over. My winning streak was in jeopardy, and pandemonium was breaking out.

My arm hit the table with a boom. Freddie Blassie had done the impossible, like the 1969 New York Mets the year before. It was a storybook ending until the Great Goliath and Black Gordman hit the ring.

Paul Heyman: *Back then, there was a simple formula: the good guy (Blassie) rides into town wearing the white hat and beats the bad guy wearing the black hat, and all is well.*

Gordman and Goliath were two Spanish-speaking heels who'd incense Latino fans by publicly denying their heritage. When ring announcer Jimmy Lennon listed their homeland as Mexico, they'd protest, "No, no—*New Mexico!*" They also were exceptional at what they did. Black Gordman was seamless in the ring, absolutely methodical. Goliath was balding, and smaller than some of his American opponents, but incredibly vicious. When he kicked someone with a foot to the side, it looked like a shoot. And he had the facial expressions of a killer.

Before Blassie could exult in his arm-wrestling win, Gordman grabbed the hammer from the ring bell and hit the man our Chicano enthusiasts lovingly called "El Rubio de Oro"—"The Golden Blond." Freddie went down and got juice. The three of us swarmed all over him, kicking and stomping, leaving Blassie in a scarlet clump.

With blood running down his face, Blassie challenged me to a match in his personally designed cage—"La Jaula de Freddie Blassie," or "The Freddie Blassie Cage," according to the Mexicans. I was thrilled to be rewarded for all those weeks building up my character with a battle against the promotion's number-one babyface. My only disappointment was the location—the town of Northridge, a thirty-minute drive from downtown L.A., in an arena that the territory only ran sporadically.

Still, the place was sold out. I was nervous, of course, because this was my first Cage match and I was really green. If I hurt a guy of Blassie's stature, there would have been enduring repercussions. When we locked up, I barely showed any offense. It was sell, sell, sell, take a bump for Blassie, punch and kick him a little bit, then sell some more. To no one's disappointment, I got color and did the job.

I later wondered why our feud was confined to one match. Today, I understand. No one really knew what I could and couldn't do in the ring; they only knew that I was big, strong, and capable of making mistakes. At Blassie's age, he couldn't risk an injury that would send him into retirement. There were many times in my career when I'd feel the same way. In professional wrestling, as the saying goes, you give your opponent your body, and he's supposed to take care of it. That's not easy for some inexperienced guys.

Jeff Walton: *We were at a show in El Monte, and I said to Billy, "What can you do?"*

He said, "What do you mean, what can I do?"

I asked, "Do you have any finishing holds? How long can you go?"

And he said, "Well, you tell me."

I said, "Look, you're a big guy. Can you do a bear hug where you pick the guy up and shake him?"

He said, "Oh, yeah, yeah."

I didn't want the match to go too long because I realized the guy didn't have much seasoning. So we kept it short. He got in the ring, went down on one knee, and started posing. He beat up his opponent a little, whipped him into the ropes, put him in a bear hug, and that was it.

The next week, he came back and wrestled two guys in a Handicap match. Both times, the fans reacted really well. I told Charlie Moto, "This kid's got a lot of potential."

But Charlie still wasn't happy with him. Billy was a bodybuilder, and he was wearing those fringed jackets and headbands. Charlie may have done an anti-American gimmick, but he was actually kind of conservative. He didn't like hippies.

I was younger than Charlie, and the hippie thing didn't bother me at all. But I didn't like the name Billy Graham. "Nature Boy" Buddy Rogers had a problem here because there was an actor named Buddy Rogers. When we brought in a guy called Gorgeous George Jr., Gorgeous George's widow wanted to sue him. Calling yourself Billy Graham seemed pretty serious to me. You know, it's like playing with fire when you mess with the evangelicals. I expected to hear from Reverend Billy Graham's lawyers, ordering us to cease and desist. But the call never came.

At times, it seemed like Jerry was more my manager than my Tag Team partner, doing the talking for our team while I took the bumps. Not that I was complaining—that's what I wanted to be doing. But when Jerry had to wrestle, he could still work. The man had incredible balance and ring psychology.

I was learning a lot from Jerry, and a bunch of the other guys in L.A. I'd observe the way some wrestlers exaggerated their facial gestures, and did the same thing with my mannerisms. I also copied Muhammad Ali—and believe me, I wasn't alone. We've all seen the photos where Ali is taunting an opponent, opening his mouth really wide. It was a pretty easy technique to rip off.

Rocky Johnson was another Ali fan. Like me, he had a bodybuilder's look. But Rocky was one of the most agile big men pro wrestling ever saw.

His patented sequence was taking a backdrop, landing on his feet, and delivering three perfectly timed dropkicks to his opponent's head. It requires a tremendous amount of skill for a man weighing 265 pounds to jump into the air, hit you with both feet, and never extract any of your teeth. And Rocky was so quick that when we wrestled, I couldn't get off the mat fast enough from his first dropkick to feed him my body again. Once he hit you with those three dropkicks, he'd excite the fans by going into the Ali shuffle.

Because of his African heritage, Rocky—whose son later honored him by adopting the ring name The Rock—was called the "Soul Man." In one Olympic Auditorium wrestling program, he was also referred to as "The Colored Matador," but fortunately, time was passing by those types of nicknames. Although he was later billed from Washington, D.C., Rocky came from Nova Scotia—the descendant of slaves who took refuge as far from the plantation as possible—and didn't talk jive. He was an old-school babyface—an intelligent, refined athlete.

Johnson's Tag Team partner, Earl "Mr. Universe" Maynard, was another black muscleman—who happened to come from England. Earl rarely got interview time because he spoke in a British accent and, black or white, the fans just couldn't relate. Between the two of them, Rocky had a lot more soul.

I liked wrestling Rocky because he was such a light worker; you never knew he touched you. But one night in San Diego—while I was laying on the apron, selling for the Soul Man—a fan came up to the ring and busted me in the eye. Rocky stepped back as I jumped onto the arena floor and pounded my attacker like we were in a street fight. It may sound cruel, but when a spectator dared place his hands on you, he willingly entered a no-man's-land. In 1970, a wrestling heel lived in constant fear of being shot or stabbed. The only way to stop these guys was to go into attack mode. It sent a message to others in the audience harboring similar fantasies.

Whether you like his product or not, credit must be given to Vince McMahon Jr. for ending these types of assaults on wrestlers. Because of the label "sports entertainment," and the revelation that matches are predetermined, the creed today is that wrestlers are athletic, versatile actors, working very hard to make a living. This full disclosure may have eliminated some of the emotion from the matches, but—in this regard, at least—the wrestlers are safer.

I know that Jerry Graham was happy in Los Angeles. He'd sit in the dressing room, holding court about training under wrestling's original "Golden Greek," Jim Londos, and shooting with Tiger Jodingar Singh in

India. The boys loved it. But there was something inside the Good Doc-tor—maybe even a genetic malformation—that continuously forced him to sabotage himself. Sooner or later, you sensed, he was going to self-destruct.

The Graham brothers only had a few Tag Team matches, and we were sometimes booked in separate towns on the same night. It didn't look like LeBell wanted to revive the Golden Grahams the way Jerry had hoped, and I think that was getting to him. In fact, I seemed to be getting a push as a singles wrestler. Over time, I noticed Jerry becoming disconnected.

One night when I was working for Jeff Walton in El Monte, Jerry was supposed to wrestle in San Diego. News filtered back to me that he didn't show up. I'd soon find out that he ended up in Hollywood, going on a drunken rampage from one club to the next, causing fights and destroying property. He was arrested and taken to the Los Angeles County Jail. The police called Mike LeBell at 3:00 A.M. Mike arranged for Jerry to be bailed out and taken back to the hotel.

When I woke up that morning, I noticed the message light blinking on my phone. The hotel clerk had written the following on a slip of memo paper: "I want you both in my office immediately. Mike LeBell."

Rousing Jerry, I told him about the message. "You have any idea what this is about?" I asked.

Jerry stared blankly ahead. "I don't have a clue."

On the drive to the Olympic, Jerry continued to work me, maintaining that he was puzzled about the communiqué. We walked up the stairs to face a livid LeBell. "You're both fired," he announced.

It was then that I learned the true story.

"Why am I being fired?" I asked LeBell.

"I think you remember that it was *your* job to be responsible for this guy."

"Look at your booking sheets," I pleaded. "I was in El Monte last night. And Jerry was booked in San Diego. I know you told me to babysit him, but come on, Mike, if you put us in two different cities, I can't do that."

I was mad that Jerry had lied to me all morning. Working on television in Los Angeles was a very big deal. I'd never had a chance like this before, and I couldn't let it slip away. Taking a breath, I prepared to distance myself from my gimmick brother.

"Do what you want with him, Mike. But it's neither fair nor logical to fire me. My arm wrestling is over with the marks. And I want to stay here and work—with or without Jerry."

The Good Doctor said nothing in his defense. He just stood there, mute. LeBell said nothing, either. And he was the judge in this situation. I shifted my feet, praying for him to render the proper decision.

Finally, the promoter spoke: "Billy, you can stay. Jerry, I'm giving you two weeks' notice."

Those would be the longest two weeks I'd ever endured in my life—hellish, you might say.

Jerry and I were still paired. Every night after the matches, he demanded that I pull over at a liquor store or bar. Jerry imbibed by himself; I was a nondrinker who just took tons of pills. The Good Doctor was totally out of control.

You may be familiar with the song "It Never Rains in Southern California." Well, on more than one night—as we drove to Bakersfield or Long Beach—I was convinced that it was raining inside my Pontiac. But the horrific noise I heard was Jerry urinating on the floor. It was one of the countless indignities I had to suffer. When drunk, the man was repulsive.

The two weeks were drawing to a close when my car broke down on the San Diego Freeway, right at the San Clemente exit. I sputtered into a gas station and was told that the mechanic was off duty until the next morning. We'd have to stay overnight.

At the hotel, I went into the restaurant and had dinner. Then I returned to the room, watched TV, and fell asleep. Jerry, of course, headed to the bar.

While I was sleeping, Jerry went berserk, shoving people around and spewing grandiose insults. He was run out of the bar, and stumbled back toward the room. Because this occurred on a nightly basis, the incident might not have made this book if we weren't in San Clemente. Its most famous resident at the time was the president of the United States, Richard Milhous Nixon.

I awoke to the sound of Jerry beating on the door. When I let him into the room, he rushed to the wall, spreading his arms and legs apart. You have to remember that Jerry was more than just a drunk—he'd been institutionalized several times for mental illness. Now he appeared to be hallucinating. He clawed at the wall with a frozen, paralyzed look on his face, his eyes bulging from their sockets.

"They're everywhere!" he yelled. "They're trying to kill me! Machine guns! Hand grenades!"

I remembered Jerry once telling me that he'd served in World War II, and wondered if he was having some kind of flashback. As I reflected on this, the room's dark walls were suddenly illuminated by a burst of flashing red light coming through the window. The police were surrounding the hotel.

Seconds later, cops and FBI agents stormed the room and placed Jerry in handcuffs. The authorities wanted to know who we were, and—in a calm, reasonable tone—I explained that we were professional wrestlers who would be departing San Clemente as soon as my car was fixed the next morning. As for Jerry, I added, he'd be leaving the state in a few days.

Remarkably, the cops removed Jerry's cuffs. "Okay," one of the officers told me. "You're responsible for him."

Where had I heard that before?

"Neither of you leave the room tonight. As soon as your car is fixed, we want the two of you to get out of town and never come back."

"You've got a deal."

Evidently, Jerry hadn't done that much damage to the bar or hurt anyone. Otherwise, I'm sure, assault charges would have been filed. With the president in town, the lawmen probably had better things to do than deal with another drunk and disorderly. Apparently, they were happy just to get rid of the Good Doctor.

Nonetheless, I wonder if law enforcement would be as flexible if someone caused the same type of disruption in Crawford, Texas, today.

After everybody left, I turned off the light and attempted to go back to sleep. Jerry sat at the edge of his bed and forced me to endure one more insult. As I buried my head into the pillow, I heard the familiar sound of Jerry urinating—this time on the carpet.

Finally, Jerry's two weeks with the company expired, and my living nightmare ended. After our final show together, we exchanged curt good-byes and went our separate ways. I never saw the Good Doctor again.

Jeff Walton: Despite everything, Wayne was wise to link himself to Jerry Graham. This was a very closed business, and I don't think Wayne would have made it in here as fast if he wasn't a Graham Brother. After Jerry Graham got fired, Billy Graham still had the name.

Before the end of 1970, I had my first wrestling magazine cover—flexing in a headband, hippie beads, striped trunks, and my moccasin boots with peace signs on the side. The headline read, INTRODUCING BILLY GRAHAM. HE TALKS PEACE BUT HE RAISES HELL.

Joyce Sampson: The whole family was really happy to see Wayne as a professional wrestler. I can remember seeing Gorgeous George in Arizona, and everyone knew that Gorgeous George made money. Because of wrestling, Wayne was eventually able to give our mother some financial help. We all knew that Wayne would do something with his body one day. Now, he'd figured it out.

After Jerry left, I mainly worked singles matches, wrestling opponents like Rocky Johnson, Earl Maynard, La Pantera Negra, Pedro Morales, and Don Morrow—later repackaged as Don "The Magnificent" Muraco—a young guy whose parents happened to be Freddie Blassie's landlords. Another foe was Mil Mascaras—Spanish for "A Thousand Masks"—possibly wrestling's biggest Latino drawing card. Like the legendary El Santo, he took his masked gimmick very seriously, and used it to cross over to a movie career in his native Mexico. But Mascaras was never one of the boys. Here's an example: after his matches, he'd shower with his mask on. I understand protecting your image, but the guy was kayfabing *us*.

I'm not the first person to say that it wasn't fun wrestling Mascaras. He was mechanical, and because of his mask, fans couldn't read his facial expressions. Pro wrestling is all about facial expressions. How can you tell if a man is hurt if you can't see the pain on his face? In L.A., I actually saw some Mexican wrestlers blade themselves while wearing a hood. What a waste—cutting up your head for a barely visible dot of blood on a dark mask!

Mascaras was also an absolute prima donna, prancing around on his toes and sticking out his chest. He hated to sell your moves; whatever you got, he gave grudgingly.

As the months passed, though, I found that I was the one being asked to sell more and more, jobbing for Mascaras and a number of Mexican wrestlers half my size. There was a pattern developing. The promotion that had put me over so strong seemed to be washing its hands of me. Thanks to the Good Doctor, the Graham name had too much baggage in L.A.

As unscrupulous as the wrestling business was back then, it was common courtesy for a promoter to call a colleague in another part of the country and say, "Hey, I've got a guy here who's a good worker. He's a little green, but he has lots of potential. You want him?" This policy benefited not only the wrestlers but the territories; new faces made a promotion interesting.

One day, Charlie Moto mentioned that the promoter in San Francisco had heard about me and wanted to give me a tryout. I was also told that I'd make more money in northern California. That wouldn't have been very hard to do.

I didn't know anything about the promoter, Roy Shire, or the San Francisco territory. But I'd clearly overstayed my welcome in L.A. Shire was going to book me at his main arena, the Cow Palace, then decide whether I'd fit in his promotion. I honestly didn't feel any pressure. After all, I'd been invited to this party.

THE DEAN OF THE COW PALACE

You ever strut? It's not easy.

—Roy Shire to sportswriter Richard Hoffer

When a San Francisco livestock show drew turnaway crowds, the concept of a permanent "Cow Palace" was born. The first event at the cavernous arena—one of FDR's Works Project Administration (WPA) endeavors—was a rodeo paying tribute to the late Will Rogers. A few weeks later Pearl Harbor was bombed, and the government converted the building into a launching point for troops departing to the Pacific Theater.

In the early 1960s Roy Shire took over the Palace, following his own war with the established promoter in San Francisco, Joe Malcewicz. Malcewicz was getting older and losing his touch, but he was backed by the gigantic National Wrestling Alliance (NWA)—a conglomeration of promoters who ganged up on upstarts like Shire by sending top talent to each other's shows, obscuring whatever cards the renegades hoped to promote.

Nonetheless, Shire—who'd wrestled as Professor Roy Shire—was a very aggressive guy, and knew how to use television to sell his product. Not only did he trample over Malcewicz but, in 1968, the NWA invited him to join the organization.

Shire had graduated from "professor" to dean of the Cow Palace.

By the time I had my first match at the fabled arena, on October 10, 1970, Shire's Big Time Wrestling Group was a major attraction there, along with the Roller Derby and another local phenomenon, the Grateful Dead.

Shire had heard all about me, and now he wanted to see me with his own eyes. As I headed from the airport to the Cow Palace, I was stunned by its size. With a seating capacity of nearly 15,000 fans, it sat there, with its six-acre concrete-and-steel roof, like a giant cube, shrouded in fog, looking somewhat foreboding. Peeking through the taxi window, I marveled at the cars parked blocks away, and the hordes of people marching up the sidewalks from all directions.

I knew one thing for sure—they weren't coming to see me.

The misty night muted the light of the marquee, which added to the mystique of the man headlining the show. "The Blond Bomber," Ray Stevens, was a household name in the Bay Area. Stevens—who'd once wrestled as Shire's younger brother, "Ray Shire"—was a legend to the fans, and a folk hero to the wrestlers. Now I was just minutes away from meeting him and shaking his hand.

I felt completely awkward as I entered the building. I nervously inquired where Roy Shire could be found, and someone pointed him out. With his gray hair swept back, Shire gave me a firm handshake and smiled—something I wasn't used to in Los Angeles. Stevens and his on-again-off-again nemesis, Pat Patterson, were funny guys, and projected their personalities onto the rest of the talent. So I noticed that a lot of the wrestlers were joking around—another contrast to the atmosphere I'd encountered at the Olympic.

When it was time for my match, I paraded toward the ring and was greeted with a roar of boos. These people—who'd never seen me wrestle before—hated me already. How could that be? The secret was that, in San Francisco, the heels walked down the same aisle for every match. I already had guilt by association on my side. Now I dropped down to one knee and gave the fans a one-minute posing routine. The result was unbelievable. The Cow Palace didn't have entrance music, videos, or bursts of fireworks, but it had a lot of heat. And I got it instantly.

My opponent that night was Kenny Ackles. His purpose was putting me over, and he did it well, raising the bar for jobbers everywhere. I returned to L.A. to finish out my commitments to Mike LeBell.

On November 7, I was invited back to the Cow Palace, and this time Bobby Nichols was anointed with the task of doing the honors for me. Unfortunately, I didn't realize that my moccasin boots provided little ankle protection, and I hurt myself in this confrontation, slinging Nichols into the ropes, then lifting my leg to meet his stomach with a size 15 boot. As he fell, I turned, diverting my eyes from him, and he came down with his full body weight on my left ankle. I dropped to the mat as if I'd been shot. I told my opponent what was going on, and we ended the match early, going straight to the finish.

The dressing room at the Cow Palace was located two floors above the arena. I limped back up the stairway, the pain exploding in my lower leg every time my foot touched the ground. I finally made it past the curtain, where Shire was waiting.

"Hey, Graham," he said, uttering the words that wrestlers in the San Francisco territory dreaded, "I wanna talk to you."

"I think I just broke my left ankle."

"Well, just stand on the other one. I want to tell you something."

As I leaned against the wall in anguish, he delivered a short lecture about how I'd lost my heat after I stopped posing. "What you want to do is attack your opponent right away. Take your vest off, stay on him, tell the referee to ring the bell to start the match. Build more heat."

I didn't realize that he'd been watching so closely; it *was* a very constructive piece of advice. I thanked him and, wincing, added that I needed to get off my ankle.

Since my match was early on the card, I had enough time to catch a flight home the same night. I won't describe every stabbing burst that went through my ankle on the trip back to Los Angeles. Unfortunately, this was just a microscopic sample of the catastrophic pain awaiting me later on in life.

As soon as the plane landed, I drove myself to the hospital for X-rays. Although nothing was broken, the prognosis was equally bad. I had severely torn the ligaments that wrapped around my ankle. The doctor told me that the condition would take between six and eight weeks to heal. I was issued a pair of crutches, told to keep my leg elevated, prescribed a collection of pain pills and anti-inflammatories, and sent on my way.

I followed doctor's orders the next day, a Sunday, positioning my left foot on a stack of pillows, popping pills, and staring at the ceiling. At times, I felt like I was drifting in and out of a trance as I lamented over my circumstances, wondering if I still had a job in the wrestling business. According to Shire, my performance had been mediocre—and getting injured and cutting the match short hadn't helped matters. What was I going to do for money?

It didn't seem like I would ever see the inside of the Cow Palace again unless I bought a ticket.

On Monday morning I called LeBell and began to tell him about my injury. He cut me off: "I know all about your ankle. I just got off the phone with Shire. He wants you to start for him the second week of January."

The second week of January was eight weeks away—perfect timing. I told LeBell that since I was in no condition to work his territory, I was going home to Phoenix to recuperate before beginning my run in San Francisco.

He didn't seem to care. "Fine," he muttered, and hung up the phone.

The next seven weeks were blissful. My ankle was coming along, and I was training hard every day. I had lots of time to bask in the sun, working on that all-important bronzed look. Sometimes, as I lay on a blanket, I thought about the people in Calgary, freezing and locked in their homes like inmates. This was far better. Being tan has always helped me feel healthy— even when I wasn't.

I didn't feel like driving the 750 miles up to San Francisco by myself, so Brick took the week off from J.D.'s and went along for the ride. In the summer, the Arizona heat can feel hostile. But now, in January, the dry, cool air had tamed the desert. We talked about Jerry Graham a little bit, and analyzed the wrestling business. It was a strange world of trickery.

"Do you ever feel bad about conning the fans?" Brick asked.

It's a subject I'd contemplated a lot. "I think we're doing them a favor," I responded. "Living in a delusional world of fantasy is good for them. It's an escape hatch for their frustrations. The violence is organized. They can scream obscenities at the heels, right in our faces. But imagine what would happen if they did the same thing to their bosses, or some cop who just gave them a ticket."

I glanced over at Brick, smiling broadly at my dissertation.

"You go to wrestling to release stress," I continued. "Then, you go home calmer and relaxed. I mean, they call us 'wrestlers.' But really, we're kind of like mental therapists."

I drove on, feeling pretty good about myself and my most recent career path.

My first match as an official member of the San Francisco roster was scheduled on a Sunday afternoon in San Jose. Prior to the card, Roy Shire entered the dressing room and asked me to step out into the hall, proclaiming the all-familiar phrase, "I have something I want to talk about."

Shire was meticulous about everything he did. On those rare occasions when he came out of retirement for a special match, I noticed that we shared a philosophy about our appearance. Both of us laced up our boots perfect and tight. And we would each use a toothbrush to push the extra lace inside the boot. "I don't go out there looking sloppy," he boasted, and meant it. He was absolutely immaculate in his appearance.

But he could also be a bit of a tyrant, and now he proceeded to deliver the type of lecture a new recruit hears on the first day of boot camp: "Starting here and in every town, I want you to watch every match before yours, and every match after you shower." Shire informed me that a wrestling match is made up of three ingredients—street fighting, high spots (the predetermined highlights of an encounter, preceding the finish), and scientific wrestling.

I wondered where I was going to learn that last one.

Before proceeding with the address, Roy betrayed his one disgusting habit—a trait so vile that he would later lose a television contract for refusing to restrain himself in the studio—spitting tobacco juice onto the spot where the floor joins the wall. "And only the main event gets blood," he continued, working toward the one axiom I'd never heard before. "And when you're in the main event, I want you to build the heat until the people are ready to riot. Then, back off."

That seemed like a pretty difficult skill to master, but I remained silent as Shire spat a little more, segueying into the next phase of his speech. "I want you in the dressing room one hour before the matches start. The first time you're late, you'll be fined $25, the next time $50, and the third time $100. And if I ever catch you riding with a babyface, you're fired."

The exchange felt much more like a reprimand than a conversation, although in years to come, I'd admire the philosophy of his territory. Every angle and every finish in every town was thoroughly plotted. There were never any helter-skelter finishes concocted five minutes before a match went into the ring. It was a promotion built on logic. Matches ended in a believable fashion. The show built towards the main event. And it was only in the main event that you saw the use of steel chairs and heads rammed into ring posts.

With San Francisco as the crown jewel of the promotion, the drive to the other towns on the circuit—Richmond, Sacramento, Fresno, and Stockton, among others—was relatively simple. Unfortunately, the miles were catching up to my old Pontiac. It had survived the most unmerciful terra firma that Arizona had to offer, but never quite recovered from those Indian reservation expeditions. I needed a new car, a reliable one, but—as usual—I had no money.

As soon as I'd entered the territory, Pat Patterson became my Tag Team partner and mentor. Now it was time to test our budding friendship. I explained my situation to Pat, and asked to borrow $3,000. Without hesitating, he loaned me the money.

It was typical of Patterson—who was just as generous in sharing his wrestling insights. Pat was a bleached blond French Canadian whose birth name is Pierre Clemont. At one time he'd contemplated becoming a Catholic priest, but was told by his monsignor that his personality was way too restless. Pat loved spectacles—the circus, the Ice Capades—and would generate many in his long, illustrious career, becoming the first Intercontinental Champion in the history of the World Wrestling Federation—the name the company used in between WWWF and WWE—and eventually one of Vince McMahon Jr.'s most valuable assistants.

Pat was smart with his money—he owned a beautiful home in San Francisco—and had the ability to pull the people around him up to his level. I was still learning carny, and Patterson loved to rib me when we were in the ring, spouting out instructions in deliberately unintelligible gibberish. Like a complete mark, I'd struggle to decipher the sounds, repeatedly asking, "What? What did you say?" Pat's response was hiding his mouth with his forearm, and laughing at my confusion.

Being Tag Team partners with Patterson gave me instant credibility— and heat with the fans. I could never duplicate his wrestling style—he was light-years ahead of me, and would remain there—but I emulated him as best I could. He was a flawless heel, vicious and aggressive, and did everything with precise timing. To this day, there's never been anybody who can throw better mounted punches from the ropes. When his head was run into the ring post, it recoiled, with hair flying backward, like it was about to pop off.

In 1971 in San Francisco, flesh meeting steel equaled blood. And when Patterson got color, it always came down from the right side of his forehead, over his eye. Blood flowing down just one side of the face was very impressive to me. It seemed to give the injury a more credible look.

Just as Shire expected, Pat would build the heat to a fever pitch. One of his favorite gimmicks was keeping a mask in his trunks. At a certain moment—usually when he was thrown to ringside—he'd pull out the mask and slip it on.

"He's got the mask!" the television announcer would yell, as the audience rose to its feet. "He's got the mask!"

Then, when the referee's back was turned, Patterson would reveal a foreign object—actually a large rubber eraser wrapped in very visible white tape—and slide it under the mask, like it was a big chunk of metal. As his opponent surged forward, Pat gave him a head butt, seemingly knocking him out and getting the win.

Shire eventually had me get a mask, too. Mine was red, white, and blue; I had started calling myself "The Real American" and "The True Spirit of America." Then Pat had the option of handing *me* the weapon, while the referee was busy checking *him* for the smuggled item.

What made this even more interesting was that Pat didn't always use the foreign object. So when the mask came on, fans were never sure about what they would see next. But the expectation was always there. It was just a brilliant gimmick because it kept the people engaged, and always guessing.

Ultimately, of course, the top babyfaces would thwart our scheme. And when the hero made his comeback, Pat—the ferocious heel a moment earlier—cowered and begged, feeding himself to his foe to avoid the impending riot.

In San Francisco, Patterson and Stevens were such celebrated names that one of the ring announcers actually named his kids Pat and Ray. And he probably wasn't the only one.

You see, anyone who ever saw Ray Stevens in his prime became a slobbering mark for him. I should know because I was the biggest mark of all. I'd been a fan since the first day I peeked through the slit in the curtain and beheld a master craftsman performing his art. Stevens was so fluid, his timing unassailable. Nothing was ever rushed or delayed. He took big bumps on a hard ring, and watching him sell made a believer out of me. In my opinion, there wasn't anything that "The Blond Bomber" couldn't do. There'll never be another one like him.

Out of the ring, Stevens was a very charming crazy man. Shortly after I arrived in the territory, he strolled into the dressing room, gripping a thick chain attached to an enormous, mutated dog. He announced that his pet weighed over 200 pounds, and was half Chow and half bear. I looked down at the animal and noticed that he was foaming at the mouth.

Stevens shackled the beast to a water pipe and scanned the stunned faces of the wrestlers. Taking a few steps back, Stevens proclaimed in his raspy voice, "His name is Chubby. Anyone want to pet him?"

The dressing room got quiet. Stevens's round, man-boy face widened as his eyes watered and he burst into laughter, literally bending over, holding his stomach. It was just another day for Ray Stevens, but the cumulative impact of these antics had transformed the man into a mythic figure among his peers.

Ray liked me from the start, and told everyone that I made him laugh. "Billy," he'd declare, with the rest of the dressing room listening, "you're the

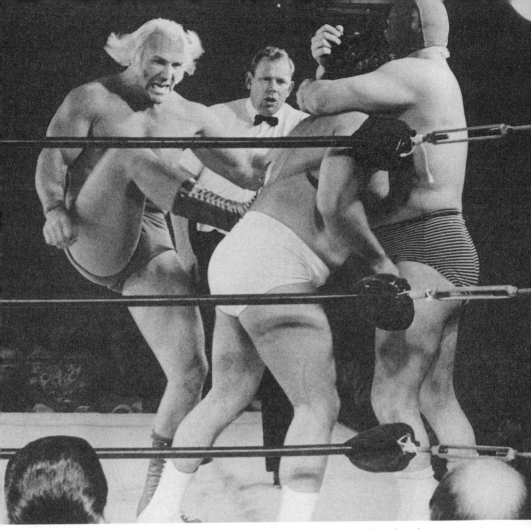

As I put the boots to Jerry Montie, a masked Pat Patterson lends a hand.

oldest-looking hippie in the world." Old? I was only twenty-seven! But I didn't mind being the butt of a Ray Stevens joke. He was becoming my hero.

Neither Stevens nor Patterson ever threw punches, kicks, or elbows that seemed pulled. All their shots looked legitimately brutal. Sometimes when I watch tapes of my old matches today, I wish I'd delivered blows that looked as hard as theirs. But I didn't have their self-confidence. I knew how strong I was, and was trying not to potato people. As a result, I held back a little too much.

One thing that I did incorporate was a subtle reaction after I hit somebody. On occasion, I'd shake my hand to give the impression that I'd hurt my fist on impact. If I was punched, I'd jerk back my head, like I'd been whiplashed—the same way Stevens and Patterson did.

There were different ways of selling, Shire pointed out. Sometimes, you wanted to "register"—or acknowledge—a shot. This didn't mean a full-blown sell job. You subtly registered that contact had been made.

The entire year felt like a semester at college, working on my M.M.—or Mark Manipulation—degree. I was getting an education, being subsidized for it, and making lifelong friends.

Paul DeMarco—whose manager, Dr. Ken Ramey, occasionally wound up in my corner—took the most beautiful backdrops, landing squarely between his shoulder blades. I wasn't ready to do that yet—it was too scary. When you're backdropped, it's natural to twist toward your side, like a cat trying to turn over.

I learned to play to my assets. When someone gave me a dropkick, I'd remain on my feet, but wobble slightly. This would inspire awe in the fans. *Wow, he's so big and strong that he didn't go down from that dropkick!*

But I wasn't being selfish. "Hit me with another one," I'd whisper to the babyface—then take a big bump.

Before raking someone's face, I'd tell him, so he could sell it like he lost an eyeball. If I chose to jam my opponent with a thumb instead, I'd hold it up to the audience, allowing them to see what was coming.

Early on in my run, Shire summoned Patterson and me to the babyface locker room of the Cow Palace, to go over our match with the Tag Team Champions, Ray and The Rock's maternal grandfather, High Chief Peter Maivia. I was still uneasy about being in the ring with talent of that stature, and now Shire told me something that literally made me nauseous. Pat and I were going to win the NWA World Tag Team title that night.

It would be a Two-Out-of-Three-Falls match, and I would take the last fall, lifting up Stevens and dropping his neck across the top rope before covering him for the pin. I listened as these three professionals discussed what was going to transpire in the ring. Every few minutes, one of them would show me the courtesy of asking if everything sounded okay, and I'd nod.

I flashed back to that day less than a year before, when I'd plodded along in the ring in front of a few listless Apaches. And I wondered if Shire comprehended the ramifications of putting such an unproven talent in this position. The only thing that the man must have seen in me was potential. Snapping back to the here and now, I realized that it was time to stop daydreaming and start absorbing the specifics of the most important match of my life.

I don't have a tape of the Tag Team title change—most likely the footage was erased or thrown out—but I do know that Pat, Ray, and Peter carried me. They worked around my inexperience, and the match got over despite the fact that I was part of it. I stepped on and stumbled over three connoisseurs of the squared circle—and they had the class not to laugh at me but to do everything to enhance my performance. In the jealous world of pro wrestling, Pat, Ray, and Peter shined like the stars they were.

If I'm going to be completely honest in this book, I have to say that I don't like the way titles switch back and forth today with such regularity that I frequently forget who's holding the championship. It wasn't like that in 1971. Those belts had value. And even though this business is a work, I felt like I was really making it. I was very proud.

Shire was waiting for us in the dressing room after the match, and—as I predicted—he motioned me into the corner with the phrase, "Graham, I've got something I want to tell you."

His calm tone of voice caught me off-guard. Following a spatter of chewing tobacco against the bottom of the wall, he expounded on the match, then stated prophetically, "I can put you over the boys—but you have to put yourself over with the people. I've done my part. Now, you have to do yours."

Initially, I lived in a hotel in San Francisco. But despite the beauty of the city, there was no room to park my car, and the rents were just too high. What plagued me most about Frisco was the ever-present fog, and the accompanying gloom. Everything was damp, and the sensation of always feeling wet didn't appeal to me. Because of the weather, Patterson and Stevens looked ghostly pale. I'd tease them and say that they appeared sickly and anemic. Ray was already a bit bowlegged, and I constantly asked him if he'd had rickets as a kid, adding, "I can't believe the bumps you take when you look so feeble."

Emitting his hoarse laugh, Ray's comeback was, "Well, Billy, you still look like the oldest hippie in the world."

I even noticed that Peter Maivia's natural Samoan tan seemed to be fading in the San Francisco weather. And that was a bad sign to me. Anticipating another struggle with the elements, I opted to move fifty miles south to San Jose, where it was warmer and dryer.

It was inevitable that Terry Gee, my old running buddy from my waning days on the evangelical loop, would find me. He arrived in a van with a girlfriend, and I put them up in a back bedroom with these big windows that let in the breeze. Terry was still into working out, and wanted to put on muscle mass fast. So I got him on my regimen, taking handfuls of Dianabol. We bought crates of eggs, stacked them in the kitchen, and each consumed about two to three dozen a day. In about three weeks, Terry gained about twenty extra pounds of muscle.

Terry really wanted to see the hippies in Frisco, so I sent him up to North Beach and Haight-Ashbury, where he purchased all the pot he could grab. Then, while I was busy wrestling, he and his girlfriend hung out in the bedroom with the windows open, getting high. The nearest house was something like six feet away, and the smell of marijuana permeated my neighbor's rooms. And that wasn't the only problem with Terry. He was kind of an exhibitionist. After he and his shapely girlfriend got stoned, they'd take off their clothes and make whoopee in broad daylight. When my neighbor's wife finally got me on the phone, I was stunned. Her husband was evidently spending more time watching Terry Gee than tending to his duties at home.

Through much of 1971, Pat and I worked against my old friend Rocky Johnson and his future father-in-law, Peter Maivia. Maivia was probably the toughest guy in wrestling. In England, he allegedly came close to popping out Billy Robinson's eye with a finger in a shoot. And he and his wife, Lia— The Rock's grandmother, who could fight like a man—once got into a crazy brawl with a bunch of drunks in a bar directly across the street from the Cow Palace. It took an army of cops to subdue the High Chief, and when they succeeded, they decided to torture him. With his face down on the floor, two officers put their boots on his back, while each grabbed an arm. They cranked him so hard, they pulled out the muscle insertions connecting his pects to his deltoids.

Yet Peter was one of the gentlest men I ever came across. If you treated him well, he loved you like family, always with a smile on his face and a laugh in his belly. In match after match, he tolerated my wrestling immaturity, even when I'd miss high spots, punch him too hard, or step on his bare feet. Back in the dressing room, he never complained. He'd simply take a seat next to me and chuckle, saying, "Brutha, what happened out there?" Then he'd compassionately explain what went wrong, and offer suggestions about improving our matches in the future. To me, he truly was a prince.

Maivia's High Chief title was not a work. He'd been given the honor in his native Samoa—as well as the ceremonial tattoos extending from the middle of his chest to just above his knees. Peter told me that the process should have taken six months. But he only had three days on the island, in between wrestling commitments, and said, "If you want to make me a chief, that's how much time you have." When so much ink went into his body at once, he developed an infection that nearly killed him.

I never realized how many Samoans lived in San Francisco until I saw the crowds that turned out when Peter wrestled. Afa and Sika Anoai were two gargantuan Maivia supporters who believed that everything they saw in the ring was real. They'd come to the Cow Palace with their families and literally rip out chairs bolted to the floor. The heels were petrified of them. Maivia kayfabed the Anoais for a long time, but eventually smartened them up and trained them for the business. As the aptly named Wild Samoans, they became World Wrestling Federation Tag Team Champions—and very good friends of mine.

Pat and I were Tag Team Champions for eight months, until September 18, 1971, when we lost to Rocky Johnson and local icon Pepper Gomez. The Soul Man took the third and deciding fall on me—the illegal man in the ring, by the way—with a Boston crab submission.

In the middle of our run, Shire decided that I had come far enough along to challenge Stevens for his United States championship, the number one singles title in the territory. I knew that the twenty minutes I'd spend in the ring with Ray would be electrifying—not necessarily for the fans or Stevens, but definitely for me.

It was important to impress upon the people that I was capable of taking away the Blond Bomber's title. Being one-half of the NWA Tag Team championship duo helped. But a week before the matchup, I made a huge mistake on television, selling too much for a guy who was out there to put me over. It was a total mental breakdown on my part. I was so preoccupied with the Stevens clash that I forgot that the whole purpose of this televised event was to make me look infallible—prompting fans to flood the Cow Palace to see Stevens's toughest challenge yet.

The moment that I stepped through the dressing room curtain, a livid Roy Shire was in my face. If the house at the Cow Palace dropped because of this poor performance, he vowed, he was going to fine me $1,000.

I'd messed up, but didn't think that the threat was fair at all. The gross for house shows—or nontelevised events—goes up and down. You can't always pinpoint exactly why a gate might drop. I felt like momentum was shifting against me.

On the night of the show, I was sitting next to Ray, talking over our match, when Shire walked into the dressing room and pulled up a chair.

"The house is down," he announced. "Graham, that's gonna cost you $1,000."

I was devastated, not because of the money but because I let down Ray Stevens. Shire was furious. He said that he was going to give us two finishes. If the match was good, we'd use the finish that led to a return encounter. If the match was bad, Ray would beat me right in the middle of the ring. He looked at Stevens: "The decision's yours. Make the call during the match."

Earl Maynard looks on as his partner flies out of the ring.

When the promoter left, I began apologizing to Ray. "I'm really embar-
rassed," I told him.

Stevens laughed. "Billy, don't pay any attention to Shire. We're using
the return finish. Don't worry about anything. It'll be a great match."

Of course, Ray Stevens could have had a great match with a punching
bag. But he went out of his way for me that night, even blading when he
wasn't supposed to. When we got backstage, Shire asked him why.

"The match was so good that I had to get juice."

Only Ray Stevens could get away with something like that. As Shire
walked away, Ray looked over at me and winked. With his blade job, he'd
convinced every fan in the Cow Palace that Billy Graham was more than

equipped to defeat him for the United States championship. It was just a matter of time.

I was definitely starting to branch out beyond my strongman routine; there was no room for a one-dimensional wrestler in the San Francisco territory. Prior to another match with Stevens, Shire told me, "Okay, Graham, I want you to take a backdrop over the top rope."

I was horrified. "What are you talking about?"

"That's the high spot. I want Stevens to give you a backdrop over the ropes."

I began calculating. The ring rose about four feet off the ground, and the ropes extended another five feet above that. Both Shire and Stevens immediately understood that I hadn't done this before. So they coached me. As Stevens flipped me over his back, I'd hook the top rope with my left arm and hold on, while tumbling to the floor. I was agile enough to land on my feet and quickly roll onto my side.

When we finally did it, things went so fast that the fans never grasped the fact that my feet touched the ground. The rookie phase of my career was coming to a close. I was one of the top heels in the territory.

But there was a price to pay for that. Fans took their wrestling very personally back then. When Pat and I teamed up around the horn, we often parked our cars in different locations, blocks away from the building. But all it took was one guy seeing you leave your car, and your vehicle became a target for destructive spectators who'd never dare challenge you to your face. On more than one occasion, I left the arena to find all four tires slashed.

The quaint city of Modesto was surrounded by fruit orchards that gave the place a sense of tranquillity. The wrestling fans, however, were anything but tranquil. Most of the time, they were nothing less than rabid.

On Friday nights, the wrestling matches were literally the only show in town. With seating for about 500 fans, the Uptown Arena should have been torn down years before. There were low-hanging rafters, dim lighting, dingy, soiled walls, and ultra-narrow aisles. In the dressing room, we sat wedged together on benches, hung our clothes on nails, and showered in a stall that only dribbled water.

This was the only town that Roy Shire didn't grace with his presence. Instead, he'd give the finishes over the phone to Pat. This was the beginning of Pat's schooling toward becoming one of the best bookers in the industry. He wrote down every detail of every finish on paper, and transmitted the intelligence to each guy. Shire protected Modesto like it was Frisco, with the same complicated high spots and finishes. The fans responded like their lives hung in the balance if the babyfaces didn't win.

Pat Patterson listens as I make my point to the television audience.

Modesto was the town where I did my first blade job in the territory—right in the middle of the ring, as opposed to lying on the floor in the shadow of the ring apron, with my head hidden from the crowd. Pat, my partner that night, had coached me on the technique, using my left forearm to hide my right hand as I gigged—a term originated by fishermen describing the way they speared their catch. After getting juice and getting pinned,

I was helped back to the corner by Patterson, who was effusive in his praise: "Good job, Billy. You covered up perfectly. Nobody saw you cut."

After one mishap in a match against Ray Stevens—where I sliced myself so deeply that the blood stained my lips, smeared under my arms, and poured down to my belly button—I began understanding the specific way that a heel was supposed to juice. If you bled too much, you got sympathy from the people. And the last thing you wanted was for them to respond like you were a babyface.

Pretty soon, I became so adept at juicing that I created a term of endearment for my defacing tool: Blue Steel, after my favorite brand, Gillette Blue Blades.

In a place like Modesto, where fans seemed to wait around all week to go after the heels, blood could really rile up the crowd. During one Uptown Arena encounter, I was concentrating on my match when a mark slid under the bottom rope and latched onto my leg. Had I seen him coming, I would have greeted him with a kick to the face. Instead, I was getting an education on how some poor beast felt with a South American anaconda wrapped around it. The difference was that I wasn't this guy's quarry, and he definitely wasn't a water boa. I walked around the ring like my left foot was stuck in a tub of cement, attempting to snatch the intruder by the head. But his hair was so short that there was nothing to grab. My Tag Team partner, Pat, was laughing too hard to be of any assistance. So I looked pleadingly at a collection of police officers who were now storming the ring. The man was coiled so tightly around my limb that it took three cops to pry him away. Pat didn't stop laughing for the rest of the match.

When I left the arena that night, I discovered that another group of fans had gotten to my car first, caving in the windshield with their feet and kicking it onto the front seat.

I didn't develop any of my promo skills in Frisco. When we teamed together, Patterson did most of the talking on our interviews, and besides, Shire told us—word for word—what he wanted to hear on television. But I did have the freedom to be creative with my ring appearance. I started wearing long tights that I eventually tie-dyed—a look that many others would imitate later on.

Before I'd left L.A., I found a Chinese woman around the corner from my hotel with a seamstress shop. I handed her a terrycloth robe, and an American flag I'd cut into different pieces. I told her what I wanted—stars on the sleeves, stripes going around my midsection.

She was appalled. "You cut up American flag?" she asked.

All over the country, young people were burning their draft cards and, on certain occasions, setting ablaze the emblem of our great nation. Now, this immigrant—whose home village was probably overrun by the Communists—was sitting there, as I began explaining that I'd sliced up Old Glory because I had a good idea for *a wrestling robe*.

Had the woman had a thriving business, I know that I would have been banished from her shop. But times were tight, and I was a paying customer. With apprehension, she made me my robe.

When I wore it in L.A., the fans were blasé; I'm not sure if they always got my whole hippie routine. But I kept the robe around, and decided to try it in San Francisco.

I altered my ring jacket slightly. From bodybuilding, I realized that horizontal stripes make you appear wider. I had the stripes turned into a vertical position to give the impression that I had a thin waist, and stars trimming the collar.

Because the hippie movement had essentially started in San Francisco, I expected a better reaction there. I'd already gotten into the habit of shopping for my gimmicks in the hippie stores in North Beach, where I bought some psychedelic-looking Grateful Dead T-shirts and a fringed white leather Indian-style vest.

But two hundred miles north of San Francisco, it was a whole different world. This was mountain country, and hippies were scum. Yet I was as unaware of the cultural nuances of the Golden State as I was of the emotional backlash one might suffer for defiling the symbol of our country. I wanted to debut my American flag robe in this region at a "spot show," or location that the promotion only ran sporadically.

I opened my dressing-room door and walked toward the ring, where five police officers were going to escort me down the aisle. As soon as they saw my robe, their faces reddened with indignation. "You're not wearing that to the ring," they all seemed to say at once.

"Why not?"

"Don't you know that it's a crime to desecrate the American flag in public?"

I guess I'd missed that in civics class. Now the cops were threatening to arrest me if I dared step through the ropes in my star-spangled attire. I pondered my options, and realized that I had no choice. Off came the robe, and I had my match.

It's incredible how one individual could set the tone for an entire promotion. Throughout the years, that has been the case with Ric Flair in the Carolinas, Dusty Rhodes in Florida, Freddie Blassie in Los Angeles, and Ray Stevens in San Francisco. In July 1971, Ray left us for the more lucra-

tive American Wrestling Association (AWA), out of Minneapolis, only returning to the Cow Palace for an occasional shot. The magic was now gone,
and residing in Minnesota.

I knew that my time in San Francisco was coming to an end, as well, a
few months later when—over the Christmas season—Shire handpicked me
as the heel to go around the loop with Terrible Ted the Wrestling Bear.

Ted was a trained 725-pound Alaskan brown bear that had been declawed. I can still feel the beast's coarse, wiry fur, smell its foul breath, and hear it snorting through its muzzle as it looked me dead in the eyes. Ted wasn't a happy bear, and I wasn't a happy wrestler.

The wrestling bear gimmick was used a lot in the South during that era, but here it was in San Francisco. The bear was trained to lift its arms so I could place my head between its paws and snapmare myself. Ted was brought in to add some comic relief, and he did just that. I wrestled the bear, and people laughed. When fans laugh at a heel, he loses his heat, and mine vanished.

All of Ted's teeth had been pulled out—except for his rear molars—so we could do spots where the bear would appear to bite me. In one finish, I'd rip the muzzle off the bear, and stick my forearm in its mouth. Its natural instinct was to clamp down, but of course there was no impact. Still, I'd sell it, sell it, sell it. The fans would scream as I left the ring, charging down the aisle to safety.

When we did this at the Cow Palace, a small African-American boy came rushing by Shire, who was standing toward the back, taking in the display. "The bear bit Billy!" the hysterical child screamed, running in circles around the promoter. "The bear bit Billy!" It was one of the few times that I saw Shire laugh uproariously.

To the spectators, there seemed to be nothing more entertaining. But I wasn't very amused when, the morning after a show in Reno, Nevada, I opened up a newspaper in the taxi to the airport. There, in the sports section, was a photo of Terrible Ted and me doing our snapmare spot.

Here's an excerpt from the article: "He does not talk to reporters, and he will not sign autographs, but Terrible Ted knows how to wrestle. . . . Wednesday night, after three minutes and 52 seconds had elapsed, he pinned Billy Graham for the pleasure of 983 fans."

As I stepped out of the cab, I was spotted by two baggage handlers, whose eyes broadened as they broke into grins.

"Hey," one of them laughingly inquired, in a voice almost identical to that of my friend Sylvester Ritter—the late Junkyard Dog. "Is you dat man who wrestled dat Gooo-rilla?"

"Yeah," I answered. "I'm that man."

Shire should have hired thirteen more clowns like me, two jugglers, and a high-wire act to complete the circus. I welcomed my two weeks' notice at the end of January 1972. But I've never regretted my time in San Francisco. Under the tutelage of stars like Patterson and Stevens—as well as the dogmatic Roy Shire—I had the best technical period of my career. As I drifted more toward entertainment, tie-dye, and interviews, I'd never reach that level of wrestling skill again.

MOTHER'S LITTLE HELPER

Bright star, would I were stedfast as thou art.

—John Keats

Before I left San Francisco, I asked Roy Shire if he'd recommend me to another promoter, preferably someone he knew personally.

"Sure, no problem," he answered, scribbling a phone number on a piece of paper and spewing a chunk of chewing tobacco on the floor.

Ed Francis was the promoter in Hawaii, and apparently he was looking for talent. "Give him a call," Shire urged. "I'm sure he can use you."

I'd expected Shire to make the call himself and do the personal endorsing. But, as my experiences generally proved, once a promoter was through with you, he was unwilling to lift a finger on your behalf. It was one of the reasons why so many wrestlers grew to consider themselves little more than prostitutes, using their bodies to scrape a few dollars together, and discarded when the lust for their services dissipated.

Nonetheless, Hawaii sounded like my kind of place to work. With visions of lounging in the sand and tanning on Waikiki Beach, I made the call.

Francis was delighted to hear from me. But then came a very strange question: "By the way, Billy, did Shire tell you that I'm closing down my territory in seven weeks?"

No, Roy hadn't mentioned that Francis was going out of business. But at that point, I really didn't care. "That's okay, Ed," I replied. "I'll take those seven weeks if you don't mind."

This journey to paradise was nothing more than a blip on the radar screen of my wrestling career—a paid vacation. Francis ran weekly shows at the Pearl Harbor naval base, as well as the Hawaiian International Center, or HIC. Everything was done at a leisurely pace; your only responsibility was going out there and doing your job. Ed even let me bring Brick along as an opening match referee.

Francis was past the point of using formulas to book his cards. Ironically, this led to some spontaneous—and intriguing—matchups. I remember wrestling against the team of Manuel Soto, a Puerto Rican middle-of-the-card guy in the WWWF, and Jimmy "Superfly" Snuka—who, believe it or not, happened to be my age, but had yet to hit it big in the continental United States. My partner was Sputnik Monroe, a unique Alabaman with a shock of white in his hair—a heel to his fellow Caucasians in the fifties, and a babyface to the African-Americans he played to in the upper reaches of the arena. Because he was so over with the black fans in Memphis, Sputnik manipulated the Ellis Auditorium into liberating them from the balcony, and was ultimately successful—molding a place for himself in civil rights history.

In Hawaii, Sputnik and I both discovered that the islanders loved their wrestling—and their wrestlers. At the HIC, fans brought in coolers filled with iced-down chunks of pineapple. Fresh mangos and cold guava juice were sent back to the dressing room. Fans were friendly to both the babyfaces and the heels, and shuttled us back and forth from the buildings.

At first, when I needed a lift, I'd catch a ride with some of the wrestlers staying at my hotel, the Waikiki Circle. When I grew weary of that, I bought a broken-down, rusted-out Chevy. The floorboards were so rotted that you could actually see the ground. Brick and I would cram in there with the other wrestlers at the motel: "Moondog" Lonnie Mayne, who'd established a reputation for swallowing live goldfish on TV, Mighty Brutus—later known as Bugsy McGraw—and Sweet Daddy Siki, a charismatic black man from Toronto with a curled Elvis lip and a bleached blond Afro.

Siki used to bring his guitar along, so he could play it in the dressing room. Strangely, his favorite tune was a Merle Haggard song, "Okie from Muskogee."

At the Waikiki Circle, tourists were always curious about Siki's ethnic background. Talking out the side of his mouth, he'd tell them that he was a legit descendant of Hawaiian royalty.

"Oh, really?" they'd answer excitedly. "Can we take a picture with you?"

One night at the motel, Lonnie Mayne wanted to see what would happen if he bodyslammed a friend off the first-floor balcony. He had no desire to really hurt the guy, so he slammed him on top of my car, caving in the roof. The guy stood up, laughing, jumping on the vehicle and denting it some more. It was fun, fun stuff.

I only remember leaving the island of Oahu once—for a show on the island of Molokai, a former leper colony. I was booked against a true legend of the islands, Sam Steamboat—whose resemblance to a young wrestler named Richard Blood would induce him to rechristen himself Ricky Steamboat. Sammy was old-school all the way. I heard that he even kayfabed his wife at home, working injuries while she pampered him. According to rumor, when she smartened up, she left him.

Before our match, Sammy told me, "I think the fans in Molokai deserve the best we can give them, so I want to build as much heat as we can before they go over the edge."

For a moment, I thought that I was talking to Roy Shire.

"Billy, I'm going to do a blade job."

My copper complexion turned as white as Ray Stevens. "Are you insane?" I countered. "We're in a high school gym with a bunch of islanders who think you're God. Are you trying to get me killed?"

Sammy remained composed. "We need to do this thing right, brutha."

I walked away from Steamboat, shaking my head and reaching for my Blue Steel. I'd learned crowd psychology in San Francisco, and now I was going to apply it. Thirty seconds into our match, I told Sammy, "Run my head into the ring post."

"Why?"

"Just a little high spot."

When Steamboat complied, I carved myself open.

Sammy gave me an incredulous look. "What are you doing, brutha?"

"Protecting myself."

Right there in the ring, Sammy started to laugh. "Billy, I wasn't going to get juice. It was a rib."

"Now you tell me."

A few days later, as I walked around Honolulu alone, I had another frightful encounter. There, staring at me from the street corner, was that mammoth Samoan football player who'd stormed into J.D.'s, screaming, "I want Wayne Coleman!"

The guy was even bigger now, and—despite my bleached blond hair—recognized me immediately. He tore toward me—and embraced me in a hug.

"Man, I'm glad you were drunk," I remarked, as we laughed about our mêlée.

The only real problem I had with the state of Hawaii was its prevalent and suffocating humidity. As a man who treasures the bone-dry climate of the desert, I fought that sticky feeling every day—even at night, when my shirts stuck to my body. The oceans and beaches were beautiful, but treacherous. Volcanic rock, sharp as broken glass, littered the sand, making it hazardous to get to the water for a swim. I didn't quite realize that there was a lot more to Hawaii than the small section I saw—and I'd make many more trips to the state. For now, though, it was time to get back to California.

I didn't even bother looking for a parking spot when I pulled into Honolulu International Airport in my decomposing Chevy. Leaving the key in the ignition, I grabbed my bags and walked into the terminal. Maybe someone saw the car and commandeered it as his own. More likely, the vehicle remained unclaimed for the afternoon before a tow truck came and took it to the junkyard.

Desperation is a pitiful state, and that's why I called Mike LeBell. I thought long and hard before picking up the phone, and concluded that LeBell wouldn't have an inkling of my dire situation unless I revealed it to him. In contrast, I'd act as if I were doing him a favor.

"Hey, Mike," I began with worked self-confidence, elevating our relationship to a first-name basis. "This is Billy. Billy Graham. You know, I just finished up a really good run for Shire, and wanted to tell you that I'm available for the summer. Then, I'm going back east for the winter."

Of course, the last time I'd been "back east" was when I was TKO'ed at Madison Square Garden. Still, LeBell was aware that I indeed *did* have a good year working for his partner in crime, the Warlord of San Francisco. He now viewed me in a new light, and spoke the words that I needed to hear: "Billy, we'd love to have you come in for the summer."

So I started my second stint of the Los Angeles territory, making my home the Flamingo Hotel in Santa Monica—where the boys were always given a good rate. The "good rate" mentality practically became a gene instilled in professional wrestlers, particularly in L.A., where Mike LeBell was hardly known for his generosity. My neighbors included a number of women of the night, a few drug dealers, a spattering of bikers, and about two dozen tourist families who didn't know any better. Yet the location far outweighed the seedy atmosphere—I was only blocks away from the mecca of bodybuilders everywhere, the original Gold's Gym.

At the Olympic Auditorium, the best perk was my relationship with the "official physician" at ringside, Dr. Bernhardt Schwartz. I've never seen any doctor anywhere take your blood pressure faster. He'd wrap the cuff around your arm, pump three times, and release you. That was the extent of an examination by Dr. Schwartz. But Bernie loved being around the boys, and was always eager to please us. As a result, I took full advantage of his aptitude for writing prescriptions.

Bernie gave me codeine and the grand champion of painkillers, Demerol, for physical discomfort; Valium—the "mother's little helper" of Rolling Stones fame—for stress and anxiety; and Seconal and Tuinal for sleepless nights. The "Green Monster," Placidyl—the 750-milligram, gel-filled capsule as thick as the pen I'm using to write this paragraph—put some people to sleep forever. "Black Beauty"—Biphetamine 20—was the speed of choice. And rounding out this demonic list of "aids" was the usual medley of steroids.

Dr. Schwartz was a pleasant enough, funny guy who seemed a little bit hyper—either from all the coffee he drank, or from his access to speed. As you'll read, there were mark doctors like him in just about every territory.

Sometimes I ask myself how I lived with all that toxic waste flowing through my bloodstream. But the truth is, I almost didn't.

I renewed my friendship with Arnold Schwarzenegger, who was consumed with becoming the most acclaimed bodybuilder of his era. In 1972, he was preparing for his third Mr. Olympia—a contest conceived by the Vince McMahon of the bodybuilding galaxy, Joe Weider. When there are already contests like Pro Mr. America, Pro Mr. World, and Pro Mr. Universe, and you want to establish your supremacy as the world's premier bodybuilding promoter, you invent a new competition to overshadow them all— hence, Mr. Olympia. In time, Arnold would win seven Mr. Olympia titles.

Weider owned a chain of bodybuilding magazines, and Arnold ranked as perhaps the entrepreneur's favorite model. I still have some of the publications from the early seventies—and in each one there's the same picture of Weider, arms folded across his chest with a proud, stately countenance, next to the inscription, "The World's Greatest Builder of Virile Men." Since one of the Webster's Dictionary definitions for "virile" is "sexually potent," Weider must have truly been consecrated with extraordinary gifts.

Occasionally, I'd accompany Arnold to some of his photographic marathons, watching him balance four or five bikini-clad models as he lounged on a Corvette convertible or some other type of muscle car. I can recall the future governor of California telling me that it normally took up to 300 photographs before Weider determined that one was suitable for his select publications. I don't know if I really believe that one.

Regardless, I humbly offered my services to Arnold as a training partner, and he happily accepted. There is no way to adequately describe pumping iron with someone so driven. Every movement during Arnold's workout was precise. Nothing was ever sloppy. As I kept up with Arnold set for set and rep for rep, my body was gradually transformed from the smooth, bulky look I'd had in San Francisco to the harder, thinner-skinned, more muscular appearance later replicated by others in the wrestling fraternity.

My steroid ingestion instilled a constant feeling of euphoria, and a deceptive belief that I was stronger than I was. It was in this frame of mind that I dubbed my massive arms "pythons," in tribute to the largest known snake in the world. Any wrestling fan who heard the Hulkster use the same term later on now knows the source.

Like clockwork, after every set, Arnold struck a pose in front of the gym's mirror-lined walls. This habit was an annoyance to some of the other guys in the room, but I couldn't get enough of it. I was learning from the best on the planet, and would integrate more than a few of Arnold's techniques into my own flexing routine in the ring. As Arnold's celebrity prospered, I got the rub—as we say about someone who profits from his association with a superstar.

Each day at 11:30 A.M., we'd wrap up at the gym and go to lunch in Marina Del Rey, where Arnold never wavered with his order: ground round beef patty—medium rare—scrambled eggs, cottage cheese, sliced tomatoes, dry toast, and iced tea. For a man so possessed, Arnold consistently maintained his cheerful demeanor, and we laughed and cracked jokes throughout the meal. Then, we moved on to the beach for two hours of tanning.

One day, as I walked behind him on the sand, I found myself studying the size of Arnold's calves. "Hey," I joked, "your calves are so huge, they make your knees look insignificant."

Arnold stopped dead in his tracks and turned around, the wheels turning in his mind. "Wayne," he asked, "what does en-sugg-neff-ah-gant mean?"

I answered, and Arnold stored it with everything else he was accumulating in his mind at that time.

After these tanning sessions ended, we'd go to Arnold's apartment, where he'd load the blender with fruit juice, bananas, strawberries, raw eggs, and protein powder. Over our protein drinks, we'd joke around some more—until it was time for Arnold's two-hour nap. I'd head back to the

Flamingo and get some sleep as well. When I woke up, I'd pack my bag, drop some speed, have a meal, and drive to the arena to perform my nightly ritual.

Arnold was baffled that, when we were out together, I was so much more recognizable. I explained that his image was only familiar to people in the bodybuilding community who read Weider's publications. And while he was only seen once a year on national television, during ABC's coverage of Mr. Olympia, residents of southern California could watch me twice a week—on LeBell's English- and Spanish-language broadcasts.

Those who chose not to simply view me from the other end of a black-and-white monitor may have noticed that I was enlarging my ring wardrobe. All those colored pills seemed to be expanding my already exploding rainbow of wrestling colors. Like the Tinseltown stars who wore sunglasses at night, I entered the arena in purple and rose-colored lenses. As my budget allowed, I ordered tights in every new color available: pink, orange, yellow, green, and—the most important of all—white. White gave me the option to dye my attire any shade I wanted. I bought white wrestling boots as well, and spray-painted them to match my tights, dying the shoelaces for contrast.

At the sporting goods store one day, I spotted some wristbands and came up with an idea. If I randomly tied a few rubber bands around these strips and dropped them into a pot of boiling purple, fuchsia, or gold dye, I'd have a pretty sharp costume accessory.

In my suite at the Flamingo, I hauled in sheets of leather in an abundance of tints, and carved out a half dozen new vests. For a long time, I was so deep into the vests that I overlooked the most obvious accoutrement to my presentation: the tie-dyed T-shirt. I think I understand why. I wanted my apparel to look color-coordinated, not gaudy, à la early Elton John. I'd leave *that* for my friend Jesse Ventura.

Under Pat Patterson's supervision, I'd become a valuable commodity in the ring. Now, like good heels everywhere, I could lead a match, telling the babyface when to start selling, make his comeback, do the high spots, and go home. I'm not implying that the babyface never had a say, but the heel was generally charged with being the ring general.

Backstage, I'd notice "The Golden Greek" of the L.A. territory, John Tolos, pacing back and forth like Jerry Russell. There was no resemblance between the two, but the mannerisms were strikingly similar. My eye was drawn to Tolos, and I began imitating his twisted mouth and macho promos.

Nonetheless, I was still very green to the political realities of the wrestling business. Occasionally, Mike LeBell flew in Ed Farhat, the original Sheik, and

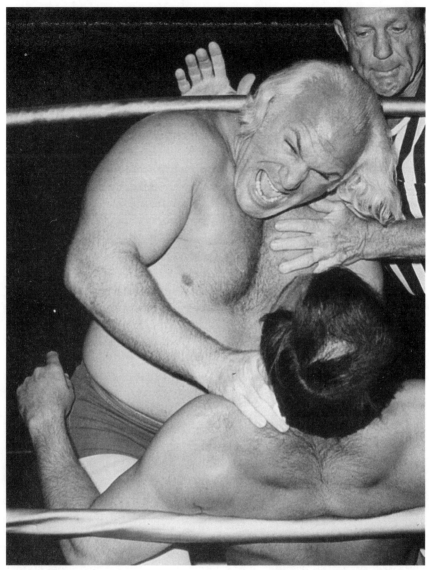

I was doing more singles wrestling for LeBell. Here I am with "The Golden Greek."

his manager, Abdullah Farouk—Ernie Roth, who was already double-dipping as the Grand Wizard in the WWWF. Like Abdullah the Butcher, the Sheik played a total maniac, darting out of the dressing room in an Arab headdress, doing a frenzied "camel strut" around the ring, and throwing fireballs from his fingertips. On the drive to the arena one afternoon, I looked in my rearview mirror and spotted LeBell and the Sheik together in the same car. I was overcome with a strange feeling of unimportance; now I knew how jobbers felt watching a promoter lavish attention on a main-eventer. I didn't understand that, in addition to being the city's number-one attraction, the Sheik was the promoter in Detroit. He and LeBell were professional peers, and were undoubtedly talking business and promotional strategies.

I should mention that, by this time, I was married again. Madelyn "Bunny" Miluso was a teller at a Bank of America branch in downtown Los Angeles. I was surprised when she became pregnant. I didn't want to get married—and for a very simple reason: I didn't love the woman.

We drove up to Reno for a quick wedding ceremony. I was anything but elated. "I don't want to do this," I told her in the car, "but I will—out of respect for the child."

Still, the birth of my daughter was one of the happiest moments of my life, up to that point. The doctor had calculated the little girl's arrival in early June, and I wanted a name beginning with a "C"—to match Coleman. Believe it or not, I actually considered Cinderella. But when my mother and sisters contemplated the name Cinderella Coleman, they suggested that I drive over to Arizona State Hospital and commit myself. After I gave the name further thought, I also realized that it might inspire some taunting from her playmates.

Looking and thinking in earnest, I opened up *The Atlas of the Universe* and searched for a star that began with the letter "C." I settled on Capella, the sixth brightest light in the heavens. From the beginning, Capella was just as beautiful as her name—both in appearance and in her heart. I only found out later that the name has another meaning in Greco-Roman mythology—"She-Goat." Sorry about that, Capella.

At midmorning on June 8, 1972, Capella was born at St. John's Hospital in Santa Monica—missing my birthday by a mere twenty-four hours. Although she was perfectly healthy, my first glimpse of my daughter was through the glass of an antediluvian incubator—standard, needless protection for a newborn in 1972. There she was, the youngest of the billions of living souls on the blue planet—a stunning pink, long arms stretching, toes curling, boasting something that I had long since lost: a full head of hair.

Capella spent the night in the hospital, and I wrestled in Long Beach, a thirty-mile shot down Interstate 405—but two and a half hours away in stop-and-go traffic.

As I mentioned earlier, when you got heat from the fans, it meant that they cared about you. But their ways of showing it were not always convenient. On this night, as I departed from the old Long Beach Arena to the dimly lit parking lot, a familiar, sickening sensation came over me. It was ab-

normally quiet, and even before I saw my car, I sensed what I would find. My suspicions were confirmed when I stepped on one of the auto's spark plug wires. I looked over at my parking spot to see that the hood was up. One by one, the spark plugs had been pulled out of the engine, the battery cables cut in half, and the electrical wires ripped out. The distributor cap was crushed, and two of my tires were slashed, giving my auto the Leaning Tower of Pisa look. It resembled a crime scene—but, then again, I guess it was.

I rode back to Santa Monica with the tow truck driver, dropped off the car at a Cadillac dealership, called Arnold, and told him the story.

"What's wrong with these idiots?" he asked in his Austrian accent, offering his services as the Coleman family chauffeur. Today, Capella's children can boast that the governor of their state is the same man who drove their mother home from the hospital.

When we arrived back at the Flamingo, we uncovered the baby, and Arnold gleefully posed for pictures with the naked newborn. He never forgot this episode. In fact, after being elected governor, he spoke to Capella and invited her to an official function.

"This time," he emphasized, "you can keep your clothes on."

Capella was right at home at the Flamingo. At poolside, after the bikers and their mamas finished passing her around, I'd feel like grabbing for a can of Grease Release to remove the Hog smell from her pink little body. With no air conditioners in the room, I'd leave the windows open to catch the sea breeze. Because of this, when the bikers cranked up their Harleys, there was no buffer for the noise. The walls literally shook, but Capella never stirred from her deep sleep.

Every so often, "Classy" Freddie Blassie showed up at the hotel to escape the fans at the beach and hang out with John Tolos, Blassie's archenemy in wrestling storylines, and a fellow resident of the Flamingo. Blassie was so obsessed with tanning that he'd bring his half-moon-shaped UV reflector up to the base of his neck and insert these devices that looked like pencil erasers between his digits to ensure that his fingers were perfectly bronzed. The first time the gruff headliner spotted Capella's bassinet at poolside, he unwrapped her blanket, lifted her up to his face, and barked, "She's the most beautiful baby in the world! Who does this little angel belong to?!"

"She's all mine, Freddie," I answered.

"Oh . . . uh . . . yeh . . . hmm . . . yeah," he grumbled, dumping her back into the bassinet. "Nice kid."

Despite this, I could feel the stain of Jerry Graham receding from my flesh; Blassie was starting to treat me like a human being, instead of a mongrel street dog. Conversely, the Graham name also continued to help me. A worked wrestling magazine article around that period suggested that my maverick ways were embarrassing the rest of my famous family. Of course, I hadn't yet met Eddie or "Crazy" Luke Graham. But I'd bet that, by that point, they'd finally heard of me.

When my mother came out to L.A. to visit the new baby, I asked her if she'd like to go to the arena and see the way her son made his living. She agreed, but I was a bit concerned about what might transpire if the fans figured out her identity.

Once again, Arnold came to my rescue, volunteering to serve as my mother's escort and bodyguard. Because I'd been indoctrinated to believe that everyone outside the wrestling business was a mark, I felt it imperative to place my upcoming exhibition in the proper context for my mother.

"Now, Mom, this is the deal," I told her, with Arnold listening closely. "We're putting on a show. There's a large Mexican community here in L.A., and I'm wrestling this little guy, Ruben Juarez, who the promoter wants to build up as a star. When I lay down for him, everyone's going to be impressed because he beat a guy twice his size."

My mother listened for a while, then rolled her eyes. "I know that stuff is fake," she cut in. "I'm not stupid."

Arnold doubled over in laughter as my mother looked over at him and shook her head.

The two of them sat about five rows away from the ring, and I remember paying more attention to their reactions than I did to my opponent. Every time I took a bump, my mother grimaced. Meanwhile, my buddy Arnold was roaring, and—yes—booing whenever I showed any offense. There wasn't a bodybuilding fan in the arena, but occasionally spectators looked over at the big guy and wondered why he seemed so amused over an absurdly boring match.

Arnold told me that, despite my mother's claims beforehand, she suddenly became a true believer when Juarez pinned me. "Oh, no," she yelled, "he had his shoulder up!"

Arnold Schwarzenegger: Billy was huge, yet he had the agility of a gymnast, performing flips and other physical feats around the ring. And, man, he was crazy. The way he knew how to work an audience was truly fantastic.

But more importantly to me back then was that he was just great to hang out with. He and his wife used to have me over for dinner. She made this wonderful pasta, and I remember eating a lot in those days. They were very good to me, and I'll never forget it.

One day, Arnold told me that he was driving over to Santa Monica Community College. He was enrolling, and needed assistance filling out the forms. I went along for the ride, and we stood in line at the registration office, laughing and joking with each other.

"They don't want a big musclehead like you," I said. Then, turning to the others in line: "He doesn't even have a visa. He can't speak our language."

Arnold got to the front of the line and immediately signed up for a business administration course. It was obvious that Arnold was going all the way with this. There's only one other man I've ever met with the same focus and drive: Vince McMahon. Because of these qualities, in 2004, I was sitting on my living room couch, watching Arnold address the Republican National Convention, proud of my friend, but plagued by one recurring thought.

I should have registered with him.

According to the arrangement I had with LeBell, I was supposed to be leaving the promotion after the summer. But between wrestling, my escapades with Arnold, and the birth of Capella, I hadn't made the time to contact another territory. By September, I could feel the walls of the Flamingo closing in on me; I knew that the "End of Days" for me in Los Angeles could come at any time. The last thing that I wanted was to walk into the Olympic one Friday night and have Mike hand me a pink slip with my paycheck. I had to beat him to the punch. I just wasn't sure how.

On September 22, 1972, Shire brought me up to the Cow Palace for a one-shot deal, a special match against Ray Stevens, who was now firmly rooted in the AWA. When I arrived, I told my old friend that, because of the Terrible Ted series, my name probably wouldn't mean anything on the card. Ray called Shire an "ignorant moron," punctuated by a few choice obscenities. With compassion in his voice, he asked about the way I was being treated by Mike LeBell, even though—as an erudite veteran—he clearly knew the answer.

Three or four days later, the phone rang at the Flamingo. It was Ray Stevens.

"Billy," he began, "I want you to come to Minneapolis. It's a great territory, and you'll make tons of money. Give LeBell your two-week notice and start on October 15."

Ray was speaking with such assurance that I wondered if he'd purchased the AWA himself. But when Stevens advocated for a wrestler, promoters always accepted his words as gospel. With the exception of my WWWF title reign, I consider the endorsement of Ray Stevens the highest compliment I ever received in the wrestling business.

Of course, once the conversation ended, I felt like calling back and asking if he'd said Miami instead of Minneapolis. I shivered at the prospect of a winter filled with snow, ice, and sleet. Looking down at Capella in her bassinet, I knew that my chubby cherub was about to lose her tan. We were moving to the land of 10,000 lakes and 10 billion mosquitoes—and replacing her tiny tank top with a parka.

CHAPTER NINE

LAY SOME YELLOW ON ME, DADDY

I am the light of the world.

—John 8:12

The American Wrestling Association was a colossus that extended out of Minneapolis to such far-off points as Chicago, Denver, Omaha, and Winnipeg—an enormous territory for that era. We flew to most of the major cities. But you needed a car to reach the "in between" places. I can't even calculate the thousands of miles I spent behind the wheel. When you drive endlessly, without sleep, you develop what truckers call "white line fever"— all you begin to see are white lines, flying by. I know that I could not have done it without amphetamines.

Yet with my twenty-two-inch arms, psychedelic wardrobe, and arrogance projected to antagonize midwestern sensibilities, something clicked for me in the AWA. The period would mark the beginning of my glory years in professional wrestling.

The AWA was not part of the NWA, or associated with the WWWF. It was big enough to have its own world champion, who—conveniently—also happened to be its owner. Verne Gagne was an excellent technical wrestler, a former NCAA champion and alternate on the 1948 U.S. Olympic team. In the ring, he had tremendous endurance but a lily-white, middle-aged appearance and no identifiable muscularity. Verne looked more like a bank executive than a pro wrestler, his hair gone except for a rim just above his ears. He loved wrestlers with amateur backgrounds, but since he was a shrewd businessman, he brought in gimmick guys like myself to make the money.

Gagne seemed to smile a lot—and who could blame him, since his company looked like it would be around forever? He paid his top guys well. Publicly and privately, he portrayed himself as the ultimate wrestler, the ultimate athlete, the ultimate promoter. Backstage, he was overbearing and hypercritical, always yelling at the wrestlers.

Every year, Verne ran a training camp for promising talent, and his son Greg was a recent graduate. In some ways, Greg was blessed with the Gagne genetics—no one could ever question his athletic skills—but the kid looked very skinny. At one point, Verne asked me about methods his son could use to bulk up. I recommended steroids.

I'm not sure if Greg ever followed my advice. Although he was a very hard worker, the fans generally perceived him as a bit too thin.

Another graduate of Verne's 1972 training camp was a classmate of Greg's from the University of Minnesota. Ric Flair was thrilled to have an entry-level position in the business, and took a liking to me right away. When we drove to far-off towns together, I'd occasionally opt to get a motel room and fly home the next day. Flair would drive my Cadillac back to the Twin Cities and, without fail, pick me up at the airport when I returned. In every instance, the car had been washed and the gas tank topped off.

From the day I met him, I knew that Ric Flair was going to be a success. He was—and, as of this writing, still is—the hardest-working man in wrestling. Even now, on Monday evenings, I look forward to turning on *Raw,* assured that—regardless of story lines—Flair will always give me another reason to mark out.

And I'm proud to have played a small role in his journey to the top. During a visit to my home in the Minneapolis suburb of Bloomington, Bunny gave the "Nature Boy" his first bleach job. Ever the gentleman, Flair brought over an expensive bottle of wine to show his gratitude and celebrate the occasion.

Without a profusion of Gold's Gyms in places like Waukesha and Duluth, I decided that the only way to maintain any semblance of the physique

I developed in California was by working out at home. Flair eagerly supplied me with a couple of hundred pounds of twenty-five-pound plates, a dozen ten-pound plates, a six-foot bar, and a couple of dumbbells. Later on, he introduced me to a friend specializing in what was then a cutting-edge concept: bodybuilding equipment for the home. With the Nature Boy's help, I purchased everything that could fit into my basement.

> **Richard Fliehr, aka Ric Flair:** *I was just mesmerized by Superstar Billy Graham's charisma. Like Ray Stevens, he was one of the guys I really looked up to when I first started. Even though he was a star and I was a young guy, he treated me like a million bucks.*
>
> *We did a lot together. Billy and I even went to the movies, and saw* The Exorcist. *We were both fascinated by the film. It was awesome. Linda Blair, with her head spinning around, was just great. She was one of my favorite characters of all time.*

As creepy as *The Exorcist* might have been, the Chicago Amphitheater was worse.

Running the ropes was like bouncing off a collection of rubber bands; there was no support. A few times, I actually slipped through the strands onto the arena floor.

From the ring, I would look out at a curtain of smoky blackness. The old-school way of thinking was: the darker the building, the more uninhibited the fans. Well, the amphitheater held some very uninhibited psychopaths.

There was a full-blown bar in that house of horrors, so people would get as drunk and unruly as they did at J.D.'s. When there were fights in the stands, we'd slow it down in the ring, wait for the brawl to subside, then pick up the action again. One night, a deranged lunatic fired off six shots at the ring. The shooter missed the wrestlers, wounded a few fans, put away his pistol, and left the building, undetected.

Verne and Dick "The Bruiser" Afflis, who based his operation out of Indianapolis—where, of course, he was the number-one star—promoted together in Chicago. Bruiser was a legitimate barroom brawler who billed himself as "The Most Dangerous Man in Wrestling," even when he was years past his prime. Backstage, he was a lot like the way he acted in the ring: loud, vulgar, chomping cigars. He was an obnoxious fool.

In the ring, Bruiser gave me nothing. If we locked up for a test of strength, he'd go down a little bit, then come up right away and seem to overpower me. I'd sell his shoulderblocks all over the place, and double over when he hit me in the midsection. When I'd take a bump, Bruiser would push the ref out of the way and beat on me some more.

Nonetheless, when Bruiser came around, he brought other members of his Indianapolis troupe, including "Pretty Boy" Bobby Heenan—later known as "The Brain." Bobby had one of the smartest mouths in the industry, and was an extremely good bump taker. He managed me a few times in Chicago, and I was richer for the experience.

Once in a while, I was still taken to task for a stunning breach of wrestling etiquette. For instance, before a card in Moline, Illinois, I slid into the front seat of a taxicab at the airport while Ray Stevens, Nick Bockwinkel, and "The Russian Bear" Ivan Koloff occupied the back. It seemed like we were running late, so I glanced over at Koloff and asked, "What time does the show start?"

Stevens lowered his voice a few octaves and scolded, *"Biiiilly."*

In the dressing room, my idol let me have it. What was I thinking when I blurted out the word "show" to describe a professional wrestling event? In front of a cabdriver, no less? Hopefully, the man wasn't listening. Otherwise, he might come to the conclusion that we were nothing more than entertainers.

The first time that I saw Dusty Rhodes, I was driving, scoping out a place to stay for the night. As I came toward a motel, I noticed a wide-bodied guy with his shirt off—and a cotton head of curly blond hair—going through a trunk in the parking lot.

When Dusty spoke, I was entranced, the way I'd been when I heard those black preachers during my evangelical days. He was a total free spirit. Once, after we landed in Chicago and were waiting outside the terminal for a ride to the amphitheater, Dusty reached over, scooped up my bag, and just hurled it in front of a giant bus.

"Hey, man," I protested, "my stuff is in there."

It landed in the road, where people were dropping off relatives, cabs were stopping and going, and passengers were boarding shuttles to get their rental cars. As I plunged into traffic to retrieve my valuables, I looked back at Dusty—and watched him laugh. He was crazy, but spontaneous. And I loved him for it.

Virgil Riley Runnels Jr., aka Dusty Rhodes: *I always felt like a simple twist of fate brought us together. Verbally, it's almost like we were clones. Music was changing. The industry was starting to change. And we figured out that it was important to tell a story in an interview. That's the deal that was cool with me—talk them into the building, then give them the product.*

We both loved Bob Dylan. It was Bobby D, and me and him. I think the connection was that a lot of times, Billy Graham and I knew what Dylan was saying—or at least we thought we did. We'd break it down. Billy and I would call each other in the middle of the night when a new album came out. One time, Billy played a whole Dylan album over the phone. I put the receiver on the floor and walked away for a little while. But I didn't hang up.

Over the years, there was a lot of Dylan influence in both of our interviews. In Florida, I'd say, "I offered up my innocence. You paid me back in scorn. Orlando, Florida, come in, I'll give you shelter from the storm."

I mean, we would laugh over things like that. We would make up poems. We talked about things that other people didn't understand. They thought we were nuts.

Dusty rented a Minneapolis town house with his Tag Team partner and fellow Texan, Dick Murdoch. There was a big basement in the place, where we'd all hang out and do speed. At least in my experience, speed could make you feel very amorous. I remember that Dusty was romantically involved with a female wrestler, and they'd speak on the phone and get each other worked up. Once, she was in Milwaukee, and Dusty told her to go to the airport and catch a plane right away to Minneapolis.

"I talked to her, man," he told me, rapping at a hundred miles a minute. "She's coming over. She's flying in now."

By the time she arrived, the speed had worn off—and Dusty had lost his desire. In fact, Dusty didn't even want her in town anymore.

The only negative about my friendship with Dusty was that I couldn't stand Murdoch. Even though his favorite show was *Sanford and Son,* he was a real bigot. Once, the three of us were at a restaurant with Ray Stevens, and Murdoch called the waitress the n-word.

Stevens was furious. "I don't care what you do in Texas, you stupid redneck, but you don't do that here!" Ray shouted. "If I ever hear you say something like that again, I'll punch your lights out!"

Dusty and Murdoch were together for years—as Tag Team partners, opponents, and best friends. But Dusty was an intelligent guy who made me laugh. Murdoch was an absolute racist loser.

After calling myself the "Real American" and "True Spirit of America," I felt that it was time to alter my nickname. And the song *"Jesus Christ Superstar,"* from the 1971 rock opera and 1973 movie, struck a resounding chord in me. The word *Superstar* defined exactly what my heel character was trying to portray. While I don't have indisputable evidence of this, I believe that I was the first member of the sports entertainment fraternity to use this term to describe myself.

Larry "The Ax" Hennig and I were seated across the aisle from each other on a plane as I was working out this concept. He watched me write out the words "Jesus Christ Superstar," then cross out Christ's name and scrawl "Billy Graham" instead.

"Oh, my God," he protested. "Not with *me* on this airplane."

I gave him a quizzical look—and a very slight, sardonic grin.

"You're scratching out the name 'Jesus Christ.'"

"No, man," I answered. "It's a work."

Larry shook his head, convinced that I was a little too cavalier. But I wasn't concerned. The Lord knew that it was a work, too.

Greg "The Hammer" Valentine: The name "Superstar" really fit Billy Graham. He was slick, the cool cat on the block. To me, he was born to be something special. Mr. Big Time.

My stay in the AWA endured the end of 1972, and was now extending into 1973. In my mind, I was prospering—not realizing that, compared to the salaries of today, I might as well have been paid out of a petty cash fund.

I bought myself a new Cadillac Eldorado—in cash!—and actually didn't have to ask anyone for a loan. The beauty probably averaged six miles to the gallon, but who was counting? The car was a glimmering jet black with a cranberry red leather interior. I was so proud of my Caddy that I drove directly from the showroom to Ray Stevens's house.

Ray came outside, and gazed long and hard at the elegant machine. Circling around the vehicle, he scrutinized the car a little more before offering his analysis. "Billy," he began in his throaty voice, "what I think you have here . . . is a first-class . . . *pimp* mobile!" Stevens howled with laughter while I stood there, grinning.

Slowly, though, our relationship was beginning to change. One afternoon, the two of us were among a group of wrestlers in the Dykeman Hotel in downtown Minneapolis, where the AWA office was located. "Billy," Ray began, "you're taking all the main events."

I expected Stevens to smile, like he was just goofing around, but he didn't. My hero was feeling left out.

"Ray," I explained, "I'm not *taking* these main events. Verne is booking them."

I'd caught on fire, and in the process, Ray's feelings were hurt. My soul

was bleeding over our conversation. How could this be? I asked myself. Me passing by Ray Stevens?! Was this really happening?

I always knew that I could talk. But in San Francisco and Los Angeles, my mic work had yet to click. When we taped our television shows at a small Minneapolis television studio, though, something triggered my inventiveness. For all of Gagne's other faults, he allowed the talent to be spontaneous in their interviews. Because of this, the promos rarely sounded contrived, and I became even more creative and original.

I bought a record album called *Cassius Clay Speaks*—featuring a succession of Muhammad Ali promos—and resynchronized the rhymes. For example, Ali would say, "I float like a butterfly, sting like a bee. There's nobody as pretty and as beautiful as me." So I said, "I float like a butterfly, sting like a bee. There's nobody as beautiful or *as powerful* as me."

On Hennepin Avenue—the downtown Minneapolis strip then favored by hippies, thieves, and assorted lowlifes—I bought a big butterfly necklace, along with a fuzzy, raccoon-colored pimp hat, to heighten these words. It was just a piece of costume jewelry, but I'd tell the television audience, "Can you dig this butterfly on my neck? A $300 butterfly, baby."

Because of my years preaching, I could pick a concept and go "free-style"—as today's rappers do. Before one championship challenge, I said, "I need that belt. Baby, it's a heavy belt. It's got gold on it. It's got silver on it. It's got platinum. It's got calcium, magnesium, and zinc. It's got uranium and titanium. It's got cobalt and asphalt . . . my fault, your fault, San Andreas fault!"

One by one, the rhymes just flowed out—and I appropriated them into Superstar Billy Graham institutions:

"I'm the reflection of perfection, the number-one selection."

"I am the women's pet, the men's regret. What you see is what you get. And what you don't see is better yet."

"I lift barbell plates. I eat T-bone steaks. I'm sweeter than a German chocolate cake. How much more of me can you take?"

And perhaps my best-known saying: *"I'm the man of the hour, the man with the power, too sweet to be sour."*

My steroid habit had me in such a grandiose mindset that I actually boasted about it in my promos. During one interview, I vowed to increase my intake of Dianabol and Delatestryl to prepare for a match.

Marty O'Neill was the AWA television announcer, a diminutive man with a receding hairline, partial to dark glasses and checkered suits. The AWA fans loved Marty O'Neill. But they were also amused when I played with him a little:

"Marty O'Neill, you're as slippery as a banana peel. I got a hot scoop for you, but I ain't gonna tell you 'til you squeal. . . ."

I'd pat down his coat pockets. "Are you packing any heat?" I'd continue.

I continued making wardrobe alterations, purchasing a burgundy velvet cap—with a small lip, rather than a brim—and fur-lined jackets with animal panels on the back. On Hollywood Boulevard, I'd found a muscle shirt with the word "God" written in psychedelic letters. I wore a Rolling Stones *Sticky Fingers* tongue across my chest, and Mickey Mouse and Donald Duck insignias—when those images were still considered pop art, before the advent of Disney stores in shopping malls. After I spotted a cloth shower curtain with an illustration of a bare-breasted Renaissance-era statue, I had it made into a robe.

It was censored off the television show.

How ironic that, today, in WWE, the Divas strip each other semi-nude. In those days, a *drawing* of a sculpture was considered morally unacceptable. Once again, I was way ahead of my time.

"This is what the world waits for," I announced on television, resplendent in canary yellow, with Marty O'Neill at my side. "The world out there asks, 'What's the Superstar going to wear next?' Not, 'Who's he going to *whip* next?' but what in the world the Superstar is going to wear. And I've got millions of letters saying, 'Superstar, would you *please* lay some yellow on me, Daddy?'"

By now I was a bona fide expert at heckling fans. I'd make eye contact with specific people in the audience, and lay into them. It made the exchange more personal than general, and the audience could feel the tension. When I had an opponent on the mat, I'd stand over his body, giving the crowd a "crab shot"—leaning forward and flexing my arms, pecs, and shoulders—to infuriate the spectators even more. Unlike today, there was nobody in the back worried that we had to go to a commercial in twenty seconds. So I didn't rush the pose. I'd always hold it for at least three or four seconds, milking the drama of my presentation.

However, Superstar Billy Graham was just my disguise. I never forgot that I was Wayne Coleman. When I was out in public and fans wanted autographs, I signed them. Back then, heels were expected to live their personas twenty-four hours a day, but I left mine in the building.

I remember being on a Central Airlines flight from Minneapolis to somewhere in North Dakota. The way the seating was arranged was that my back was to the pilot, against the wall. There was a nun sitting next to me, two in the row facing me, and one across the aisle. I noticed the contrast between them in their habits, and me, with my bleached blond hair, muscles, and bandages across my recently gigged forehead.

Apparently, they made the same observation. "Excuse me," my neighbor asked. "Do you mind if I ask what you do?"

"I'm a pro wrestler."

The nuns suddenly became animated. Although they weren't wrestling fans, they wanted to know more about my way of life.

"Well, I tell you what," I said. "How would you like to come to the matches?"

I got all of them tickets—at ringside. In their penguin outfits, they stood out in the crowd. As I stomped and beat down my opponent, they were the only ones clapping for me and laughing. They loved the whole spectacle—as ornate as a papal mass, in some ways—and instantly understood what it was all about. I even corresponded with a few of them for a while. Later on, I'd wonder if I ever tempted any of these pious ladies to kick the "habit."

Gagne had heard reports of my arm-wrestling gimmick in other territories when he called me into his office and proposed an angle that forever changed my stature in the wrestling world: "Superstar, I want to shoot an arm-wrestling angle between you and either Wahoo McDaniel or Billy Robinson. I just don't know which guy to do it with."

Besides the fact that Robinson's highly technical, scientific wrestling repertoire would clash with my basic approach, I explained to Gagne that Robinson didn't like football players or weightlifters who wanted to become wrestlers, and I was both. I didn't work with Robinson in Calgary because I never made it to main-event level. But I knew that he had intentionally hurt some underneath guys with his amateur, collegiate-style moves. He reeked with arrogance, and I wanted nothing to do with him.

Oddly enough, it was at least a year later when Verne did book me with Robinson. That night, before our match, I sat down next to the devious shooter in the dressing room, holding some athletic tape and a razor blade. While telling him that I knew he had deliberately hurt some guys in Calgary, I broke the blade into quarters and taped a piece to my finger. Giving Robinson a piercing glare, I issued this warning: "I don't like you or trust you. If you want to shoot or hurt me in any way with your technical garbage, I will shred you from your face to the tip of your toes." I'm positive that it isn't necessary to expound on the man's change of heart—or the quality of our match.

As for Verne's earlier multiple-choice proposition, I declared, "Wahoo's the man."

Chief Wahoo McDaniel was a former linebacker for the New York Jets, Miami Dolphins, and other pro football teams. Despite his Irish surname, Wahoo really *was* part Native American and had the demeanor of an Indian brave—solid in appearance, with big thighs, wide shoulders, and a thick chest. In the ring he wore a headdress and cut into opponents with his "Wahoo chops." Just from looking at his six-foot, 260-pound frame, you knew he was tough. From watching some of his matches, I also knew that he wasn't afraid to sell, and his comebacks were fierce. This man was a brawler, a fighter who kicked, punched, and once in a while threw a little wrestling into the mix (very little, I might add).

Another big plus for Wahoo was that he wasn't afraid to bleed. The abundance of scar tissue on his forehead was a testament to that. This humble, well-mannered, yet tenacious Native American would definitely arouse the sympathy of the fans. And no one opponent was more responsible for thrusting me to the top of my profession.

For three weeks, I strutted out on television, arm-wrestling jobbers, slamming their hands onto the table, then circling the ring, gloating and flexing my twenty-two-inch guns. On week four, when my opponent and I locked hands, Wahoo burst through the studio door and rolled under the ropes. I jumped out of my chair, hurling insults at him and the people in the audience.

Wahoo took the microphone. With passion in his voice, he told the fans that he was tired of seeing me humiliate people. He didn't know if he could beat me, but he wanted to try.

As the crowd popped, I snatched the microphone out of his hand, vowing to break his arm, rip it off, and send him back to the reservation in shame.

We sat down, locked arms, and started pulling. There was a momentary deadlock as we glared at each other. Then I made my move, slowly pulling down Wahoo's arm until it was about three inches from the table. Looking crazed, the warrior yanked my arm back to the starting position. Another stalemate, with our arms quivering, brought the crowd to a fever pitch. Now—just like in the Blassie angle—the unbelievable was occurring: my arm was going down. With the fans in a frenzy, I came across the table with a forearm to Wahoo's face and neck.

Earlier in the day, I'd cautioned McDaniel about the force of this assault. "It's gonna have to be a hard one, because the cameras will be right on top of us," I warned.

Wahoo was amused. "Graham," he replied, "you couldn't hurt me if you had to."

He was probably right.

Now I picked up the table and brought it down on his skull. A river of red flowed from the Chief's forehead. I stayed on top of Wahoo, breaking off a table leg and gouging the wound. Wahoo struggled to one knee and threw some wild punches. As he held the ropes to boost himself up, I stomped him down.

Wahoo fought back, swinging frantically. Finally, one of his blows connected. I took a bump, and rolled out of the ring to safety.

But not for long. Wahoo took the microphone and made this fervent plea: "I want you tonight, Billy Graham! *Tonight!*"

How convenient. The AWA television show aired at 5:00 P.M. on Saturdays in Minneapolis. The matches started at 8:00 P.M. Even in blizzard conditions, the building was sold out.

This was a classic matchup, epitomizing good vs. evil, conceit vs. humility, the cowardly vs. the courageous. In Minneapolis, and everywhere in the AWA's vast territory, Wahoo juiced and sold. When I'd choke him, he'd contort his head at a 45-degree angle to the canvas and drool saliva onto the mat. Then he'd rebound with fiery kicks and punches, delivering blistering chops to the chest. In time, I convinced him to hit me with Tomahawk chops instead—raising his hand high and coming down with a knife-edged chop to my head. I'd sell it for all I was worth, relieved that he wasn't beating my chest to a pulp.

Either way, Wahoo always ran my head into the ring post, and I'd bleed. In the ring, I'd cower, begging off in the corner, seemingly trapped—a routine I'd learned from Pat Patterson in Frisco. As Wahoo was about to strike, I'd slide out of the ring, wave my hands in disgust, and escape to the dressing room—leaving the fans incensed, but willing to lay down their money for the rematch.

"Wahoo McDaniel," I asserted in one promo, "do you know what I'm going to do to you? I'm going to introduce you to *pain*. I'm going to introduce you to *agony*. Professional wrestling is *pain* and *blood* and *pulled tendons* and *broken bones* and *strained ligaments* and *torn sinew* and *headaches* and *backaches* and *pain*."

We finished up our feud with a series of Indian Strap matches. Wahoo just happened to have a ten-foot bloodstained strap in his closet to resolve these types of conflicts. There was a loop on each end for the combatants to wrap around their respective wrists. To win, one had to drag his opponent around the ring, touching all four corners with the free hand.

Despite the fact that there was no championship at stake, we set attendance records around the territory. The dignity of Chief Wahoo McDaniel was on the line—and that seemed far more important than a superficial title.

Wahoo had apparently won scores of these lawless battles. There were no rules to speak of—Wahoo could choke, lash, and drag me up and down the stairs leading to the mezzanine section. What wholesome midwestern family would want to miss a bloodbath like that? Even more importantly, I couldn't run away, like I had in the past. The strap would prevent me from escaping the wrath of Wahoo.

These matches had a pattern in every town. With little variation, here's what the fans would see: after taking a quick beating, I'd crawl out of the ring and try to make a run for it. Wahoo would give me as much lead as he could, then pull me back into the ring, battering me again. I'd attempt another getaway, and now—with the fans programmed to telegraph the next maneuver—Wahoo jerked the strap one more time, generating a deafening pop.

It was clear that I wasn't going anywhere. In the ring, I'd be on my knees, pleading with Wahoo to halt the attack. Instead, he'd begin flailing on me with the strap. Every lash made a loud, smacking sound as it hit my back and welts rose up on my flesh.

The fans would be in a frenzy: *"Wahoo! Wahoo! Wahoo!"*

At this point, McDaniel wielded the edge of the strap in a sawing motion, to simulate the shredding of skin. I'd blade—and bleed heavily. Wrapping the upper part of the strap around his wrist to get better leverage, Wahoo would make his first attempt to end the contest, touching three of the ringposts—until I saved myself by hooking my legs around the bottom rope and rolling onto the arena floor. Wahoo would follow me, tie a section of the strap around my neck, and return to the ring over the top rope— hanging me.

Despite the free-flowing nature of these matches, the ref would intervene and save my life. Shortly afterward, I'd take the advantage again. Wahoo was always liberal in his selling, and beseeched me to lay it in as stiffly as possible. Once I swung a chair at him with such fury that I actually cracked open his head. It was the one time that I saw Wahoo display a touch of regret about encouraging me to whale on him.

"Graham," he mentioned as blood poured down both the front and back of his skull, "you hit me a little too hard."

This would be the stage of the match where I'd fight back and take over. I'd try dragging a seemingly prone Wahoo around the ring. He'd assist me, digging his heels into the mat and pushing as I pulled. When I was inches away from the fourth turnbuckle, I'd stop to adjust my grip. That would be the signal to Wahoo to kick up into my chest with both feet, knocking me off balance.

It was time to go home. Wahoo would resurrect himself, flailing at and chopping me with new vigor, until I was the one being dragged around the four corners. This time, Wahoo would make it to the final ringpost—as pandemonium broke out. Then, apparently weakened by my blows and his excessive blood loss, the mighty brave would collapse.

I'd ascend from the canvas, demanding that the referee free my hand from the strap. When he did, I'd lay the boots to Wahoo to get my heat back. But there was no quit in this Indian. He'd rise and lash into me as we went at it again, punch for punch. It would take another referee and a half-dozen wrestlers to pull us apart. Right until the end, we fought like the mortal enemies that we were supposed to be, grabbing for each other's throats, drenched in blood and sweat.

When you trust a man to thrash you around like that, your respect for him grows. Wahoo and I became very friendly during this period, and would regularly banter about a variety of things unrelated to wrestling.

The Big Chief was a very fancy dresser—wearing slacks and a sports coat with ostrich boots out in public. The two of us were getting on a flight to Denver once when he noticed that my traveling attire consisted of Levi's, a T-shirt, and a pair of leather sandals.

"Graham," Wahoo noted, "you're the best-dressed wrestler in the ring, and the worst-dressed outside the ring."

"Wahoo," I shot back. "Is Denver sold out tonight?"

"Yes, it is."

"Case closed."

The day after a Strap match in Winnipeg, Wahoo and I were in the airport in Minneapolis, at five-thirty in the morning, standing six feet away from each other. Suddenly, I heard a sound behind me: *"Kayfabe! Kayfabe!"*

It was Gagne, freaking out and twitching and gesturing. He was afraid that some marks would see us in such close proximity and wonder why I wasn't choking out Wahoo with the velvet rope leading to the reservation counter, or carving him up with the ticket agent's pen. The thing was that, with the exception of the AWA guys, the terminal was empty.

It was absolute madness. The guy was completely paranoid—a total kayfabe maniac.

One of my wintry wars with Wahoo was booked in Fargo, North Dakota. I arrived early and decided to venture into the subzero climes to the local YMCA for a workout. As I was training, a very polite redheaded kid apologized for interrupting me.

"I recognized you, and wanted to say hello," he said.

We shook hands. I was accustomed to being approached. And at least this guy wasn't obnoxious.

"Can you help get me into professional wrestling?"

That was a bit of a bold remark. Usually, people would inquire *how* to become a wrestler. I'd never had a stranger request my personal intercession. I figured that the guy didn't mean to be rude. It was just the way that the words came out.

Very modestly, he listed his credentials. He'd won the NCAA Division II wrestling championship—in the 190-pound division—at North Dakota State in 1971. I told him about Verne Gagne's training camp. Verne was always looking for athletes with potential; in addition to Flair, Ricky "The Dragon" Steamboat, Ken Patera, and the Iron Sheik were among the graduates. One of Gagne's latest finds was 1972 U.S. Olympic bronze medalist Chris Taylor. Chris was now pushing the 500-pound mark, and seemed to have such little regard for his personal hygiene that I'd occasionally drag him into the locker room shower. But he'd signed for a remarkable $100,000 annual contract, and was helping the AWA receive a lot of national publicity.

The kid thanked me for my advice, and apologized again for interrupting my workout.

"No problem, brother," I told him. "Good luck."

Bob Backlund eventually *did* become a professional wrestler. He beat me for the WWWF championship in 1978.

In the summer months, the wrestling business slowed down in the AWA. Who wants to go into an arena when he's been stuck indoors all winter? Gagne booked a bunch of outdoor shows, where I teamed with Ivan Koloff—another strongman, and a former WWWF champion—against Wahoo and Dick the Bruiser's "cousin," Reggie "Crusher" Lisowski. Ivan was the workhorse of the team, while I did all the talking. Among my boasts: Wahoo might have dragged me around the Midwest, but he never pinned me.

My body had adjusted to Wahoo's hard blows. But before those outdoor cards, I winced at the knowledge that I was about to be gnawed by the mosquitoes that commuted to the shows from Minnesota's celebrated lakes. These winged invertebrates became such an obsession that I cut a televised promo about them:

There I was, lounging by the pool
Getting a tan and looking cool
Drinking a Coke and eating Fritos
And being attacked by giant mosquitoes.

The mosquitoes disappeared soon enough. In Minnesota, the summers are short, and there are no autumns. When that Siberian train loaded with polar air leaves the station, there's no turning back. Can a man raised in Arizona's Sonoran Desert ever forget the trauma of shoveling out a driveway in below-zero weather? I can't. But when those blasts of frigid air hit the Twin Cities of Minneapolis and St. Paul in the winter of 1974, Ivan Putski came along, too, bundled up in a lamb's-wool coat.

The "Polish Power" was among the last stragglers to pass through Ellis Island in the early 1950s. Before developing an excellent bodybuilder's physique, he was as thick as a polka barrel, carrying 300 pounds on his five-foot-nine frame. Alternating between English and Polish—to play to the ethnic fans around the Midwest—Putski was a carefree character on his AWA interviews, smiling, laughing, and claiming to have a stomach made out of steel.

That sounded like an angle to me. So Gagne set up a demonstration in the television studio. Putski lay flat on his back in the corner of the ring while a sequence of jobbers jumped onto him from the second turnbuckle, bouncing off his stomach like tennis balls. The fans loved cheering this human trampoline act.

Then it was time for the Superstar to ruin their good time.

Bolting through a side door, I swept up the ring post and balanced myself on the top turnbuckle.

"Watch out!" the spectators screamed, hoping to startle the Polish grappler out of his miasma. Some went up to the ring and actually pounded on the apron. But their gullible hero looked like he'd just eaten a large meal and fallen asleep—all he needed was a toothpick—as I soared through the air and came down with my left knee over Ivan's neck. He grabbed his throat, coughing and choking, while I continued the ambush, stomping him until the ring filled with wrestlers, pulling me away.

Working with the Polish Power forced me to do some innovating. His definition of selling back then was dropping to one knee while we locked fingers, and smiling at his fans. Our matches came down to tests of strength, standing chest to chest, pushing and shoving and slogging around the ring. Compared to my explosive encounters with Wahoo, the ritual of muscle vs. muscle felt like slow motion. In fact, sometimes we wouldn't be moving at all. This may sound a bit boring, but it was much easier on the body.

After Ed Francis folded his promotion in Hawaii, Verne came in and made the state part of the AWA. Our television show ran there, and we regularly flew into Honolulu for shows. I even became the Hawaiian champion for a while, beating Francis, who still wanted to be part of things and got along with Gagne.

But the commute was a terrible grind. We'd fly from Minneapolis to Los Angeles, then on to Hawaii. Immediately after the matches, we'd get on an 11:30 P.M. return flight. We had to be in Winnipeg the next night to wrestle.

Gagne also arranged tours to Japan, where we worked on shows with names like Rusher Kimura, Tadaharu Tanaka, and Great Kusatsu. I didn't love Japan at first because the rooms were so small, and the arena commodes were literally holes in the ground. I didn't understand why a country so advanced couldn't manufacture a modern toilet.

I grew a goatee on one of these early excursions, and got over very quickly with my muscled look and posing routine. The people were great and very respectful—there was never any carryover of ill will from the arena. The streets, the shops, and the produce markets were immaculate. Because of the strict prohibitions on gun ownership, the crime rate was bewilderingly low.

In June 1974, Billy Robinson won a tournament in Tokyo for the Inter-

Posing for the Japanese press.

national Wrestling Alliance (IWA) version of the world championship. I don't know what kind of arrangement the promotion had with Gagne, but on August 16, I defeated Robinson for the title in Denver. The next morning, I boarded a plane to defend the belt against Mighty Inoue in the Japanese city of Saitama. The IWA treated the match like it was something out of the Olympics, playing the Japanese and American national anthems.

"The Star-Spangled Banner" at a pro wrestling show? I thought. It didn't seem to fit.

As arranged, I laid down and relinquished the title. Once again, the next morning, I was on a flight back across the Pacific. I felt like a zombie. The money and so-called prestige were not worth the aggravation.

In hindsight, I wish that I'd put greater effort into my trips to Japan, and established more than a superficial rapport with the fans. I could have built a real legacy there.

Along the way, I was booked to challenge Verne for his AWA belt. To state it mildly, we didn't have a lot of chemistry in the ring. As a pure athlete, Gagne wanted me to curtail the strongman stuff and put more wrestling in there. But I will give the boss credit for this: he'd sell—so much that, in Peoria, Illinois, a crazy fan felt compelled to charge the ring to offset my advantage.

The clash took place in a high school. The principal wouldn't allow chairs on the new gym floor, and Gagne certainly wasn't going to pay for a refurbished basketball court. So the ring posts had padding below them, and the fans sat in the bleachers. Verne was tangled in the ropes as I strangled him—and saw a spectator stand, work his way down the bleachers, and sprint across the court.

I had plenty of time to prepare. I waited for the out-of-control mark as he dove headfirst through the ropes and kicked him in the face. Even I was revolted by the echo of bones cracking and teeth being dislodged. With blood spattering, he slumped to the gym floor, where the local cops caught up with him and hauled him out of the building.

I went back to Verne, still tied up in the ropes, and continued where I left off. "Good job," he said, as I choked him. "You better not kick me that hard."

"I won't as long as you keep selling."

James Janos, aka Jesse "The Body" Ventura: *I was home on leave, just before I got out of the navy, and all my friends were busy one night, doing other things. I'd been a wrestling fan as a kid—following Mad Dog Vachon, The Crusher, Verne Gagne, Larry Hennig, and all these people—and I saw that wrestling was down at the Minneapolis Auditorium. I went there by myself, walked up to the ticket counter, and said, "I want the best seat you've got."*

The lady said, "I think I have one in the front row."

Superstar was in a Six-Man Tag match with Horst Hoffmann and Baron Von Raschke. They were wrestling against Wahoo Mc-Daniel and two other babyfaces—who remembers babyfaces? I'll never forget that Billy was wearing a fishnet top, and he was ultra tan. He came into the ring, and his eyes locked on me. We looked at each other for three or four seconds, which was a long time. He probably noticed me, too—look at that big kid.

Graham got down on one knee and did that pose. It was at that point that I thought, "This is something I want to do. I want to be Billy Graham."

After I got out of the navy, I started going to the matches with a group of five or six guys, and we used to cheer for Graham. Of course, we'd get heat from the crowd because Billy was definitely the most dastardly villain in the AWA. But we were heel fans—college kids going against the status quo.

Billy was the transition between the hippie era and disco—because he had the tie-dye and the flashiness. He was hip and in-

sightful enough to go after that generation of rebellious youth. He deserves more credit for his impact—in many ways, he changed interviewing.

I started training for wrestling with Eddie Sharkey in downtown Minneapolis. One of my friend's wives was a hairdresser, and she dyed my hair blond. The next day when I walked into the gym on Seventh Avenue, Leroy, the owner, said, "Hey, your idol's here."

I thought he was lying to me. I quickly looked and saw Billy doing pulldowns. I changed as fast as I could because I wanted to talk to this man. When I came out, Billy was going around the corner to the drinking fountain. Billy looked at me like he was looking in a mirror because here's this younger kid, buffed out, too, with the bleached blond hair. We were even balding in the same place.

The gym was a dingy building with cold, cement walls, but Jesse brought warmth to it the moment that we shook hands. He couldn't stop smiling. I knew that this was one happy man.

Jesse told me that he was training with Sharkey, who also ended up teaching pro wrestling to Bob Backlund. I knew that Gagne wouldn't give Jesse a shot in the AWA because we were too much alike. "You've got to go on the road," I told him. "Get experience somewhere else, and come back."

Because of the bias against marks, Gagne and others in the AWA front office did not want me associating with Jesse. To them, he was a pest who liked the business a little too much. Wally Karbo, one of Verne's partners, specifically told me to ignore the aspiring wrestler.

"He's a wacko," Wally said.

"Oh, come on," I answered. "The kid just wants to be a wrestler. What's wrong with that? And I like the guy. I'm his hero. Is the business going to rise and fall if the two of us talk?"

Jesse "The Body" Ventura: Whenever he wrestled in Minneapolis, Billy would come out of the dressing room and talk to me before the matches. He gave me advice. My friend tape-recorded all of Graham's interviews off the TV, and put them on cassettes. When I was in my car, instead of listening to music, I listened to Billy's interviews.

I met my wife when I was working the door at a club. I asked her for her ID, and she said, "You know, you look just like Superstar Billy Graham."

"Well I ought to," I told her. "He's my older brother."

Jesse made a career out of mimicking my persona. He even chose a ring moniker that would have been perfect for me—"The Body." Like his hero, Jesse was not the best technical wrestler. His main attribute was his ability to communicate. He was not the first, but he was by far the best heel commentator in the business.

At times, people have told me, "Jesse ripped you off." But he did a good job at it. Through all the turns in my life, he has remained a devoted, consistent friend. I'm happy that I had something to give him.

CHAPTER TEN

HARD RAIN

Ceaselessly scanning the earth and sky
Feeding the need for warmth and beauty
Always examining the how and why
Reconciling freedom with duty

—Paul Boesch,
Houston wrestling promoter

By the fall of 1974, I was on the threshold of a third, flesh-numbing winter in the upper Midwest. I just didn't have it in me to face another one. Wahoo was already living in the Dallas area, and suggested that I do the same. It was relatively warm, with a good airport to fly anywhere in the country. There were several promotions in Texas, and—by this point—everyone wanted me on their shows. On one of my days off, I flew down to Dallas and purchased a home. The only thing left for me to do was give Verne my two weeks' notice.

This had to be a first—the hottest heel in a territory, on good terms with his boss, quitting a good-paying job because he hated the weather. But if you look at the real world, it's not that odd. There are thousands of people in my hometown of Phoenix who arrived because they couldn't cope with the blizzards in Chicago and Michigan. And there are thousands of other transplants who bail out as soon as the thermometer hits 115 degrees.

I walked into the Dykeman Hotel coming off a sellout the night before in Green Bay, and dropped the bomb to Gagne. He didn't yell or threaten, like I feared, but shook his head in disappointment. "I was going to do a weightlifting angle with you and Patera," he said.

That sounded great to me. Ken Patera had been a genuine Olympic weightlifter. He was now one of Verne's newcomers, overflowing with potential.

"After that," Verne added, "I wanted to turn you babyface."

This seemed a little too good to pass by. "We can do all that," I offered, "even if I am in Dallas. I can fly up."

I proposed shooting Gagne's planned angles, but only working the big cities. That would get me off those ice-covered roads to the AWA's smaller towns—and allow me to wrestle around Texas instead. Gagne agreed, but with a stipulation. I'd have to cover my airfare. If he conceded anything more, he'd be setting a bad precedent.

That was fine. Weary of hazardous car travel, I already *was* paying for flights to every little town with an airport. For the first time in my wrestling career, I had some say over my own destiny.

I converted my garage in Dallas into a home gym, running air-conditioning ducts from the house to the place that should have been reserved for my Eldorado. Carpenters sealed the room by installing glass into three gaps on the west wall. I found the perfect panels in Dallas's thriving antique district—salvaged from an old Episcopal church that had fallen victim to the wrecking ball. The stained-glass panes were nothing less than stunning—radiant scenes held together by lead seams. The adjustment forced me to look inward, and back to something that used to be. For all of Superstar Billy Graham's outer success, the soul of Wayne Coleman was in a state of decay. The young man who used to talk to God like a best friend barely uttered a prayer. Sure, I invoked the Lord's name while going through turbulence at 35,000 feet. But I'd stopped giving thanks for my daily bread, my money, my health. Essentially, I was treating God like an errand boy.

I'm sure that a lot of you can relate to what I've just written.

Beverly Swink Welch: *I hadn't heard from Wayne since he stopped going to church. I'm not a wrestling fan, but I flipped on the TV one* *night, and there he was—with the biggest biceps. "Oh, that's what happened to Wayne," I said. I wasn't surprised. I knew why he was calling himself Billy Graham, too.*

After a few home workouts, it was time to go back to Minnesota for the big angle with Patera. Although he'd fallen short in his quest to win a medal at the 1972 Games, Patera was still billed as the "World's Strongest Man." And why not? After all, I was the so-called Arm-Wrestling Champion of the World.

During the strategy meeting with Patera and Gagne, I explained that I had a bad lower back, and knew I couldn't put the amount of iron over my head that Ken could. "What we need to do is find someone who can make *replicas* of these weights," I suggested.

Patera became animated: "I've got a friend who can do it. He has a giant lathe. He can make anything out of wood."

The idea was to duplicate a bunch of 45-pound plates, using precise Olympic dimensions. We'd spray-paint the wood black and rub it down with chalk, creating a worn look. A few genuine weights would be slipped in, as well, so fans could hear that authentic metal-against-metal clang. Under these conditions, it would appear that we were loading the bar with more than 500 pounds.

Gagne's main concern was that a wooden plate might break apart when dropped to the mat, exposing the swerve. "You better not let anyone catch you at this," he warned.

Verne now laid out his vision. Ken would lift first, and I'd have to match him. We'd go back and forth three or four times, until the World's Strongest Man tired of playing my silly games and filled the bar with 550 pounds. Seeing this, I'd realize that I was about to become the loser—and a sore one at that. During Patera's next—and most impressive—lift, he'd rest the bar on his front deltoids, pausing before pushing it over his head. But he'd never get the chance, because I was going to kick him in the chest, and—as the plates fell in all directions—put my Size 15s to the former Olympian.

"I don't know, Verne," I responded. "We're using a lot of real weights and a real bar. It sounds kind of dangerous."

Before Gagne could argue, I offered a different approach: using a chalk box wrapped in athletic tape. There would be an inch-thick layer of baby powder in the container, with four or five broken bars of chalk. Between lifts, each of us would walk over, and chalk up our hands. When we got to the spot where the bar was resting on Ken's deltoids, I'd throw the chalk and baby powder in his face. This would have a shocking effect, like a bomb exploding. In the confusion, Ken could safely dump the loaded bar and sell the notion that he was temporarily blinded. As he fell to his knees, I'd run his head into the plates. Of course, he'd have juice.

What the fans would see was the disturbing sight of a onetime Olympic hero, his face and upper torso plastered with white powder and chunks of chalk—with streams of blood zigzagging through the mess and clumping in spots.

Gagne agreed to my concept. But Ken was nervous.

"I've never done a blade job," he disclosed.

I looked at his virgin forehead, and figured that this wasn't the time for him to learn. "I'll do it for you," I offered.

Patera leaned back on his swivel chair and thought for a moment. Then he grinned and replied, "Superstar, if you don't mind, I think I'll take a pass on that one."

We laughed and closed the meeting.

A short time later, I went on television and told our audience that Ken Patera's Olympic team selection was a fluke. It should have been *me* representing the United States. I was the Superstar—the man with the twenty-two-inch arms. "Bring your weights to any arena," I challenged, "and I'll expose you for the fraud you are."

Patera went on the road, lugging around our gimmicked weights. While entering Canada, a customs agent opened up Ken's suitcase and asked, "What are these?"

"These are plates," Patera answered.

"What kind of plates?"

"Weightlifting plates. We're going to have a weightlifting contest up here."

The guy shrugged. "Oh . . . okay." He fixed up the bogus weights and handed them back. That suitcase should have weighed 600 pounds!

At the Chicago Amphitheater, we had one of our biggest scares. A group of weightlifters found their way into the front row and sat on the edge of their seats, clearly suspicious about the validity of our contest. They stared so intently that their faces could have been in suspended animation. Then again, that may have been the result of the cannabis being passed around ringside.

The referees had the unenviable job of sliding the weights onto an official, 45-pound Olympic bar. First, they loaded on four actual plates—producing that metal "gong" sound that we wanted. After that came the gimmick plates. As the refs pretended to exert themselves, I grabbed the chalk box, pacing and rubbing the white mixture against my hands while ridiculing—and distracting—the weightlifters at ringside.

Yet I never completely diverted their attention from the bar. Every time that a referee reached for a phony plate, I felt the veins on my forehead twitch. Remaining in character, I pointed tauntingly at Patera.

"Hey," I said through gritted teeth, "those guys in the front row are watching us a little too closely."

Patera called for two more plates. But now the referees were nervous, too. One of them slipped on a gimmick plate too fast and too hard. It smacked against another one with a flat whoosh.

Jumping out of his seat, one of the lifters screamed, "They're fake! The weights aren't real!"

"Time to go home," I told Ken. He lifted up the bar, and I let him have it. The chalk mixture looked like it had been shot out of a cannon. The cries of the crowd drowned out anything that the weightlifters had to say. In fact, the fans were charging the ring, followed by the cops—just the way we wanted it.

The subsequent grudge matches made Gagne a lot of money, and helped jump-start Ken's career in the AWA.

As promised, Verne did turn me babyface, distinguishing himself as one of the few promoters who recognized that—with my rhymes, psychedelic outfits, and outlook about the public at large—I could connect with the people. The transformation was relatively uncomplicated. After a Six-Man Tag loss, my partners—World War II era heels Baron Von Raschke and Horst Hoffmann—took me to task for my "poor performance." Out of the blue, Hoffmann hit me in the stomach, circled around, grabbed my arms, and pulled them behind my back. Squinting hatefully, the bald-headed Baron reached into his tights, retrieved a "loaded" black leather glove, and busted me open. Unable to control his genetic impulses, the despised German next grabbed his wrist, widened his fingers, and goose-stepped around the ring.

Now he delivered the coup de grace, the dreaded "Iron Claw," clamping his fingers over my temples. According to one wrestling magazine, the evil Baron hoped to crush my skull—the only protection for the frontal lobe of my brain.

In the weeks following the double-cross by the horrible Huns, none other than "The American Dream" Dusty Rhodes—the "son of a humble plumber," fans were reminded—rushed to my defense, delivering jive-talking promos that blended with mine. Our confrontations against Hoffmann and Von Raschke didn't set any attendance records, but Dusty and I had a great time, listening to Bob Dylan in the car, contemplating his lyrics, and impersonating his nasal singing voice. We'd joke about how Dylan would sometimes end a concert by simply walking off the stage without saying goodnight or a thank-you—a true heel. Yet it only made marks like us want to see him more.

A photo I keep at home reminds me of my happy days with Dusty: the two of us in the dressing room, nose to nose, laughing over some joke that no one else thought was funny.

While all this was going on, I was also wrestling in Texas, where I remained a heel in the Dallas territory. During one Saturday afternoon show in Austin, I was working in front of a heavily intoxicated, largely Mexican audience. I don't recall the name of my opponent, but I had him in a chin lock when I noticed the referee looking over my head, his mouth hanging open. I looked behind me to see a mark coming my way with a knife. Automatically, I swiveled around and smashed the guy with a forearm across his face. This was a lifesaving shot; knives kill people. The crowd was riled up, and I couldn't back off and show any fear. As the referee lifted the knife from the mat, I punched and kicked my attacker bloody. There had to be a lesson there for all to see.

Like Baron Von Raschke, Dallas promoter Fritz Von Erich had made his name as a Nazi heel. But after purchasing the territory, he renovated his image to portray himself and his wrestling sons as the All-American Christian family. It was such a work! Fritz was a cutthroat guy with an off-the-wall ego. His office was above the Dallas Sportatorium, and mortals were generally forbidden to ascend that hallowed staircase. There had to be a monumental reason to be granted an audience with Fritz.

By contrast, the Dallas booker Red Bastien was one of the most respected guys in the industry, who—despite his exalted position—remembered that he was a wrestler, just like the rest of us. With Bastien's help, my friend Steve Strong began working beside me in the territory.

After I'd left J.D.'s, Steve filled my shoes, and for a period became Brick's roommate. While I was visiting Phoenix in 1973, Steve told me that he was ready to change professions. At six-foot-five and more than 300 pounds of muscle, Steve was a perfect candidate for the Mentor of Mayhem's training academy in Calgary. Stu Hart was elated to have a very athletic bodybuilder to physically torment. Who knew? Maybe Steve would even learn a little wrestling as a bonus. So he entered the Dungeon—and ended up lasting a full year in the territory, seven months longer than I did. Because of this, I had full confidence when I dropped his name to Bastien. Red took me at my word. While it meant nothing to the rest of the world, a tag team of J.D.'s alumni was a pretty big deal to our friends in Phoenix.

> **Steve Strong:** *I think Superstar and I bonded as much over art as anything else. We both painted. If you're born and raised in Arizona, you're totally connected to the Indians. Billy was always finding wood and sanding it down and painting bow hunters and other American Indian stuff. We both embraced the Indian in Southwest art.*
>
> *And we both loved to train hard. For a while, we were training with Tony Atlas, who billed himself as "Mr. Universe." We would get off the bench press, then stand up and curl two and a quarter. Tony seemed to think that Billy had some formula for getting bigger. So Billy ribbed him. He said, "Tony, after you eat your best meal, you need to get a bag of cement, and take a big teaspoon." Cement!*
>
> *I think Tony believed him, too. When we'd see him after that, he'd say, "I'm getting bigger every day. Feeling stronger!"*

Steve was a very good driver—I bought a van to work the Dallas territory—and an even better workout partner. We'd train at my house on Monday and Tuesday when we wrestled in Fort Worth and Dallas, as well as Wednesday, prior to traveling to San Antonio. After working out at a local YMCA the next morning, we'd drive to Padre Island and tan, then make our Thursday-night shot in Corpus Christi. After the matches, we'd head straight to Houston, home of the Sam Houston Coliseum—and a great gym to pump iron on Friday mornings.

The reason Steve never really broke out of mid-card matches—except when the two of us were teaming together—was that he was such a talented artist. Under his real name, Steve Cepello, Strong was selling his paintings to galleries. When you're not willing to sacrifice everything else in your life for wrestling, promoters view you as a subversive.

Although part of the Dallas loop, Houston was an entity all to itself. Wrestlers from the far points of North America flew in specifically for promoter Paul Boesch's shows because he was different than his contemporaries: he had a rare sense of integrity, and the audaciousness to treat the talent like they were human beings. This jewel of a man—with his broad smile and cauliflower ears—never forgot that he was part of a larger community; a blood drive he organized for the Veterans Administration netted more than 500 pints of blood from wrestling fans.

Paul himself was a decorated war hero. But his biggest legacy in wrestling may have been introducing Stu Hart to his wife, Helen, on a beach in Long Island.

On Friday afternoons before the shows, I'd frequently visit with Paul in his office—decorated with plaques and wrestling memorabilia—where he wrote every line of the Houston program, as well as poetry:

On some star-filled ecstatic night
When Heaven brings to earth sweet rapture,
Halt the hours! Stop time's mad flight,
Forevermore this Eden capture.

The ring in Houston was gigantic—22 by 22, compared to the standard NWA ring at the time, 18 by 18, or even today's 20-by-20 WWE ring. I had the privilege of wrestling Jose "El Gran" Lothario there. After he retired from wrestling, Jose became a trainer, and I can see a lot of him in his most famous student, Shawn Michaels. Lothario was an incredible worker, and threw punches like a professional boxer. Because he was a legend—the fans revered him—I let Jose get my arm almost to the table in the now-familiar arm-wrestling angle.

When Andre the Giant and I had *our* Houston arm-wrestling match, the behemoth emitted a bellow like a wounded animal before bringing my arm all the way around and crashing it into the table. As planned, I followed this embarrassment with a couple of forearms to the head.

Andre sold nothing. "How are you doing tonight, Boss?" he said, eyes gleaming while looking across the table at me with a gummy smile. "Are you ready to wrestle?"

For a moment, my heart jumped. This was one guy who really could have crushed me. But Andre was just having a good time. He quickly let me get the heat on him, and even asked me to lift him off the mat with a bear hug. I could barely reach around his body and lock my hands. At that time, I think Harley Race was the only other man to pick up Andre. To be given this license meant something very important:

That big giant liked me.

Houston was the place where I cultivated a lifelong friendship with Ernie "The Big Cat" Ladd, who'd transitioned from pro football to pro wrestling because, amazingly, he earned more money in the squared circle. Ernie claimed to have made $98,000 the same year that football's highest paid player, Johnny Unitas, received $15,000. Despite the racism of the time, Ernie never let a promoter mold him into anything other than what he was—an educated man who made his points with cerebral street talk.

Another football player, my friend Ron Pritchard, turned up in Houston during my run, hoping to reprise our Navajo reservation match at the Sam Houston Coliseum. Ron had one specific request that night—he wanted to get juice. His ring career was so sporadic that he hadn't experienced this rite of passage.

Before we left the dressing room, he showed me a razor that was almost as long as a knife.

"Ron," I said patiently. "You'll sever your head with that—and probably kill me, too."

I took the blade, broke it up for him, and taped it to his finger. Then we went out and had our match.

"You happy?" I asked, when I saw the first trickle of blood on his fore-head.

Ron nodded. "Not yet, brother. Now *you* need some blood!"

Eventually I finished up my AWA commitments. But I wasn't beyond repeating angles that worked there. When I told Boesch about the weightlifting deal with Patera, Paul called Verne and got an open date on Ken. This time, I threw a gallon container of iced tea with lemon rinds in Patera's face during the attack. The plot generated heat with the fans and—not intentionally—the boys. Because we went on last, and needed bodies to load and unload the weights, a number of the wrestlers had to stay late in the arena before driving home to Dallas—a major inconvenience when you have a 240-mile ride ahead of you.

Other AWA stars found their way to Houston as well. Bald, bearded, and gravelly-voiced, Maurice "Mad Dog" Vachon was a mark for his own gimmick. He'd rake his dirty fingernails across your back and deliberately scrape off skin. The night after Steve Strong received an eighteen-stitch gash in a match, he had to face Mad Dog, and told him to stay away from the eye. As soon as the bell rang, Vachon tried to tear open the cut.

When *ABC's Wide World of Sports* did a story on U.S. Olympian Chris Taylor's AWA debut, Maurice—who'd represented Canada in the Olympics—seemed jealous. Taylor was overweight, with high blood pressure, among a plethora of health problems (he died at just twenty-nine years old), and had frequent nosebleeds. As the ABC cameras rolled, Vachon stuck a thumb in Taylor's mouth, grabbed his nose, and wrenched it, releasing a red cascade.

Ivan Putski was once in a private plane with Mad Dog when he opened the door in midair, dropped down the stairs, and announced that he was going to jump. Had I been there, I would have pushed him.

I generally enjoyed Cage matches—but not when I worked with Vachon. In one Houston clash, he tossed me over the ropes, and I twisted my body, midway, to hurtle against the hurricane fencing. This was a standard spot for me, but in this case I caught my left leg on a loose barb that cut through my boot. I ended up hanging upside down, with a sharp piece of wire jabbed into my skin.

Since wrestlers are supposed to trust and cooperate with each other, I expected Vachon to unhook me while we continued the match. Instead, he stomped on me and laughed.

"As soon as I'm up, I'm gonna kill you," I grimaced.

Vachon just kicked me relentlessly until I unfastened myself—and whacked him around with a few potatoes.

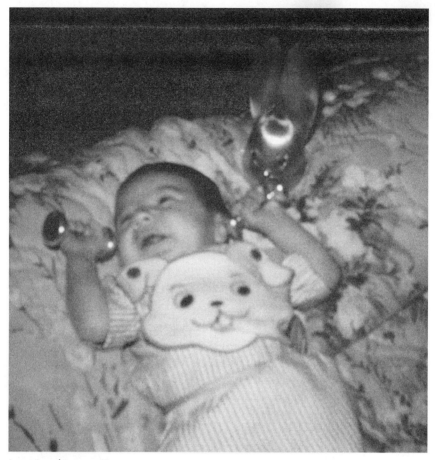

Joey "working out."

I'm not sure that he even cared.

Because I was home at least three mornings a week in Dallas, I was able to spend time with Capella, as she was learning to talk and figure out the world. I took her with me one day to meet Dusty at the airport, after he called and said that he was going to have a long layover there. To create the right mood, I played some Dylan on the way over.

She liked Bob Dylan as a child. Later on, as our relationship became more challenging, she'd claim that she never did.

There was another Dylan tune, unfortunately, that would signify the turn my life was about to take: "Hard Rain." It began on a day that should have been magnificent—March 18, 1975, when my son Joey was born.

The reason why my kid is so tough today is that he's been fighting from the instant that he drew his first breath. While Capella was born with the pink skin of a healthy newborn, Joey's flesh was clammy and bluish. It still chills me to remember that first sight of Joey in an incubator, as nurses flashed him by me. He wasn't getting enough oxygen. Despite my physical strength, I felt absolutely powerless. Joey was going to have to struggle for his own survival.

> *Joe Miluso: I was basically almost dead when I was born. My heart was enlarged. They immediately rushed me to intensive care to help stabilize my vital signs. And I actually developed pneumonia, which caused a hole in my heart. In 1981, they patched up the hole and reduced the size of my heart. But in 1983, the hole broke open again— it turned out the aortic valve was leaking. So they replaced that with a metal valve, which is what I still have now.*

I wanted to be at Joey's bedside every day, but the demands of professional wrestling sometimes took me away. If you've read other wrestling autobiographies, you know about this pattern. The business can be like a thief, stealing hours that turn into days that turn into weeks that turn into months that turn into years—causing deep emotional wounds that never quite heal.

I still have wonderful memories of Joey's earliest days. Paul Boesch had his jeweler make my son two sterling silver rattles shaped like dumbbells. And Dusty Rhodes became Joey's godfather.

CANAAN

I have the comforting certainty that mankind is real flesh, and I myself am not a dream.

—Helen Keller on visiting New York City,
in *Midstream: My Later Life*

I never contemplated entering the Mr. Olympia contest, against luminous posers like Lou Ferrigno and Arnold. But when I heard that bodybuilding promoter Dan Lurie was staging the 1975 Pro Mr. America contest in New York, I was interested. Lurie's World Body Building Guild (WBBG) events tended to be more low market than those sanctioned by Joe Weider. Pro Mr. America was one contest that I believed I could win.

I was still living in Dallas, but now wrestling almost exclusively for Paul Boesch, who began promoting my preparation for the event in the Houston program. I was planning to take a month off before the contest to train. But a few nights before my final match, someone gave me a running powerslam,

and I landed wrong. Instead of coming to rest on the flat of my back, my left shoulder and neck hit the mat.

When I looked in the mirror the next day, my pec and tricep had both dropped. My left arm could barely move. It was a struggle to bench-press 135 pounds.

Steve Strong was there when I visited an orthopedic surgeon with an outstanding reputation among local pro athletes. After some X-rays, he said, "You pinched a nerve from your neck down your left side. It will probably be with you the rest of your life."

"But what can we do about it?" I asked. "I'm supposed to be in the Pro Mr. America contest next month."

The doctor and I looked at each other. We both knew the solution to this dilemma.

> *Steve Strong: The doctor gave him a script for injectables and a script for ingestibles. He asked Billy, "How much do you want? What do you think you'll need to take?"*
>
> *He wasn't doing anything illegal. In 1975, there was no FDA (Food and Drug Administration) statement on steroids. If you were found with steroids in your possession at the airport, nothing happened to you. No one could prove that you were taking more pills than your doctor prescribed. And if they could, you weren't breaking any laws.*
>
> *I don't think the doctor had any ethical questions at all. It was all about hanging up a picture of Superstar Billy Graham in his office and saying, "Oh, he's a patient of mine."*

The normal dose for my condition should have been something like one or two Dianabol a day. I took about thirty—including tripling up on my injectables. The combination gave me enough retention to go ahead with the contest.

I also had the good fortune to befriend a fellow bodybuilder who happened to own a pharmacy, a guy who'd do some prison time after steroids were reclassified.

I'm not going to give you a term paper on anabolic steroids. I can only tell you what I know. Through my experiences, these are the benefits I found in taking the drugs: increases in muscle mass, strength, training capacity, and recuperative abilities from sports injuries. The drugs also heightened my libido and sense of euphoria. But steroids are definitely addicting—so much so that I used drugs labeled in languages I couldn't understand, and packaged with the warning: "FOR VETERINARY USE ONLY."

Now, some more negatives: steroids can cause headaches, nosebleeds, acne, cramps, kidney failure, high blood pressure, testicular atrophy, strokes, heart enlargement, hepatitis, heart attacks, and cancer. Women have been known to suffer menstrual dysfunction, diminished breast size, deepened voices, aggressiveness, and facial hair, among other syndromes. In other words, they start turning into men.

I'd always been well-read, and aware of the rumors that steroids could cause long-term health damage. Yet after taking massive doses, I'd lie in bed and literally feel my body stretching. It felt so good that I didn't care about the side effects. The mindset was, "It'll happen to someone else. Not me."

> **Steve Strong:** *If Superstar had been a fat, bloated guy, I'm sure that his charisma would have still made him some money in wrestling. But it was essential at this particular point of his career that he be better, stronger, more cut, more developed than any other man in the business.*
>
> *He was just ridiculous. He was one of those guys who you'd see the next day, and you'd say, "Oh my God. His arms grew a quarter of an inch overnight." We were fighting for every quarter inch, every eighth of an inch, and he would just grow and grow.*

I have a cool picture of myself in bed at the Ramada Inn in New York, with a portable sunlamp hooked onto the frame, so I could tan before the contest. I ended up turning red—flipping around like a hamburger on a grill—and dehydrated. But you want to get dehydrated. Then all the judges see is muscle tissue and definition—no puffiness.

Unfortunately, if you get too dehydrated, your electrolytes are thrown off kilter and you have a heart attack. I know of one Australian bodybuilder who actually dropped dead on the posing dais. While I didn't suffer *that* fate, I did start cramping up while I was on the posing platform at Manhattan's Beacon Theatre. I was bone dry.

I didn't win Pro Mr. America, but I took first place in the "Best Developed Arms" category—posing with the right side of my body toward the judges to hide the nerve injury. I now had a bodybuilding title to exploit for the rest of my wrestling career. More importantly, the contest gave me visibility outside of wrestling—something that members of our fraternity rarely received in 1975—and even more clout with wrestling promoters.

The most important one in the country was Vince McMahon Sr., a dignified second-generation impresario with a swept-back mane of grayish white hair. McMahon had Madison Square Garden, the crown jewel of all wrestling arenas, and perennial champion Bruno Sammartino, the humble immigrant who arguably connected with fans better than anyone else in history. Every time a heel rained a blow down on Bruno's compact, muscular body, his fellow Italians—in addition to the Greeks, the Irish, the Jews, the blacks, the Ukrainians, and the Dominicans—in the arena felt it.

Just before the Pro Mr. America contest, I received a call from Vince at my home.

"Billy, this is Vince McMahon," he began, and quickly cut to the chase. "How would you like to come to New York and work for me?"

I stated the obvious. "That would be great."

"I'm sure you know about Bruno Sammartino up here. We bring in guys to feed Bruno." What he meant was Bruno cycled through the top heels in the country, enhancing their value in other territories with his rub. "And he said he would love to have you come in with us."

That was a major endorsement. I called Boesch and told him about the situation. I wasn't supposed to start in the WWWF for several months, and then the company would introduce me on TV for a few weeks before booking me on a regular schedule. In the interim, I'd continue appearing on Paul's Friday-night shows, making a very good cash payoff each time.

In the midst of all this, though, I was called into emergency service in the Charlotte territory. On October 4, 1975, Charlotte headliners Johnny Valentine, Tim "Mr. Wrestling" Woods, Bob Bruggers, and "Nature Boy" Ric Flair were involved in a private plane crash outside of Wilmington, North Carolina. Flair, Bruggers, and Valentine suffered broken backs. Local TV commentator David Crockett—brother of Charlotte promoter Jim Crockett Jr.—received a concussion and slight compression fracture when his head crashed through a seat, cracking and bruising Tim Woods's ribs. The pilot, Mike Farkas—who'd dumped out fuel to load the plane with wrestlers, then ran out of gas—died.

The booker, George Scott, was in a panic. Four of his top talents were out of commission. I came into the territory for a temporary run, filling in for Flair at a number of venues, and took Steve Strong with me.

The promotion was concerned because Woods—a babyface—had been onboard with a bunch of heels. Putting the business first, Tim checked into the hospital under his birth name, George Burrell Woodin, listing himself as a wrestling promoter on the medical forms. Still, rumors were swirling. Before the wall of kayfabe could crumble, Tim checked out of the hospital and—two weeks after the accident—had a very short match with me in Richmond, Virginia. Now the fans were convinced: no one who'd been banged around that badly would have ever been given medical clearance to wrestle.

Unless, of course, a wrestling promoter said it was good for the business.

My main concern was Flair, that good-natured kid who'd gone from picking me up at the airport to igniting the Charlotte territory. He was on his couch, in traction and surrounded by orthopedic equipment, when I walked into his home. Flair greeted me with a beaming smile.

"Superstar!"

He pointed at an assortment of dumbbells. "You want the dumbbells?"

"It's okay, Ric. You gave me enough in Minnesota. So how you doing, man?"

Ric ignored my question. "Come on," he offered, rising from the couch and hobbling over to the weights. "Take some dumbbells."

He swore to me that he would be back in the ring soon. There was never any doubt in my mind.

Bruggers also recovered, but opted to leave the business. Johnny Valentine, a superstar since the 1950s, was paralyzed from the waist down. About the only positive thing about that situation was that it created a void for Johnny's previously underrated son Greg, who nearly thirty years later would join me in being inducted into the WWE Hall of Fame.

> **Greg "The Hammer" Valentine:** *Guys were starting to pick up some of the things that Billy was doing—his flashy outfits, the cockiness. I had a much quieter persona, but even I began copying him— pausing and looking out at the crowd before a match, with an arrogance that said, "Don't you wish you were me?"*

The Charlotte run was short, but Strong and I had a good time. We freaked over Rufus R. Jones, an African-American babyface who mumbled in an unintelligible southern accent. His TV promos were the most entertaining in the business. We'd laugh at every line, because we couldn't understand a word of this Deep South dialect.

My mother had a wing of her family in the Carolinas, including her sister Launa, who was a dwarf. Her son Gordon looked exactly like me— except he was a dwarf, too. Strong couldn't get over this. When he finally met Gordon outside the arena in Asheville, Steve clutched his head and ran around and around our car in disbelief.

> **Steve Strong:** *When Superstar walked in the locker room, it was as if E. F. Hutton talked. All conversation stopped. People fixated on watching him take his clothes off.*
>
> *We were in Norfolk, maybe Raleigh, and—this is the God's*

honest truth—a mark snuck into the locker room in the middle of the afternoon. He hid there all day waiting for Billy to show up. Superstar was finally in the toilet stall, and this guy stuck his head underneath and went, "Superstar Billy Graham! Oh, my God! I always wanted to meet you!"

Superstar jumped off the pot. He was scared to death.

When Vince McMahon Sr. greeted you, he'd wink with a little sparkle that charmed and reassured. Before shows, he ambled through the dressing room, offering advice and pearls of wrestling trivia. It was Vince who told me why the term *pencil* was used in reference to the booker—as in "Who has the pencil in that territory?"

Bookers wrote down long-term plans in pencil because the industry was always in a state of flux. If a wrestler got injured, took a better offer, or did something to upset the company, he could be easily erased.

With his disarming smile, Vince also recommended that I inscribe my friends' names in ink in my address book, but their phone numbers in pencil. "People change their addresses and phone numbers," he pointed out, "but not their names."

Still, in wrestling—as in the traveling carnivals from which our business is derived—nothing was permanent. People came and people went.

Like his son, Vince Sr. exuded the McMahon charisma, and wrestlers measured their own sense of self by his approval. I'd often see him shuffling quarters from one hand to the other, and wondered if he was juggling our fates at the same time. Yet I loved working for Vince, and the WWWF would be my Canaan—a carny version of the biblical promised land.

After my first WWWF TV taping, I returned to my room at the old Savoy Hotel in New York, dropped some speed, got down on the carpet, and did 1,500 leg raises, followed by 500 sit-ups.

Then I headed for Times Square.

After the Pro Mr. America contest, I was in the best shape of my life, with a refined, ripped physique. But I was surprised that when I arrived at the arena, Vince instantly steered me to manager Ernie Roth, better known as the Grand Wizard of Wrestling.

"This is Ernie," Vince said. "He's the greatest mouthpiece in this business."

I looked down at Ernie, slight and smiling, with his shades, medallion-studded brown turban, orange pants, and maroon jacket with checkered pockets. He looked like he'd stepped out of a Saturday-morning cartoon—which was exactly the impression that he was trying to convey.

I didn't know much about Ernie at that time—other than what I'd seen when he'd come to Los Angeles, as Abdullah Farouk, with the Sheik. Nor did I understand that every major heel in the WWWF was immediately assigned a manager, either the Wizard, Captain Lou Albano, or Freddie Blassie—who'd basically retired from the mat wars and now paced around at ringside in lime green and bubblegum pink spangles, periodically bashing his protégés' foes with a cane.

"Hello, Ernie," I said, shaking his hand. But I was a little bit distressed. I didn't need a *manager*.

I tried explaining this to Vince later on: "I don't really have to have anyone talk for me. That's my deal, you know, cutting a promo."

"I know, Billy, but that's how we do it here," Vince countered, not like a hardnosed promoter but like a guy who sympathized with my internal struggle. "Just give it a try for me."

For me? This guy was smooth; I'd just met him!

I decided to make the best of things. I went looking for Ernie Roth and huddled with him. "What do you do?" I asked. "What is your rap? Let's try to get something going here."

Ernie began talking, cutting a Grand Wizard promo, and drew me right in.

"I know you're good on the stick," he said, using the carny term for microphone. "Don't worry. I won't get in your way."

We came up with a strategy for my first match—and executed it when the cameras rolled. I did my posing routine in the ring, then the Wizard attempted to remove my tie-dyed muscle shirt. However, he worked it like my arms were so massive that he couldn't slide the material over my biceps.

At ringside, Vince's son, Vince McMahon Jr., was doing play-by-play, selling his heart out: "Oh, my goodness! The Wizard can't get the Superstar's shirt past his twenty-two-inch pythons!"

The Wizard stood behind me, combing my hair with a pick and whispering in my ear, playing manservant as well as manager. The crowd popped, reaching an intensity level that would never waver throughout my run in the WWWF.

Vince knew that he had his guy.

When I'd seen managers in the past, they often seemed like window dressing. The Wizard was a talent unto himself. I can't remember him ever having a bad night. From the outset, we melded as one.

Greg "The Hammer" Valentine: *A lot of managers would try to hog the microphone, and wouldn't let their protégé speak. They wanted all the air time. Ernie would say a few words, then go, "Tell them, Super-*

star." In the ring, Billy would pose while Ernie pointed with both hands, then opened his palms as if to say, "This is my shining light."

Because Ernie was so skinny, he rarely got involved in the action. Captain Lou Albano, on the other hand, was a former wrestler and could take big bumps. Like the Wizard, Lou—bearded and wild-eyed—was very colorful, and could go on some memorable verbal tirades. But he drank, and did goofy things that persistently irritated the McMahon family. At every other Garden show, I'd hear Albano telling someone, "Vince fired me again. But I'm back."

Instead of juicing the regular way, Albano carried around a straight razor. He told me that he once slipped doing a blade job and ripped open his cheek. As a result, he began piercing his cheeks and hanging rubber bands from the loops.

On another night, in Madison Square Garden, Lou ran into the ring after his protégé lost to Bruno, and attacked the champion. As planned, Bruno turned around and belted Albano. Albano juiced, carelessly tossed his straight razor up in the air, and went back to the dressing room.

This was one of the few times that I saw Vince Sr. go crazy. "Lou," he screamed, "this is the *Garden!* We can't lose the *Garden!*"

With the state athletic commissioners seated at ringside, Albano had left what appeared to be a bloody switchblade in the ring.

Despite his drinking, you just had to love Albano. The man consistently delivered. This wasn't the case with another erratic personality with whom I'd barely missed crossing paths at a TV taping in 1975.

Vince McMahon Jr.: My dad had a soft spot for Jerry Graham. He even sent Jerry to one of the best rehabilitation clinics for alcohol at one time, but he managed to sneak a bottle in there. Jerry would periodically dry up and lose weight, and my dad would take him back. But it always failed.

This last go-round with Jerry, just prior to Billy Graham's arrival in the company, was simply charity on my dad's part. He was a mere shell of himself. He still had the gift of gab, but by then there was nothing new or innovative about it. Unfortunately, the alcohol had pickled his brain.

My dad flew him back and forth first class. Which was a mistake, because you can get all the booze you want in first class. On the way home, Jerry got drunk and proceeded to paint the entire first-class cabin in his own feces.

This was not going to go over well with the flight attendants, or anyone else around first class. And you could smell all of that way in back of the plane. So the pilot came back and said, "Please sit down." And Jerry wanted to fight. At that time, he couldn't beat his way out of a paper bag. But you didn't know that when you saw him.

The pilot wisely recognized that the best way to handle the situation was to have Jerry pass out. So the pilot said, "Just give him more booze."

When Jerry fell asleep, the plane made an unscheduled stop, and the federal marshals took the illustrious Jerry Graham into custody. And it was the last time that we heard from the Good Doctor for a long time.

My first match at Madison Square Garden took place on December 15, 1975, against Dominic DeNucci. Like Bruno, DeNucci was a native of Italy. This was not a coincidence. Vince Sr. wanted to create interest in my impending confrontation with the champ by having me whip his *paisan.*

"Billy, we're putting you over strong," Vince told me in the dressing room. "You're going to beat DeNucci as fast as you can."

I could feel the currents pulsing through Madison Square Garden even when I was backstage, listening to the reactions to other matches. When my name was finally announced, I strode down the aisle, taking note of the multitudes of loud, impassioned fans. I did my posing, and the Wizard did his primping. Before the bell, I extended my hand to my foe. The streetwise New York audience, sensing a plot, shouted, *"No! No! No!"*

But DeNucci, the trusting babyface, accepted the gesture, allowing me to grab his wrist with my other hand and sling him into the corner, just as the bell rang. Then—*boom, boom, boom*—I beat him with the bear hug. Total time of the match: nine seconds.

DeNucci was still wearing his ring jacket.

Back in the dressing room, the boys were ribbing DeNucci: "You're not really going to take a shower, are you?" I'm not sure if either of us had ever touched the mat.

Dominic just laughed. He understood his position and had a wonderful attitude. It's a mindset he'd eventually pass along to the aspiring wrestlers he trained at his home near Pittsburgh, including future World Wrestling Federation Champion Mick Foley.

DeNucci was one of several opponents I battled during my buildup to Sammartino. I also engaged in a series of matches with Chief Jay Strongbow, who played a Native American—and may have believed it himself—but had some heat from legit Indians like Wahoo and the Brisco brothers because he was actually an Italian from New Jersey.

I never connected well with Strongbow because, among other reasons, he was incredibly cheap. During an earlier incarnation he'd worked in carnivals, sleeping in the wrestling tent, so I understood his frugality. But the man was always on edge over saving a penny.

I think we started off on the wrong foot when I cut a promo on him in the old Philadelphia Arena. The building was empty except for the wrestlers, who were gathered around an empty ring where Vince Jr. stood, interviewing us one after another for segments to be inserted into the broadcasts.

"Despite Chief Jay Strongbow being in the twilight of his career," I stated, "I will show him no mercy."

The boys laughed and nudged Strongbow: *"Twilight of your career."*

The Chief stood up and stormed away, disappeared backstage, then came back yelling.

I tried to calm him down: "It's just a promo, brother." But from that point on, there was tension between us.

We never had fun together in the ring. I felt that he was rushing our matches, and wondered whether he was trying to blow me up—get me out of breath—a condition that "real" wrestlers believed impaired muscleheads like myself.

Still, nothing could set me back. I altered my wardrobe for the WWWF, making a mini poncho of animal hide with the kind of jagged look that would later be associated with punk rock. I wore a T-shirt inspired by Andy Warhol's pop art depiction of Marilyn Monroe, telling Vince Jr. on a promo, "Marilyn Monroe looks her best when she is sitting on the Superstar's chest."

I'd often forget these lines after I said them, but the fans didn't. Years later, at a church in Philadelphia, I was introduced to a blind keyboard player who claimed that he never missed one of my televised matches.

"But didn't your condition kind of lessen the experience for you?" I wondered.

"There was just something about your rap that kept me in front of the television."

Paul Heyman: *Speaking in a way totally different than anyone who came before him, Superstar Billy Graham didn't just demand attention—he commanded it. His words were poetic, yet delivered like a heel. His prose was hysterical, yet he sold thousands upon thousands* *of tickets as a heel with real-life, genuine heat. He was the most popular wrestler in the world, and yet the moment he walked into the ring and squared off against his opponent, people salivated at the mere prospect of the Superstar getting his butt kicked.*

Diamond Dallas Page: *My fondest memory as a teenager is being at my friend John Rossi's house in Point Pleasant, New Jersey, wearing tie-dye and watching the Superstar. We didn't even care about his wrestling. We wanted to hear him talk. We were humongous marks.*

Paul Levesque, aka Triple H: *If I had to pick one wrestler and say, "This is the most copied guy in the business," I'd pick Superstar Billy Graham. He was the guy who broke the wall in terms of where you could go with entertainment. He paved the road for* Hulkmania. *He paved the road for all of us.*

On January 12, 1976, one month after trampling over DeNucci, I had my first match with Bruno in the Garden. This was it, man: the venerated, unpretentious peasant, powered by the love of his followers, defending his precious gold belt against the narcissistic, flamboyant intruder, tanned and in tie-dye, scoffing at the values that Bruno's people held so dear. I had fun putting him down in my promos leading up to the clash—"Bruno has varicose veins now"—then putting him over big to embellish his stature: "Bruno is at the pinnacle of his career, the zenith of his strength, I know for a fact that he can bench-press over 500 pounds. But I'm the man with the twenty-two-inch pythons, and I will show no mercy."

Heels usually called the matches in the WWWF back then, even against Bruno. So before we left the dressing room, I respectfully suggested capitalizing on our mutual might. "I know the fans idolize you for your strength. Why don't we do some strongman stuff—the grip of the hands, the top wristlock, the powering out of it? You know I'm going to put you over—there'll be no doubt that you're stronger than me. But let's really tap into that part of your strength."

Bruno agreed with everything; even before we touched each other, we had real chemistry.

I'd never been in a building anywhere with that type of atmosphere. I came out to the ring with the Grand Wizard and watched Bruno's entrance—as fascinated as any fan. I was standing where every wrestler in the world wanted to stand—in the ring with a wrestling icon.

The champion passed an ocean of outstretched hands, trotting, with no robe, no ring jacket, just a belt. It almost seemed like Sammartino was in slow motion. Because of all the people milling about, fans in the corners of the building couldn't see Bruno at first. But as Bruno hopped up the steps and came into full view, throwing his right arm into the air, pandemonium broke out.

With his manager, Arnold Skaaland, standing on the apron, "the Living Legend from Abruzzi, Italy" was introduced and took a small bow. There was no nonsense about him. This humble warrior was ready to fight, and the people believed it.

We locked up just like we planned, our fingers intertwined. I raised my elbows and seemed to power Bruno all the way down to the mat, torquing his body. Leading him, I pulled Bruno up, real slow, as he started to make a comeback. Now I was the one going down, contorting my face in dismay and disbelief. I dropped to my knees, and Bruno began turning me until my shoulders were touching the canvas. The formula was simple—WWWF fans hadn't been exposed to a lot of cruiserweight-style, high-risk moves back then—but the execution was often more effective than today. I couldn't outmuscle Bruno—we'd just established that—so I broke up the pinfall by placing a foot on the ropes.

The entire match went like that. I wrapped a bear hug around Bruno, gritted my teeth, and repositioned my legs, apparently tightening my grip. This was the move I'd used to defeat DeNucci the month before; there was consistency in the storytelling. Bruno sold it like I was crushing his spine, wilting his body while I dug my clasped hands into his lower back, his eyes shut tight, his mouth hanging open in agony.

"Grab my wrist and power out of it," I told him, and Bruno rebounded again.

The match ended as the two of us crisscrossed the ropes and charged toward each other. We collided, and—with the momentum going against him—Bruno tumbled out of the ring. I remained on my feet, wobbly, while the referee counted to ten, called for the bell, and raised my arm, to the shock and anger of the crowd. These were knowledgeable enough fans to know that a title couldn't change hands on a countout, but the fact remained that I'd outdone their hero. To maintain his pride and purpose, Bruno would have to beat me decisively.

We were going to meet again.

Oreal Perras, aka Ivan Koloff: *I understand how the fans felt about Bruno because he was my hero, too. I just fell in love with him. I beat him for the WWWF Championship in 1971 (he won back the title in*

*1973), but a lot of people don't know that I also wrestled him before
I was Ivan Koloff.*

*I'm French Canadian, but I was working as an Irishman, Red
McNulty, with an eye patch. Another wrestler, Bull Johnson, was
supposed to wrestle Bruno on TV, and he got sick. Somebody called
me up in Canada: "Hey, kid, do you want to take his place?" I remember being so excited because I'd be wrestling on TV against the
champion. I was nervous and really green in the business. When I
kicked, I kicked hard. When I punched, I really punched.*

*Some of the old-timers in the dressing room told me, "If you
want to be a big star in this business, you have to take chances." So
before the match, when Bruno kneeled down in the ring and made
the sign of the cross, I put the knees to him, kicked him, and stomped
him. I remember him looking up like, "What is this kid doing?"
Then he just manhandled my body, got me in a bear hug, and put
the squeeze on me. When Bruno made the sign of the cross, it wasn't
a joke.*

A blizzard blanketed New York on the day of my second Garden clash
with Bruno, February 2, 1976. The Bronx-Whitestone Bridge swayed back
and forth in the gusts. Sections of Long Island Railroad tracks froze over.
But Madison Square Garden was still packed, with the overflow filling up
the adjacent Felt Forum, where a closed-circuit telecast of the match was
shown.

Along with reports on school closings and transit delays, the next day's
New York Daily News ran a photo of Sammartino and me in a test of
strength, under the headline, THE ONLY GAME IN TOWN.

This match ended with Bruno thrashing me so badly that the referee
had no choice but to halt our encounter "due to blood." Still, Bruno had
once again failed to score a decisive win over his most demanding adversary. Therefore, the feud would have to go on.

George Napolitano, wrestling photographer: *Bruno's matches with
Superstar Billy Graham really hit a nerve with people. You already
had all the emotion associated with Bruno Sammartino, and now
you had an opponent who was very different from anyone he'd ever
wrestled before. In those days, if you were good, you were good. If
you were bad, you were bad. But Graham was something more than
that. I mean, he was more than just a wrestler.*

When Billy wrestled in the New York area, I'd sometimes drive him around, almost like a chauffeur. I'd pick him up at the airport and take him to his hotel. Then we'd drive to wherever he was appearing—Elizabeth, New Jersey, New Haven, Connecticut, Philadelphia for TV every three weeks. At my house in Brooklyn, we could get wrestling from Florida once a week on UHF, and he'd come over to watch that. The reception wasn't great, so we'd adjust the aerial. I remember him watching a Dusty interview and moving his chair up to right in front of the TV. "Man," Billy laughed, "he's taking my whole rap."

Sometimes Billy would eat over at our house, and train at a gym here in Brooklyn. Not everybody there was a wrestling fan—but they knew that he was somebody.

My wife, Jackie, always made Italian food—veal cutlet parmigiana, chicken parmigiana, macaroni—and a big bowl of salad. The first time Billy came over, she put the salad bowl in the middle of the table, and he grabbed it and started eating. He thought the whole thing was for him.

Because he was living in a hotel, he sometimes used my house as an address. I remember some girl in Hawaii sent him a gift set of colognes. He didn't want it, so he gave it to me. Then my wife wanted to know, "Who's sending you all these presents?"

He'd also given my address to a doctor, so I started getting these packages of Dianabol. I didn't question it—I wasn't a gym guy, and it wasn't illegal. I'd just hand the steroids to Billy when I saw him.

I also grew friendly with another wrestling photographer and writer named Bill Apter. Bill's magazines, *Inside Wrestling* and *The Wrestler,* had the highest circulation in the country. He featured himself prominently in the publications—so much so that there were fans who referred to them as the "Apter mags"—and made it a point to cover most of the wrestling territories. Because of this, some of the boys attributed their national exposure directly to him.

One of my favorite photo shoots with Bill took place in Times Square. It was a raunchy but famous neighborhood, a place where I felt very much at home. Koloff and I would explore the area after the matches and study the faces of the people we passed. We'd get absorbed in watching a heroin addict, a cigarette burning down to his fingers, eyes nodding, body weaving on a single chunk of sidewalk as if he were swept by a breeze.

"What's the story with these guys?" I once asked a cop.

"We really can't bust them," he said. "We just let them float around."

On every block we'd see the same sign: LIVE NUDES.

"Not dead ones," I'd remind Koloff.

On this photo shoot, Apter and I wandered around the same way, past the theaters showing kung-fu movies and XXX features, and took pictures with the people. On the street, I never received any heel heat in New York—a city former mayor John Lindsay described as not only the nation's melting pot but "the casserole, the chafing dish, and the charcoal grill." Everyone crowded around me for autographs—men in leisure suits, kids from Harlem coming out of the video arcade, subway workers on break, junkies looking to cop dope. It reminded me of Jesus, preaching the word alongside beggars, tax collectors, and Mary Magdalene.

With the denizens of Times Square trailing behind us, I made open-mouthed Muhammad Ali faces in the lens and signed people's arms. Then, on a traffic island on Broadway, I jumped up on a cement garbage can, tore off my shirt, and flexed against the wintry chill. As Bill snapped away, the crowd stood around him and cheered. Even at that early stage, I knew that I was ready to pop as a babyface.

Bruno and I took our feud to Baltimore, Providence, Toronto—where the promotion had a working relationship with the WWWF—and Augusta, Maine, among other venues. WWWF fans were incredibly intense in Boston; there was a net over the ring on poles to catch hurled debris. During one clash in Madison Square Garden, I rolled to ringside after a bodyslam and headed back to the dressing room, waving the match off. Special referee Gorilla Monsoon chased me down the aisle, ducked under one of my right crosses, and carried me back to the ring like a sack of potatoes. There, Sammartino finished me off.

The fans went insane, literally leaping into the air, pumping their fists.

The people just never grew tired of us.

Even Bruno's teenage son David—who later wrestled in the World Wrestling Federation—seemed to lose his senses over the rivalry. Before a match in Bruno's hometown of Pittsburgh, the kid approached me in the dressing room with an unusual proposition:

"Hey, Superstar, do you mind if I walk to the ring with you?"

I didn't know if David was just having fun, or trying to spite his father in some way. "Ask your dad," I told him.

David did, and Bruno shrugged his shoulders. "Go ahead," he said. "I don't care."

So instead of the Grand Wizard that night, I was escorted to the ring by David Sammartino, who raised my arm in the air and heeled for the crowd. A group of Pittsburgh Steelers were in the front row. Everyone knew the Sammartino family in Pittsburgh, and these guys were truly bewildered. But they were having a blast.

Cowboy Stan Hansen was a big, strong guy who began going around the horn with Bruno after we played out our program—string of matches— in different cities. During an April 26, 1976, challenge at Madison Square Garden, Hansen tried an unconventional type of bodyslam, crossing arms and turning Bruno around in the middle of the move. Both guys were sweaty, and Stan was still green. Somehow, the champion slipped out of his grasp and went straight down on his head.

Bruno was so tough that he kept wrestling for another fifteen minutes with a broken neck.

The promotion tried to turn a negative into a positive, telling fans that Hansen used his signature clothesline, the Lariat, to injure the champ. But Stan had never wanted to make a name for himself *this* way.

The two of us were together in Maine when Bruno was let out of the hospital, and I could see that Hansen was badly shaken. I suggested that he call Bruno at home.

"Well, I'd like to, Billy," he admitted. "But I'm afraid."

I told Stan that I'd dial the number for him and actually speak to Bruno first, emphasizing how much regret Hansen had over the incident.

"What do you think I should say to him?" Stan asked.

"Well, apologize for starters. Then ask how he's doing. When's he coming back? You're looking forward to seeing him again. You're looking forward to working with him again. He's gonna make a full recovery."

I stood next to Stan, giving him reassuring looks as he spoke to Bruno: "I'm sorry, Bruno. Man, I'm so sorry. You know I would never do anything like this on purpose. . . ."

There was nothing disingenuous about Stan's remorse, and Bruno forgave him. Fortunately, he did recuperate quickly, and had a very exciting grudge match with Hansen that summer at Shea Stadium, the home of baseball's New York Mets.

Still, anyone who knows Bruno can pretty much guess what he would have thought if he'd *never* received that phone call.

He'd still hate Hansen today.

At a certain point during this WWWF run, I was reunited with Ernie Ladd, and he immediately became my personal career adviser. If we were staying in Manhattan and I wanted to walk to a restaurant, Ernie insisted on taking a cab.

"Save your knees, Superstar," he counseled. "Never walk more than two blocks."

Television was transitioning from film to video, and Ernie urged me to begin collecting tapes of my matches. "Build a library," he said. "If you wanna go into a new territory, you can send tapes of your stuff."

Ladd would travel with Koloff and me, and talk about the things that he wanted to change in the industry. One of his biggest gripes was that our payoffs dropped when we weren't in the main event. This might have been fair if we were career mid-carders, but all three of us were box office maineventers. While Koloff and I were willing to accept the status quo, Ladd went directly to Vince Sr. to confront this perceived inequity.

Ernie "The Big Cat" Ladd: *I felt that I deserved more money than the guys who were down in the deep, whether I was in the main event or whether I was in the middle of the card. I was big talent, not little talent. Promoters knew what would happen if they tried to short-*

change me. I'd walk out. I would leave the arena. I wouldn't stick around. I'd done it on more than one occasion. But when I told Vince Sr. about the money I wanted, it didn't have to go that far. He gave it to me.

I'm not sure if the Big Cat was trying to use the race card. Ernie was too savvy to come right out and accuse a promoter of racism, but he was more than capable of implying it. Back then, you could push the race card pretty far—especially with a guy like Vince Sr., who never broke things down in racial terms but didn't want that kind of trouble.

Either way, Ernie's agitating raised my income.

Joyce Sampson: It's amazing how many times my husband Buddy tried to get Wayne to invest money. "Save some," he'd tell Wayne. "Give it to me. I'll invest it for you." I remember that a group of us went in on a property. We put in $5,000 each, and came out with $96,000. But Wayne wasn't interested.

Buddy Sampson: It was very frustrating. Wayne's always been this person who has to have it so perfect that he misses the window. You've got that window of time when you're doing well. If you miss it, you screw it up.

Buddy was a smart businessman, but I never took his advice. My attitude was, "It's my life, and it's my money." Plus, in 1976, I had my own idea about the way I wanted to multiply my earnings.

Ivan Koloff and I were going to become wrestling promoters.

THE
COVENANT

Walk before me, and be thou whole-hearted.
And I will make My covenant between Me and thee.

—Genesis 17:1–2

Mike LeBell's promotion was teetering when Ivan and I decided to come in and take southern California. We weren't going to work through the NWA, and we weren't going to ask LeBell's permission. Like Roy Shire in San Francisco some fifteen years earlier, we would simply go on TV, give the people a better product, and make the territory our own.

Without even naming our promotion or procuring a TV station, we flew out to L.A. and bought houses there. We paid $2,000 to have a beautiful belt crafted for our World Champion. Our roster at the time consisted of two: Ivan was going to be the top heel, and I would be the top babyface. Steve Strong was essentially a lock to join us, and I assumed that every other name we wanted would follow.

Before we departed for the West Coast that April, we told Vince Sr. about our plan.

"Well, you know what I have to do, guys," he responded, as the three of us stood around backstage. "I have to call Mike and let him know."

That was only fair. LeBell and McMahon were professional peers who occasionally exchanged talent.

Reaching into his pocket, Vince fished up a handful of coins, then—right in front of us—went over to the pay phone and dialed L.A.:

"Listen, Mike, this is Vince McMahon. Uh, Ivan Koloff and Billy Graham want to go into business for themselves, and they're coming to L.A. to work against you."

Vince looked over at us and winked. He listened to LeBell for a few seconds, then replied, "No, Mike, I think they've made up their minds."

LeBell wanted to know when he might expect the insurgency to begin. Vince gave him an honest answer, "They haven't told me yet, but I suppose right away."

Vince hung up and came back over to us. "All right, guys," he shrugged. "Whatever you do, don't run your first show on Memorial Day. You never draw money on Memorial Day."

> **Ivan Koloff:** *We didn't understand this philosophy of* I own this area. *To us, wrestling was free enterprise. If you have one gas station in town, why can't there be two gas stations?*
>
> *We thought we'd get a license, and draw the first few crowds with our names. We'd start off as Tag Team partners, then I'd double-cross Billy and turn him babyface big-time. After that, we'd have our program—the Russian vs. the American.*
>
> *We didn't realize how tight Mike LeBell was with the athletic commission in California. First, we were told that you couldn't own a promoter's license and be a wrestler at the same time. We said, "Okay, we'll make our* wives *the promoters." Then, suddenly, the rules changed again. Now you couldn't wrestle if one of your* family members *had a promoter's license.*

We spent the entire summer of 1976 battling Mike LeBell in court. We were operating on a shoestring, and now had to calculate a lawyer into the budget. Obviously, LeBell had been through this before, and his attorney knew how to stall the case and eat up our resources. In fact, I had to book myself with Paul Boesch just to make some extra money.

On July 17, 1976, I did a job for Jack Brisco in Houston. Brisco was a recently dethroned NWA titlist whose NCAA championship background and technical skills placed him in a category later reserved for men like Kurt Angle. Unfortunately, our styles didn't mix. Like Gagne, Brisco was more of a wrestler's wrestler, and we just couldn't get a groove going in the ring.

What I remember most about the match was Brisco's concern for his looks. Jack was a very handsome guy, and he knew it. He once told me, "You know, Billy, if I had your body with my face, I could get any girl I want."

Ivan Koloff. I posed while the "Russian Bear" did all the work.

Now, he made it very clear that he didn't need some jacked-up body-builder ruining his features. "You can potato me anywhere you want," he said, "but not in the face."

In August Koloff and I both toured Japan, working with Seiji Sakaguchi, Strong Kobayashi, and Antonio Inoki, among other talent. Inoki had recently fought Muhammad Ali in a controversial Boxer vs. Wrestler match. With the two unable to agree on the rules, the contest was a clinic on monotony—but it helped solidify Inoki's standing as a cultural icon. The man was absolutely phenomenal in the squared circle, more because of his energy level than the moves he executed. When I wrestled Inoki, he set the ring ablaze.

Back in L.A., I was beginning to figure out that Koloff and myself had been a little presumptuous to start a wrestling territory with a grand total of maybe $25,000. During courtroom breaks, Mike LeBell grimaced at us in the halls. Koloff and I would laugh, then visit another courthouse, where Mike's brother, "Judo" Gene LeBell, was on trial for his alleged participation in a murder.

Gene—a judo champion and Hollywood stuntman who occasionally stretched uncooperative wrestlers on behalf of the family—had fallen in with a group of guys who played rather malicious ribs on one another. When one of these characters turned up dead after a trailer where Gene kept his motorcycles caught fire, Gene was implicated in the crime.

Heads always turned when Koloff and I entered the courtroom, usually in the middle of proceedings. From the defendant's table, Gene would give us a friendly nod. When we'd see him during recess, he'd joke and laugh out loud. I guess he knew that he was going to be acquitted—and that we didn't stand a chance of ever obtaining a promoter's license.

By the fall, Ivan and I folded and became full-time wrestlers again. The only positive thing that I took away from the whole experience was an autograph—from singer Harry Chapin, who happened to be on the flight to L.A. after I wrestled Brisco.

Dusty was now the booker for the Florida territory, so I gave him a call and told him about my situation. "Let's do it, man," he told me. "Come down here."

I started working the Sunshine State on November 16.

Dusty's style of booking matched his unrestrained personality. There were fights at the announcer's table, matches with violent stipulations, and long, entertaining promos. But the power behind the Florida territory was Eddie Graham—Dr. Jerry's partner from the Golden Grahams' heyday, and the gimmick brother I'd never met.

Dusty wanted to push an emotional family feud angle, but Eddie chose to be subtle. The fact that we were "brothers" was never stated on TV, but highly suggested. It created an air of mystery about the relationship—*What transpired between these two guys if they don't even acknowledge their kinship?*—and a buzz among fans who thought that they were "smart" to the business. That was the genius of Eddie Graham.

Eddie and Shire were considered the two best finish men in the industry, creating climaxes to matches and feuds unlike any who came before them. Both would pass on their wisdom—Shire to Pat Patterson, Eddie to "Cowboy" Bill Watts—shaping the wrestling business through the work of their disciples for at least another era.

I found Eddie to be an absolute gentleman; the kind of guy I really *would* have wanted as a brother if I didn't have Vance.

When I'd wrestle "Sailor" Art Thomas, an aging African-American bodybuilder who preceded me in the industry with a highly muscled look, Eddie always came up with complicated finishes, involving numerous high spots leading to the crescendo. But Thomas was a gentle, childlike soul, and became confused by all the detail. Eddie never barked at him or shook his head in exasperation. Instead, he'd smile and patiently go over the ending of the match again.

Even so, I really had to guide Art through the match, relying largely on the strongman stuff both of us had done so often. When he sold, he rarely exhibited the drama I'd learned from people like Ray Stevens and Pat Patterson. Thomas would simply fall back to the mat, like he'd been shot by a rifle. At this point of our careers, I was the one generally winning our encounters, but I still found a way to put him over, wincing and "collapsing" from exhaustion after the pin.

In reality, the person I really wanted as an opponent in Florida was Dusty, and the feeling was mutual. We launched our feud by doing an updated version of the old weightlifting angle. But it wasn't Dusty competing against me on the bench press. It was Jos LeDuc, a French Canadian lumberjack type with grooves in his forehead to rival Abdullah. The way that we worked Dusty into the equation was by having him act as LeDuc's spotter. Steve Strong was mine.

This time, since I'd be lying on a bench, we used real plates. We started with 225 pounds and kept loading until the bar was arching with 550 pounds. I did the lift first. Then LeDuc slid onto the bench press, with Dusty spotting.

That's when I grabbed the chalk box and hurled the powder into *Dusty's* face. LeDuc was simply the setup. He sold the chalk, too—some of it *had* actually filtered down to him—while Strong and I doubled on Dusty.

Then I ran the American Dream into the steel plates, leaving fans with that indelible image of chalk-clumped blood running down their hero's torso. The heat was on.

Despite the diminutive size of the TV studio, the exchange was a textbook example of Shire's philosophy about bringing the people to the brink of a riot.

On November 22, 1976, Dusty did the job for me in West Palm Beach, relinquishing his Florida Heavyweight Championship. Eddie had given us a brilliant finish: Dusty *submitted* to my full nelson, then collapsed on the mat, adding yet another dimension to our feud. Inspired by Wahoo McDaniel, I'd designed my very own Indian strap, with a motif reminiscent of the Navajo and Apache symbols I'd seen in Arizona. This was newer than Wahoo's strip of leather, but I stained it to create an older, worn appearance.

Dusty and I hotshotted all over the Sunshine State, flogging each other with the Indian strap, as well as in Bullrope, Cage, and Lumberjack matches. In Tampa, fans were told that I was putting up my limo against Dusty's pickup—and we parked the vehicles grill to grill in the parking lot to lend "authenticity."

There was a fan at the Fort Homer Hesterly Armory that night who I'd noticed before. Terry Bollea was a tall, skinny blond guy who dressed in black leather and boots like a rocker. From the ring, I'd see his big head hovering above the rest of the crowd about ten rows back. While everyone else was screaming, he sat there, transfixed, never darting his eyes, dissecting my every move and facial gesture. His gaze was so piercing that occasionally I found myself looking back at him.

One night at the Imperial Room, the nightclub where the boys hung out in Tampa, Terry approached me. I was seated, and he was standing, towering over me. Like Jesse, Terry wanted to become a wrestler, but he felt like the local promoter—in this case Eddie Graham—was shutting him out. Terry was frustrated, but not discouraged. "I'm not taking no for an answer," he vowed.

It was the first of many encounters. Another time, Terry confessed that he felt too thin for the squared circle, and asked Steve Strong and me about the types of steroids we used.

"We're not on anything," Strong answered, looking the future icon dead in the eye.

Terry acknowledged the rib with a nod and a grin.

In time, Terry would convince Hiro Matsuda, a Japanese taskmaster who trained a number of wrestlers in Tampa, to take him on as a student. A few years later, he'd hit the World Wrestling Federation as Hulk Hogan, where he'd brag about his "pythons" and ask, "What you gonna do when

Me and Dusty. We hadn't seen each other for twenty years.

Hulkamania runs wild on you?"—borrowing from my standard line, "What you gonna do when the Superstar comes down on you?"

Up north, Bruno Sammartino was approaching the third year of his second title reign. At forty-one years old, with barely a day to spend with his children or aging parents, he was weary of taking bumps on hard boxing rings, particularly after his broken neck. At some point, while working with Ken Patera, he'd hyperextended his elbow, and was never able to straighten it out again. He still ran twelve miles a day and trained hard—albeit with lighter weights than in the past—but was anxious to pass the torch.

On a surface level, the two of us were very different. He was righteous, old-world, and drug-free. I was a steroid-abusing showman. Yet he liked me personally, and we had exceptional magic together. I still believe that no one has ever replaced Bruno in the business. Like Muhammad Ali, this was a once-in-a-lifetime superstar.

He wanted to lose the WWWF Championship to Superstar Billy Graham.

I first found out about this during a phone call from Vince Sr. He needed a long-term babyface champion. But the kid he'd slated for Bruno's slot, Bob Backlund, wasn't ready yet. So Vince asked me to take the title and hold it for close to a year, while Backlund developed as a wrestler and a personality—which he never did.

> ***Ivan Koloff:*** *Bob Backlund was a great technician and a great ama-*
> *teur wrestler. Even though he was quiet and led a clean lifestyle, he*
> *was a tough guy. In the ring, he'd do a short-arm scissors and pick*
> *me up with one arm. He wasn't built like a strongman, but when you*
> *can pick up a 280-pound man with one arm, you are one.*

Vince suggested that I recount the details of our conversation to Eddie Graham. Vince and Eddie had become very close, and—even though Florida was part of the NWA—Graham wanted to feature WWWF title defenses on his cards. This would be unprecedented, appealing to native Floridians and those who'd migrated with their WWWF bias, as well as their New York accents.

I have to admit that I had a WWWF bias myself. Although the NWA had dozens of affiliates, there was no comparison between their title and the WWWF championship. The WWWF had the crowds, the excitement, the aura of its title, Bruno, and Madison Square Garden. How could you compare walking through Ybor City in Tampa or Buckhead in Atlanta to Times Square? You couldn't.

"Listen," Eddie said when I relayed Vince's plans to him, "let's fly over to see Vince now. We better seal this thing before he changes his mind."

The two of us boarded Eddie's private plane and flew down to Fort Lauderdale, where Vince Sr. had a home. He picked us up at the airport and drove us to a beautiful beachfront restaurant. As we were talking and people-watching, I glanced at the ocean and noticed that the Gulf Stream was moving north.

So was the flow of my life, it seemed.

After the meal, Vince invited us to his home. On the way there, though, he was pulled over for a minor traffic infraction. Vince was trying to negotiate his way out of a ticket when the cop peeked into the backseat and spotted me.

"Ah, Superstar Billy Graham," he smiled, waving Vince free.

I had saved the day, and this was good!

Vince lived in a picturesque house alongside a canal on an inlet. He walked Eddie and me onto his yacht, and we made ourselves comfortable in a well-appointed room belowdecks. Eddie sprawled out in a big chair, I stretched out on the floor, and Vince laid out his scenario:

"On April 30 in Baltimore, we're going to have Bruno drop the title to you. Then, on February 20, 1978, we're going to put the belt on Bobby Backlund in the Garden."

It was that specific. There was only one thing that bewildered me. Although I'd met Backlund years back in North Dakota, and wrestled him recently in Florida, his name didn't really stir me. He'd always been just another babyface on the card, a guy who meant nothing when it came to drawing money. Was Vince really going to take an unknown and make him a champion? It seemed impossible for Backlund to follow the Living Legend *and* Superstar Billy Graham in Madison Square Garden.

"This is going to be the longest run for a WWWF heel champion ever," Vince continued.

"I'm honored," I replied. "I'm ready to do business."

With Eddie Graham as our witness, we closed the deal with a handshake. No lawyers. No contracts. No demands.

I had a few months left in Florida, and was expected to kayfabe the other boys about my impending fortune. That was pretty close to impossible. Gossiping is as much a part of wrestling as a headlock. People were talking about the proposed title change immediately. I shared the information with Steve Strong, as well as Dusty—who immediately had visions of the two of us transferring our feud to Madison Square Garden.

I found a house in Atlantic Beach on Long Island. By then, my marriage of necessity had all but fallen apart. I was on the road often—and not too concerned about being faithful.

Valerie Coleman: On Tuesday night, January 11, 1977, my life was changed forever. I was eighteen years old. My sister Shirley and I were in an IHOP restaurant when Superstar Billy Graham and Steve Strong walked in. We were the only two customers in the place, but Wayne and Steve sat down at the table right next to us.

Both of my parents had been wrestlers, so naturally I was smart to the business, and well aware of who these two guys were. I have to admit that I thought Wayne was the most amazing-

looking man I'd ever seen. He was perfect, the personification of masculinity.

Wayne introduced himself as Steve Strong, and Strong as Billy Graham. He was trying to have some fun with us. "You girls are so beautiful, you must be models," he said.

He then claimed that he and Steve had just returned from Paris, where they'd eaten crêpes suzette.

It was all so corny, and that made him all the more charming. There was nothing crude or out of line with Wayne. I loved the fact that he didn't try to portray the ultra-cool, arrogant persona I'd seen on TV. He was sweet and funny, and had the most incredible smile. For me, it truly was love at first sight.

Strong asked where the good nightclubs were. I told him I didn't know. "I don't drink," I explained, "so I don't go to clubs."

I had no idea of the impact that simple statement would make on Wayne.

Steve Strong: *It was like a trigger going off in Superstar's head. He didn't drink or like bars, either. Between you and me, he was not a real womanizer. Right then and there at the IHOP, he fell head over heels for Valerie. You know, you're in coffee shops and restaurants every day and every night, and you hear jabber back and forth. But it doesn't go anywhere. This was instantaneous. They were a soul couple.*

Valerie Coleman: *I became a Christian when I was thirteen years old, and was determined to remain a virgin until I married. At the time I met Wayne, I was managing a clothing store called Pants Towne. I'd met a guy there who wanted to date me, but I didn't want the hassles that always seemed to go along with dating. I had no desire to mess around. So when I now told this guy that I liked Superstar Billy Graham, he looked at me like I was the biggest idiot in the world: "You've got to be kidding. He'll never want you, you're a virgin!"*

Shirley was going to beauty school, and Wayne said that he needed someone to bleach his hair. When we'd met at the IHOP, he'd taken her number—which was actually the number of our house—then called her and said, "Don't forget to bring your friend."

We arrived at the motel, but I was painfully shy. There was no way that I was going into his room.

My beautiful Valerie.

I opened the door and didn't see Valerie. "Where's your friend?" I asked Shirley.

"She's in the car."

I peeked out the door, and there she was—ten feet down the sidewalk. Valerie was a beautiful girl, with dark brown hair and round, hazel eyes.

"You can't sit in the car," I said, pushing the motel door open wider. "I'll leave the door open. Everything's cool."

Valerie Coleman: I walked into the room, and there, on Wayne's dresser, were all of these books about the Lord, about the Bible, about Noah's Ark. For me, it was confirmation that this was the guy.

He called me a few days later to ask me out. I was talking on one of those wall-mounted phones in the kitchen. He said, "Okay, we'll go out to dinner. And then, if the chemistry is right, we'll go back to my room for a little romance."

My heart sank. "You know what?" I told him. "There's romance, and then there's romance. And the kind of romance you're talking about, I don't do."

"Oh," he said. "Well, maybe sometime we'll get together and talk." That was pretty cold.

I hung up the phone and slid down the wall to the floor, just like in the movies, with tears streaming down my face. I thought my friend had been right, after all—Superstar Billy Graham didn't want me. We'd never be together.

But the very next day, he called me at work and said, "Can I take you to dinner when you get off? Just dinner, and then I'll take you home." He told me later that he had just been testing me.

The first movie that we saw together was *The Texas Chainsaw Massacre*. I'd decided to work Valerie a little bit. When the date was over, I shook her hand. And I did the same thing on the second date and the third date. Now *she* was starting to get worried.

Valerie Coleman: It was like the Scope mouthwash commercial, where the guy shakes the girl's hand at the door because she has bad breath. A handshake instead of a kiss?! I appreciated the respect he was showing me, but this was ridiculous. I was beginning to worry that our relationship would remain platonic.

Suffice to say, we eventually consummated our friendship. Despite our fifteen-year age difference, I was really falling in love with this girl. And she was definitely falling in love with me.

After only four weeks of dating, I knew that I wanted to spend the rest of my life with Valerie. This marriage would be born out of love, not a whim or necessity. I asked her to marry me, and without hesitation, she said yes.

That was the answer that I needed to hear. Because—between my scheduled championship win up north, and that wife I'd neglected to mention—there were a few things that would keep Valerie in limbo for a while.

Valerie Coleman: When Wayne asked me to marry him, he told me that he wanted to spend the rest of his life taking care of me. Neither one of us thought that, almost from the outset of our marriage, I would be the one taking care of him.

CHAPTER THIRTEEN

JACK OF HEARTS

There's only one diamond in this business, and you're looking at him.

—"Nature Boy" Buddy Rogers,
upon meeting the new "Nature Boy," Ric Flair

The WWWF had been launched in 1963 when Vince and partner Toots Mondt splintered away from the confederation of NWA promoters. I assume that there were bad feelings at first. But a lot had changed in fourteen years. Now, Vince and the NWA were working together.

Like Houston, St. Louis was a self-contained promotion that featured the best talent from around the country. The fans were avid in the best kind of way. They'd been exposed to a range of styles and performers, and respected a good match. Their wrestling education was administered by promoter Sam Muchnick, the former NWA president and sportswriter, who presented the matches as legit athletic contests. Gimmicks were discouraged, and promos were short. This might have enhanced Sam's status with his friends in the St. Louis sports community, but to me it was stifling.

On New Year's Day, 1977, I was in St. Louis, wrestling Pat O'Connor, NWA Champion from 1959 to 1961, in a miserable match. O'Connor was hung up on the past—with a shooter mentality and an obnoxious personality. This boring relic of yesteryear seemed obsessed with proving that he could manhandle the star of tomorrow, hitting me with stiff shots and working too "tight"—really cinching down on holds. I'd never taken a suplex before, but in the middle of the match—without warning—I suddenly found myself up in the air. Pat brought me up a little too high, and now I was crashing down, trying to tuck in my chin as best I could. I landed on the back of my head on a very hard ring, felt my neck crack, and for a split second feared that it was broken. That's how quickly everything can end in professional wrestling.

I was definitely dazed—and very mad. I actually contemplated retaliating and going after O'Connor's eye. But it was a total waste of time just being in the ring with this creep.

On February 6, 1977, Harley Race began his second NWA championship reign. Harley was, in many ways, everything I was not—a no-nonsense performer who could carry any type of opponent through a thrilling sixty-minute match. Our differences exemplified the distinctions between the NWA and WWWF.

Still, it was good business to have me work with Harley before I beat Bruno. It would illustrate that I could hang with not only the rival champion but a guy who was technically unassailable.

The week before our first matchup in St. Louis, in front of some of the most intense and knowledgeable fans in the country at the time, I was told that there were only two minutes *total* allotted on television for promos—one for me, one for Harley. Instead of complaining about this absurd time limit to talk people into an arena, I good-naturedly focused the interview on Sam Muchnick.

"We all know that Sam Muchnick is the godfather of professional wrestling. He's the man who controls the worldwide business, and he's responsible for this match. And he'll be responsible for the pain and suffering I cause Harley Race."

Wrestling Harley at this juncture was an extremely valuable experience for me. He was a master worker, always under control, never hurrying through one move to get to another. One of Harley's distinctions in the business was his unusually hard head. This enabled him to deliver his signature flying headbutt from the top turnbuckle—a maneuver later replicated by Chris Benoit. When he sold my bear hug, he did a lot more than simply bend his fingers in despair and shake his head. Harley *arched* his entire body, holding out his arms at his sides, then dropping them limply in resignation. He was just incredible!

The match ended with the referee disqualifying me, prompting the promotion to announce a rematch the next month. This bout ended in a draw, establishing me as Harley's equal, even though I was far from it.

In Tampa, I'd already dropped my Florida title back to Rhodes. Yet on April 2, 1977—just before I was scheduled to leave for the WWWF—Ox Baker and I won the Florida Tag Team Championship from Jack and Jerry Brisco. I'm not sure why Eddie Graham and Dusty made this decision. I guess it still tied me to Florida—and there was something to be said for having one of your wrestlers beat Bruno for the WWWF title.

It's hard to describe Ox Baker if you've never met him. He certainly had a menacing appearance—bald, with a dyed-black Fu Manchu mustache and bushy eyebrows—but he was just screwy. He'd paint his toenails red and talk in a booming voice that you could literally hear across the street. Sometimes I'd ask him to sing "Old Man River," and listen to the backbeat coming off the locker room walls.

Tom Renesto, one of the masked Assassins and a booker in a number of territories, noted that Ox looked like an amazing heel until he opened his mouth. There was something about his voice, his countenance, and his general manner that seemed comical, and it translated to fans. For whatever reason, it was hard to take him seriously.

A few weeks before my match with Bruno, I took time off to cosmetically prepare. I went back to Arizona to pump iron and tan in the desert. I wanted this moment to live up to everyone's expectations.

Titles didn't normally change in places like Baltimore, so the members of the so-called wrestling press usually skipped the cards there. This prompted me to buzz my friend, Scott Epstein, a photographer, and some others about what was going to occur. Kayfabe wouldn't do me any good. I wanted a historical record.

George Napolitano: *The two of us were driving down to Baltimore, and Billy said, "It's gonna be a big night tonight. I'm gonna get Bruno. You might be driving home with the champion." And I said, "Yeah, okay." I'd heard that story before.*

I was having fun with George: "Stay close to me. I just have a feeling that something might be happening."

On April 30, we walked into the Civic Center and immediately noticed a number of television cameras, and Vince McMahon Jr. directing people. The first thing I thought was that the fans in Baltimore had never seen this type of arrangement before. Maybe they'd know that something momentous was about to occur. But spectators were not that analytical in 1977. I was giving them far too much credit.

Outside, a line of people were already winding around the building from the box office. But inside, where the illumination was dim and the seats were empty, I was struck by a feeling of eerie calm. I stopped to glance at the ring, empty and dark under the overhead lights, sitting there mute. In just an hour or so, the lights would blare, the bell would clang, and that ring would speak.

I walked alone toward the back of the building, where I could hear the echo of the boys—Gorilla Monsoon, Baron Mikel Scicluna, and my old Tag Team partner and rival, Baron Von Raschke from the AWA (yes, two barons on one show!)—talking and laughing. They knew that the Civic Center was sold out, and that meant a bigger payoff. I passed a table where a doctor was taking blood pressure readings, shook hands with a few guys playing cards, found an empty stall, and dropped my bag on the floor. Like radar, I scanned the dressing room for Bruno.

He was in one of the changing rooms off the main hallway, and welcomed me in to sit down and go over our match. Bruno seemed relieved to be finally getting some time off. I was so grateful to him for putting me over for the championship that once our conversation ended, I taped on a blade.

"This occasion calls for some juice," I said to myself.

The fans had poured into the building by this point, and I heard a voice shout, "First match! Let's go!" Bruno and I were number four. Main events on WWWF shows were always held in the middle of the card. The policy was implemented during Pedro Morales's championship reign, when his challengers frequently found themselves rumbling with the Puerto Rican kingpin's overzealous supporters while exiting the arena.

Quietly, I contemplated the enormity of this night, while unpacking my outfit: a beautiful green-and-white batik T-shirt with a spiderweb design, yellow patent leather boots, and mint green tie-dyed wrestling tights that I'd made myself.

During the third match, Bruno's manager, Arnold Skaaland—who also worked backstage for Vince—yelled, "Graham, you're up next!" I went over to the entrance area, just behind the dressing room curtain. I stood there nervously, pacing back and forth, waiting for the preliminary match in the ring to end and the boys to return to the dressing room.

In the lull between matches, I could hear the energized murmur of the crowd, anticipating the championship bout. Finally, an escort of police surrounded me, and we headed to the ring. We didn't have entrance music or pyro in 1977, but man, how I would have loved some that night!

Nonetheless, I was able to generate a lot of heat, doing my posing routine for the fans. When Bruno began his walk down the aisle, I climbed onto the second rope and glared at him in defiance.

The Civic Center began to rumble.

As soon as Bruno's foot touched the lowest ring step, I jumped off the turnbuckles and melted into a corner, allowing the champion to command center stage. Sammartino was introduced first. The ring announcer referred to me as the "capable challenger." With Vince Jr. commentating at ringside—leaning forward and watching us so intently that I expected his nose to touch the ring apron—the timekeeper rang the bell.

The ring in Baltimore felt as large as a tennis court. When you ran the ropes, it seemed like you were in a marathon; it took forever. But Bruno and I used the size to milk the drama, stalking each other for a good minute before we ever locked up. Finally, we tied up, and I shoved Bruno into the turnbuckles—twice. He came bounding back, whipping me into the opposite corner. I ricocheted off the buckles at him like being shot out of a cannon—into a Sammartino arm drag. On the canvas, the champ applied a hammerlock. I draped a foot on the bottom rope, forcing Bruno to break the hold, and rolled onto the arena floor.

I caught my breath—and fixed my hair.

"Boooooo!"

There was nothing out of the ordinary about the match, nothing classic. Bruno and I pushed each other around the ring like two snorting bulls, while I positioned myself in places where George Napolitano could snap some good shots.

Biding my time to measure the man, I punched and kicked, taking over the match, generating old-school heat to incite the crowd. Bruno sold and sold, then made his comeback. "Run me into the ringpost," I told him.

Bruno slung me into the pole, and I toppled from the ring apron to the floor. There, I pulled off the little piece of tape I had covering the Blue Steel on my index finger, and cut myself two inches long—not once, but twice. When I crawled back up to the canvas and the lights hit my face, there was a huge pop from the crowd. In photographs I have of the match, some of the ringsiders are actually recoiling from the sight. I feared that I'd cut myself too deeply, and the fans might become sympathetic.

We were going to have to end this quickly; I couldn't afford to lose my heat. After a few more exchanges—I wanted to show that I still had the will to fight—Bruno crunched me in a bear hug. Resting my shins on his thighs, I leaned back and held out my arms like a crucifixion. Finally, I broke loose by raking his eyes, then fell to my knees in the corner, placing my hands behind my back and begging for mercy.

Over the noise, I shouted for Bruno to come closer. As he did, the referee ordered him away. With Bruno's attention seemingly diverted, I reached down, grabbed his feet, and tripped him, placing his legs over my shoulders in a pinfall effort. When the ref slid down to the canvas to count, I slipped my feet onto the ropes.

Vince Sr. had been very explicit about this. If I was going to cheat Bruno out of the championship, there couldn't be any subtlety. On Vince's orders, I placed my feet all the way up on the top rope, tottering there as the ref counted to three.

All 12,000 fans jumped to their feet. This was not a celebration. But, with the exception of Stan Stasiak's title win in Philadelphia in 1973, the WWWF title had always been won and lost in Madison Square Garden. It was incredibly exciting for something this monumental to occur in Baltimore.

The first thing that I did was look for the photographers at ringside. I held up the belt, let the cameras flash a few times, then—satisfied that the event had been documented—formulated my exit strategy. Already, tons of spectators had made it down to ringside, pounding on the canvas with their fists. Garbage was starting to fly into the ring. Bruno remained there with Skaaland to deflect attention from me. But that could only work for so long.

Usually, the signal for fans to calm down was turning on the house lights. However, the person commissioned with this task had forgotten to perform it; I imagine him being as awestruck as everyone else. Security was supposed to keep the aisle clear. But the barrier consisted of a thin piece of rope, and a wave of irate fans flooded the walkway. I jumped off the apron into the darkness of the arena, getting blasted with beer, Coke, and saliva. A couple of marks landed kicks and punches. Some cops managed to fight their way over to me and act as shields as I swung my belt over my head like a helicopter propeller to keep back the hordes.

To use a wrestling cliché, it was true pandemonium in Baltimore. Superstar Billy Graham had stolen the title and gotten away with it.

I returned to the dressing room, bloody and sweaty, my eyes burning from the tossed fluids. No one said anything to me as I dropped the belt at my stall and flushed the blade down the toilet—a postmatch ritual I fol-

Sammartino always found a way out of my bear hug.

lowed for purposes of both safety and kayfabe. After a quick shower, I threw my gear into my bag with the championship belt, got dressed, rushed over to Bruno's cubicle, shook his hand, and said, "Thanks, man, but I've got to go."

"No, go, go. We'll talk later."

I needed to escape the wrath of the fans. There was another match in the ring when I darted out the arena exit and found myself on the sidewalk.

How was I going to get to my hotel? George was still in the Civic Center, taking pictures. I raised my arm to hail a cab. The feeling was absolutely surreal. Inside, 12,000 people were ready to lynch me. Yet here I was, all alone, on a calm, empty street. Eventually a taxi stopped, and I crammed inside with my gear. My bandages were already loosening on my forehead from a combination of blood and sweat. But I managed to relax my shoulders and fall back against the seat. It was springtime, and the fragrant smell of cherry blossoms came in through the open window. I tried to enjoy it for the rest of the ride.

Once back in my room, I unpacked the bloody contents of my bag. Everything—my boots, tights, shirt, even the belt—was smeared. And the bag itself reeked. Once again, I was drenched in sweat, and I took another shower. Drying off and rebandaging my head, I called room service. After my meal, I sprawled on the bed and phoned Valerie. I told her that the match went well, there was more heat than I expected, but I was all right.

We stayed on the phone for the next four hours, talking about things far more important than winning a title. Just before the sun came up, I said good-bye and drifted off to sleep.

I'd been scheduled to wrestle Gorilla Monsoon on the next Madison Square Garden show, while Bruno was slated to defend his championship against George "The Animal" Steele. Both matches proceeded as planned. But when I came out for my bout with the gold around my waist, the fans went wild. Vince Sr. had thrown them a swerve. Communication between wrestling fans in different cities was virtually nonexistent back then. Breaking news was passed on through wrestling magazines two or three months late. Along with the crowd's disappointment over the end of Bruno's reign, there was a sense of indignation over being cut out of the excitement. How dare we change a title, and not do it in New York?!

Yet when I tore off my shirt and teased tossing it to the crowd, there was also some applause—mainly from young people looking forward to a new era.

Paul Heyman, former owner, Extreme Championship Wrestling:
Superstar Billy Graham came through my television like nobody I

had ever seen. He flexed his biceps. He talked in prose. He'd talk about the toaster oven system coming at you from inside the radio waves that transponded into a picture in your living room. It was just an amazing television experience.

Anybody on the inside of the industry will tell you that he was far from a great technician. But he knew how to mask it. He knew how to accentuate all his strengths and hide all his weaknesses.

He was the talk of the town. His momentum was enormous. But I don't think the company was prepared for this phenomenon. He probably could have sold out Yankee Stadium, and I don't mean just once. He could have done it on two back-to-back shows. He was ridiculously hot.

When Bruno came out for his match with Steele later in the night, the place erupted into a standing ovation. The fans didn't know that I'd pinned Bruno with my feet on the ropes—that news would be conveyed on an upcoming television show—but his longtime supporters assumed that, if Bruno lost, the finish had to be tainted. This was a groundswell of protest from those people who loved Bruno for defending the title—and defending their worldview—all these years. There was so much magnetism in that building, and it set up my return matches with Bruno perfectly. The scene was just so intense. It will never be replicated ever.

We drew sellout crowds almost everywhere. But shortly before one of these encounters, I was wrestling Chief Jay Strongbow in a soiled boxing ring in Albany, New York, and took a halfhearted bump. The mat was so dirty that my right leg stuck to it. As I twisted free, I wrenched my knee. A couple of days later, I rubbed against another dirty canvas in St. Petersburg, Florida, coming away with a mat burn on my elbow. When the grime penetrated the raw, exposed skin, the bacteria traveled down my body and settled in my already inflamed knee.

A few days after that, outside Philadelphia, I was startled awake in my hotel room. My knee was inflated like a balloon, with red lines streaking up my thigh to the groin area. I called the desk clerk, who directed me to a hospital in Chester, Pennsylvania.

Hobbling into the emergency room, I told the doctor on duty, "I need to get this knee drained. I'm the World Wide Wrestling Federation Champion, and I have to defend the belt tonight against Bruno Sammartino."

The doctor was unimpressed: "Fine, let's take the fluid out, send it to the lab, and find out what's in your knee."

When the results came back, he was far more frantic. I had a staph infection, and needed to be checked into the hospital.

"Can't you just drain the knee?" I implored.

"We can. But if we check you out, you are going to die."

In the operating room, the doctor gave me a local anesthetic, tied down my arms with Velcro straps, sliced me down to the bone, pulled apart my skin and tissue with a pair of grippers, and began scraping chunks off my knee bone. The bone itself wasn't numb, and when the scalpel scratched against it, I nearly leaped through the ceiling. The pain was unbelievable.

"You can't do this," I yelled. "This is torture. Put me under."

Remarkably, Vince Sr. was incredibly understanding when I told him that I'd be missing close to a month's worth of commitments. Still, before a scheduled rematch in Baltimore, I was suddenly asked to make a personal appearance.

"Billy, the Civic Center is sold out," Vince explained. "How about we bring you down to ringside to cut a promo?"

It was probably the first time we'd disagreed since the day Vince decided to put me with the Grand Wizard. Only, on this occasion, *I* was right.

"Vince, I can't do that. I can't even walk. The only way to get me to ringside is on a gurney, with the paramedics wheeling me to the ring."

"Well, maybe we can do something with you on a stretcher."

"We *can't,* Vince. I had to fight for my life in that building when I won the title. And you want me to lay on a gurney and get rolled down the aisle—in front of rabid fans who want to kill me? It's too dangerous. I can't do it, Vince."

No one—save for Jerry Graham or Captain Lou Albano—spoke to the distinguished promoter like this. Vince was disappointed—if I made it to the ring, he wouldn't have to give the fans their money back—but definitely not offended. After all, he understood his audience as well as I did.

One of the luxuries of being the champion was that I didn't have to turn up at the arena as early as everyone else. In New York, I'd have one of the boys reassure Vince that I'd be arriving at the Garden an hour or so into the show—and work out at the Mid-City Gym until about 8:00 P.M.

I'm proud to say that, as champion, I didn't need a strong undercard to support me. My name sold out buildings by itself. But if I dared ask for a ticket for a friend, I was sent on a guilt trip, like the company was going to collapse because of my request. This didn't come from Vince Sr. but from the cabal that surrounded him—old-timers like Phil Zacko, Willie Gilzenberg, and Skaaland. I'd walk into the Holland Hotel, the rat-infested dump where the office would set up shop before the Garden shows, and knock on their door. With the exception of Vince, who always had color in his cheeks, along with a smile and flash in his Irish eyes, everyone was grumpy. All these old men—stranded with broken teeth and without love, to paraphrase Dylan—seemed depressed. I mean, we'd sold out Madison Square Garden! What else did these guys want?

My understanding with Vince was that I'd receive 5 percent of the gate from larger arenas, like Boston Gardens and the Philadelphia Spectrum, and 8 percent from the small clubs. That's 5 and 8 percent of the net, by the way, not the gross. The question that was never answered was, "What constitutes a small club?" Were Binghamton, Rochester, and Worcester big buildings or little ones? The lines were blurred. Despite the seating and demographics, small towns suddenly became big towns.

Every three weeks, when we taped our syndicated broadcasts at the Philadelphia Arena, Vince Sr. would lead me down a hallway to a dilapidated room with one light hanging overhead. Zacko, the company's treasurer—a shuffling, skittish fireplug of a guy—would be sitting there, going over my payoff. As we reviewed the list of towns, the math could get very confusing. After one three-week period, for instance, Zacko wanted to pay me $17,000. That's a lot of money, but I caught a few miscalculations. Zacko was stuttering, embarrassed, and flushed. But he owed me an extra $3,000. And, after a struggle, he paid it—in that run-down, gloomy den of thieves.

There were no agents, of course, in those days. And wrestlers didn't run these kinds of things past lawyers. Not long into my championship reign, Vince Jr. presented me with a contract backstage in New Haven: "Well, Superstar, we need you to sign this now," he stated, sounding almost as smooth as his dad.

"Okay, brother."

Who knew what was in the contract? Who cared? What was I supposed to say—"I don't like this. Take the belt off me"?

Occasionally, I'd marvel over the way I'd become the biggest star in professional wrestling. Jerry Graham had lent me his name and brought me to the L.A. office. But I was the one who created my persona. I was the one who composed the promos. I was the one wearing green felt hats and feathered headbands and boas. There'd been no one before me to copy. I'd done it all myself. I was an original.

Joyce Sampson: Wayne had always been doing this, doing that, one thing and then another, and never staying with anything. He got into wrestling and he stayed with it. All of a sudden, he was champion. We had a celebrity in our family. It was great.

The Grand Wizard and I were even more in synch than during my first WWWF run. Both of us were always on speed, a condition that stimulated some very funny promos from the Wizard—and accounted for his pacing in and out of frame. Vince Jr. had a hard time trying to insert his own hurried commentary into interviews.

"If you'd let me finish, *McMahon,*" the Wizard would rebuke him on television, "you might even learn something."

As always, the Wizard would warm up the viewers, then let me ride the rest of the promo to its finale. "I'm on the sunlight system. I'm on the laser beam system. I'm on the microwave system. Superstar Billy Graham being beamed all over the world. I'm the man with the biggest arms. I'm the man who does the most harm. I'm the man of the hour, the man with the power, too sweet to be sour."

Before a match, I'd outstretch my arms, slowly swaying back and forth, as the Wizard removed my robe. After raising my fists to the crowd, I'd drop down to a side chest shot, with one knee on the mat. The Wizard would stand behind me, licking his fingers and patting down my hair. Then he'd gently pat my head. We'd embrace before he sent me into battle.

This got heat in a lot of places. But people were also amused by our routine, and appreciated the fact that we entertained them. I was beginning to notice banners praising the Superstar. This was also unheard of for a heel. No one brought signs to the arena for Nikolai Volkoff, Toru Tanaka, or Killer Kowalski—a multifaceted guy who, in addition to training Big John Studd, Chyna, and Triple H, photographed several of my magazine covers.

I found myself invited to functions by people who knew that I could engage the audience with words as well as charisma. At a bodybuilding event, I was featured alongside my childhood hero, Steve Reeves. "I'd rather be here with Steve Reeves than any man alive," I told the crowd, "even President Jimmy Carter . . . Steve Reeves is God."

When I noticed Reeves and his wife wince at this declaration, I quickly amended it to, "Steve Reeves is the true god of bodybuilding."

As anticipated, I became the first WWWF champion to defend his title in a variety of territories. At Detroit's Cobo Hall, I wrestled Bobo Brazil— long after he and the Detroit territory had faded. Although there were only about 500 fans in the building, it was a pleasure to step into the ring with the "king of the Coco Butt," a future WWE Hall of Famer, and an angel of a man. Bobo worked so lightly that I could barely feel his grip on my body. It was a sign of courtesy and respect.

I went to Japan and, on the spot, challenged Rusher Kimura to an armwrestling match in a Tokyo television studio. Kimura couldn't speak English, but I led him with the force of my arm—he didn't have to do anything but hold on. Of course, I jumped him like I always did in those situations. Had this been anything but an impromptu angle, I would have remembered to punctuate the moment with a little juice. Regardless, the fracas made the papers, and our subsequent Cage match drew a big crowd.

In St. Louis, I faced Dick the Bruiser and—just like in the AWA—had another horrendous match. This time, at least, I didn't have to lose. But don't think Bruiser did the honors for me, either. We wrestled to a double countout.

Sometimes I questioned the logic of these interpromotional encounters. When I traveled to Atlanta, I was matched against Ray Rougeau, a French Canadian who didn't mean a thing to those southern fans. My impression was that the NWA guys didn't want to see the WWWF champion outshine their stars, so they put me in the ring with someone who wasn't over. I had the same experience at Memorial Hall in Kansas City, Kansas, against a long-bearded guy named Black Angus. As much as I tried, I couldn't get any heat on him because the people didn't care. The experience did nothing to enhance me or the WWWF.

"Why are you sending me to the middle of the Midwest, where no one's interested?" I complained to Vince Sr. later on. "I'd rather be someplace where I'm over."

Someplace like Florida.

Because of my run there prior to my title win, and the trusting relationship between Vince and Eddie Graham, the territory felt like an extension of the WWWF. At the beginning of my reign, the fact that I was a WWWF Champion *and* Florida Tag Team titlist meant something to people in the Sunshine State. When Ox Baker and I lost the title to the Brisco brothers, it was portrayed as big news, as well.

Here, Dusty became my most voracious challenger—and all-time favorite opponent. We shuttled between the North and South like a couple with homes in the Hamptons and South Beach. In Boston, Dusty would get off the plane from Tampa and stroll into the arena at about 8:00 P.M. Vince would put us on third instead of fourth, so Dusty could catch the last plane out.

In the ring, we'd make each other laugh. Outside of it, we'd listen to Reverend Ike, a Harlem preacher who promised his followers great wealth—after they sent him their jewelry and money in the mail.

"The best way to help the poor is *not* to be one of them," he said. "The *lack* of money is the root of all evil."

I suggested using some of Reverend Ike's stuff in our promos. But according to Dusty, the preacher was already taking *his* stuff from us.

Dusty Rhodes: *We had a great time. We tried to teach Andre the Giant to sing a few lines from the Bob Dylan song "Lily, Rosemary* *and the Jack of Hearts." And we tried it with "King" Curtis Iaukea from Hawaii. Andre said he was the Jack of Hearts. Superstar was Rosemary, and I was Lily. Andre would come over to me and say, "Hey, Lily, what's going on?" And everybody would look. That's what I mean about great times, and a great era.*

My fondest memories of this industry are with Billy at Madison Square Garden. It was like the Beatles, the Who, and the Rolling Stones in the same building on the same night. It was the electricity that he and I had. It was just a dream thing that happened, the plumber's son from Austin, Texas, against a real bodybuilder who could actually do something in the ring, who had that impact. I mean, George Steinbrenner and my mom were sitting three seats apart. It was her first trip to New York. That's why it was so special. The titles I won later on in the NWA, my matches with Ric Flair and Kevin Sullivan, they were special, too. But this was different for me. It wasn't hard yet. Everything didn't feel like a job.

We were on the biggest stage in the world. Andy Warhol and Halston and these guys were in my limousine after the show. I'm not name-dropping. It's true. They just hung on us. It's like we came to New York and took it by storm.

There was a rhythm to the way Dusty threw his "bionic elbow," as if he was dancing to a melody in his mind. He'd hold you in place, pause a moment, and mutter, *"Dit, dit, dit, dit, dit,"* conducting his personal opera while dropping the elbow. The shots were stiff—I blame Dusty for my compressed vertebrae that grinds whenever I look upward—but I was too caught up in the dance. Dusty had a cadence to his selling, to regaining his strength, to his comebacks—when he'd do a wiggling shuffle unlike any white man I'd ever seen—and I was proud to join him in this waltz.

Our tests of strength were very different than the ones with Bruno. With our fingers locked, Dusty would appear to power me down until my palms were on the mat. Then he'd release the hold and stomp—his toes would hit the mat, but the ball of his foot would graze my fingers—and I'd leap up, grabbing my wrist and frenetically shaking my hand.

After every match, I'd go on TV and put Rhodes over in my promos, rubbing my fingers against my temples and complaining about the migraines inflicted by his mighty blows. And the war wasn't over, fans were told, until the two of us met in a Bullrope match. Dusty might have had the advantage because he was from Texas—where, apparently, people regularly

tie themselves together with bullropes and fight outside shopping malls in Dallas, and movie theaters in Austin—but I would win because I was stronger.

"These are official police handcuffs," I pronounced during one interview, dangling a pair of manacles in front of the camera. "And soon, very soon, on this very stage . . . I will pull apart steel, among other fantastic things, to prove to the world that I am the greatest and strongest athlete in the world. That's how I will win the Bullrope match. I will pull the cuffs apart with my two bare hands and wrap it around his throat and choke him literally *to death*."

The matches were guaranteed gorefests. Dusty loved to juice, and even had cuts all over his arm from Barbed Wire matches. In the course of our battle, he'd manage to "hang" me from the ring apron, with the bullrope extending from my neck, over the top ring cable, into Dusty's tugging hands. The cue for the finish generally started while I was choking Rhodes with the rope in the ring. Apparently fearing for Dusty's life, the referee would order me to stop. I'd turn and voice my dissent, forgetting about Dusty, who'd regain his senses and snatch the cowbell attached to the rope. Now I'd turn back around and feed myself to Rhodes, who'd blast me with the cowbell like he was swinging for the bleachers. I'd sell it, rolling outside the ring and falling to the floor, seemingly unconscious. The referee would count me out of the match. But because of that rule about titles not changing hands this way, the gold remained on me.

> ***Tony Garea:*** *Graham was always stealing a victory, but the fans didn't hold it against the company. I remember having to wrestle him for the belt in Philadelphia. I drove down there from Connecticut on a beautiful summer's day. It took me about three hours, and the whole time I was thinking, "Nobody's going to be there. It's too gorgeous." It turned out that we had 19,500 people, and we just tore the house down. We locked up and stayed in a lockup position for two or three minutes. He pushed me. I pushed him back. I went to one knee. I got back up. The crowd was going nuts. In wrestling, it takes two to tango, and we tangoed that night.*

When former WWWF Champion Stan "The Man" Stasiak and I wrestled in Toronto, where he was a babyface, he asked if I could mention the city's Croatian community in my promos. I was happy to accommodate, putting Stan over at the same time: "I will make your Croatian hero beg for mercy."

Ivan Putski was already entrenched as a Polish role model. And he made it a point to catalog other ethnic groups on interviews and include them in his "Polish army." By the summer of 1977, he'd come a long way from his days in the AWA. Ivan had shed sixty pounds, and he was ripped. It was basically effortless for the two of us to sell out buildings, doing strongman matches. I'd always liked Putski, and enjoyed selling for him. If I gained the advantage, I often did it through devious means, like unwrapping the tape on my wrists to choke my opponent. When he'd surge, I'd play the coward and run away. And even though I maintained the championship, it was often by a countout or some other fluke.

It was good business for the people to watch a guy like Ivan handle me and think that, on any given night, some babyface could take my title.

Yet I would never elevate Haystacks Calhoun to that category. Calhoun was listed at 601 pounds and did a hillbilly gimmick, wrestling barefoot in overalls. He was the epitome of a nonwrestler, a guy who had no place in the ring with opponents who were athletic and believable. Abdullah may have been huge, but he could deliver flying elbows, take bumps, and help you through a match. Calhoun was a horrible sideshow fat man, and nothing more. What made it worse was that he didn't like to sell, and became annoyed if you tried to make him work. In one bout at Long Island's Nassau Coliseum, he deliberately sat on me too hard and wouldn't get up for a while. When he finally did, I lost my temper, kicked him in the stomach, and shoved him on his backside.

Calhoun rolled out of the ring and went back to the dressing room, whimpering like a baby.

On November 1, 1977, at Madison Square Garden, I finally had the opportunity to show High Chief Peter Maivia my gratitude for good-naturedly enduring my inexperience back in San Francisco. New Yorkers didn't believe that a Polynesian chief was going to win the championship in their city. But I decided to work as hard as I could to pull as many fans into the building as possible.

Before a television taping, I suggested that Peter rip the head off a live lobster, like a savage. Vince Jr. liked the idea. His more conservative father did not. The elder McMahon did not want any repercussions from station managers or the ASPCA. He was a wrestling promoter, not an activist for change.

Instead, we had Peter play a happy islander, plucking away on a ukulele, when I jumped him from behind and lashed him with the instrument across the back of the head. This was a hardway shot, and it shattered the ukulele. But Peter was tough enough to take it. After he bladed, I turned him toward the camera and simulated gouging the open wound with a jagged edge. This was my tribute to the High Chief; I wanted a sold-out show.

Captain Lou Albano was our official attendance barometer. Before a card, he'd stick his head through the curtain and survey the crowd. Most of the time, he'd saunter back to the heel dressing room and announce, "It's all the way"—his term for a sellout. In this instance, he said, "Billy, there's a few empty seats. Almost all the way."

This was the only Garden show that I didn't sell out during my championship reign. But for Peter's sake, I was glad to see that we were pretty close. Over 18,000 fans showed up.

Before our match, Maivia came over to the heel side of the dressing room. "Billy, what do you want to do out there?" he said.

I was humbled by the notion of this legend asking me to conceptualize the bout. "Brother," I replied, "we'll do whatever you want to do. This match is on me."

That night, I did everything within my limited ability to make my friend look like a world champion. I bumped. I sold. I cowered. The only thing that I couldn't give him was my belt. But when the fans left the Garden after the show, cascading onto Thirty-third Street and downstairs into the E train, they had no doubt about which of us was the better man.

It was the least I could do.

CHAPTER FOURTEEN

BUT I LIKE MY ROBE

Glory is fleeting, but obscurity is forever.

—Napoleon Bonaparte

I never liked the way that some of the bigger stars treated the jobbers, throwing them around with no regard for their safety, then breezing by them backstage without an acknowledgment. I made it a point to talk to these guys after our matches and show some appreciation. They were sacrificing their bodies for my career.

As cliché as it sounds, some of my good friends were jobbers. I caught rides all the time with Pete Sanchez and "The Unpredictable" Johnny Rodz, two tough Puerto Rican guys who jobbed for everybody. We'd drive to spot shows in New Jersey or Pennsylvania, with the two of them passing a joint around and periodically offering me hits.

"Nah, I'll pass." I wasn't a dope smoker, but I sure got a contact high.

When we'd arrive at the building, fans would often be surprised to see

Rodz and Sanchez step out of the car, while I trailed behind them. It all seemed natural to me. I never believed in separation of power. Who drew what meant nothing to me.

Yet here I was, on January 25, 1978, at the Orange Bowl in Miami, ready for what may have been the most intriguing match in pro wrestling history at that time: the first confrontation between a WWWF and NWA champion.

During Bruno's first reign in the 1960s, there had been some discussion about fusing the titles. From what I heard, Bruno was supposed to defeat Lou Thesz, but nixed the idea. At the time, he only had two Sundays a month to spend with his family. Sammartino claimed that between his NWA and WWWF commitments, promoters would have him booked on thirty-two shows a month—working afternoons and evenings on the same day when necessary.

This was an entirely different situation. Nobody was talking about uni-fication. Harley Race and I were going to wrestle to a Two-Out-of-Three Falls Broadway—an inconclusive finish—with both titles remaining distinct and equal entities.

Harley Race: What I really wanted was to hold three separate matches in three separate venues. In the first match, either I'd beat Billy or he'd beat me. The next event would go through (end in a draw). The following match would have the guy who lost the first time winning again, so you're right back to where you started.

At the time, I felt that the WWWF needed this match more than the NWA. They wanted to show the world that their guy could hold his own with the NWA Champion. It was an honor for me to do it because Vince Sr. was one of the nicest men I ever met. I was helping his organization, and furthering the wrestling business at the same time.

I think Billy's working ability has been underrated. He could get in the ring and wrestle most people and have a decent match with them. A lot of guys his size couldn't do that. People compare him to Hulk Hogan, but I think he was better. Hogan was a person who just wanted to run over the top of you. If Billy was in the ring with a per-son who wasn't calling stuff to him, he wasn't bashful about being in-ventive. He could come up with things to do in the ring.

The problem we had in the match was that a downpour started. I don't remember how many people were there, but it was a lot of them before it rained. Then half were trying to stay covered up. The attention was not in the ring, where it should have been. When wrestling rings get wet, they get slick. Even in a regular wrestling match, you're trying to keep from twisting an ankle and hurting yourself and the other person. Add that rain to it, and it becomes a lot harder.

I gave Harley a shoulderblock at one point, and slipped on the canvas. With the weather and excitement, though, the fans barely noticed. The match continued, and Harley gave me my first and only piledriver. Normally, when someone tried to put me in that position, I pulled away. But I felt safe with Harley, even in the rain.

Harley and I had a side bet going: who would the fans treat as the heel? Despite the way that I was depicted on TV, I thought that the transplanted northeasterners in the crowd would cheer for the WWWF representative. Harley was also a villain when he wrestled in Florida. But as the NWA champ, the fans responded to him like the hometown hero.

The only issue I had with the Orange Bowl format was that I didn't see the need to wrestle to the sixty-minute time limit. Like all great NWA champs, Harley could work an hour-long match every night. I never wrestled for more than fifteen or twenty minutes. Of course, I could do the basic stuff in the ring. But I couldn't exchange holds like Harley; my style was brute force. I would have preferred having us each take a fall, then double-juicing and fighting on the fifty-yard line. After thirty-five minutes, the ref could have counted both of us out.

Harley Race: *The hour went fairly well. Billy blew up three different times, but that's no big deal. We've all done that at some point. He knew that I'd never take advantage of him. I wish everybody else associated with the match felt the same way.*

There were two referees—Gorilla Monsoon for the WWWF, and Don Curtis for the NWA. The reason for this was so somebody could stop me if I tried to double-cross Billy. Word got out that I might try to pin him, and take the match as a shoot. I have no idea where this came from. Why would it make any difference to me when I was already the heavyweight champion to start with? I don't know.

The first fall went to me when Race submitted to my bear hug. Harley won the second fall after a suplex. Just before the sixty-minute mark, he locked on his sleeper hold. I slid down to the canvas, but remained in Harley's grasp. Slowly, my body went limp, and Harley dropped me onto the mat, where he covered me for the pin.

Harley Race feeling the wrath of Superstar.

NWA referee Don Curtis counted, *"One . . . two . . ."*

Clang!

Just as his hand hit the canvas a third time, the bell rang. Monsoon—suddenly revealing his WWWF partisanship—jumped into the ring, waving his arms. The Floridians booed this very subtle heel gesture—conceived, I'm sure, by either Dusty or Eddie Graham.

The match was ruled a no-contest.

"The mat cover was wet from rain," I protested to a Miami newspaper. "This made it difficult to utilize the leverage my superior strength gives me. Also, I found it demoralizing that Race was escorted to the ring by a vision of loveliness [local beauty queen Susan Fox], while the NWA assigned *me* [local wrestler] Bubba Douglas as a second."

Today, when I watch the tape of the Orange Bowl clash, I realize that my physique was not as cut as it had been a few months earlier. With less than a month to go before my scheduled title loss to Backlund, I was starting to neglect myself.

When Vince first told me about his plan to crown me champion, I felt like he was giving me a gift. I knew that I was a temporary titlist, but it didn't bother me. Now I believed that I *deserved* to have the title. I was selling out arenas everywhere—including the Philadelphia Spectrum, where my title defenses turned away fans three months in a row! The people were basically turning me babyface. In their eyes, Superstar Billy Graham was not a transitional champion. Superstar Billy Graham was a *legitimate* champion. Why should I have to lose now?

Had Bruno been scheduled to replace me, I would have kneeled in the center of the ring and handed him back his belt on a velvet pillow. If Dusty were programmed, what could I really gripe about? But *Bob Backlund?* Bob was a fine athlete and a nice guy, but those weren't necessarily prerequisites for becoming WWWF Champion. He didn't have the look, he didn't have the rap, he didn't have the "C.C."—charisma connection—with the audience. He was boring.

I pleaded my case to Vince Sr.: "I'm just a flash away from becoming a babyface. All we need to do is have Koloff turn on me, and we'll have an explosion. One more year of automatic sellouts. Automatic!"

Vince nodded. "I know your drawing power."

"Vince, Backlund's not there yet, and in my opinion, he never will be. Everybody knows it. He isn't the new Bruno. Give him another year in the bullpen. Let me have my babyface run as champion."

Vince shook his head. In the most compassionate voice he could muster, he replied, "Billy, my mind's set on Bob Backlund. I'm committed."

Taking time out to hit an ab shot.
Courtesy of Wayne Coleman.

The Wizard declaring that "Superstar Billy Graham is the greatest champion of all time."
Courtesy of *Pro Wrestling Illustrated* Photographs.

Minneapolis, 1974. I had my daughter Capella hitting *the* pose.
Courtesy of Wayne Coleman.

Weightlifting against Ken Patera. Unknown to the fans, half of the plates are wooden.
Courtesy of Michael Gordon.

At the wrong end of a head butt from High Chief Peter Maivia.
Courtesy of *Pro Wrestling Illustrated* Photographs.

My pre-match ritual of posing. Courtesy of *Pro Wrestling Illustrated* Photographs.

At *Wrestlemania XX* with one of my favorite ladies, Stephanie McMahon-Levesque. Courtesy of Wayne Coleman.

In 2003, after years of estrangement, Vince graciously invited me to *SummerSlam.*

I'll give Vince credit for being a man of his word. He told me that I'd win the title on April 30, 1977, and lose it on February 20, 1978, and he meant it. For the past year, he'd been selling the other promoters on Backlund. In a business where people pounce on your vulnerabilities, Vince would not be seen as indecisive. But he was wrong. He put pride and stubbornness in front of good business sense.

Vince McMahon Jr.: All the stars had lined up for Superstar Billy Graham, and I wish it lasted longer than it did. I thought he would have been an extraordinary babyface. But my dad didn't see it that way. It wasn't traditional. The way of thinking back then was you couldn't have someone his size as a babyface. How could you get sympathy for him?

I always thought that we missed the boat with Superstar, and quite frankly, had I been in charge at the time, he would have been Hulk Hogan for me.

To add insult to injury, I had to wrestle Mil Mascaras in the two Garden shows preceding the title change. Despite the fact that I was the champion, Mascaras still refused to sell for me. Vince put Backlund in Mascaras's corner for the second confrontation. When I tried pinning Mil with my feet on the ropes, Backlund broke up the fall, igniting a brawl to lead to his championship challenge.

Two nights before the Garden card, I arrived at the Philadelphia Spectrum to a record gate—with some 5,000 turned away—for a Cage clash with Bruno. As we went over our match, I mentioned that I was dropping the title on Monday.

Bruno seemed floored. Although I'm sure that he knew about Vince's long-term designs, Sammartino had been distancing himself from the business and wasn't keeping up with late-breaking gossip. He didn't realize that I'd be losing the championship at the peak of my popularity.

Bruno suggested that I protect myself in the eyes of the fans. "Let's do something tonight to hurt your knee," he said. "Then you can limp into the ring at the Garden, and the people won't think you're at a hundred percent." That's how much Bruno didn't believe in Backlund. I'm sure he was insulted that Vince was going to try and make Bob into another Sammartino.

Of course, no one had given us permission to fake a knee injury. In fact, this went beyond going into business for ourselves. Backlund's long reign needed to start with him winning the gold from a healthy man, not a cripple. We couldn't let anyone else find out about our idea and stooge to Vince Sr. Only Bruno and I were in on the scheme.

In the course of our match that night, we did a spot that involved me charging at Bruno. Sammartino slipped out of the way, and my knee crashed into a corner of the cage. I sold the purported injury, and Bruno began stomping it. Then, to swerve the boys, I gestured to Bruno that the knee was really hurt. He responded by going for my head instead, apparently to give the knee a rest.

Two nights later—after a detour, wrestling Edouard Carpentier in Toronto on Sunday—I hobbled into the dressing room at Madison Square Garden. Vince Sr. observed my performance and asked what was wrong.

"I hurt my knee in the cage with Bruno on Friday."

"Okay," Vince responded, "let's get Monsoon in here."

By this point, Gorilla Monsoon owned a percentage of the company, and wanted to protect Backlund at all costs. He asked me to hop up on a table, where he taped up my knee and asked if it felt any better.

"I don't know," I said, contorting my face.

Vince and Monsoon looked at each other, sensing that something wasn't right. McMahon spun around and found Backlund. "Bobby," he said, "as soon as the match starts, go after his knee."

Now I could sell my limb as much as I wanted. In the fans' minds, Backlund would be the one who hurt me.

For the first time ever, I wore white tights into the ring. It was a subliminal message. White was too bland. It wasn't me. Therefore, the man the people saw losing the championship was *not* Superstar Billy Graham.

I didn't call much of a match this night (Backlund won with an atomic drop). I was giving Bobby my belt. That was enough for me. It wasn't really Backlund's fault; he was simply the guy anointed. This was a protest against Vince McMahon Sr.—even though he allowed me to drape my foot on the bottom rope while the referee was counting the pin. After all, I'd beaten Bruno with my feet on the ropes. It was only fair that, after the work I put into being champion, my defeat should be something of a question mark, too.

I was so despondent after the loss that I nearly gave Vince my two weeks' notice. I thought better of it, though, when I considered the amount of money I'd make in rematches. New York had been my city for the last ten months. Now I wanted to flee the place in shame. I left the Garden and drove to a nondescript motel on Long Island, where Valerie was waiting.

George Napolitano: *His psyche was shot. I know it doesn't make sense. People think, "Why do you care? Are they real matches?" Well, when your pride is hurt, it becomes real.*

Billy's whole up demeanor changed to downcast. He felt invincible on the way up. Even when he lost on the way up, he felt invincible. But once you've been to the top, the only place to go is down. I'd tell Billy, "Look at you. When you walk down the street, people don't say, 'There's the guy who lost.' They say, 'There's Superstar Billy Graham.' They love you."

"It's different now," he'd say.

I think what really got to Billy was that Backlund didn't look the part. He was a redheaded guy from Princeton, Minnesota. The bad guys called him "Howdy Doody" in their interviews. Then the fans began saying it, too. Yeah, Backlund sold out the Garden. So did Graham and so did Bruno. There was no Pay-Per-View. If something big was going to happen, it was probably going to happen in the Garden. But this was the beginning of fans hating the good guys.

With the exception of a one-week period—when he exchanged the belt back and forth with Antonio Inoki in an unreported sequence of matches in Japan—Bob Backlund held the championship until December 26, 1983. Although Backlund certainly had his fans, I felt that the company always had to stack its cards with other attractions, like Andre the Giant and Jimmy "Superfly" Snuka, to maintain the crowds.

Backlund's promos were monotone. And while he spoke about admirable values on his interviews, I know he wasn't delivering what the fans wanted to hear. There were moments when he seemed completely oblivious to the fact that we were in a gimmick business. Before our first rematch at the Garden, the two of us came down opposite corridors in the dressing room and met in the center with Vince Sr. I had the tie-dye and the color. Bob was wearing a black full-length boxing robe, tied over his belt.

"Bobby," Vince said, "the *belt*. The fans have got to see the belt. You can't hide your belt. It's all about the belt."

Backlund didn't seem to understand. "But I like my robe," he answered in a childlike voice.

Vince McMahon Jr.: *I guess maybe, to look at it from my perspective, Bob Backlund would have been black-and-white movies with no sound, and Superstar Billy Graham would be like the movies we see today, with Dolby sound and wraparound screens.*

Kevin Sullivan: *It was cookies and milk against Jack Daniel's and weed.*

Nonetheless, I sold my rematches with the new titlist hard on my promos, leaving many with the impression that maybe Backlund was just holding the belt for me for a while. "How will your body feel," I asked before a card that also featured my third gimmick brother, "Crazy" Luke Graham, "when I take my precious belt back? . . . Don't you dare steal any of the jewels because the Superstar will be wearing the championship belt, just as brother Luke Graham will also be victorious in his first appearance at the Garden in recent years. Graham night at the Garden! Victory is ours!"

Our first New York City encounter after the title change called for the match being stopped because of Backlund's bleeding. Unfortunately, Backlund didn't know how to blade yet, so Vince asked me to cut him instead.

You might imagine that I would have taken out my frustrations on this innocent farm boy. But I wasn't that cruel, and Bob had done nothing to warrant a permanent mauling. We were professionals, and I assured him that he'd be safe in my hands.

"I might have to cut you two or three times," I warned him in the locker room beforehand. "I'm not going to cut your head off. It's going to feel like a fingernail going across your forehead. We just have to give them enough juice to stop the match."

Bob was fine with that. And I believe that I was the one who suffered the most from the gig job. I could feel the razor blade on my finger, grinding into another human being's skin. The first cut didn't go deep enough to draw much blood, and I had to slice Backlund again. I was so sickened that I was afraid that I couldn't do it. It was like I was stabbing a guy, under the pretense of a wrestling match, and it was very disturbing for me.

On the other hand, some guys—like my good buddy, Ric Flair—don't have this aversion. At *SummerSlam* '03, I watched him cut open his friend Bill Goldberg with a smile from ear to ear. And Goldberg thanked him for it later!

In the 1990s, Philadelphia's heel-oriented fans turned Extreme Championship Wrestling (ECW) into a true phenomenon in the industry. But two decades earlier, the sons and daughters of the City of Brotherly Love were mesmerized by Superstar Billy Graham. When I walked the aisle for a title challenge against Backlund, they applauded me with both hands over their heads, waved banners, and shook my hand—thumb over thumb, seventies soul brother style. Quite understandably, this rattled Backlund. Despite the trust he invested in me for the blade job, these public displays of affection told him that I wasn't really fighting on his side. So when I called a "false finish" spot in the ring, he feared a double-cross.

I had Backlund covered for a near-fall. "Count to three," I told the referee. "But, Bobby, get your foot on the bottom rope by two."

As planned, the sound of the official hitting the mat three times got a huge pop from the crowd. I rose up with fists raised until the referee spotted Backlund's foot, still on the rope, pulled down my arm, and ordered the match to continue.

Backlund—always paranoid about being double-crossed—had turned whiter than he already was. When we got backstage, he lost it. "Bobby," I reassured him, "it was just a high spot. I'm not going to steal your belt."

I didn't tell him that I *wanted* to. I just said I wouldn't.

Although the title was no longer at stake, my rivalry with Dusty had been so hot that Vince chose to continue it. Unlike Roy Shire and Verne Gagne, McMahon did not prohibit babyfaces and heels from sharing the same car, so we decided to travel together to a show in Binghamton, New York, about three hours from the city. Dusty was supposed to meet me on a street corner, near his Manhattan hotel. But when he got there, he was surrounded by fans chanting, "Dusty! Dusty! The American Dream!" Suddenly, I pulled up, and the focus shifted: "Superstar! Superstar!"

Some in the throng expected me to jump out of my vehicle, Texas bullrope in hand, and fling myself on top of Rhodes. Instead I leaned over, popped open the passenger door, and—to the absolute astonishment of everyone—drove off with my hated enemy.

> **Dusty Rhodes:** *It was a horrifying trip because he cannot drive. He had no velocity on the road, and no philosophy on the signs and the other cars. I mean, it was crazy.*

Regardless of my popularity in major urban centers, there were places that hadn't changed with the times. On March 11, 1978, I was wrestling Ivan Putski in an old wooden building in Johnstown, Pennsylvania. I'd cheated to win and left the ring, but just before I entered the locker room, I felt somebody punch me in the back of the head. I stumbled a few feet, then turned around to face a crazy mark, poised to attack me again. He didn't fare very well. I kicked the guy in the groin, broke some teeth with a foot to the face, and threw him into a Coke machine.

The fan sued me. Actually, he sued "Billy Graham." But I had to go to court anyway.

I was worried when I stepped into the courtroom with my twenty-two-inch pythons, and noticed that the judge was armless and relied on a pencil in his mouth to flip pages. My alleged victim was a local guy, who'd brought his entire family to testify as witnesses.

But Vince had provided me with a WWWF attorney. "I have a ticket stub," my lawyer announced, parading in front of the plaintiff. "Is this your ticket stub? Were you sitting in the balcony on March 11, 1978?"

"Yes, sir, I was."

"So you're telling me that you got up out of your seat in the balcony and came down to the main floor?"

"Yes, sir."

"Why did you attack Mr. Graham?"

"I was upset with the wrestling match."

"You mean, because Mr. Graham won?"

"Yes."

"So you wanted Mr. Putski to win?"

"Yes."

"So you are telling the court that you left your seat and went down the stairs to the main floor for one purpose, and that was to attack Mr. Graham?"

"Yes, sir. That's true."

Obviously, the judge had little choice but to rule in my favor. The plaintiff did not receive a dime in compensation. However, Vince did not want me coming off the road for a second trial, and offered to pay his dental bills.

With the championship or not, I was worth too much in the arena.

WASTELAND

He who was living is now dead
We who were living are now dying

—T. S. Eliot

I knew Valerie would never date a married man, so I avoided telling her about my marriage to Bunny for as long as possible. By the time I did, I'd already started divorce procedures, and Valerie was too much in love to turn back.

We married on July 1, 1978.

Still, the breakup with my ex-wife caused a tremendous fracture in my relationship with my kids.

Capella Flaherty: The main memory I have of living with my father while he was champion was when I found his belt in the closet. It was big and gold and had all these jewels in it. It was really gallant, really royal. And heavy, so heavy. I started polishing it. Right next to it were his boots, and I shined them, too. My dad walked into the bedroom and saw me, and said, "What are you doing?"

"I'm just shining this for you," I told him.

"Okay," he said, "make it pretty."

I also saw my parents break up. I was in the room, and they didn't even know it. We had a little poodle dog that I was chasing around, and I went behind the couch in the living room to look for it. I heard the word "divorce," and looked through a crevice on the side of the couch. My dad had his shirt off, and his jeans on.

"It's over," he said. My mom started crying and ran into the bedroom. My dad stayed in the living room, with his head down.

We moved to Burbank, where my mother was from, and I remember her parents being there a lot. My mom went back to work full-time at the Bank of America.

I was so upset about the divorce that I had psychosomatic stomach pains. I went to the hospital, and had to have an upper GI because of it. I didn't understand why my parents had to split. It freaked me out.

Joe Miluso: My mother told me, "Your father left me for another woman." So when you're growing up and living with your mom, of course you're going to get a negative image of your father. It didn't matter to me that he was a famous wrestler. He was just a man who hurt my mother.

Valerie Coleman: When I met Wayne's mother, the first words out of her mouth were, "You're nothing but a sexpot gold digger. And I hope you don't plan on having kids because he's already got two, and he doesn't need any more." I told her that we planned to have ten.

I knew a guy from the Arizona powerlifting scene who was—and *is*—a total psychotic. Once, at a party after a tournament, Brendan O'Connell suddenly pulled out a gun, forced the bartender to kneel, and pistol-whipped him. When people asked Brendan why he savaged the poor guy, he said, "I just wanted to do it."

If I were Brendan's defense attorney, I'd argue that anabolics affected his body chemistry. But the truth is that I think the man was born deranged. This was a person who purchased a Doberman pinscher and shot it full of steroids. It became massive.

Like so many others with borderline personalities, Brendan found his way into the wrestling business.

The two of us were leaving a convenience store one night, after a show in Portland, Maine, when I was confronted by a bug-eyed, village-idiot type.

"Graham, I hate you!"

This was an extreme mark, a guy who obviously had something wrong with him, and he stuck his face right in front of mine, spitting as he spoke: "You smell, Graham. You stink. You stink."

Honestly, the guy was giving me the creeps. But he was all by himself, and I was just a few feet from the car. Brendan, though, saw an opportunity to beat somebody up. Before I could calm the situation, he cocked back his fist and punched the guy in the face. When the fan hit the pavement, Brendan kicked him a few times in the head.

"Come on, man," I said, pulling Brendan into the car. We pulled out of the parking lot and went on to the next town. But when the cops found my antagonist in a bloody heap, they had a few questions.

"Who did this to you?"

"Graham."

That night, at a local hotel, there was a knock on the door of a room where some of the boys were playing cards. As Andre the Giant, Arnold Skaaland, and Angelo Savoldi looked on, baffled, "Crazy" Luke Graham was handcuffed and taken into custody.

He was released a few hours later when authorities figured out that not only was he innocent, but no one with the Graham moniker had actually assaulted the victim.

With my most successful WWWF run coming to an end, I wrestled Backlund once more at Madison Square Garden. Although neither of us could trace our roots to the Mediterranean, this was a "Sicilian Stretcher match"—and my final chance to show Vince that he had made a mistake. On the way down the aisle, I took off my head scarf and handed it to a fan. In the ring, I ripped open my tie-dye top and threw it into the crowd as well. People were yelling and cheering and clamoring for more, so I gave it to them. One by one, I removed every gimmick I had—headband, wristbands, knee pads, elbow pads, sunglasses—and chucked them into the outstretched arms of ringsiders. Backlund stood back like a spectator as the people trampled each other and pumped their fists at the Superstar.

When you look at the overall picture, my period on top in the WWWF was very short. I started 1977 in another promotion, won the title, had my reign, and worked the rest of 1978 as a challenger. In that small window, I made a huge impact. If I had been able to stretch out my time with the title, I wonder what could have been.

Back then, promoters always made the champion put a deposit on the belt. This way, the territory would be saved the embarrassment of having its kingpin jump elsewhere with the gold. If the company's holding $30,000 of your money, it was reasoned, you'll relinquish your title when asked.

I returned to Phoenix with my deposit and not much else. Between hotels, steroids, amphetamines, barbiturates, and my very contentious divorce, I'd exhausted my championship purse. Arnold Schwarzenegger was investing in the original Gold's Gym in Venice, California, and asked if I was interested in joining him as a partner. I blew the opportunity off.

I had a much better idea.

During this era, I'd noticed that *Star Wars* and *Battlestar Galactica* were very hot. So I made the decision to market a Superstar Billy Graham space age poster. I probably could have done the artwork myself, or asked Steve Strong, who'd been consistently grateful to me for helping him find work in all those different territories. Instead, I went to my brother Vance's wife at the time, a commercial artist best known for designing the mermaid on the Chicken of the Sea tuna can. Her fee was $5,000, and in her illustration, I was in outer space, holding back a saber-toothed tiger, with stars and planets behind us.

I took out a $5,000 ad on the back of *Starlog* magazine—the front cover depicted Christopher Reeve as Superman—and purchased time on stations that broadcasted wrestling. I also paid a television crew to shoot a commercial.

"The new Superstar space poster!" I excitedly declared in the spot. "It's finally here! Now, I want the cameraman to zoom in close and . . . see how the Superstar looks in outer space! There's flying saucers! Venus! Jupiter! Saturn! Mars! There are gas, gamma rays, and all your favorite stars! And look at my new Tag Team partner—a Stone Age saber-toothed tiger! Now, you know that you can never pin the Superstar in the ring, but now you can pin me to your wall! And think what a Christmas present this space poster would be, all wrapped up underneath your Christmas tree! Now, get a pencil and paper—because here's your television announcer to tell you how to get it!"

I believe that I sold between fifteen and twenty posters. The rest were carted to a storage facility. After a while, I could no longer afford to pay for the rental space, and the company took my entire inventory. For all I know, copies are being sold on eBay right now for $500 apiece.

Less than a year after selling out Madison Square Garden, I was digging underground sprinklers in Phoenix—for one of my high school heroes, who had a landscaping company.

George Napolitano: He vanished into thin air. Wrestlers might leave a territory, but they never disappear. Since no one saw him, and no one heard from him, people said, "He must be dead." We had no idea what happened to this guy.

Paul Heyman: There were rumors that he'd gone over to Paris and died like Jim Morrison. There were rumors that he was back in Arizona. There were rumors that he went to Mexico. It almost became like folklore. He was in deep training to become a bodybuilder. He was running from the Mafia. He was working undercover for the CIA.

I didn't want to return to the wrestling business. I was too bitter, and my heart was somewhere else. But when I was really desperate for money, I'd surface and work a show somewhere. I wrestled for Eddie Graham in Tampa against Rocky Johnson, and in Hollywood, Florida, against Jack Brisco. I did a job for Jerry "The King" Lawler in Memphis, then no-showed a bunch of dates in the territory because I was disappointed in the payoff (that's how despondent I'd become; I didn't even care about disappointing the fans who'd paid to see me). I wrestled Bruno—with my head shaved, and a brown beard—for Paul Boesch in Houston. The next week, I came back to work against Bruiser Brody. Then I took myself out of circulation again.

Abdullah the Butcher: I heard that Wayne was dead. Then, I went on a tour of Japan, and one of the wrestlers said, "Superstar Billy Graham's here."

Another one told me, "Whoever said that is a liar. He's dead."

I went up to Wayne Coleman's room and knocked on the door. When he saw me, he got a big smile on his face and said, "Aaabbbby!"

We hugged each other and started laughing. Then I asked, "Hey, Wayne, you have that $300 I lent you in Calgary?"

He told me, "I still don't have it yet."

Uncertain about what to do next, I had business cards made—WAYNE COLEMAN COLLECTION AGENCY—and contacted construction supply companies, drywall manufacturers, and restaurant equipment distributors. My offer was pretty straightforward: I will personally collect your debts for 40 percent of the proceeds. No one ever asked if I had a license to perform this task, and truthfully, I'm not sure if I needed one or not.

At first, I had Brendan O'Connell helping me out. But he was too menacing and scared people, and I had to stop bringing him along. As in the past, I never had to resort to violence to collect money. In fact, I sometimes felt a little too much empathy with the debtor. Had I made this business my primary focus, I believe that I could have developed it. But I wasn't born with a proclivity for making money, and was so addicted to Ativan, Placidyl, and other prescription medications that I could barely think.

Valerie Coleman: I was leading a very solitary existence because my husband was always unconscious; he was sleeping all the time. One Thanksgiving he was drugged out, as usual, and I was completely alone, and the only place open to eat was Jack in the Box. I went there and ordered a ham and cheese sandwich because it was Thanksgiving, and I knew my mom was home in Florida making a turkey and a ham. I called and told her about my Thanksgiving Day meal, and I remember her crying. She had thought we were going to be spending the day with Wayne's family when, of course, we weren't invited.

Joyce Sampson: Wayne would try to act like things were going fine when you knew they weren't. On New Year's Eve, we were dressed and ready to go out when Val called us, hysterical: "We have no money. We have no place to stay. We have nothing." They came by, and Wayne was calm. Then he went into the bathroom, and we could hear him sobbing and sobbing and sobbing. He came out and said, "God, I don't know what brought that on."

I said, "I do. You're on drugs."

We gave them $500, and told them to get a hotel room somewhere. But I knew that Wayne would use some of that money for drugs. Valerie was a young girl who didn't know what she got herself into. I told her, "If you want to live your life as a normal human being, you'll leave him. He's not normal, and he probably never will be normal."

I understood how my sister felt. Our marriage was still young, but behind Valerie's beautiful face, there was so much pain. She couldn't sleep at night, watching me destroy myself. I even told her, "You'd be better off without me."

But she stayed.

Valerie Coleman: I was only twenty-one years of age and married less than two years, so it was very difficult having my husband's family tell me that, for my sake, I needed to leave Wayne. As well-meaning as they were, I knew they were wrong about him. After all, they weren't there when he and I would sit out on the pier at Clearwater Beach, talking about the Lord until the sun came up. I realize this isn't the way fans would have pictured Superstar Billy Graham spending time with his wife. Maybe I hadn't known him for very long, but I already knew him better than anybody else.

I'm very blessed in that God has given me a huge capacity to forgive, along with the strength to ask forgiveness from others. I'm also a very tenacious woman. If there is something that I believe in, I don't let go. I've never been a quitter, and there was absolutely no way that I was going to walk away from Wayne or our marriage.

I thought that the World's Strongest Man contest might help me turn the corner. The competition was televised on ABC each year, and featured the most powerful guys on the planet performing feats like bending steel around their necks, wheeling 700-pound engines up inclines, racing with refrigerators on their backs, and—at least in 1980, when I competed—squatting with a bar attached to two platforms holding as many as ten *Playboy* bunnies.

Despite Valerie's protests, I sold our furniture to subsidize my training—highlighted by as many steroids as I could obtain—and we moved into the Riviera Hotel by the River Bottom area, near ASU. To prepare for the eighteen-wheeler pull event, I spent hours pushing my car around the block. A dairy man I knew would meet me at a preselected spot every morning and fill up three one-gallon bottles—or "protein containers," as I called them—of raw milk. In total, I'd drink those three gallons of raw milk each day, and eat all the food that I could consume. When I arrived at the *Playboy* ski resort in Great Gorge, New Jersey, for the contest, I weighed 325 pounds.

Aware of the television cameras, I contemplated getting some color during the log lift to generate more mainstream coverage. While picking up the log, I'd "accidentally" bump my head against the timber, drop it, and blade. With blood running down my face, I'd crawl over to the log and valiantly lift it again. I decided against the stunt because I didn't want to get caught and thrown out of the contest. Although there was a definite show-biz element to World's Strongest Man, my competitors and the judges would not have welcomed the introduction of Blue Steel.

As it turned out, I pulled my hamstring during the log lift, but continued the contest with my thigh dramatically taped. Because of this, I did become something of a sentimental favorite, but—since we weren't allowed to book the finish—that wasn't enough to win. I came in fifth in a field of ten—not bad, considering my injury. The ultimate victor, Bill Kazmaier, would win the next two contests as well, before going up to Calgary to train for the squared circle with Stu Hart.

While Stu may have envisioned Kazmaier as another Wayne Coleman, it was not to be. With no Abdullah to protect him, the other boys—most notably "Flying" Brian Pillman and Stu's son, Bruce—ribbed Bill mercilessly, calling him "Quagmire," and tainting his view of the wrestling business for life.

My payoff was $3,350, but I never considered using that money to solve my financial burdens. Instead, I tried promoting again—not wrestling, but powerlifting. I called powerlifters from around the country—lining up people like Joe Bradley, a 132-pounder who'd recently squatted 650 pounds, and Dave Waddington, who'd squatted 968 pounds—and drove out to California to recruit my friend Dave Draper, a former Mr. Universe, as a guest poser. Dave was making custom furniture at the time, and agreed to handcraft the plaques for the First Annual U.S. Invitational Powerlifting Championships. Feeling motivated, I contacted health clubs and companies specializing in gym equipment, and persuaded them to take out ads in our program. The Amateur Athletic Union (AAU) would serve as our official sanctioning body.

Jim Profitt, a retired cop who knew my brother Vance, became our master of ceremonies, and performed feats of strength like breaking official police handcuffs, bending horseshoes, tearing two decks of cards simultaneously, and blowing up hot water bottles until they burst. After leaving the police department, Jim had become a successful jeweler, and now he put down a $1,000 deposit to reserve the Celebrity Theatre in Phoenix for December 6, 1980.

"Maybe that's not such a good day," my high school buddy Bob Calvan pointed out. "Isn't the Mr. Arizona contest the same night?"

It was one of those coincidences that epitomized my life. Out of 365 nights, I happened to pick the one with a competing event in the same city. But I'd already lined everything up, so—as always—I rolled the dice.

With my shaved head and black mustache, I didn't feel like Superstar Billy Graham anymore. So I stayed in the shadows, listing myself in the program as Wayne Coleman, president of Super Star, Inc.—my brand-new promotional company—and codirector of the event with Brick. Interestingly, several of the records set that night remained unbroken for years—and that's with the powerlifters using old-school weightlifting belts, improvised wrist wraps, and Ace bandages around their knees instead of rubberized elastic pads and high-tech supersuits that now can increase a bench press by as much as 200 pounds.

Unfortunately, we never had more than four hundred paying customers in the 2,500-seat theater at a time. I started the event at about noon, and—like other powerlifting shows back then—went deep into the night. With competitions spread so far apart, the experience was monumentally boring. Excluding a handful of hardcore fans, most of the attendees wandered in and out, stopping by the building for an hour or two, then leaving to go somewhere else.

By the time Mr. Arizona let out across town, the box office had closed. So hundreds of new spectators just strolled into the Celebrity Theatre for free. They all came to see Dave Draper's posing routine. I'd purposely scheduled it last to keep people in the building. He took the stage at about 3:00 A.M., and stole the show. But I still left the contest with my pockets empty.

The powerlifters had all been lodged at the Desert Rose hotel. I worked the manager, who allowed me to reserve a block of rooms and host a banquet there with a credit rating of zero. I was a former wrestling champion and local personality. The notion that I'd stiff the place wasn't even feasible.

But I did anyway. I had no choice—once again, I was broke.

Jim Profitt felt so badly about my predicament that he gave me a gorgeous 1963 Cadillac convertible that he'd restored. He made Valerie an exquisite hand-tooled gold cross pendant with four rubies at each end, held by a solid gold chain.

A month later, I was so destitute that I couldn't even place an ad in the paper to sell these items. I pawned the cross and sold the Cadillac—then, hoping to conserve the price of cab fare, walked eight miles back to our hotel.

I'm sure that every mid-sized city in America has a street like Van Buren, a last resort for rotting souls—a busy street with no one going anywhere. In Times Square, I communed with those blighted spirits while passing them in the night. Now, back in Phoenix, I was one of them.

The south end of Van Buren was a pocket of aging hotels with weekly rates and kitchenettes, with western-themed names like the Alamo and the Pioneer. There were auto repair shops, strip joints, nightclubs, vacant lots, and a mental hospital. Transient hookers roamed Van Buren for blocks, too withered to ply their trade in Scottsdale.

It was the type of place where I imagine the "Reverend" Jimmy Swaggart went to sully himself in sin.

In our dreary hotel room, Valerie prayed for my redemption. I'd sit on the commode, unshowered, nodding in and out of sleep, unable to urinate because my kidneys were shutting down. Then I'd wake up and go out, looking for drugs.

Valerie Coleman: Wayne and I were in a place called Furr's Cafeteria, going down towards the cashier with our trays. I looked to the left, and suddenly, I felt the rail shake. It started slowly at first, then became a violent vibration. I turned to my right to see what was causing it. Wayne's eyes were rolled up in the back of his head. His hands were clenched around the rail, shaking it like he was being electrocuted. He couldn't let go. I thought he was having a heart attack, and completely lost it. A woman came over to help. "Don't worry," she said, trying to calm me but still speaking frantically. "I know what's happening. He's having a grand mal seizure."

I'd been sleepless for the past few days and had run out of drugs. Now my body was going through major withdrawal. This electrical field was blasting in my brain; all the neurons were misfiring. I'm amazed that I didn't split open my head as I fell backward to the floor. Then the paramedics were there.

"Do you want us to take you out on a gurney?" one of them asked.

"No, it's okay," I replied. "I can walk."

I stood and practically sprinted through the cafeteria, taking giant steps. Every word that came out of my mouth was rapid-fire. I didn't know anything, not even my name.

"Do you know who this is?" a paramedic asked, motioning at Valerie.

I shook my head from side to side, yet asked her to stay with me. Even though I couldn't remember who she was, I wouldn't let go of her hand. Our connection was still there.

Some Christians would analyze this period in my life by concluding, "Satan was after your soul. The devil was beating you up." Others might say that I was demon-possessed and needed an exorcism. In reality, I was just a backslider, one who was doing a pretty good job of hurting myself without Satan's assistance.

At Maricopa Medical Center, I was put in a detoxification program. For the first time in years, I felt clear-headed. Brick's grandmother, Lucy Thorbecke, invited Valerie and me to move into her small two-bedroom house. Valerie slept on the couch; I took the living room floor. Brick owned a gym by now, and gave me a key, so I could work out at any hour of the day or night.

It was a touching gesture from a friend who obviously thought of me like a brother. And everything was going great as long as I was drug-free.

But I wasn't ready to walk that path. Soon I was sneaking into the gym to steal three or four dollars at a time from a container next to the cash register for vitamin and protein pill exchanges.

When Brick found out, he told our friend Ron Pritchard, who confronted me with a tough-love approach: "I can't talk to you anymore. I love you, Wayne. But I won't be in your life and watch you kill yourself like this."

I had to move. But like many addicts in this position, I was defiant. I didn't have a problem, I convinced myself. Everyone else had become too rigid. But now I was *really* out of choices. On more than one occasion, I picked grapefruits off a tree for a meal. And, in a desperate attempt to make money, I tried salvaging the few items we had at a swap meet.

I arrived early at the location, the parking lot of the greyhound racetrack across the street from the Ramada Inn that was the site of my first wedding. At the crack of dawn, I opened the trunk of my car and set up a little display. I had some clothes, purses, jewelry, and shoes that all belonged to Valerie, and several of Steve Strong's paintings.

"You can't sell those," Valerie had argued beforehand. "He painted them for *you.*"

"I have to," I said. Strong's work went for thousands of dollars in galleries. If I sold two of his paintings at a huge discount, I'd probably still earn a couple of hundred dollars.

Like a beggar ashamed of his vocation, I huddled in a folding chair in disguise, pulling up the collar of my coat, pushing a sailor's cap down my forehead, and wearing a pair of shades. Sure enough, once the sun came up, I spotted a group of guys from high school.

They passed by and tried to make eye contact. I looked at the ground. They walked a few feet and glanced back again. I went around to the front of the car and bent down, pretending that I was readjusting the license plate.

"Is that Wayne Coleman?" I heard one of them ask.

"I think so."

"What in the world is he doing?"

They all exploded into laughter.

Of course, I never sold a painting. People come to swap meets for blouses and shoes and jeans—things they really need—not fine art. At the end of the afternoon, I left with maybe $25.

Valerie Coleman: After the embarrassment and the trauma of the swap meet, Wayne came home infuriated. I'd taken a job at a cosmetics company, but we still didn't have enough money for gas. Wayne tried to get around this by stealing gasoline—pumping the gas, then getting into the car and taking off. That would cause huge fights. I couldn't stand it. I've always had zero tolerance for thieves.

On one particular day, Wayne was all drugged up and tearing out of the gas station. We were fighting. And a report comes on the radio that Harry Chapin, one of our favorite singers, had just died in a car accident.

"Aaaaaah!" Wayne started screaming. He was in such a rage that he reached up and ripped the rearview mirror off the car.

I was so caught up in my own depression that I didn't realize that, on the East Coast, people still spoke about me, and speculated about my whereabouts. On November 4, 1981, Gorilla Monsoon showcased his skills as an investigative journalist with the following item in his weekly column in the *Philadelphia Journal:*

This week's column begins on a sad note. The wrestling world has been shocked by the death of former World Champion, Superstar Billy Graham, who died of cancer recently in his hometown, Paradise Valley, Arizona.

Although I had many controversial matches with Billy, he was always one of the more respected men in our business. He will surely be missed.

Gorilla might as well have been telling the truth. At night, when I'd wake up to get something to eat, I regularly fell down in the kitchen, smacking my head on the tile. Valerie would come running after me, using every fiber of her 113 pounds to drag me off the floor and sit me up.

"I want to die," I'd cry to her. "I can't take it anymore."

What I needed was a reason to live—a goal that I presumed could be attained by making one phone call to Vince McMahon Jr. But why couldn't I make that call?

CHAPTER SIXTEEN

WHATEVER HAPPENED TO SUPERSTAR BILLY GRAHAM?

No mercy in the desert in the Arizona sun
You either move, adapt or burn away
. . . Look at Billy Graham
His eyes are scorched with fire
And the ravages of every single ray

—"The Genius," Lanny Poffo, former pro wrestler

In 1982, Vince Jr. and his wife, Linda, purchased his father's company, then called the World Wrestling Federation. Vince was different from his father—who still maintained an advisory role in the organization—in a lot of ways. The elder McMahon was a diplomat, while Vince Jr. celebrated his rough edges. The old man adhered to the codes established by the wrestling promoters of his generation. To Vince Jr., the traditions cherished by men like Verne Gagne and Sam Muchnick were as obsolete as idol worship. Those promoters only existed, Vince believed, to be put out of business.

Yet both father and son had fond memories of Superstar Billy Graham. I'd made the McMahon family a lot of money, and they were sure that I could again.

As soon as Vince Jr. gave me the green light to return, I started loading up on steroids, tanning, and weaning myself off the downers and substituting speed. I reconciled with Brick, working out hard in his gym. By April 1982, when I debuted at the company's television tapings in Allentown, Pennsylvania, I was in great physical shape.

But mentally, I remained a wreck. I was still depressed about losing the title to Backlund, and mad at the company. So—instead of returning with the bleached blond hair and tie-dye, like Vince Jr. expected—I arrived with my head shaved, and a karate gimmick. I didn't explain my new appearance, but left it up to the fans to assume that I'd been with the monks and come back as a new, mystical figure. My *gi* was deliberately black—since I'd probably never win back the title, I wanted to wear the color of mourning.

Because I'd gone to the trouble of purchasing a *gi,* I threw a few weak karate thrusts at my first television opponent. As excited as the fans were to see me, they weren't buying my gimmick. It wasn't me, and I'd never taken a martial arts class. After winning the match, I kicked at the air, then froze in what I assumed was a karate stance.

From ringside, Vince Jr. announced, "There's a very big difference between this Graham and the Graham we knew some four and a half years ago." He was seething.

When we saw each other backstage, he and Pat Patterson—who did color commentary with McMahon, and played a large role in the company's booking—asked me to explain myself. "You know, Superstar," Vince said, "it would've helped if you told us what this gimmick was all about. We're trying to commentate this thing. You just walked out there, and we don't know what you are or what's going on."

> **Vince McMahon:** *This faux karate type thing was hard to believe. I think he could have devised something a little better. It seemed that, psychologically, he had broken down. He was a shell of what he was in his heyday. It reminded me of Johnny Unitas playing for the San Diego Chargers the year before he retired from the NFL. It was tough to watch.*

> **Paul Heyman:** *Nobody believed that this was Billy Graham. He looked dramatically different. Everybody thought, "Billy Graham really died, and this guy is replacing him."*

It was demoralizing to see that Bob Backlund was still the champion, and hadn't developed his personality since the day I left. As part of his campaign to modernize the company, Vince had ordered a new championship belt. Rather than place the older one in storage, he suggested that I desecrate the title in an angle. I wasn't going to have to fake that one—I really *did* want to destroy the belt.

While Backlund was wrestling during a TV taping, I appeared at ringside, watching the match and riling up the fans. Then I grabbed the belt from the timekeeper and began walking back to the dressing room. Backlund attempted to pursue me, but his opponent, Swede Hanson, held him back, and they started exchanging blows. The champ ultimately prevailed, rolling up his foe with a neck bridge for the pin. But now I began beating Backlund with the title belt until he collapsed on the canvas. Then I lifted up the belt and repeatedly smashed it against the arena floor.

It was very hard to tear apart; with all the leather and metal and rivets, we could only loosen it so much beforehand. I tugged on the pieces of the title, but nothing seemed to give. At this point, Vince came toward me, microphone in hand. But I hadn't accomplished my mission yet. I slammed the belt against the floor again, and managed to yank off the main insignia. Then I threw up my hands in disgust and left the broken treasure on the floor.

Mark Lamonica, aka Bubba Ray Dudley: I had respect for Bob Backlund as a child, the white-bread babyface who stood up to all the big, bad bullies. So I was really shocked when Superstar Billy Graham ripped his title. I had never seen anything like that. My God, this guy destroyed a belt! *After that, I couldn't get enough information about Superstar. I'd read old magazines, and look at pictures of when he was champion. He used to hold the title hanging down straight out in front of him. It was like he was taunting the fans: "Look what I have. Look what you wish you had. Look what you wish you could be." It was the kind of white heel heat I'd try to emulate in ECW. I was almost mad at myself for being too young to really remember him as champion.*

Once I exited the ringside area, Backlund crawled over to his battered title and lovingly lifted it off the ground. On his knees, he pondered the damaged possession, like a child pouting over a broken toy, then wept: "Why? *Why?*"

His manager, Arnold Skaaland—who'd been strategically placed with

Backlund to continue the link to Bruno—stood behind the champion and rubbed his head. It should have been a moment of heart-stirring emotion. But the World Wrestling Federation's hard-edged northeastern fans concluded that the champion looked like a weakling. In his subsequent matches, they peppered Backlund with taunts of "Crybaby."

Still, Backlund and I sold out the Garden—not once, but three times. Was it Backlund, or did I have some kind of magical hold on New York City? In our final encounter, special referee Swede Hanson refused to show solidarity with me as a fellow heel, and ruled the match in favor of Backlund. I attacked Swede, he turned babyface, and the two of us had a return match in Madison Square Garden.

But even this didn't make me happy. I knew that, like every other contender, I was looping through the World Wrestling Federation before being sent on my way. I became indifferent to my appearance, and began filling myself with Valium, Tuinal, Seconal, Codeine, Ativan, Demerol, Doriden, and Quaaludes. One of my regular suppliers was a Harrisburg, Pennsylvania, doctor who had access to the boys through his work on the state athletic commission.

My promos lacked fire. I'd look into the camera, dazed, with the Grand Wizard behind me. I still knew what to do on the stick. But there was little jive talk or inventiveness. Nothing resembled the old Superstar. He'd been left in the seventies.

In Hagerstown, Maryland, one night, I was so stoned in the ring that my partner, Don Muraco—not the most temperate guy himself—didn't want to tag me. When I finally got into the bout, I tried to compensate for my condition by overselling for Andre the Giant, bumping for his head butt, then flapping around like I was having an epileptic seizure. My spastic display ruined the flow of the match and diminished whatever believability we were trying to portray. In the car later on, I repeatedly mumbled apologies while Muraco blasted me with reprimands.

On another occasion, Gorilla Monsoon sent me home from a TV taping in Hamburg, Pennsylvania, because I was so impaired and anemic looking.

I call this period my "dance with death," because I was killing myself so publicly.

Tony Garea: *Billy kind of kept to himself at this stage, and away from everybody. But I think that's where you go when you fool with the synthetic.*

One of my few close friends was John Minton, aka Big John Studd, a former Killer Kowalski trainee listed at six-foot-ten and 364 pounds. Like me, Studd was an introspective guy who'd become overwhelmed by the availability of prescription medication. "Before I got into this business, the strongest drug I ever took was Tylenol," he admitted one night in the dressing room in White Plains, New York. "Now look. . . ."

He opened a bag full of speed, sleeping pills, and pain medication.

In late spring, I received word that another dear friend, Peter Maivia, was confined to a hospital in Hawaii with inoperable cancer. I phoned him and tried to invoke the old days. But neither of us could bring back that long-departed energy. In the middle of our conversation, Peter began coughing, then said, "Brutha, I'm not feeling too good." After a few more coughs, his wife, Lia, took the phone and said good-bye. Two days later, on June 13, 1982, the High Chief passed away at age forty-seven.

The loss darkened my mood even more. By contrast, my periodic traveling buddies, Curt Hennig—later billed as "Mr. Perfect"—and "Playboy" Buddy Rose, seemed to find everything hilarious. When we'd drive through aging mill towns in upstate New York, I'd take note of the architecture of the beautiful Catholic cathedrals.

"Architecture?" Hennig would cackle. "Why would we wanna look at architecture?"

After I'd made a particularly large purchase, the three of us were watching the news in my hotel room. A disturbing story came on about a group of children dying, and I began to sob, "Children? Oh, my God. This is a tragedy."

Hennig and Rose exchanged bewildered smiles, nodded at one another, and left.

Certainly, the sedatives had added to my despondency. But I believe that I was also bemoaning the state of my relationship with my own kids.

I still have drawings that Capella made at that time—with me in the ring with the karate gimmick. But we didn't have the closeness I desired. I blame my drug use, as well as the influence of her mother. For instance, as she grew older, Capella told me that she hated Bob Dylan—even though she'd enjoyed listening to him with me when she was little. Today, she's a big Tom Petty fan. But she won't listen to Dylan. How can you like Tom Petty—whose music is totally influenced by Bob Dylan—but not Dylan himself?

As foolish as this sounds, I've always interpreted this attitude as a personal rejection.

Capella Flaherty: *That's very funny. I understand how my dad could see it that way. My mother was very vocal about the way she felt about Bob Dylan's music: "I couldn't stand it when he put that*

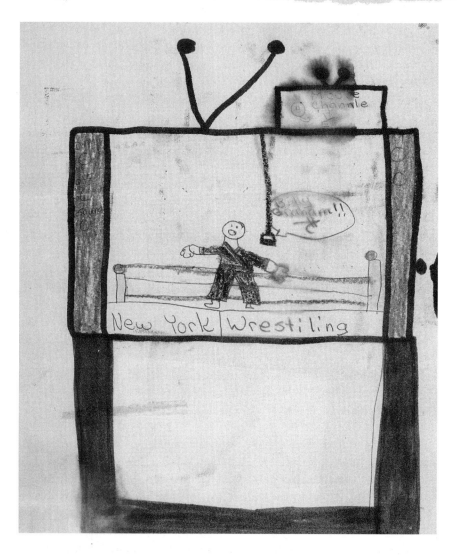

on. How can anyone listen to that clanging voice? That's not music. Elvis Presley—that's *music.*"

Music is a huge thing in my life. I listen to all genres of music. But—regardless of what my mother has told me, or what my father has told me—I don't like Bob Dylan's music.

Honestly, I think the drugs were a more serious problem in our relationship. My brother and I would always be excited when my dad visited because we didn't get to see him that much. He'd come over to hang out, and just fall asleep on us. We'd turn around from watching TV, and his head would be tossed over.

One time, I was talking with him on the phone, and in mid-sentence, he just passed out. He didn't wake up for a half hour, and I stayed on the phone the whole time. I was like, "What's wrong with my dad?" Finally he woke up, but the whole thing freaked me out. I was old enough to figure out that there was more to it than just being tired.

I loved him so much. I looked at him, and it would be pure love. If he wanted to be with another woman, I could understand that. My mom was not the right person for my dad. Valerie was that person. But for him to act the way he was acting, it really hurt.

Joe Miluso: *There were times when my dad wasn't around that I'd actually hang out with Valerie. She'd take me and my friends to the movies or the arcade. Even when my dad was gone, Valerie was there. It was like somebody didn't leave.*

Like my father, I was a big kid—I'm now six-foot-two, and weigh 255 pounds—and I wanted to play football at Burbank High. I was asked to join the football team. But I couldn't join because of my heart condition. The doctors wouldn't sign a release. I wanted to join the marines. I couldn't do that because of my heart. So I kind of thought for a while that my heart condition came about because of my dad's steroid use. I'm not saying that's true. But as I grew up, I felt resentful. I felt that what my father did for his career ruined what I wanted to do in my own life.

One of the side effects of my steroid use was a low sperm count. This was catastrophic to Valerie, who wanted to have a large family. But I'd been a steroid user for so long that I didn't want to stop—especially now when I had a job again in the World Wrestling Federation.

Valerie Coleman: *Wayne would ask me to inject him with steroids. I felt that, by doing that, I was contributing to his infertility. That was incredibly painful for me, but his drug use made him very unpredictable and intimidating, so I relented. It got to the point where I would purposely jab the needle into his scar tissue because I knew that there were a lot of nerves in there. I'd think, "All he cares about is his physique, not whether we have babies." I did it like I was stabbing him with a dagger.*

Sometimes I'd think to myself, "Whatever happened to Superstar Billy Graham?" This thought was never stronger than when I wrestled Rocky

Johnson in Madison Square Garden. It didn't seem that long ago that we were both starting out in Los Angeles and San Francisco. Now, Rocky looked even better than he did then. When we'd lock up, he'd occasionally shoot me a questioning glance. Was he curious about the next spot, or did he wonder how I'd become a gaunt apparition taking apathetic bumps?

After that particular show, Valerie and I returned to our room at the Ramada Inn on Eighth Avenue, at the far end of a still-seedy Times Square. A group of wrestlers were having a party in the next room, and I could hear Stan Stasiak, intruding through the walls in a booming voice like Ox Baker.

Suddenly I said to Valerie, "I have to get out of here."

At 3:00 A.M., we packed up and left the hotel, shooting up to Massachusetts, where I had a match the next night in Boston. At daybreak we pulled into a hotel in Worcester, where I poured a random handful of downers into my hand, washed them down, and walked over to McDonald's to get breakfast.

Valerie was still unpacking when I returned to the room with the food and sat down on the edge of the bed. I'd just started eating when I slumped over and fell, lodged between the bed and the wall, unconscious.

> *Valerie Coleman: I had to clear the food out of his throat because he was choking. I called the front desk. "My husband's having a drug overdose!" I shouted. "He's dying!"*
>
> *It so happened that the desk clerk that morning was a registered nurse, filling in for a friend at the motel. She wasn't supposed to be there, but there she was. She came into the room, and the two of us pulled Wayne out from between the bed and the wall. When we placed him on the bed, he wasn't breathing. He had no heartbeat, no nothing. She had to straddle him because he was still so big, and brought her hands together like a sledgehammer.*
>
> *"Come back," she yelled, beating his chest. "Don't you leave. Don't you die on me. Come back!" I always believed in divine intervention, and now I knew—beyond a shadow of a doubt—that it was true. The Lord provided just the right person when we needed her the most. There are no coincidences.*

Finally, the paramedics arrived and strapped me onto a gurney. I was still unconscious, but I remember this feeling of looking down at the whole scene from above. I saw the medical technicians pounding on my chest as they carried me down the winding stairwell, turning the hard corner onto the main floor. It was a definite out-of-body experience.

I was conscious when I arrived at the hospital, where a nurse poured a charcoal-like fluid down my throat to make me vomit, and absorb what was left in my stomach. As always, Valerie—the strongest person I've ever known—was right by my side, cleaning up my mess. It was obvious that I wasn't going to make the show in Boston that night.

"Tell Vince that I had an allergic reaction," I told the doctor. He didn't even hesitate before accommodating my request.

The doctor was a mark.

I was discharged a few hours later, and Valerie and I went back to the hotel, where she placed a call to Howard Finkel. Besides being the World Wrestling Federation's most visible ring announcer, Howard was one of Vince's right-hand men. Everyone was very kind to her; I think they felt sorry that this beautiful young woman had fallen in love with a guy with such serious addictions. Howard, in particular, was extremely compassionate, and did his best to comfort her with his words.

I spent the next three days sleeping.

Valerie Coleman: Thankfully, I didn't use drugs or drink. If I had, I really don't know if Wayne would be alive today. Staying straight allowed me to be there for him and to get him the help he needed. Believe me, there were many times when I was tempted; it would have been nice to escape for a while. But I had seen enough to know that pills were not the answer to my problems. And besides, it just isn't my nature. I've never been big on taking the easy way out.

The New Jersey State Police had a reputation for being particularly aggressive in searching for drugs. So I either drove out of my way to avoid the New Jersey Turnpike or rented a room at the Ramada in New York and filled the drawers with industrial amounts of sedatives before leaving for a show in Pennsylvania or Maryland.

After a match with Salvatore Bellomo at the Capitol Center in Landover, Maryland, I found an old motel between Baltimore and Washington. I had a day to kill before my last shot at Madison Square Garden, and decided to ingest some drugs I'd brought and just sleep in the room. At one point, I stumbled into the hallway to go to the Coke machine and, as I was entering my room again, started to feel lightheaded. Falling forward, I grabbed onto the bathroom door for balance and ended up pulling it into my chest, leaving a giant gash. I plunged onto the bathroom floor, solidly wedged between the door and the commode.

Looking back, I think about how this would have been a pathetic way to die—from a drug overdose, draped over a commode.

This time, the paramedics had to come with firefighters to chop the door away with axes so I could be transported into the ambulance. I woke up on the operating table to face some very pointed questions from a female doctor.

"Why did you try to commit suicide?"

"What do you mean?"

"You had enough drugs in you to kill three men. Why do you need so much Valium?"

Now I was feeling defiant. "Because I'm a hyper guy. I need the Valium to tone me down."

"What about the codeine?"

"I'm a professional wrestler. I'm always hurting. I'm in pain."

"And the sleeping pills?"

"I can't sleep."

She shook her head. "Well, we believe that you were trying to kill yourself. And we're going to have to keep you overnight for observation."

That wasn't going to work for me. "You know what? I have to wrestle in Madison Square Garden on Monday. I'm leaving for New York tonight."

I sat up, glaring at the medical team, and yanked out my IVs. Blood shot onto the floor as I hopped off the table, and Security rushed in.

"What are *you guys* gonna do? I'm leaving."

"I can't authorize that," the doctor intervened. "If you're going to leave, you'll have to sign a release, indemnifying us of whatever happens to you later."

"Well, give me a pen," I snapped. "I'll sign it."

I returned to my room—still overturned and littered with splinters—grabbed my gear, and caught a flight to New York. At the Ramada, I hurried into the room I'd rented, and pulled open the bottom dresser drawer to take inventory of my drugs.

Everything was gone; the drawer was empty.

I looked around. The bed was made. The towels were folded. Nothing had been disturbed. It didn't seem like I'd been burglarized. So who took the drugs? In my mind, I began listing other people I knew at the hotel. I stopped at Ernie Roth, who, like me, frequently camped out at the Ramada for extended periods.

"The Wizard."

I stomped downstairs and knocked on his door. "Ernie, have you seen my drugs?"

Beneath his toupee, Ernie's face twisted into a cockeyed smile. *"Biiiillly,"* he replied in a nicotine-scorched voice. "Of course. I heard about what happened to you in Maryland, so I called the manager and got your medicine."

He wouldn't say "drugs." "I didn't want the police coming to your room and finding anything."

I wondered why the police in New York would suddenly appear at the Ramada over an incident that occurred three states away.

He opened his dresser, and I reached in. Everything was accounted for.

"I'm going to take these back. Okay, Ernie?"

Ernie's face dropped. "I was just protecting you. I didn't want the police to get them. Not only would it be bad for you, but it would be bad for the boys. It would be bad for the business."

"I appreciate that, Wiz."

This was getting ludicrous. How much longer could I live this way? My World Wrestling Federation run was about to end. After that, the future was uncertain.

For the past several months, Big John Studd and I had analyzed the circumstances of our lives, and developed a kinship that would last until his untimely death in 1995. But in 1983, everyone assumed that I would be the one to pass first. After my last shot with the company in Madison Square Garden, John watched me pack my bag in the locker room, then hugged me with tears streaming down his face.

"Please, Billy," he begged. "Take care of yourself."

"I'll see you soon, brother," I said. But I wasn't sure if I believed that. I was out of control, and frightened that next time, I really *would* die. I closed the locker room door behind me and burst into sobs, walking down the hallway to the elevator by myself.

I felt like I was walking the last mile.

CHAPTER SEVENTEEN

PASSION, COMPASSION

No man is rich enough to buy back his past.

—Oscar Wilde

Within months of my departure, Bob Backlund's championship run came to an end. Vince had big plans, and installed the Iron Sheik as transitional champion. Four weeks later, on January 23, 1984, Hulk Hogan charged into the ring at Madison Square Garden and dethroned the Iranian bad man. For the next nine years, on and off, *Hulkmania* would rule the World Wrestling Federation—thanks in part to a gimmick Hogan himself admitted that he took from me.

I wasn't in any position to enjoy it.

Valerie and I drove down to Florida to see her family after my World Wrestling Federation run, then started working our way cross-country to Arizona. On my own, without consulting a doctor, I began cutting down on my drugs—I'd take large doses of one, fewer doses of another, and eliminate other pills completely. At one point, I spoke with a doctor, who told me about an incredible deal on Ativan—a much stronger sedative than Valium.

"I'm gonna pass," I told him. "I'm trying to get clean."

The doctor appeared to be livid about the possibility of losing a good customer. So much for this doctor's creed of "First do no harm."

In New Mexico, just before the Arizona border on I-10, I began to hallucinate. Pulling over at a rest stop, I attempted to use the restroom. But it was dark outside, with mobs of people around, and I couldn't see the door. There were spots in front of my eyes, and flashes of light. Everything was confused.

We managed to drive further until we stopped at a little town near Tucson. I was exhausted, and decided to get a motel room. Valerie stayed in the car while I went into the office to register.

The clerk looked like he'd been roused from his sleep—it was about 2:30 A.M.—and wanted to get this over with quickly. He handed me a pen and asked me to fill out a registration card, but I couldn't. I couldn't speak, either. I was stuck, and just stood there, feeling frozen in time.

I'd imagine that this wasn't the first encounter that the clerk had had with someone materializing out of the desert in this type of state. "Is there anyone else with you who can do this?" he asked tersely.

I was lucid enough to get Valerie, and have her register for us.

Valerie Coleman: When we got into the room, Wayne couldn't undress himself. I had to undress him, put him down in the bed, go back to our car, and get the rest of our stuff. I'd been through this before, and knew what to do because this time I understood what was happening. I sat on top of him, then held him down so he wouldn't fall out of the bed while he had another grand mal seizure. Once he was safe, I called the paramedics.

The funny thing was that by the time the medical technicians arrived, the seizure had passed and I felt fine. I was sitting up on the bed, chatting with them. I seemed straight. Valerie was straight. They didn't understand why they'd been called.

But I did. When they left, Valerie flushed all my drugs down the toilet. The next morning, I checked myself into rehab in Phoenix.

I remained in the facility for ten days. I had to go to group meetings, but didn't participate—I'm not big on sharing in large settings. One night, I developed an enormous craving for junk food and left, cruising right past the front desk and into the street. I came back a few minutes later, after finding a 7-Eleven, with a bag full of candy bars.

A few days after my discharge, I was sitting in a chair, relaxing, when my hand suddenly reached for the phone. Automatically, I dialed the doctor I knew in Pennsylvania and placed an order, like a dog returning to its own vomit.

For a while, I was a functioning drug addict. And I even had money left over from my karate run. It had been a long time since Vince Sr. promised Ernie Ladd that I would be among those receiving championship payoffs—and, as with Backlund and his scheduled title win, Vince never went back on his word. Even now. As a result, I returned to Phoenix with about $30,000.

With that kind of cash, I purchased a nice white Cadillac, drove to Burbank, and rented a room at the Safari Motel, where Valerie and I spent a very enjoyable summer with my kids.

In October 1983, I returned to Minnesota and Verne Gagne. This was just before Vince Jr. snatched up Hogan and Jesse Ventura, and it looked like the AWA would never go out of business. Verne tried to resurrect the Superstar Billy Graham name, but it was pretty hard to do that with a drug-ravaged guy in a karate gimmick.

> *Jesse "The Body" Ventura: I was going out to do an interview, and Verne turned to Billy and said, "Hey, Graham, listen to this. You can hear somebody do Superstar better than Superstar." It was meant as a low blow because Billy ran off to New York and became famous there. But I told Billy later, "Take that as a compliment because I wouldn't be where I am if it wasn't for you. Whatever I achieve, feel that you are part of it."*

By November, the storms were pounding Minnesota. We had four and a half feet of snow on the ground by Thanksgiving—*and it wasn't even winter yet!* With the temperatures brutal outside, I retreated indoors—and into myself, keeping Valerie as isolated as ever.

Verne had incorporated Phoenix into the territory by now, and one night a group of my old friends came to a show to watch me wrestle "Jumping" Jim Brunzell.

Verne's son, Greg Gagne, was doing the finishes for the matches that night. I'd always liked Greg, and I hope the feeling was mutual. "This is your hometown," he told me before the show. "Do you want to do a disqualification or something, and not get your shoulders pinned?"

"It doesn't matter," I answered. "Pin me." I was completely indifferent.

By Christmas I was ready to leave, but agreed to fulfill my AWA commitments through January. On the way out, I was asked to do a job for Billy Robinson. How appropriate, I thought, losing to a man I detested, while

Valerie was all alone, stuck in a frozen house in the middle of a snowbank somewhere.

Valerie and I went back to Tampa to escape the deep freeze and give her some time with her family, while I decided to try my luck with Eddie Graham. The territory was going through some changes that I couldn't comprehend. Vince Jr.'s aggressive expansion of the World Wrestling Federation had all the regional promoters uneasy. Dusty, the Florida booker, seemed preoccupied, and was noncommittal when I asked about a job. Eddie Graham was in the hospital with a very serious infection, and I stopped in to visit him there.

The promoter's face had lost a lot of its gleam; as with Dusty, there were issues weighing on his mind. But he lit up when I walked into the room. My gimmick brother and I joked and small-talked, enjoying each other's company, before Eddie asked, "When are you coming back to work for us?"

"I don't know. I spoke to Dusty about it, and—"

Eddie waved off the rest of my comment, grabbed the telephone, and told Dusty to make a spot for me.

Compared to the AWA, traveling around Florida was infinitely more bearable. From Tampa, the promotion rented a plane called "Old Blue" so we could make our shots in Fort Lauderdale, Key West, and other south Florida locations, and fly home the same night. On Wednesday night, Lester Welch, a promotional partner in Florida, personally flew us in his aircraft to go to the matches at Convention Hall in Miami Beach.

On one of these Miami Beach flights, I was suddenly jolted by the vibration of a sputtering engine. I was seated next to Kevin Sullivan, and across the aisle from manager Sir Oliver Humperdink. Outlaw Ron Bass was in the shotgun seat next to Lester.

"What's happening?" Ron asked, as the plane began to drop.

"We're losing a fuel pump," our pilot answered.

I had a death grip on my arm rest. Sullivan turned to me with his eyes bulging, and muttered in his Boston accent, "This is probably it, Superstar."

My heart was racing and my clothes soaked with sweat as we continued to lose altitude. I looked over at Humperdink, and noted that he resembled a man in the electric chair, poised for the first jolt.

There was a suspension of reality, a suspension of time. My ears hummed with the racing of the engines. We made a wild turn in midair, dropping fast as we headed back to the airport in Tampa. Through the pilot's window, I could see ambulances and fire trucks, with sirens flashing, lining the runway. We barreled onto the tarmac and rolled at least 300 or 400 yards, as the second engine conked out.

A few more seconds in the air, and this would have been a tragedy.

Our airplane was towed to a private terminal, where we wobbled out of the plane and into the lobby. There, all of us dropped to our knees—but not to pray or give thanks to the Lord. Every wrestler on board dumped his pills on the floor, as we kneeled in a circle like a group of kids playing marbles. Then, each of us snatched up the sedatives and downed them, calming our nerves before boarding a commercial flight to Miami.

Despite my frame of mind, Dusty treated me like the star I'd been, putting me in a program with Billy Jack Haynes, a powerhouse from Oregon believed to possess infinite potential. We did an arm-wrestling angle, culminating with me slamming the table onto his wrist and hand. Then we went into the locker room, where Dusty mixed up some plaster and placed Billy Jack in a cast.

He wore the cast in public for five weeks—it was still like that in 1984—and the two of us engaged in a successful series of Full Nelson vs. Full Nelson matches. I beat Haynes for the Florida championship in June, and held it for about a month.

But backstage, there was always a kind of tension in the air. Before a big show in Tampa one night, Dusty announced that he was leaving to become booker for Jim Crockett Jr.—who, like Vince, had designs of expanding nationally out of his Charlotte-based territory. Former NWA champion Dory Funk Jr. was taking over for Rhodes that night.

Dusty exiled himself on the spot.

If it had been a few years earlier, I would have sought out Dusty and asked about his thought process. But there were clearly things that he didn't wish to discuss. Eddie Graham, in the meantime, was not approachable, either. When I'd see him backstage, he was depressed and often intoxicated—a very sad and perplexing sight, given Eddie's reputation as a well-organized businessman and local civic leader. I later heard rumors that he was about to be indicted for real estate fraud, and there was a high probability of prison time.

Immediately upon Dusty's departure, business declined. For example, during one week in May 1984, I earned $1,125. During the same period in October—after Dusty was already in Charlotte—I received $75 apiece for St. Augustine and Fort Meyers, $100 for Fort Lauderdale, Miami Beach, and Fort Pierce, and $150 for West Palm Beach and Tampa—or $750 for a seven-day week.

In total, I was paid $23,883 in 1984.

Yet once Kevin Sullivan replaced Dory as booker, I participated in some of the most satisfying story lines of my career. Sullivan portrayed himself as the head of a demonic clique that included, at various times, "Purple Haze" Mark Lewin, Jake "The Snake" Roberts, and myself—all individuals who'd embraced the influence of the Prince of Darkness, as both a work and a shoot.

Kevin Sullivan: *I used a lot of terminology that suggested Satanism. One valet was the Fallen Angel. I'd cover the face of another one, The Lock, to keep out the "forces of light." When The Lock teamed with Luna Vachon, I called them the Daughters of Darkness.*

The funny thing was that I never used the word "Satan." People just took that on their own. I'd make references to the Chairman of the Board and Abudadeen, but that name was based on a Hindu fertility god I heard about during a trip to Malaysia.

John Sutton, aka Sir Oliver Humperdink: *I was the manager of this group, and we wanted to do something with snakes in the ring, big, long pythons. There was a guy in Miami who had snakes, and we used his. But Superstar didn't know about the snake bit beforehand. He was actually afraid of snakes. When we put a snake around his neck, he grabbed that thing and had such a tight grip that I thought he was going to kill it.*

After Dusty left, we needed someone strong on the babyface side, so Kevin decided to turn Superstar. The fans already loved him. Even as a heel, they loved him. I don't know if they identified with his street lingo or the fact that he was a free spirit, but they loved him.

Kevin Sullivan: *Billy and I were working as a Tag Team. We did something where I rolled out of the ring and bumped into The Lock. It was like the second time I bumped into her in two weeks. I slapped her in the face. She wanted me to lay it in, and I slapped her so hard that the referee, Bill Alfonso, jumped out of the ring, and yelled, "That's too much." The next thing I knew, Billy was on my back, saying, "What's going on here?" I went to slap The Lock again, Billy grabbed my hand, and the place went silent.*

The angle had been going toward the Windhams (Blackjack Mulligan and his son, Barry Windham). We were really pushing it so the fans were thinking, "All right, this is the week that the Windhams are going to rescue the girl." And we turned it on them. No one expected Billy to rescue her instead.

He turned around, and I threw a chair at him and hit him, blood streaming down. It was such a perfect shot that it couldn't be duplicated. We hung Billy by his karate belt from the ropes. The fans who thought they were smart—we caught them for that minute.

Then Billy went away for a few weeks. He went to Arizona, and took these pictures in the desert. Not video, but still pictures—we used the still pictures on TV with voiceover. It had never been done in the wrestling business before. His arms are stretched out, like he's crucifying himself in the desert, to purge himself of his sins, and of Kevin Sullivan. When he came back, he was a huge babyface. We did big business all over.

Subliminal messages were very much a part of this presentation. Billy's wearing white now. He's fighting for the sins of the world. He's walking in the light. When you have blood on those white tights, it's symbolic, like the devil is recrucifying Christ.

On January 20, 1985, Eddie Graham ended his internal agony with a fatal gunshot. I didn't even have the chance to attend his funeral. My babyface turn had given me renewed prominence in professional wrestling, and Dusty invited me up to Charlotte to work with him.

Once I arrived, though, I felt like just another slab of beef. The company turned me heel, and gave me Paul Jones as a manager. Jones had been a regional star in the South, but he was not a great talker. In fact, I felt that the partnership reduced my stature rather than improved it.

After the WWWF and Florida, I felt disconnected in Charlotte, not necessarily from the boys, but from the system—and the territory as a whole. Along with the Mid-Atlantic states, Crockett had become a power broker in the Atlanta territory, after taking control of the valuable two-hour Saturday-night slot on Ted Turner's "Superstation," TBS. That meant that I had to deal with Ole Anderson, the periodic booker in Atlanta, and a belligerent, obnoxious presence in the dressing room. Once, prior to a show, I was standing on the second tier of the arena, and Ole crept behind me, scooped me up, and pretended that he was going to bodyslam me over the railing. Maybe I would have laughed if Ole were my friend. But I had no time for that man, period.

Fortunately, I had Abdullah around again to keep an eye out for me. Before a squash match on TBS, Abdullah claimed to have heard some gossip about my opponent refusing to sell for me. There was no validation that this was true. Why would a jobber take it upon himself to sit down on me before I delivered a backbreaker? But paranoia runs deep in the wrestling fraternity, and Abdullah was adamant.

"Change the finish," he insisted. "Beat him with a head butt. He can't mess up a head butt."

So, when the time came to end the match, I called a head butt. The jobber sold it well, and I won without any complications.

With Vince buying up syndicated time slots and using cable television to muscle the other territories off the airwaves, a group of promoters—led by Gagne and Crockett—banded together into a short-lived group called Pro Wrestling USA. Their goal: pooling talent to allay the World Wrestling Federation's national incursion. At the coalition's first TV taping in Memphis, it was obvious that the various anti-Vince camps were not united. The story lines were arbitrarily thrown together. The matches were rushed. The Gagne and Crockett factions were competing for air time. In the chaos, I was given Jimmy "The Mouth of the South" Hart as a manager, and didn't even cut a promo. It's too bad because Jimmy could have been another Wizard for me—if we'd had the time to mesh.

Back in the Charlotte territory, Jimmy Valiant was calling himself the "Boogie Woogie Man," a biker-hippie type babyface with a ZZ Top beard and backward trucker cap, who'd dance with fans, and occasionally kiss a redneck for a laugh. The two of us were wrestling each other in South Carolina one night in a beaten-up field house with creaking stairways, spiderwebs, layers of filth in the dressing room, and a grimy mat. Jimmy was often in an altered frame of mind, and he proved it here by deciding to blade while I held him in a reverse chinlock. There was absolutely no logic to this—who ever bled from a chinlock? But Jimmy wanted to do it. When he reached up to cut himself, though, he missed by about half a foot, and sliced my nose instead.

"Star," he muttered, "you're bleeding on me."

"I know, brother," I replied.

Even though the blood was mine, Jimmy now had the juice that he wanted.

After the match, I told Valiant, "You just cut me wide open for no apparent reason. How can you miss your own forehead?"

Jimmy hugged me and apologized. "Star," he explained, "I just wanted to make that comeback." Clearly, nothing made sense at this time with the "Boogie Woogie Man."

"It's okay," I answered, still bleeding. "But how'd you manage to cut me like that?"

"Oh, I started using a scalpel."

"A surgeon's scalpel?!"

"Yeah, it's much sharper than a razor blade. And it won't leave as much scar tissue because it's a small incision."

With Paul Jones in my corner, I'd been teaming with the Barbarian, a tough Tongan guy, around the horn, but never had the feeling that the fans were invested in me. So one day I walked into Jim Crockett's office with an announcement: "It's time to go back to who I am. I want to do my old gimmick. The tie-dye, the promos, everything else."

Crockett nodded. "You know, Superstar," he said, "that's the greatest news I ever heard. When Dusty brought you in, that's who I thought I was getting."

Obviously, Crockett didn't keep up with wrestling outside his territory. But he was ready to put his faith in me.

"I need $5,000 to make this thing happen," I added.

Crockett was unfazed. "That's fine, Superstar."

He called the accounting department and authorized a check. Then he let me leave, without any type of notice, to work on my gimmick.

Capella was about fourteen now, with a highly developed artistic sense, and she and I prowled high-end boutiques all over L.A., picking up scarves, earrings, and new ring attire.

"I need a new look," I told Valerie, and we came up with a two-tone goatee.

After a few weeks, I returned to Charlotte, met up with the Barbarian and Paul Jones, and headed for a TV taping. "On the way back," I told Paul, "I'm going to have to ride with someone else."

"Why?"

"I'm turning babyface."

When it was my turn to wrestle that night, I came out to George Thorogood's "Bad to the Bone"—it was Valerie's brother Steve's favorite song—with my tie-dye, the sunglasses, the scarves, and the earrings. Automatically, the people were cheering. Crockett had seen me in my gimmick earlier in the night, and ordered a five-second match. As soon as I stepped into the ring, my opponent charged toward me. I hit him with a boot to the stomach and, when he bent forward, picked him up in a backbreaker. The bell rang, and the referee raised my hand to a huge pop.

I was reborn. From ringside, I could hear Dusty selling my revised image in his color commentary: "He's back! The Superstar is back!" I could tell that this was a shoot; he was genuinely excited for me.

Dusty Rhodes: Billy went into the closet and brought out the old Superstar Billy Graham. In that era, the bodybuilding types in wrestling were all copying Superstar. But he was the original. Now, it was like he was never gone. It was still there.

My first rivalry under my old persona would be with my former Tag Team partner, the Barbarian. And since I was in the South, I was able to cut an evangelistic promo. "The Superstar got down on his knees and said his prayers," I began, sounding like Oral Roberts. "And I said, 'Dear Lord Jesus, thank you for the food in my belly. Thank you for the clothes on my back. And thank you for the shelter over my head, even though it's a shack. And thank you for forgiving me for all my sins. But, dear Lord, there's one sin I haven't done yet you have to forgive me for. And that's the sin of what I'll do to the Barbarian.'"

Ric Flair: I liked the old Superstar. I thought he did great in Charlotte. But I remember watching one of his interviews and noticing that one of his arms was atrophied, and a little bit smaller than the other. As a friend, I told him to turn that arm away from the camera the next time.

I loved listening to Flair's promos. They were the most believable interviews in the business because of his energy and the fact that he probably believed his words while delivering them. There was never a stammer, never a second take during pretaped segments. He put his whole soul into every promo every time.

I also loved the interviews I could now do alongside my new Tag Team partner, Jimmy Valiant. "We not only got passion, but we got *com*passion," I declared on one broadcast, like Jesse Jackson at the Democratic Convention. "Passion! Compassion! To the soul! To the bone!"

Pentecostals like to say that when someone's personality is compatible with yours, you bear witness to his spirit. Well, Jimmy and I definitely bore witness to each other.

"Me and Jimmy Valiant," I enunciated before an encounter with the Midnight Express and their manager, Jim Cornette, "we love the sick, the afflicted, the lame. We love the ones who can't hear us. We love the ones who are blind and can't see us. We love all God's children. But the Midnight Express and Jim Cornette are so low that if a snake crawled across the top of him, and he looked up and saw the dew on the snake's belly, he'd say, 'That dew looks like the stars in the Milky Way.' That's low."

Regrettably, my payoffs were not as invigorating as my promos. In fact, I only earned $22,902 in 1985—less than my salary the year before. The situation was so dire that, much to Valerie's dismay and heartbreak, I pawned our wedding rings. And before a TV taping in Atlanta, I slipped out of a cab, promising to return with the fare. I expected the driver to leave. Instead, he angrily trudged through the building. Dusty was in a meeting with the talent when a production assistant entered the room and pulled him aside.

Dusty nodded sternly as the assistant spoke, then turned sharply to me: "You stiffed the cab downstairs?"

"You know why, brother," I said. "I didn't have any money."

In front of the boys, Dusty pulled a $50 bill out of a money clip and threw it onto a table. "Go down and pay the cab," he scoffed.

It was one of my most humiliating experiences in professional wrestling. But—while I was justified in resenting the way that I was compensated—I couldn't really blame Dusty for his reaction. What I'd done was an insult to him and the Turner company. There was something haywire in the way that I was conducting my life.

Depression set in, and I was soon back to my abusive ways. My drug of choice was Ativan. I'd begun taking work on indie cards—shows unaffiliated with any of the major wrestling organizations. Before one event in New Jersey, the promoter brought me to a local radio station to hype my appearance. The entire staff gathered around me, reminiscing about my matches with Bruno and Dusty and Putski. But midway through the interview, I began to crave some Ativan. I'd run out of my supply and was experiencing withdrawal symptoms, stuttering through answers and seeing lights flash in my head. I was on the verge of another seizure.

"We have to stop," I told the interviewer. "I need to go to the doctor."

I told the secretary at the radio station that I'd run out of medication, and she called a local doctor to write me a prescription. The promoter drove me to the physician's office, then a pharmacy.

"Oh, I'm sorry," the druggist said, when he looked at the script, "I don't have the strength that you need."

"It's okay," I replied, shaking. "Just give me more tablets, and I'll double up my dosage."

"I'm sorry, sir. I can't really do that."

I could feel the withdrawal indicators worsening and began to argue, becoming more erratic and rageful with each sentence. Eventually the pharmacist relented, and I tossed some pills in my mouth right in the store, with everyone watching. Once the feeling of normalcy returned, I was mortified. An hour earlier, the staff at the radio station thought that I was the coolest guy in the world. Now they'd go home to their friends and families, and talk about how "sad" I'd become. They'd witnessed Superstar Billy Graham going through drug withdrawal.

Yet it was a thrill to wrestle in New Jersey, in the heart of World Wrestling Federation country. Everybody in the high school gymnasium had grown up with me, including my opponent, Bam Bam Bigelow. Bigelow was relatively new to the business, and euphoric about working with the man who defeated Bruno. "Whatever you want in the match, I'll do," he told me.

I opted for an entertaining brawl. I pulled Bigelow onto the arena floor, grabbed a microphone cord, put it in his hand, and wrapped it around my own throat. Bam Bam was shocked. He couldn't figure out how he'd ended up choking me.

We continued battling on the floor. "Superstar," he said, "throw me into the wall."

"How about the door," I mumbled back to him. "It's more flexible."

"No," he insisted. "The wall."

I slung him by the arm, and Bigelow took off from mid-court like a sprinter out of the blocks—so fast that I could barely keep up with him. He hit the wall full force, then bounced back at me. I grabbed him, throwing a couple of gimmicked rabbit punches to his sides, and whispered, "I'm putting you over."

"But that's not the finish."

"I'm rearranging it."

I laid down for Bigelow, exhilarated by the noise of the crowd, with its northeastern accent and attitude. For a brief moment, I flashed back to 1977, and I liked how it felt. Would I ever feel that way again? I wouldn't know until I returned to the World Wrestling Federation.

CHAPTER EIGHTEEN

"I KNEW HE WAS A HULKAMANIAC"

I wasted time, and now doth time waste me

—William Shakespeare

Vince McMahon Sr. had already died when the Good Doctor showed up in the World Wrestling Federation for the very last time. In 1985, Vince Jr. brought in Jerry Graham for an interview on *Tuesday Night Titans,* a sports entertainment version of *The Tonight Show.* Nothing really scandalous occurred, but Jerry wasn't asked back, either.

Fortunately, Vince wasn't done with all the members of the fictional Graham clan. When I called him in the early part of 1986, he invited me up to his office, greeting me like an old friend. Vince asked me if "those pythons" were back, and I took my shirt off and hit some poses. I'd been training hard for the past few months in the event of such a request. Vince gave me not only a September starting date, but a $10,000 advance.

The two of us spoke about the state of the industry. The World Wrestling Federation was now marketing tons of merchandise, incorporating celebrities into story lines, and leading the rest of the sports and entertainment fields in Pay-Per-View technology. "How have you taken it this far?" I questioned.

"I keep giving the people something fresh. I bring in new talent, or talent they haven't seen in a while, like yourself, and just work really hard."

I couldn't wait to get on board, and intentionally neglected to inform Vince that I was a little worried about my left hip. There was really no need, I thought. I'd experienced the first twinge of pain there in 1983, told myself that I had some type of strained tendon, and tried to push it out of my mind. When the pain was particularly bothersome, I deadened it with cortisone and went about my business.

That's what I'd done in Florida, and that's what I'd done in Charlotte. I didn't want to imagine that it would be any different in the World Wrestling Federation—even though, deep inside, I had an uneasy feeling.

Valerie and I moved out to Burbank, near my kids, and began preparing for my return. By now, I was feeling a continuous, intense burning sensation in my left hip. During a visit to an orthopedic surgeon, I received some shocking news that I didn't want to hear.

"You need a hip replacement."

This sounded like something out of *The Six Million Dollar Man*—science fiction. I didn't know that this type of medical technology existed.

"A hip replacement?" I asked. "What does that mean?"

"It means you need your hip replaced, a total hip replacement—the socket, the ball, everything. You've worn your hip out. You're walking with bone on bone."

I couldn't believe the timing of this. How could I have a hip replacement before my World Wrestling Federation return? I needed to get a second opinion.

But the other surgeon, Dr. Lawrence Dorr, reached the identical conclusion. I was suffering from avascular necrosis, or as he put it, "the death of a bone"—more specifically, my hip joint. And he had a reason why I'd ended up in this quandary.

"It's the steroids," he said. "They've eroded your joints."

I shook my head. "I think it's from all the bumps I've taken."

"It's the steroids," Dorr repeated. "And you're going to have to stop taking them now. Otherwise, you run a very high risk of destroying your other hip, your ankles, all your joints."

I couldn't quit steroids! Not at forty-three years old, with no money saved, and a good run ahead of me. The fans were not through with me yet—and they wanted to see my pythons.

"I don't think you should keep wrestling," Dorr added. "If you do, the trauma will loosen up your joints even more."

Well, that was completely out of the question. What could I possibly do instead? There were no wrestling books to write in 1986. And like almost all of my peers, I was not prepared for life after wrestling. This was the only choice I had.

So I came up with a strategy: I'd pump myself full of cortisone until I got over with the fans again. That wouldn't take long. Once I was a valuable commodity, I'd tell Vince that I needed a hip replacement. Then it would be worth his while to pay for it, and do some type of angle to set up my comeback.

I wouldn't be the first wrestler to return after hip replacement surgery. The original Sheik had done it, as well as Al Costello of the Fabulous Kangaroos. I might not be able to take the same kinds of bumps as in the past, but I had my bear hug and the rest of my power moves.

There was no other alternative. I had to have one more run.

Valerie Coleman: We were lying in bed one night, and Wayne thought that I was asleep. He was crying. I sat up and asked him what was wrong. It was his fear over the hip replacement. He didn't want to miss this opportunity, or this money.

The day before I was scheduled to leave for the World Wrestling Federation, I had my hip injected full of cortisone and pain-numbing medication. But less than twenty-four hours later, as I was climbing the stairs onto the airplane, my hip started bothering me again.

"Oh, no," I said to myself. "This stuff is wearing off already."

And wouldn't you know that when I arrived at the arena in Baltimore, the first person I ran into was Vince. He was walking out of the building. I was limping through the door.

"What's wrong, Superstar?"

"Oh, nothing. Just a tendon that flared up at me. I'll just ice it down, and be good to go."

Vince nodded, not really buying the story. But he didn't know the seriousness of the situation, and had me do an interview with color commentator Jesse Ventura.

"Tell him he stole your gimmick," Vince said.

That was going to be fun. Wrestlers didn't use insider terminology like "gimmick" on TV. It would be one of the few times that Jesse was ever caught off-guard.

This is an insight into Vince McMahon's unique sense of humor.

The promo began with Jesse loudly pontificating about some issue. Suddenly, I cut him off: "Wait a minute, Jesse. The big problem is that, to this day, you're ripping off my gimmick."

For a fleeting moment, Jesse actually looked concerned. Then he realized that this was a Vince-endorsed rib, and got a little smile on his face. "There's no way I ripped you off, Superstar!" he bellowed in character. "That was *my* stuff. *You* ripped *me* off!"

I knew that three hours of syndicated television were being taped that night. In our impromptu dressing room—the arena was being renovated, so the wrestlers were forced to change behind the curtain of a stage overlooking the ring—I spotted Vince again, and asked if I could be on more than one show.

"I'll do my best," he said. As each territory crumbled, there was a mass exodus into the World Wrestling Federation. It felt like the company now had more guys than they could use.

Vince put me into a match against Bob Bradley, a very competent jobber. I was already struggling to carry my own weight on my hip, and when I lifted Bradley for a bear hug, I added another 250 pounds. Bone scraped against bone, and my hip popped out. The pain was so excruciating that I dropped my opponent.

"Let's go home," I grimaced, rolling him over and pinning him.

Everybody backstage knew that something very serious had occurred. I tried to downplay my condition, but Vince asked his limo driver to take me back to my hotel. There I tried to get something to eat, but it was excruciatingly painful to even sit down. I knew that we had another television taping in less than twenty-four hours in Salisbury, Maryland, and frightening thoughts were beginning to overtake my mind.

By the time I settled into the dressing room the next day, I was in so much agony that I asked the backstage physician for a pair of crutches. Almost as soon as the words left my lips, Vince's radar honed in on me.

"What's going on, Superstar?"

"The hip's gone, Vince."

"Can we at least have you come out so the fans can see you?"

"You know I want to do that, Vince. But I'm in too much pain. I need a hip replacement. It's over."

Vince squeezed my arm. "It isn't over, Superstar. I will not put you out to pasture. Let's get it fixed. We're going to make a comeback."

"Vince, I don't have the money or the insurance."

"I'll pay for it." Vince cut me off. "Then you'll pay me back."

I nodded, touched by his commitment and empathy.

Since I'd been trying to wean myself off the downers, I didn't have enough pain pills to get through the day. So I hobbled around to various wrestlers, hitting them up for medication. Blackjack Mulligan invited me to stay in his room, and I bit the bullet all night, sweating and rocking back and forth in bed before my flight home.

Vince made sure that the hospital received $20,000 in advance, before I even checked in, and told me to call him as soon as the surgery was over. The moment that I was wheeled up from recovery and felt well enough to speak, I phoned Vince.

"I know you're going to make it, Superstar," he told me. "But even if you can't wrestle again, you don't have to worry. You will have a job with the company for life."

> **Vince McMahon:** *That story seemed to be going around at the time, the old job-for-life stuff. No one's ever guaranteed me anything. And I've never guaranteed anyone a job for life.*

Predictably, we turned my entire hip replacement process into a World Wrestling Federation story line, beginning with a vignette of myself in Dr. Dorr's office. Dorr displayed a model skeleton for the camera, explaining the upcoming procedure—and omitting any reference to steroid abuse. This being wrestling, he referred to me as "Superstar," as opposed to "Wayne" or "Mr. Coleman."

"Superstar has a destroyed hip with a smashed head of his femur, which is the ball of the joint," he said. "We are going to put this metal stem down in Superstar's bone, and replace that with a metal ball on top of the femur."

He ended the segment with a line I fed him, leaving my future open-ended: "It will be impossible for Superstar Billy Graham to ever wrestle again. He will be able to walk." *Man,* I thought, *this guy's not only a brilliant surgeon, but a great worker.* He'd delivered the line with a straight face.

Vince also sent a TV crew into the operating room for my surgery. Dr. Dorr and I took a gag photo of him placing me in a headlock and rubbing his knuckles on my head, while the anesthesiologist stood behind us, injecting me with an epidural. I told everyone in attendance that this had to be worse than the impending surgery.

"Dr. Dorr is the greatest surgeon on the face of the earth," I proclaimed for the camera before going under, "and he's going to replace my hip and . . . and . . . he's going to replace my hip . . ."

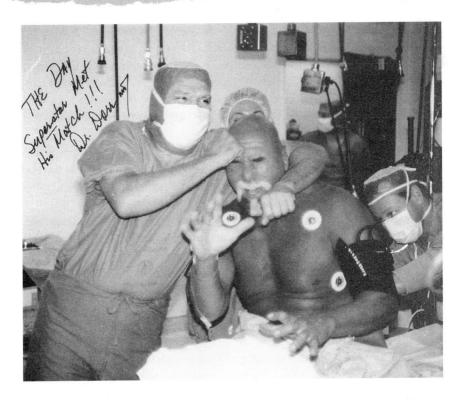

I forced myself to stay awake. "I will be back in the ring," I stated, confusing the seventies and eighties, "and I will retain my title."

"Okay," Dr. Dorr cut in. "That's enough showbiz. Let's get you to sleep."

What made this angle particularly compelling was that it wasn't an angle at all. Viewers saw doctors drilling into bone, and inserting a titanium prosthesis and plastic socket. It was one of the few times that nothing had to be overemphasized on a wrestling show. The reality was dramatic enough. In some places, the TV stations censored some of the surgery with a large white X. It didn't matter that violent crime and murder dominated the local news in these cities. Medical footage—something that was actually educational—was simply too graphic at the time.

As it was, the sound of the drilling was probably more gruesome than any visual.

When fans next saw me, I was climbing a craggy mountain in the Arizona desert on a walker, alongside World Wrestling Federation announcer Craig DeGeorge. In order for nothing to be lost on the audience, I made it a point to bandage myself *over* my sweatpants. Suddenly, I slipped and hit the ground.

"I'm going to make it," I grunted, struggling to my feet. "I'm going to make it. If I got to crawl, I don't care. I'm going to get to the top of this mountain. I'm not going to have any help from anybody. I'm going to make it."

No one seemed to notice that I actually fell on the wrong hip.

DeGeorge turned to the audience, and told them that Superstar Billy Graham was fighting both logic and nature.

In yet another vignette, DeGeorge tracked me down at the gym, doing a leg press on a slight incline. I'd placed sixteen 45-pound plates on the machine—the majority made out of wood. There was no need for all this lumber, of course. It was just the nature of the business.

Obviously, Vince was going through a great deal of expense to put me over to a new generation of fans. And, as Shire had counseled in San Francisco, he needed me to put myself over, as well.

"You have to remember who you are," Vince reminded me. "You're Superstar Billy Graham."

I learned nothing from my hip replacement surgery. Though steroids were still legal in the United States in 1987, it was, of course, illegal to bring them in from Mexico. Just before my return, federal agents had made a number of busts in border towns in both countries. The news frightened me. In my mind, there'd be no comeback without sauce, and I couldn't afford for the supply to dry up. So I called a black market contact and said, "Get me a year's worth of steroids."

The guy was happy to sell. Things were so hot that he wanted to get rid of his stash, and was willing to do so at a bargain price. He met me in the parking lot of a Phoenix gym and handed me a shopping bag brimming with every type of injectable and oral steroid that he could find. I peeked into the bag and saw a treasure trove of boxes, syringes, and bottles, along with indecipherable labels from France, Germany, and Mexico. I probably paid $1,000 for $10,000 worth of drugs. It was just too hard to resist! Then, I began using them—at literally 100 times the recommended dose.

Around this time, Jerry Russell made a brief reappearance in my life. I heard that he was living north of Phoenix, near Prescott, and wanted to see him again. I knew that he'd left the ministry, but I was surprised by his overall depraved essence. Jerry had gone back to the violent ways of his youth, and spent time in prison for drinking, fighting, and other offenses. He had a Star of David tattooed on his face, and a giant portrait of Jesus, bleeding from a crown of thorns, on his back.

"If you want the other inmates to leave you alone, you act like a nut case," he explained. "They'd take one look at me, and think I was a Jesus freak psycho."

But Russell wasn't even close to being a "Jesus freak" anymore. He chain-smoked and used the Lord's name in vain constantly. He still said, "*Jeee-sus,*" when he blasphemed.

"Wayne," he confessed, "I'm not so sure there's a pie in the sky."

Valerie Coleman: I was stunned when I finally met Jerry Russell. I told Wayne, "This is the man you've been telling me about all these years? There's something really off with this guy."

My spirit definitely did not bear witness with him. I felt uneasy in his presence.

When Jerry and I spoke, he said, "I can tell you for a fact that I love Wayne more than you do."

When I asked him why he'd say something like that, Jerry responded, "Even if Wayne molested his own daughter, I would still love him, and I guarantee that you wouldn't."

What a sickening thing to say. "Well, Jerry," I answered, "you're right. You do *love him more than I do."*

Soon Jerry was back in jail, after the cops received a call that some lunatic had marched out onto the highway brandishing weapons and firing. When I visited him, he boasted, "Wayne, I can make up some speed that will keep you awake for a week. You will love it."

"Are you talking about methamphetamine?" I asked while passing on his offer.

"Yeah. You should see the things it makes me do."

Incredibly, I learned, that included molesting his wife's teenage daughter—who, to compound the tragedy, happened to be afflicted with Down syndrome. Now Jerry's comment to Valerie made sense. In my opinion, child molesters are the epitome of evil. They can never be allowed to circulate in society because, inevitably, some other innocent will be victimized, traumatized, and corrupted. In fact, I believe that these demons from hell deserve the death penalty, and would harbor no guilt about serving as executioner. Fortunately for his family and the general public at large, Jerry spent his final days in prison, where he died of natural causes. But it confounds me that a man whose heart seemed so pure spiraled so hideously off course.

The Brooklyn Brawler, Steve Lombardi, was appointed to do the honors for me on TV when I returned from surgery in January 1987. Fans who romanticized my championship reign now had an extra incentive to salute me: my recent stretch of bad luck verified that I was as human as anybody in the upper deck. When I came down the aisle in Glens Falls, New York, spectators rushed forward to hug and high-five me. I took my time going to the ring, not because my movements were inhibited but because the ovation was as real as the surgery. I wanted to touch the flesh of every person I could to return the gratitude.

"You know what I love about him?" Jesse told the television audience. "He's got my clothes on," he said, referring to my new tie-dye ring attire. I gave him this line: "Those are my labels in those clothes."

I'd instructed Jesse to utter those words beforehand, and he delivered them perfectly. It was a great line.

After Charlotte, I'd hoped to continue using "Bad to the Bone" as my entrance music, but Vince squashed that. I was having bone problems, and he didn't like the connotation. My new theme was the melody to the very song that inspired my gimmick, "Jesus Christ Superstar."

Fans didn't want to see a long, drawn-out match, and we didn't give them one. I beat Lombardi with a sleeper hold, discarding my old-school bear hug finisher. The sleeper still showed off my arms, but I didn't have to pick anyone up—a choice that didn't exactly delight Vince.

Vince McMahon: Some of the other performers said that the only reason Superstar came back was so he could get a free hip operation. But I wanted to find some room for him in some capacity. You know, here's a man who's paid heavy dues in this business, and his contributions are enormous. You try to do something for people like that.

We tried to play up the strongman stuff. I was paired up in Tag Team matches with Ken Patera and Billy Jack Haynes. But my injuries were worse than most people understood. As Dr. Dorr had forecast, every bump loosened up my new hip. I was losing height because my spine was collapsing. And there was a grapefruit-sized, grisly-looking deformity growing on the inside of my right ankle because the bone was deteriorating there, too. In airports, I'd walk fifty yards, with the other wrestlers breezing past me, before ducking into the men's room so I could sit and take the pressure off my ankle and lower back. Then I'd hang on the stall door to create some traction on my lower spine, attempting to pull my vertebrae apart.

Valerie Coleman: I was lying out by the pool one day when Wayne came walking over to join me. Since I was low to the ground, I had a perfect view of his ankle. I couldn't believe what I was seeing. It was truly a horrifying sight. I wondered just how much more we were going to be forced to endure.

Before an outdoor show in Milwaukee, I told my opponent, Hercules Hernandez, "I'm going to do the best I can for you, but it isn't going to be pretty. Every time I get in the ring, I'm just trying to keep my balance."

Hercules was a big fan of mine, who I remembered from a few years earlier, sticking his head around the corner in the gym in Tampa to watch me work out. Now he was a solid block of granite. But in Milwaukee, he bumped all over the ring, and took care of me like I was a baby.

Harley Race: Billy and I were at the Nassau Coliseum one night, and left before the main event. It was Hulk Hogan against Paul "Mr. Wonderful" Orndorff. Please believe me, we didn't leave because we didn't want to see that match. We just wanted to go back to the hotel and not get hung up, like two old guys, in the middle of that crowd and the traffic. We were going through the parking lot when I said to him, "We were born ten years too soon. Ten years later, and it would have been us in that ring right now." What I was talking about was how the World Wrestling Federation had become bigger than anything we'd ever imagined. Would both of us have even made it as far as we had if the peak of our careers had been in 1987? I'm not sure. But we would have made a whole lot more money.

Everybody wanted to be on the shows that Hogan headlined. Hogan told me himself that he hoped that we'd be booked on the same cards because I'd earn more money. Since I was getting paid a percentage of the gate for every match I wrestled—I didn't have a contract—a Hulk Hogan card meant a difference of about $1,500 to $2,000.

Backstage at these very same shows, I remember being surprised at how some people were totally indiscreet about their steroid consumption. Dynamite Kid would inject his cousin—and partner in the British Bulldogs—Davey Boy Smith, inject himself, and just toss the syringe in the corner of the dressing room. Eventually, I figured, somebody was going to get pricked by a needle, or find this evidence to nail the company. But those guys threw caution to the wind.

Their mutual brother-in-law, Bret "Hit Man" Hart—he was married to the sister of Dynamite's wife, and Davey Boy was married to Bret's sister—pushed the limits in a much safer way. Chief Jay Strongbow was now a road agent, saddled with the unenviable job of supervising the boys backstage. Given his position of authority and notorious miserliness—he acted like every penny the company spent came from his own pocket, and was known to order eight or nine jobbers to share the same hotel room before a TV taping—the wrestlers loved goofing on Strongbow. Bret, a gifted cartoonist, would regularly search for a blackboard backstage, then sketch a profile of the Chief, with an enormous bubble waist and huge nose. Minutes later, Strongbow would come into the room, notice the portrait, and just lose it.

I guess that it was unavoidable, Vince was becoming more corporate. He was followed around by guys in suits—so humorless and cautious that, under different circumstances, they would have moved to another town if someone like Vince bought a house in their neighborhood. The overall atmosphere was more controlled than ever before. With Jim Crockett Jr. and others conspiring to take down Vince, we received memos from the boss, threatening us about revealing too much to friends in other territories. Here's one I saved from September 10, 1987:

> From time to time, it becomes necessary for me to put into writing matters of policy which I think should be crystal clear to everyone. So that there may be no misunderstanding relative to any World Wrestling Federation talent's responsibilities and obligations, please make note of the following:
>
> Should you as a World Wrestling Federation talent discuss matches, finishes, grosses or anything else related to the business activities of . . . the World Wrestling Federation with talents who are not part of the World Wrestling Federation, customers, vendors or with any former employees . . . whether or not he or she has resigned or has been terminated, you will be subject to disciplinary action. The disciplinary action may include termination of your contract with the World Wrestling Federation.
>
> Let me also call attention to the fact that magazines other than the World Wrestling Federation magazines will want to take photos, do interviews, and write about you for their own sales and publicity. Since we guard your image very closely, and put so much time, energy, and money into developing your particular character, we would ask that you neither pose for photographs nor grant interviews with any other publication.

When we received our itineraries, we'd be informed that we also had duties outside the arena. For instance, we might be expected to show up at a hotel from 1:00 to 5:00 P.M. to cut promos for our various local markets. I remember being crammed into a room with Randy "Macho Man" Savage, his manager—and real-life wife—Elizabeth, and Sensational Sherri Martel, with lights and cameras and technicians. There was no time to go to the gym or tan. There was no time to get a good meal. Our lunch consisted of these terrible hamburgers sent up from the hotel kitchen.

We'd do double shots on the weekends—Springfield, Missouri, in the afternoon, and maybe Springfield, Illinois, at night. Early in the morning, we'd get on a plane and go straight to the arena. The garage door to the street would be open, with trucks loading and unloading equipment, and wind sweeping through the building. In the winter months, it would be freezing. After the show, we'd be moving so fast that the company often stacked platters of catered food on the wing of the charter to the next town. We'd eat on the runway, then get on the plane, land, and have a shuttle bus carry us to the arena for the evening show.

It wasn't fair to compare this time to the era when I was champion because Vince had taken the business in a very different direction. But this wasn't fun. Everyone was tired, and getting on each other's nerves. And because of the fatigue, it was easy to get injured.

One night, I was doing push-ups before the show, and heard something snap. I'd blown out my rotator cuff. With all my other injuries, I didn't need one more ailment to reduce my value. So I took a few days off and went back on the road.

Nonetheless, I could sense that the end of my run was near in October 1987, when I wrestled "The Natural" Butch Reed in a cage at the Garden. Hogan was somewhere else that night, so our match was listed as the main event. My body was falling apart, but the Garden sold out anyway. The fans in New York always gave me a pass.

Reed and I were doing a deal where he was scaling the cage, and I was supposed to come up after him and pull him down. But my mobility was so limited that I had difficulty climbing. Seeing my distress, Butch reached down, grabbed me, and lugged me up to his level.

There was no way that I was going to be able to swing my legs over the top of the cage and descend to the arena floor. So we ended the match with me hitting Reed with a pair of brass knuckles, and exiting the door.

After I showered and dressed, I saw Vince talking to Pat, who was leaning with one foot on a folding chair against the wall. As I approached them, Pat gave me a sympathetic smile.

"I did the best I could," I said.

"I know you did, Superstar," Vince replied, patting me on the shoulder when I passed them. As I exited the Garden onto Thirty-third Street, I sensed that this would be the last time I'd ever wrestle in the fabled building, and hailed a taxi, overcome by a dark feeling in the city that I'd once illuminated.

I'd been scheduled to appear in the *Survivor Series 1987,* teaming in the main event with Hogan, Patera, Paul Orndorff, and my old fan, Bam Bam Bigelow, against Andre the Giant, Reed, One Man Gang, King Kong Bundy, and "Ravishing" Rick Rude. My partners and I had cut some promos for the Pay-Per-View, and I was looking forward to the payday. But a few weeks before the event, Vince called me into his office.

"Superstar," he said, "I'm going to have to put Don Muraco in your place. You're not up to it physically."

"I know I'm not," I admitted.

Vince McMahon: I probably thought that he would hurt himself and hurt somebody else. With a guy like Superstar, you do the best that you can with him, and hope that the audience is not seeing what you're seeing. But eventually, you know that the audience sees it, too. Obviously, he's not helping the company that much at that juncture. It just wasn't working.

The company came up with an angle to write me out of the plot. I wrestled Butch Reed on television, and—after he took a bump—his manager, Slick, jumped into the ring. I cornered him against the turnbuckles and nailed him a couple of times. Seemingly out of nowhere, another Slick protégé, One Man Gang, joined the fray, splashing his 450-plus pounds onto my injured hip three times. Muraco raced down to the ring for the save, and—as he tangled with Reed—Gang gave me one final splash on the arena floor.

The consolation was that I wasn't retiring from the wrestling business. I was becoming Muraco's manager. At the Slammys, a gimmick version of the Oscars that Vince did for a few years, Hulk Hogan gave me an extra rub, presenting me with a "Real American" award.

"You know," he told the audience, "the Hulkster didn't come here tonight to get this applause, man. This applause is for somebody more deserving, man, somebody that has suffered through the hard times and survived. And more than that, this big dude stands for everything America is built on, man—integrity, perseverance, the attitude that you never give up, man. Yeah, man, we are only talking about one man. . . . We've seen this dude suffer, man. We've seen him climb from the ashes below all the way to the mountaintop. . . . A lot of us patterned our lifestyles after this guy, man. He hangs and bangs. He trains. And when I saw him drop to his knees and say his prayers, I knew he

was a *Hulkamaniac.* So the Real American Award goes to"—Hulk popped out his eyes and tilted his head like Dusty—"Superstar Billy Graham."

I entered the stage with the support of a cane, in a white tuxedo that had been tie-dyed fuchsia by a hippie for life I found in San Francisco. "I accept this award from my heart," I said. "You know, the super thing about this is I get to stand next to Hulk Hogan, 'cause this is the Real American, and this is the real example that all Americans should follow." I actually did mean some of that; Hogan and I were still close. "And I'm just proud to say, 'I love you,' and thank you for the award."

We started to walk off the stage with Hulk's arm around my back. Suddenly, Hogan snatched my cane and cracked it across his knee (he'd been worried that it wouldn't break, so we gimmicked it beforehand). I held up my hands, apparently troubled about what to do without the aid of my walking stick. Hogan pointed at my hip, and motioned at my cane. I peered down, shocked that I could stand, and looked up at the heavens. What a miracle! I'd been healed by the power of *Hulkamania.*

All we needed was for Jerry Russell to burst onto the stage: *"Praise God-uh! Hallelujah, brothers and sisters!"*

Muraco and I began traveling around the horn and cutting promos together on TV. At first, my interviews were powerful. I transferred my tie-dye tank tops to Muraco, and spoke about passing the torch to a man as strong as the Rock of Gibraltar. Vince seemed confident that my talking ability would add to Muraco's aura.

It didn't. It seemed like I was talking about myself; the interviews didn't translate to Muraco. Plus, I still had to walk down the aisle every night, escort my charge through the ropes, and pace around at ringside without looking like a cripple. That was a pretty tough con to pull off.

My condition had degenerated to the point that even the pain pills weren't helping anymore. For a brief period, I began drinking wine—something I'd never done in the past—to anesthetize myself even further. Then I started urinating blood, and went to see a doctor. He told me that the alcohol consumption, combined with all my other issues, elevated the enzymes in my liver. So I stopped.

It was a horrible existence. My dressing room drug supplier was Dr. Zahorian. But one day when I came into the room where he was supposed to be taking blood pressure, he curtly announced, "Billy, I can't give you any more credit."

"I don't need credit. I have fifty dollars. Let me buy some Valium."

"Do you have the cash?"

"Yes, I have the cash."

In the middle of our conversation, Zahorian was summoned to another part of the building. He quickly motioned to a guy who looked like an assistant and said, "Watch my stuff."

So I stood there, eyeing this stranger protecting Zahorian's stash like a security guard. "Who are you?" I challenged.

Wisely, the guy remained quiet. The doctor rushed back to the scene within minutes, and we made our transaction. I'd never associated myself with street addicts because most of what I used could be obtained with a doctor's prescription. But on this night, I really felt like a hardcore junkie.

During one swing through Canada, my ankle was throbbing so badly that I contemplated not even going to the arena. "Superstar, make it to the building," Hillbilly Jim, my driving buddy that day, urged. "Don't be a no-show. Make your shot, then you can tell them about your bad ankle."

"Okay, brother. You're right."

The two of us pulled into the parking lot of a large hockey rink. But when we entered the building, we took a wrong turn and had to backtrack through the entire length of the arena to find the locker room. By the time I sat down, my ankle was on fire, and the Fabulous Rougeau Brothers—Ray and Jacques Jr.—were preparing to go to the ring for the opening match.

"You better not touch our stuff," Jacques warned the British Bulldogs, who were notorious for disrespecting fellow wrestlers' personal property.

Dynamite and Davey Boy puffed out their cheeks and bounced their heads from side to side, like grinning imbeciles. As soon as Jacques and Ray left the dressing room, the Bulldogs went through the Rougeaus' belongings, found their street pants, and cut off the legs.

I didn't bother mentioning my ankle to anyone.

I'm not sure how this occurred, but I ended up in a car another time with the Bulldogs and the Ultimate Warrior. The Warrior, who'd dethroned Hogan at *WrestleMania VI* in 1990, was a physical anomaly, who'd lie down on his towel by the locker, do 1,000 crunches, pop up, and go to work. He went through his food before every meal, and separated out anything detrimental to his diet. The man was all muscle and no body fat. He was ripped to the bone.

He also had a fuse that was usually on the verge of erupting, and I think that anyone who's ever seen a picture of the Warrior could probably guess why. When he spoke—either in promos or in person—he often didn't make sense. He legally changed his name to Ultimate Warrior in 1993 and moved to Scottsdale, Arizona.

Of course, the Bulldogs—flying on a grab bag of drugs—loved to rib him, screaming in his ear as he drove and poking him in the neck and sides. During this particular car ride, the Warrior grew weary of all the harassment and went into a trance, scrunching down his shoulders and gripping the steering wheel so hard that I feared that he would literally tear it off.

From 60 miles per hour, we went to 70, then 80.

"*Faster!*" Davey Boy shouted in the Warrior's ear. "Faster! *Faster!*"

The Warrior gritted his teeth and stepped on the gas.

"No!" Dynamite protested. "Slow down!"

"No!" Davey Boy countered. "You're not going fast enough! *Faster!*"

By now, the speedometer needle had passed 100. And I was sitting there, wondering how ironic it would be if, after all the ways I'd abused my body, God chose to take my life this way—with these guys.

The turnaround angle for Muraco and myself was shot on June 1, 1988, in Oakland, California. To the fans, this would be the watershed event solidifying the bond between the two of us.

Greg "The Hammer" Valentine had been wearing a shin guard, apparently to torture his foes while administering the figure-four leglock. He had a jobber named Ricky Ataki in the hold, continuing to apply pressure after the bell, when Muraco and I rushed the ring to break it up. In the confusion, Valentine's manager, Jimmy Hart, spat at Muraco and ran back to the dressing room, with Don in hot pursuit. In the ring, I was tending to Ataki when Valentine pitched forward, shoved a knee into my back, dropped a few elbows, and finally grinded my wounded joints with the figure four.

"Oh, my goodness," Vince reacted from ringside.

Muraco returned to run off Valentine and assist as I was hoisted onto a stretcher. After a few feet, the people transporting me dropped the gurney, and I sold it like my leg had snapped off in the process.

For the second time in less than a year, I'd done a stretcher job. It was a little humiliating. But Muraco was going to go after Valentine for revenge. I'd be in my protégé's corner, inserting myself into every confrontation and beating up on Jimmy Hart. The feud would draw money, and everyone would see that—his health notwithstanding—Superstar Billy Graham still had value.

Greg "The Hammer" Valentine: *I'd put the figure four on a guy who'd had a hip replacement. How rotten can you be? I was really looking forward to this program because I'd get to work with Billy Graham. He and Muraco both had on the tie-dye thing, and they looked really good together.*

Right after we did the angle, Muraco and I went on a World

Wrestling Federation tour of Europe. We were all at a nightclub in France somewhere, and they had these big lounge chairs around a table, a real fancy disco-type thing, and I remember watching Muraco while Davey Boy handed him a bunch of pills. Don gobbled them all down at once. About an hour later, a bunch of fans are sitting around, getting autographs and stuff. Muraco's sleeping, passed out, and I'm thinking, "I hope he doesn't go into a coma." Just then, he threw up, and it was like a tidal wave hit the table. The drinks go everywhere. Then he threw his head back and did it again. Of course, everybody cleared out of that area.

A couple of days later, we were at a luncheon in Sardinia and Nick Bockwinkel [a former AWA champion, and road agent at the time] and Don had some disagreement. It was just a small thing. Don ripped off his shirt like he was Billy Graham and screamed, "Come on! I'm sick of this!" I thought it would have blown over, but Nick had to report it.

Those weren't the only incidents on the trip. Another time, we were on a double-decker bus that the French network, Canal Plus, was providing. Davey Boy Smith had gotten ahold of this liquid Valium, and some of the boys had mixed it with beer. Everybody got whacked out. There were two ladies from the network on the bus, and when they looked up, they saw a stream coming down from the spiral staircase. It was Davey Boy and the Junkyard Dog, urinating on the bus.

I got back from the tour, and Muraco had been fired, Davey Boy Smith had been fired, Junkyard Dog had been fired. I was practically the only guy who still had a job.

I told Vince, "Don't fire Don. Please, I want to work this angle."

But he said, "I can't let someone disrespect my employees like that. We'll find someone else to work with you."

Billy wasn't part of the story anymore—he had no one to manage. There's a magazine from that time with pictures of me putting Billy in the figure four, and the two of us look at it and laugh. "Isn't that awful?" he goes. "My great career, and Greg Valentine ended it for me."

There was still hope for me in the World Wrestling Federation. Pat Patterson had approached me about doing personal appearances on behalf of the company, and on different occasions I attended a Special Olympics carnival and conference of independent television stations. It was fun interacting with the fans. And I was paid about $5,000 per appearance!

Working with Lord Alfred Hayes (left).

"Five thousand dollars without taking any bumps," Pat said. My old friend seemed sincerely happy for me. Now, *this* was easy money.

Even before the Muraco incident, Vince had been trying me out as a color commentator. This allowed me the opportunity to work with another retired wrestler, Lord Alfred Hayes, a Brit who'd earned a name as a witty, articulate man behind the microphone. "You know," he told me, "you don't have to use profanity to tell a story. In fact, if you *do* have to resort to using profanity, it's a sign of ignorance."

On August 29, 1988, I was given my biggest challenge as a color commentator, calling the first annual *SummerSlam* Pay-Per-View with Gorilla Monsoon. Since Monsoon was so much more experienced as an announcer, I followed his lead and played off his comments. Considering the fact that this was a brand-new discipline for me, I felt like I'd done a very good job. Afterward, Vince told me that my only major flaw was using the term "brother" too much.

"I counted at least fifty 'brothers,'" Vince observed. Considering this was the Hogan era, I found that critique a little absurd.

What tipped the scales against me was a show that I announced at the L.A. Sports Arena a few months later. At one point, I was supposed to switch from calling the action to interviewing some of the talent in the locker room. And I did a horrible job in the transition.

> **Vince McMahon:** *I'm trying to find something that this guy can do. You'd think that being an announcer would be one of them. He's got a great gift of gab. So let's try that. I was trying to keep him on the payroll.*
>
> *I wouldn't be at all surprised if Billy was in a lot of pain and on medication, because his material was not real sharp. He could talk for himself, but he didn't have the ability to get other individuals over verbally. And that's not good.*
>
> *I tried every conceivable way to keep him around. But dead weight is lousy for morale, and doesn't really help the individual in the long run.*

On January 3, 1989, Vince called me at home. "We're going to have to put you in the bullpen," he said.

It was like a bomb being dropped. My health was failing. How was I going to pay my bills? Was I being severed from the business forever?

At forty-five years old and with seemingly no other skills, what was I going to do?

CHAPTER NINETEEN

MY BODY HAS PLENTY OF EVIDENCE

For they embittered his spirit,
And he spoke rashly with his lips

—Psalms 106:33

I tried acting after retirement, and landed a couple of small roles: a lion tamer on *The Young and the Restless,* a guy munching hamburgers on a McDonald's commercial, a wrestler on a Miller Lite ad, and a barroom brawler in a Mexican B-movie called *The Fist Fighter.*

But even after I no longer had to take bumps for a living, my body continued to deteriorate. My right ankle was completely disfigured, a swollen collection of soft tissue and bone pressing against my skin. On February 19, 1990, doctors fused the ankle, using undamaged bone from my right hip area and shin, along with a titanium rod and seven titanium screws to hold everything in place. The surgeon, Dr. Luigi Gentile, told me that he had nightmares about the procedure. The only time that he'd seen ankles mangled so badly was during World War II, when he operated on soldiers who'd stepped on landmines.

Doctors also said that I'd eventually need to have my spine fused—regrettably, a procedure I avoided because I didn't want back surgery. Because of spinal erosion, I'm about four inches shorter than I was at the height of my career. Occasionally, I forget that I used to be six-foot-four, but my memory comes crashing back on those occasions when I'm backstage, visiting with the boys at a show. In 2004, for example, I was chatting with Triple H and David Batista before a card in Tucson, and I realized that I was looking up at them. Had my spine not collapsed, we would have been eye to eye.

In 1990, I was forced to apply for disability benefits—on the basis of what one of my doctors, Robert Watkins, called "severe spinal stenosis . . . degenerated disk and bone disease of the spine." In a letter to the California Department of Social Services, he characterized me as "totally disabled." This was no exaggeration, and I've spent much of the past two decades living largely on government payouts.

I miss my mobility. While researching this book, I watched dozens of my old matches on tape. In one, I was wrestling Bruno, and after a bodyslam sprang back up to my feet like a cat. I was amazed by my agility—I actually was a real athlete. I've been living with my injuries for so long that the Superstar Billy Graham era of the 1970s sometimes doesn't seem real.

And what a paradox it was that my downfall mirrored Arnold Schwarzenegger's emergence as a Hollywood star. His success forced me to look at the shortcomings in my own life. It was embarrassing to think that we both started out on the same playing field. Why didn't I pursue the same avenues as Arnold when I had the opportunity? Is there a gene he possessed that made him more aware and focused? While he became a household name, I was dragging Valerie through my netherworld of drug abuse and poverty—and pushing my children so far away that there were times when they wanted virtually nothing to do with me.

Joe Miluso: I always had the feeling that my dad didn't want to call the house because my mother would answer. And then, I'm not sure if she'd even let us talk. So he'd call my sister and say, "Tell Joey hi,"

At home in the Arizona desert with Val.

and things like that. I was actually communicating with my dad through Capella.

If Capella had a boyfriend, I'd make him into a father figure. The two of them would go out and take me with them because I didn't have a dad. One of her longer-term boyfriends would even come over when Capella wasn't around, and bring me places. When they broke up, I cried because it felt like my dad was being taken away again.

I saw my mom working and making sacrifices for us. As far as I knew, we weren't getting child support from my dad on a regular basis. So I started to feel more of an allegiance to my mom's side of the family. As I got older, I decided that I didn't want anything else to do with my father, and took my mother's maiden name. It was my way *of telling myself and telling my dad that I didn't need him. Just stay away, and I won't worry about it.*

My newest grandson, Joey Miluso Jr., was born in March 2005. Since my grandson's last name is Miluso and not Coleman, the final nail has been driven into the coffin. Much to the pleasure of my son's mother, a wedge has been inserted between my son and me. This is why I have to take a stand. After many years of looking the other way and sweeping the issue under the rug, I must defend myself and the Coleman family name.

When I first heard that Joey had changed his name, I felt as if I had been crushed by an avalanche of giant boulders. It was, and still is, extremely painful. The brainwashing by his wicked, embittered, and very evil mother began when Joey could barely even speak. I have done absolutely nothing to deserve something as disrespectful and insulting as my son changing his last name. It's the ultimate cruelty, as far I'm concerned. I'm relatively sure that Joey wasn't conceived through an act of incest, even though he has his maternal grandfather's surname.

> *Valerie Coleman: For nearly twenty-seven years, I've insisted that Wayne and I take the high road when it comes to the kids' mother. We agreed that they would not hear any disparaging remarks about the woman from us. In hindsight, it appears that I may have been wrong. As the saying goes, "Evil flourishes when good men do nothing." By remaining silent about the truth of things, we've let the kids grow up with a very distorted view of both their father and their mother, who to this very day continues to portray herself as a victim and a martyr. She is neither.*

Having all these health problems only plunged me further into depression. Seeing success all around me and finding myself worthless in my own eyes was almost a deathblow. I was walking through the valley of the shadow of death.

> *Valerie Coleman: I was working as a manager of a clothing store, and Wayne couldn't accept that I was our sole support. He wasn't one of those types who cared if his wife worked. He just didn't feel like a man anymore.*
>
> *With the exception of Jesse Ventura, Terry Funk, and Big John Studd, most of the boys seemed to forget about him once he left the World Wrestling Federation. And he had a bad relationship with his kids. So he started mutilating himself with forks, knives, anything*

that was sharp, cutting his arms, his face, his forehead, his cheeks. While I was at work, he told me that he'd go to the beach and think about ways that he could kill himself. Even though he was mutilating himself, he didn't want to do anything that would have me find him a gory mess. He'd think, "What would be easiest on Valerie?" He thought about hanging himself, but he was afraid that he might just break his neck and remain paralyzed for the rest of his life. An overdose, obviously, made the most sense to him. I lived in constant fear of what I might find waiting for me at home.

In 1991, my mood suddenly lifted when I learned that dressing room doctor George Zahorian was arrested and charged with distributing steroids for nonmedical purposes. To me, he was a drug pusher who'd exploited my addictive personality. And his trial would shed a negative light on a company that I believed had offered me a lifetime job, then bounced me into obscurity. So when the Justice Department contacted me, I told them that I'd be overjoyed to offer my services.

Already, the government had subpoenaed several wrestlers, including "Rowdy" Roddy Piper, Rick Martel, and Danny Spivey—all guys who admitted purchasing anabolics from Zahorian, sometimes via FedEx. I called B. Brian Blair, a close friend of Hogan's, and tried to pump him for information that I could pass back to the Feds. Blair was suspicious and guarded, but he did provide enough data for the U.S. attorney's office in Harrisburg to subpoena him, as well. Blair—a well-rounded guy later elected commissioner in Hillsborough County, Florida—never forgave me for setting him up like that.

And understandably so.

After the other wrestlers testified, I flew to Pennsylvania, where I was met at the airport by John Arezzi, a bit of a wrestling fanatic who hosted a radio show in the New York area. Obviously, I was not going to travel across the country without generating some media fanfare. And Arezzi was dedicated to assisting this effort.

Like a hot wrestling angle, the U.S. attorney's office kayfabed my presence in the Keystone State. The goal was to pop the crowd when I turned up unexpectedly in the courtroom.

Jerry McDevitt, Vince McMahon's attorney: *Billy injected himself into the Zahorian controversy, and gave the government something they needed. Roddy Piper and Rick Martel seemed healthy. But Billy was the canary in the coal mine, the crippled old warrior.*

The Justice Department hid me in the U.S. attorney's office on the morning of my testimony. I was addicted to Halcion and Valium, and found it a little odd that I was taking these drugs right in the prosecutor's office before I was supposed to help the government put away a dealer. As with my promos in the past, I knew that my mind would clear once it was my turn to speak.

I didn't own a suit at the time—except for the fuchsia tuxedo I'd worn to the Slammy Awards—and had flown to Pennsylvania in casual attire. "I don't know if the judge is going to let you testify without a suit," one of the prosecutors said.

"Isn't that a little discriminatory? Just because a person doesn't have a suit? I'm not slighting the court just because I can't afford to buy a suit to wear to trial."

Who could argue with that line of reasoning?

The government waited until the moment before I was about to be called, then positioned me outside the courtroom doors, like I was on the other side of the dressing room curtain, waiting to wrestle Bruno.

"The government calls Eldridge Wayne Coleman."

With the exception of John Arezzi, neither the press nor the spectators knew the more public identity of Eldridge Wayne Coleman. But as the doors opened and every eye turned to the back, I heard a collective gasp.

"It's him."

I was walking with a cane, and sold my limp as I passed the jurors. I had to. It's a wrestler's nature.

"Mr. Coleman, in what city do you reside?" Theodore Smith, the assistant U.S. attorney, began the questioning.

"Burbank, California."

"And do you have a name other than Eldridge Wayne Coleman?"

"Yes. Superstar Billy Graham."

I could feel another wave of excitement sweep through the room.

"Is the person you know as Dr. George Zahorian present in the courtroom?"

"Yes."

"Would you indicate where he's seated, please?"

I almost didn't recognize Zahorian without his tackle box full of drugs. But I pointed at the witness table anyway. I also identified Zahorian as a doctor with the Pennsylvania State Athletic Commission.

"And what services would he perform as an athletic commission doctor on you specifically?"

"On me specifically?"

"Yes."

"Occasionally, he would take my blood pressure, and that's it."

"Did he perform any other physical examination on you?"

"None whatsoever."

"Well, what did he do besides take your blood pressure on several occasions?"

"He sold me steroids and other drugs."

Zahorian shot me a curious look because, in reality, he didn't think he had sold me that many steroids. I usually came to him for sedatives. But the truth was that I'd also purchased Dianabol, Delatestryl, Anavar, Winstrol, and Deca Durabolin from the doctor—and he'd used the U.S. mail to ship my orders, a very important point for prosecutors trying to establish a federal case.

"You indicated that you're disabled," Smith said. "I'd like you to simply state for the jury what the name of the condition is that you suffer from."

"The name of the condition that I suffer from is avascular necrosis. It's the death of a bone in the bone joints . . . the bone joints have died from lack of blood circulation due to steroids."

Jerry McDevitt: Billy was not qualified to discuss how certain conditions came about. But despite the admonishment of the judge, he offered medical opinions. The media loved these sound bites, and printed them without any kind of verification.

"Do you suffer from any other medical condition?" I was asked.

"Yes, I suffer from liver enzymes that have been elevated to the point that at one time I was urinating blood because of the high intake of steroids."

Zahorian's lawyer, William Costopoulos, was becoming agitated. But I kept getting in my points:

"I also have ruptured tendons in my body from steroids, and I also . . ."

"Your honor!" Costopoulos interrupted.

"Excuse me, Mr. Coleman," Judge William Caldwell interceded. "Please do not—"

"Okay, I'm sorry."

"—attempt to—"

"It's just such a habit of—"

"Well, avoid the habit."

"Okay, I apologize."

As the judge requested that my last few statements be disregarded, I looked at the jurors—their eyes all glued to me, most of them fans probably—and managed to work in that I was also sterile.

But I wanted to physically communicate with this panel—telling a story with my body, as I had every night in the ring—so I asked for permission to step out of the witness box to stretch. The judge had no choice but to honor my request, and when he did, I held my hip and groaned the way I would in Billy Jack Haynes's full nelson, and hung on the witness stand like this was a physical therapy session.

Costopoulos did all that he could to depict me as an opportunistic showman. But I'd telegraphed this strategy in advance.

"Did you tell the media here in Harrisburg that if you were not allowed to testify, you were going to have a press conference?" Costopoulos queried.

"I told the media that I would hold a press conference after I testified."

Costopoulos hardened his tone: "You have a press conference lined up with the media?"

"If they want to interview me, you know what I'm going to tell them?"

Judge Caldwell shot out of his chair: "No!" He was so freaked out that I thought that he might declare a mistrial.

The media swarmed around me outside the courthouse, where I announced my bombshell. I was suing Zahorian for, among other things, not warning me about the disastrous effects of anabolic steroids, as well as six pharmaceutical companies that produced some of the drugs. Furthermore, I was suing the World Wrestling Federation for making me into a steroid addict.

"By hiring only performers with abnormally large muscles, caused by nontherapeutic AASs (Anabolic Androgenic Steroids) use," my lawsuit stated, the World Wrestling Federation "intended to induce wrestlers, including Superstar Billy Graham, to consume AASs."

And, I claimed, I wasn't the only victim in my household: "As a result of defendants' negligence, recklessness, carelessness . . . and other conduct . . . Valerie Coleman has been deprived of Wayne Coleman's assistance, society, and consortium to her detriment and loss."

The newspaper reporters couldn't scribble fast enough as I fired off a succession of promos on the company. And I kept the performance going, even after the conference ended. The press followed while I hobbled through downtown Harrisburg, stopping every few seconds to grab my hip and moan.

With the government now focusing their steroid investigation in the World Wrestling Federation's direction, I assumed that this type of spectacle would pressure Vince to settle. But when you provoke Vince, he fights back. And now he was really angry.

Vince McMahon: *Obviously, I didn't want to jump for joy. In my heart, I thought that I'd done everything possible to help Superstar. And I couldn't figure out his angle. I never thought that he'd go out of his way to hurt me.*

Everyone knew that Superstar had started taking steroids a long time before he met me. That's well documented. It's absurd that I would ask anyone to take anything that would in any way hurt them.

George Napolitano: *I was not tight with the World Wrestling Federation at the time, but when Billy Graham said that Vince McMahon forced steroids upon him, it bothered me. I knew that wasn't the case because I was the one who was getting packages of steroids sent to my house. Vince McMahon had nothing to do with that.*

Jerry McDevitt: *What I thought was the irony of the whole thing was that Billy Graham probably brought steroids to wrestling. And when he came back to the World Wrestling Federation in 1986, he had pre-existing injuries. Part of his scam was to set up Vince to pay for his hip replacement. Vince has always had a great love for Billy Graham, and Billy took advantage of it.*

The strange part is that if Billy had come to me after all his health problems—instead of trying to discredit Vince—I probably could have helped him. The way steroid companies originally marketed the drug was amazing. Steroids really do make people bigger and stronger and faster. We wanted to beat the Russians and the East Germans and the Bulgarians in the Olympics, so we got steroids out to athletes in an unregulated fashion. People started to take Dianabol like they were vitamin pills. The drug companies included the warning label, "Not For Athletic Enhancement." So every time that someone suffered side effects, the drug companies could claim misuse of the product. Billy was one of the first guinea pigs.

On June 27, 1991, Zahorian was convicted of fourteen counts, and subsequently sentenced to three years in prison. I was elated, and still am.

Yet the doctor's incarceration did nothing to ease my escalating health issues. In 1991 and 1992, I had to have my hip replacement revised—or fixed—twice. After the second procedure, Valerie dropped me off at home and went to the market for some items. A few seconds later, the phone rang, and as I reached for it on the floor—violating my doctor's edict against bending more than 90 degrees—I separated the hip again. It looked like a pool cue was pushing through my glute; the ball of my hip was bulged out, about six inches too high.

As I agonized, I felt even more animosity toward the World Wrestling Federation. I'd sacrificed my body for the wrestling business, and this is what Valerie and I were left to deal with by ourselves.

Because Zahorian claimed to have sold steroids to McMahon—a body-builder in his heart—and Hogan, the media couldn't get enough of the story. Since 1984, the Hulkster had been portrayed as a role model for America's youth. He'd transitioned from wrestling to movies, television appearances, and commercial endorsements, and the scandal had the potential to end all that. So, two weeks after the trial, he agreed to appear on *The Arsenio Hall Show* and come clean about his drug use.

Instead, Hogan made the outrageous claim that he'd only used steroids three times to rehabilitate injuries—all at a doctor's behest. Then he added, "The real steroid user and abuser is Superstar Billy Graham."

This was a very personal attack from somebody who I considered a friend, and it hit a sensitive nerve. Sure, our business is entertainment. But who was Hogan to be acting so much holier-than-thou? I found it hard to imagine that Hogan, who always acknowledged patterning his career after mine, would make this kind of statement without prompting. I thought, *Vince has to have put him up to it.*

In my media interviews, I now began lashing out at the World Wrestling Federation *and* Hogan, telling reporters that when the Hulkster lectured kids about taking their vitamins, he should have clarified that those come in both oral and injectable doses.

"I compare Hulk Hogan to [former Washington, D.C. mayor] Marion Barry," I told the *Los Angeles Times*. "Barry went to schools, and talked to kids about not doing drugs and, at the same time, had crack cocaine in his pants pocket. Hogan is a liar to the children because all the time, he is saying, 'I'm not using steroids.' I think this is the most disgusting thing you could do in this country with the drug situation the way it is."

For the local NBC affiliate in Los Angeles, I estimated the number of World Wrestling Federation performers using steroids at a staggering 90 percent—the figure sounded good at the time—and claimed that the joke going around the locker room was that if you tested *negative* for the drugs, you'd be fined.

When I heard that *The Phil Donahue Show* was going to devote an hour to the World Wrestling Federation's growing problems, I called the producers and essentially invited myself to the panel discussion.

The atmosphere in the green room before the broadcast was extremely tense. Vince was all by himself among my fellow guests, including Bruno Sammartino—who'd had a very acrimonious falling-out with the company—Dave Meltzer, founder of the *Wrestling Observer* newsletter; and a number of former World Wrestling Federation associates who'd shown up to accuse Vince of being the ringmaster of an underworld of drug abuse and perversion. Bruno refused to acknowledge Vince at all. I accepted a handshake from my former boss, but avoided engaging in conversation or looking him in the eye. I didn't feel good about what was going to happen.

I was too preoccupied with going onto the set and lying.

When the program started, I told the audience about my various overdoses and claimed that if Valerie owned a gun, she would have killed both Dr. Zahorian—that part *was* true—and Vince McMahon.

"Could you compete and survive and be a top card person in the eighties in the wrestling game without steroids?" Donahue, the white-haired, bespectacled host of the program, asked.

"No. You would have to take steroids in Vince McMahon's World Wrestling Federation to be on top."

Hogan, I added, mixing fantasy and fact, "came to me in 1977 in Tampa, Florida, and inquired about steroids because he wanted to become a wrestler. . . . I've injected the man probably a half a dozen times. [Wrestler] David Schulz, a close friend of mine, has injected him over 200 times. And Hulk Hogan himself has told me personally, 'I knew nothing about steroids when I began, and for the first year, I took a shot every day of my life. . . . That is the point, Phil."

"You're threatening a very big income here with this information," Donahue remarked.

"You can't lie to children in this country about drugs," I countered. "That's a form of child abuse."

Unfortunately for Vince, the steroid controversy erupted at the same time as another scandal. "Ring boys"—kids who worked on the ring crew, and carried the wrestlers' robes back to the dressing room—had been part of wrestling since the days when matches were staged in carnival tents, and a number even became wrestlers themselves. Now stories were beginning to circulate in the media that a few had been molested by World Wrestling Federation employees. Some unsuccessful wrestlers—and even a short-lived television announcer—also stepped forward to claim that their careers were curtailed after they rejected the sexual advances of booker Pat Patterson.

I'd traveled with Pat, and had never seen that side of him. But I was so caught up in my vengeance toward the company that I now directed my rage at a man who'd only treated me as a friend.

"I've seen ring boys being sexually harassed," I told Donahue.

"What's a ring boy?" he asked.

"A ring boy is a person who is usually employed to put up and take down the ring, travel from town to town, age group from thirteen to nineteen to twenty. It fluctuates anywhere in between."

"And you saw what?"

"I saw on one occasion, I believe in New Haven, Connecticut, Pat Patterson actually grab one of these children in the crotch while putting up the ring. I came to the arena a little bit early, walking by the ring to the locker room, and I saw Pat Patterson with his left arm on the kid's shoulder, and his right hand in his crotch. I witnessed this myself."

"Let me make this point, Billy," Donahue said. "These are pretty heavy bombs you are throwing here."

Vince McMahon: The low point for me was the accusation about Pat. If you know Pat Patterson, he's such a quality human being. We all have our sexual preferences, and his are not mine. But it has nothing to do with kids. Billy knows that when you lie like that and you use kids, that's low. That's as low as you can possibly get.

Valerie Coleman: I was sitting in the audience, crying because I couldn't believe what was coming out of my husband's mouth. I was shocked and disappointed. When we got back to the hotel room, we had a huge fight. I told Wayne, "Do you know what you just did to Pat?"

This was my most shameful moment, not only in the wrestling profession, but in my life. Because the accusations came from me—a former champion and friend of Pat's—they lent credibility to the scurrilous charges of others. The rumors followed Pat around for years. I could blame my assertions on the fact that I was on Halcion at the taping, but that doesn't absolve me. In my pathetic, self-absorbed state, I hurt a good man who I knew was 100 percent innocent.

Yet I was satisfied when the show aired. Vince seemed intimidated by the forces massed against him—in contrast to the usual state where the wrestlers live in fear of the promoter. I felt that I'd delivered a very convincing extended promo, and the company would eventually buckle and pay me some kind of settlement.

> *Jerry McDevitt: Billy's lawyer said that he wanted more than a mil-lion bucks—or Billy had stories to tell about sexual improprieties about a number of people, including Vince. And our attitude was, "Take your best shot."*
>
> *I spoke to everybody I could to get background on Billy. We re-created the past. His criminal record was easy enough to find out. I believe we spoke to his ex-wife, Bunny, and she had plenty to say. We even knew about the stolen television set that he sold to Stu Hart. Vince once asked me how I knew so much, and I said, "If I told you, you wouldn't need me."*

"What year did you marry your wife, Bunny?" McDevitt asked at my June 1993 deposition hearing.

"I can't remember," I answered. "I'm trying to forget."

McDevitt was picking apart my personal history.

"Did you ever use drugs around your previous wife?"

"I wasn't around her very much."

"Did you ever use drugs around your previous wife?"

"Yes."

Jerry had already established that I had a difficult time remembering the name of my third wife, the kleptomaniac. Jerry was a pit bull, and I understood the message that he was trying to convey: What kind of man is so cavalier that he forgets his wife's name? And why in the world had I been married five times?

My goal was to not let him rattle me.

"Do you have a preference as to whether I call you Mr. Coleman or Mr. Graham?" McDevitt asked.

"Superstar is fine, too," I answered.

McDevitt laughed; he sold it.

I then went on to link my steroid use to the McMahon family's decision to crown me champion: "The fact that I had a steroid-induced body defi-nitely influenced their decision . . . because Vince Jr. was infatuated with my physique at that time."

"Nobody told you that you were being picked to be champion because you used steroids," McDevitt said. "Is that correct?"

"They told me that I was picked as champion because of my appear-ance and charisma."

"Which is different than saying you're being picked as champion be-cause you use steroids. Correct?"

"I guess the term is different, but I assumed that my appearance, having an extremely muscular physique, steroid induced, along with my charisma, was the reason they picked me as champion."

"Why do you think they picked Bob Backlund to beat you?"

"Because Vince McMahon Sr. was convinced that Bob Backlund would be another Bruno Sammartino . . . because of his wholesome appearance."

"The fact is . . . that the man you took the belt from, Bruno Sammartino, as well as the man that took the belt from you, Bob Backlund, neither of those two used steroids, did they?"

"No. They did not."

"So both of those men achieved the stature of champion with the World Wrestling Federation without ever touching a steroid. Correct?"

"That's true."

Jerry went down a list of wrestlers who'd worked for the company—George Steele, Dominic DeNucci, Freddie Blassie, and Lou Albano, among others—and had me confirm that, according to my judgment, none of them used steroids.

"How about Andre the Giant?" McDevitt asked.

"I know Andre and . . . believe he did not use steroids."

McDevitt smiled slightly. "Everybody was very thankful for that, I'm sure."

"Yeah," I quipped. "Maybe human growth hormone." I was working the room.

Jerry McDevitt: *It was definitely theater for everyone there. The pharmaceutical firms that were also named in the lawsuit had sent these white-shoe lawyers who weren't used to this kind of character. He made a huge tactical mistake by naming* us *in the lawsuit. We already knew him. The pharmaceutical companies would have had no idea who they were dealing with.*

"You have had extensive dealings with the tabloid media, haven't you?" McDevitt questioned, in another effort to undermine my integrity.

"What is that?"

"You have dealt with *A Current Affair,* right?"

"I believe I did."

"Did you deal with *Hard Copy?*"

"No."

"How about *Inside Edition?*"

"Yes . . . I might like to add one more that I did that I'm very proud of, and that was a Nickelodeon children's program they just aired on the first of the year. I did a steroid interview for Nickelodeon. That's a real good children's program that was obviously not in the tabloid arena. It was very wholesome."

That wasn't a bad line. And I also held my own when Jerry asked me to provide validation of my steroid purchases.

"It's true," he stated, "that you don't have one piece of documentary evidence as to where you purchased them, when you purchased them, or how much you paid for them for so much as one transaction. Is that correct?"

"That's probably true," I retorted. "The only evidence that I have that I used them is in my body, not in a checkbook or receipt. But my body has plenty of evidence."

That was a great comeback, I thought. Still, the heart of my argument—that Vince McMahon and the World Wrestling Federation were responsible for my steroid abuse—was effortlessly shot down by McDevitt's questioning.

"By 1975, when you had your first affiliation with [the WWWF], would I be correct that you had been a steroid user for a decade?" he asked.

"Yes."

With that established, he continued, "Did anybody from Titan [the World Wrestling Federation's corporate name at the time] ever give you steroids?"

"No."

"Did you have any knowledge of anybody from Titan ever giving any wrestlers steroids?"

"No."

Jerry McDevitt: The deposition had been going on for two or three days. I had a couple of document bags with me. I noticed that every time I went for another document, Billy seemed to be getting a little jumpy.

"What else do you have in that bag there, brother?" he asked.

During one of the breaks, I ran into Billy in the bathroom. He started laughing and said, "You're killing me, brother." I've been in this situation with other litigants, and they usually scowl. But he was very charming.

Then he went back out and continued lying.

Even when McDevitt was trying to nail me, I kind of liked him. I'd use a line, and he'd use another one to try to top me. It was almost like cutting promos against Dusty. We definitely enjoyed each other.

The deposition took place in downtown Philadelphia, where everybody knew me. When I'd step out of the elevator or walk down the street, people would stop and yell, "Superstar! Superstar!" One of the pharmaceutical company lawyers came up to me during a break and said, "I was at your Cage match with Bruno. Off the record, do you think I could get your autograph?"

This was an attorney from the *other side!* Can you imagine if his client found out? When it comes to wrestling—except for those absolutely hardcore about "protecting the business"—there's always some humor.

There was nothing funny, though, about the Justice Department's zeal in going after Vince. I now regret feeding the hysteria, as prosecutors formulated a case to put him on trial for steroid distribution. This was kind of bewildering to me. Vince wasn't a *dealer*. I couldn't figure out the government's motive.

This had gone too far. All I wanted was some of Vince McMahon's money. I never intended to send him to the federal penitentiary!

CHAPTER TWENTY

CROSS OVER, BROTHER

He that seeketh findeth.

—James Allen, *As a Man Thinketh*

While I was embroiled in the lawsuit, Valerie persuaded me to go to church with her and try to relieve some of my inner turmoil. In particular, she wanted to introduce me to Jeff Fenholt, a vocalist who'd performed with Black Sabbath before becoming a minister. So we drove to Apple Valley, California, a beautiful location in the high desert, enjoyed the service, and accepted an invitation from Jeff to attend a barbecue afterward. Jeff had long hair and a cool rock'n'roll presence. He was surrounded by a group of bikers who'd also turned to God.

"We want to get some people saved here," he announced as his guests sat around picnic tables and balanced platefuls of food. "And we also want people who've been away from God to come back and rededicate their lives to the Lord."

He looked in my direction and smiled: "Come on, brother, I know who you are."

It was exactly what I needed. Jeff and I approached each other. "Say some prayers for me, brother," I asked. We prayed together, and my terrible burden was lifted—at least for the time being.

We spent the rest of the afternoon talking about wrestling and rock'n'roll and the Lord. The chemistry was definitely there, and we decided to stay in touch.

I soon realized that I couldn't get back with God while pursuing a fictitious case against Vince McMahon. So shortly after the deposition hearing, I wrote a one-paragraph letter to my attorney, telling him that I had flat-out lied to him about the critical contents of the lawsuit and I now wished to drop the case. I had a very guilty conscience—or, as church insiders would say, I was convicted by God's presence in my life. Lying and serving God do not mix well.

Vince was indicted on November 23, 1993, and charged with distributing anabolic steroids to World Wrestling Federation performers. He faced eight years in prison, among other penalties. In the event that the government achieved this goal, he arranged for Memphis-based promoter Jerry Jarrett to run the wrestling end of the company. But—Vince being Vince—he refused to even contemplate a plea bargain.

By the time of the trial, Hogan had left the World Wrestling Federation to work for the company's main rival, World Championship Wrestling (WCW). The U.S. attorney's office subpoenaed the Hulkster as their star witness. But that only resulted in exchanges like this:

"Did you ever hear Vince McMahon tell a wrestler he should take steroids?"

"No."

"Do you recall any conversations with Vince McMahon where he implied a wrestler should take steroids?"

"No."

On July 22, 1994, Vince was acquitted.

Meanwhile, Jeff Fenholt and I became friends, and during lunch one day, I told him about my experiences preaching. "Brother," Jeff responded, "you were called. We can walk away from the calling, but the calling is always there. The Lord has allowed you to come full circle, man. The fame you have from pro wrestling can be a platform for the Lord."

Jeff became almost like a Jerry Russell to me—a spiritual mentor. He invited me to go around with him, visiting different churches, not necessarily to preach sermons but to give my personal testimony. He also encouraged me to offer to speak to congregations on my own. Some said yes, some said no. But the rejection letters were priceless. The terminology was so unique—and different than anything you'd encounter in the corporate world.

For example, after being informed that a particular church already had enough guest speakers scheduled, a typical letter would continue, "We are excited to hear how God is using your powerful testimony to expand his Kingdom. We are sure that the dramatic change in your lifestyle after your rededication to The Lord bears witness to God's grace and mercy, and will bring glory to His name, and many souls to salvation. Praise God! However, our calendar happens to be full for the next two years."

Through Jeff, I was fortunate to meet Larry Kerychuk, the director of Athletes International Ministries (AIM), an organization of Christian athletes. Larry is a third-generation pastor, and former player in the Canadian Football League. In fact, his roommate at one point was Bob Lueck, the bouncer at J.D.'s who'd encouraged me, first, to try out for the Calgary Stampeders, and then to train with the Mentor of Mayhem, Stu Hart.

> *Larry Kerychuk: I remembered watching Superstar Billy Graham on TV when he wrestled in Minnesota. Then, lo and behold, he was back in my life again. This time, I met him in person, when I saw Jeff Fenholt coming down the hallway in my church, with Billy behind him.*
>
> *He said, "Man, this guy just rededicated himself to Christ. What do I do with him now?"*

It so happened that AIM was located in Phoenix, and Kerychuk needed help expanding the ministry. Although Valerie had a well-paying job in California, it didn't take any convincing to get her to leave it; both of us felt that a change might be healthy. So we moved to Phoenix, where I rekindled some old friendships and began working closely with Larry.

Phoenix had changed dramatically, even from the last time that I'd lived there—and few of those modifications benefited the public good. In 2004, Phoenix edged out Philadelphia as the fifth largest metropolis in the United States, and had transformed itself from a beautiful desert oasis to a crime-infested, smog-choked city. Among the dubious claims of the Valley of the Sun: supremacy in methamphetamine dealing, red-light running, and hit-and-run accidents. Arizona had broken borders with Mexico, and an estimated 5,000 illegal immigrants pour into the state every day. There are now shootouts on our freeways between rival coyotes vying for each other's load of human cargo. We have hundreds of drop houses where up to fifty people are crammed into one residence, waiting to be dispersed by the predators who brought them to the United States under the most inhumane conditions.

This is tied into the hit-and-run issue. On small fender-benders, illegal aliens may give you the middle finger and drive off—it's happened to me. The only one of these cases that I can recall involving a naturalized citizen occurred in 2003. That's when our own Bishop Thomas O'Brien had to resign his vaunted position at the Catholic diocese after fatally striking a jaywalker. Without bothering to stop, the clergyman drove home and parked his dented Buick in the garage. He told police that he thought that he'd hit a dog or a rock. In fact, it was a 240-pound Native American.

Valerie and I were welcomed as family into Larry's church, Phoenix First Assembly of God. The striking, white-walled sanctuary seats about 6,500, and occupies seventy-five acres on Shadow Mountain. Because of programs assisting AIDS victims, the elderly, and the homeless, the congregation calls itself "The Church with a Heart." Members wash off graffiti, mow lawns, and fix up homes in the inner city. The senior pastor, and my spiritual leader, Tommy Barnett, is legitimately the most sincere man on earth.

> **Valerie Coleman:** *It was absolutely wonderful to be back at Phoenix First Assembly. This was my "home church." I began attending there in 1980. I'd go alone because Wayne was using pills pretty heavily at the time and wasn't interested in going with me. At the end of each service, I'd get down on my knees at the altar and pray for the Lord to help my husband. Now it appeared that my prayers were being answered.*

Through the ministry, Mr. T and I took part in Reverend Pat Robertson's Operation Blessing campaign, distributing bags of food in El Paso, Texas. I visited prisons, and came face to face with Karla Faye Tucker, who killed two people with a pickax during a 1983 drug-fueled frenzy—boasting that she received sexual gratification from the murders. But when I met Karla Faye, who had become a Christian in prison and formed a group called the Life Row Sisters with several other death row inmates, she exuded an earnest, gentle countenance. Together, these women are credited with thousands of conversions within the Texas penal system.

It's hard to understand how God can forgive a person like Karla Faye for such a heinous crime, but as I sat there speaking with her in her death row cell, I believe that her spirit was transformed. In 1998, under orders from then-governor George W. Bush, she became the first woman executed in Texas since before the Civil War.

I'm convinced that she is in paradise.

As I traveled, I began to feel that Christian principles—well, not just *Christian* principles, but basic American principles—were under siege. Along with lessons about evolution, I think that we can make room for the concept of a divine designer. How do you explain the complicated mechanics of the human eye? Why do oceans store heat for the rest of the planet? How do the respiratory and nervous systems work in tandem with each other? All these questions point to the existence of a master blueprint created by a supreme architect, a God who, in the words of Albert Einstein, "reveals himself in the harmony of all that exists."

Fortunately, at least one school district in Pennsylvania is now encouraging students to question Charles Darwin's ideas, offering "intelligent design" as an alternative. Finally, pupils can consider the premise that nature may be too complex to have developed by chance. All I want is for my grandchildren to learn that evolution is a theory, rather than an indisputable fact.

Unfortunately, we have organizations like the ACLU that have declared an unholy jihad against anything involving the God of the Bible. The unrelenting attack on Christmas is pure evil in my eyes. I celebrate Christmas, but because it is not celebrated by a tiny segment of the American population, we can no longer say "Merry Christmas" in public. Now, it has to be "Season's Greetings." Instead of "Christmas vacation," we have "winter break." Christmas carols are banned from schools because they might offend students of different religions. Christmas scenes are forbidden on state property. The collapse of Christmas is unparalleled in American history.

The absurdity of political correctness even affects the celebration of Halloween. In 2004, one Washington State school district canceled events related to the holiday because no one wanted to upset witches and warlocks. Have we really reached that place in America where we are concerned about offending a witch?

In 1995 I learned that my dear friend, John Minton—aka Big John Studd—was suffering from Hodgkin's disease. It started as a massive tumor in his chest, and just expanded. Although it can't be proven, I suspect that the condition was accelerated by his consumption of human growth hormone. Regardless, Studd—a man who always had a spare room for me in his home—knew that his time was near. And I wanted to help him prepare to meet the Lord. He let me witness to him over the phone, and told me that he had no fear of death because he knew that he was going to heaven. He said he had spent the days gazing at a portrait of Jesus on his bedroom wall.

On a Friday, John called to say that his doctors had just informed him that his chemotherapy was no longer working, and he had a week to live. Two days later, I felt a burden to call John. His wife, Donna, told me that he could no longer speak, but she put the phone to his ear. When he understood something, he blinked. If he didn't, he opened and closed his eyes in another pattern.

"Don't be afraid," I told him. "Let go of the pain. Go on ahead to the Lord. He's waiting for you."

I'd heard the breath of life of a newborn baby in my ear, the soft spray of Joey and Capella. Now, I listened to the labor of a dying man who could do nothing more than struggle to breathe. The air passed through his lips in excited bursts as I told him, "Just cross over, brother."

Two hours later, I received word that he had passed away.

Whether you're a Christian or an atheist, you have to make corrections in your life if you want to move forward on your road through it. Religion notwithstanding, I needed to apologize to Vince, as a matter of character. One should not have to be motivated by an outside force to be a man of dignity. But with my recent rededication to the Lord, I felt a duty to make amends with Vince, and wrote the following letter:

May 29, 1996

Dear Vince,

I know that you are an extremely busy man with many important items on your agenda. I just ask that you take a few minutes of your time to read this letter. I want to express my many regrets for all the false statements and inappropriate actions that I have taken against you in the past. There is absolutely no excuse for the things I have done regarding you and your business. Having always considered you a friend in the truest sense of the word, I was caught completely off-guard when you let me go in 1989. With no explanation, I was terminated. This left me very angry but, more than that, I was hurt. So I thought that I was justified when I verbally attacked you through the media and, subsequently, through the lawsuit, but that was not the case.

Vince, the most significant event that has happened in my life is that I rededicated myself to The Lord, Jesus Christ. When God calls someone into the ministry, it is a lifetime call. How one responds to that call throughout his life is up to him, as God has given each of us a free will. Having renewed my commitment to that calling has opened my eyes and my heart, and is the driving force behind this letter.

I am asking you to forgive me for all the wrong I have done to you and your family. My prayer is that you will find it in your heart to accept my apology because I am truly sorry. I have asked The Lord to forgive me. I now ask you.

In the Book of Mark 8:36–37, it reads:

"For what does it profit a man to gain the whole world and lose his own soul? And what shall a man give in exchange for his soul?"

Also, in the Book of Psalms, King David compares our life to that of a vapor. It is here one minute, and gone the next. Valerie and I are praying that if you already haven't asked Jesus to be your personal savior, that you will do so now.

In closing, I hope that I will someday have the opportunity to speak with you over the phone or, better yet, in person.

With respect,
Billy

While my sentiments were heartfelt, when I look back on this letter, I feel that I was presumptuous in a number of areas. First of all, who was I to suggest that Vince McMahon had better get right with God? How did I know that he wasn't *already* right with God? When you get that fire in you—as I did after my rededication—it makes you stretch out a little bit.

And I shouldn't have included that quote from the Book of Mark, about gaining the world and losing your soul. It sounded judgmental—like Vince had to sell his soul to be successful. There was a good deal of conjecture in that letter that I no longer think is justified.

Fortunately, I don't believe that Vince was insulted.

Vince McMahon: I felt that Billy was telling me the truth. Sometimes with the born-agains, you wonder whether it's an angle or not. But I have to accept people for what they tell me. If they're conning me, they're only conning themselves in the long run.

I'd always been Billy's friend. I don't know if he's always been mine. I know that friendship is not 50-50. There's management, and then there's the boys. And they haven't always mixed.

In terms of getting back to Superstar right away, it wasn't a pri-

Doing the Lord's work.

ority on my list. I first and foremost owe my time to the individuals who are working for me now. I don't necessarily owe someone who has done and said the things that Superstar has done in the past.

Around this same period, I witnessed some very disturbing sights in the Full Gospel world of believers. When I was an evangelist as a young man, we passed the hat, sometimes receiving a $30 payoff for one service. And after my rededication, I conducted myself the same way—averaging $300 to $500 at some of the smaller churches, and $1,000 at the larger ones (the various ministries generally paid the hotel and airfare). The fluctuating pay scale is not unlike what I experienced working for Eddie Graham.

But as a creed of greed has infiltrated this society, more and more guest preachers want to set a fee. It's considered impolite—and un-Christian—to flat-out ask, "How much money am I getting?" So they use a working term, "I hope you'll be sensitive to my needs."

It is hard not to get caught up in this frenzy. For example, while I was preaching in the 1990s, I attempted to supplement my income by selling silk-screened T-shirts with scriptural quotes, as well as autographed photos. Other guest speakers—including the most honest ones—sold CDs and books. But in order to move your merchandise, you had to set yourself up at a table with a display near the exit of the church. So as the services were ending, and I'd give a basic altar call—"Who wants to come up and get saved?"—I found myself preoccupied with rushing over to the gimmick table. There was no time to cast out demons. Suddenly, the altar call became an obstacle to get out of the way so I could make my money.

I didn't like peddling Jesus paraphernalia. I didn't like it from day one.

For all the decent preachers, like my pastor and Del Way—a country-style singer and musician in Kerrville, Texas—I still see things as questionable as when I was doing the revival circuit. I'm going to cast some stones here. Once, I heard "prophetess" Juanita Bynum speak about how, when she desperately needed money, the Lord commanded her to go to the nearest ATM machine.

"He spoke to me," she said. " 'I'm your Redeemer. I'm your Supplier. Just put in your card.' And, lo and behold, children of God, I went to this ATM machine and out came $600! Now, that's Jesus for you."

Salvation is an unrelenting mystery. Is the headhunter in New Guinea going down because he's never heard the name of Jesus Christ? Is Mother Teresa in hell because she was a Catholic? Many people I've met actually believe that. How about my co-author, Keith Elliot Greenberg? He was raised Jewish, and does not believe that Jesus Christ is the Messiah. Is he doomed to end up in a lake of eternal fire?

Recently, a friend was having lunch with another Christian in a restaurant when a member of my church spotted them and concluded that they were seated too close to the bar. To make matters worse, the righteous congregant ratted on them to my pastor, who called them in for a conference. "Just think, man," I joked to my friend, "if you were another five feet away from the bar, no one would have had a case against you." What sick, holy hypocrisy!

My friend, pro wrestler Bill Anderson, once attended Pastor James Willoughby's church in Ontario, California, and went up for an altar call in order to have "a little closer walk with Thee."

"Hey, brother, have you spoken in tongues yet?" asked the guest speaker, Marvin Smith, a former pro football player for the Los Angeles Rams.

"Well, not really."

"Well, you better check yourself, man. Because you are not saved until you speak in tongues."

That's just an example of the laughable absurdity I've encountered in the World of God. If you watch the Reverend Jesse Duplantis, you may have heard his personal testimony about God giving him a vision of Jesus Christ, sitting on the throne of heaven. Now, in the Bible, when the Apostle Paul was allowed to see heaven, he was told not to speak of what he witnessed. But those rules were obviously waived for Mr. Duplantis. He gave a vivid description of the celestial kingdom, and claimed to be quite surprised to see angels without wings. Others had one or two, and some even had four. But the big moment came when Duplantis himself stood up and ascended to the throne, in front of Jesus. Duplantis said that he'd expected the Lord's hair to be white like his. But Jesus' hair was actually brown. He was also taller than the preacher anticipated.

"Do you like this place?" Jesus apparently asked his guest.

"Yes, sir."

Why do people who claim to be of God work us so much?

In my opinion, the biggest embarrassment is Benny Hinn. I've watched him on TV, blowing on people in the prayer line, while they fall to the ground under the anointed breath of the famous televangelist. And his expensive, custom-made suits are apparently anointed, too! Because when he hurls his rolled-up suit jacket at a crowd, at least six or seven grown men will go down at a time. Hinn claims to have healed the sick and the lame. Well, I'd like to extend an invitation to the reverend: come to the Mayo

Clinic in Scottsdale, and help the surgeons heal those livers that need transplanting, like mine. I know the people at the Mayo, Benny Hinn. I can get you in.

People who knowingly take bumps for a renowned evangelist have a working term for the process. They call it a "courtesy drop," or a C.D., and it means that they're willing to hit the floor out of respect to the preacher's celebrity. Another athlete I know told me a story about being in a prayer line with George Foreman. When the evangelist laid his hands on my buddy and the former boxing champion, they each took a C.D.—neither wanted to offend the man of God. After a few seconds, Foreman rolled his head over to my friend, winked, and asked, "How long do we stay down?"

Valerie and I were once at a church with her mother in Tampa, Florida, and we noticed that every single person who was touched by the pastor, Randy White, was going down. Some kid about ten years old was flip-flopping on the ground, and taking bumps against the poles supporting the tent.

"Are you all right?" Valerie's mother asked him.

"Oh, yeah. I do this every Sunday. I'm the pastor's son."

There are no C.D.'s allowed in my church, by the way. And I want to reemphasize that my intention here is not to demean anyone legitimately doing the Lord's work.

I'm pro-faith, but—when it comes to serving God—I'm anti-gimmick.

CHAPTER TWENTY-ONE

FOR KATIE

Hold on to life
Even when it is easier to let go.

—Pueblo Indian blessing

When Dr. Jerry Graham died of a stroke in 1997, someone from the nursing home notified me that I could come in and claim his remains.

"I won't be doing that," I responded.

"But you're his brother," the caller said with a Filipino accent.

"I'm not really his brother."

"You're *not* his brother?"

It was clear that this man wasn't smart to the wrestling business, and probably didn't have enough command of the American vernacular to understand the term "gimmick."

"I'm his *stage* brother," I finally explained.

The man didn't realize how close I was to re-forming my Tag Team with the Good Doctor in the afterlife. And I feared that, like Jerry, I'd end up in a pauper's grave.

In the late 1990s, I found that I barely had enough energy to get through the day. The release of ammonia into my system had caused "brain fog," limiting my ability to concentrate and interact on an intellectual level. I began dropping excessive amounts of speed to offset the situation, but I was still exhausted. Soon I was abusing the drug so badly that I broke out in little bruises all over my body. Speed freaks and meth addicts call these "speed bumps."

I went to see my internist, Dr. Deborah Michael, who immediately recognized that there was something wrong with my liver. A blood test revealed that I had hepatitis C, an illness that I may have acquired from those free exchanges of blood with opponents in the ring. As it turned out, the speed was aggravating the condition.

> *Dr. Deborah Michael: Wayne was a handful. He's got a hard head. And at times he was a little sneaky. He didn't inform me that other people were giving him narcotics. He was trying to increase his energy, and he wanted uppers from both me and his orthopedic surgeon. Of course, his bones are bad. That's not what he should be doing. And I'd have to say, "You can't have more than one person prescribing for you, you little skunk."*

I was scheduled for another hip replacement—this time on the right side of my body—when, at just thirty-nine years-old, Valerie was diagnosed with cancer in her left breast. This was a tragic revelation. She'd been taking care of me for so long, and now the cards had shifted. I was heartbroken.

One of the few bright spots in my life was the fact that I'd become close to Capella again, after she became pregnant. Valerie had always wanted children, and she ingratiated herself even further with Capella by showing maternal instincts toward my newborn granddaughter, Caitlin. We drove to Los Angeles to celebrate with my daughter and her husband, Mike, but it was just two weeks after Valerie's diagnosis. While we were all in a restaurant with the baby, I broke down.

I was terrified over the possibility of losing Valerie.

When we returned to Arizona, I told Valerie, "We have to be aggressive. Cut the breast off. Get rid of the cancer."

> *Valerie Coleman: From the moment I heard the words "I'm so sorry, Valerie, but you have ductal carcinoma in situ," I knew what I*

Capella and I during *WrestleMania 21*.

had to do. As much as I hated the idea of a mastectomy, a breast wasn't something that I was willing to exchange my life for. I'm very blessed that my husband felt the same way; in fact, Wayne was even more adamant about it than I was.

Valerie survived the cancer surgery, and I had yet another hip replacement. As we both recovered, I purchased Mick Foley's book, *Have a Nice Day*. Prior to this time, the attitude in publishing had been that wrestling fans didn't read. But Foley ended that delusion forever when *Have a Nice Day* shot to number one on the *New York Times* best-seller list. Foley had the ability to communicate with his reader like he was talking to a friend. I loved the book and thought that maybe, just maybe, I could pull off the same thing one day.

Mick Foley: I started watching Billy Graham when I was growing up on Long Island. Your first impression is often a lasting one, and a lot of what I consider professional wrestling to be comes from Billy Graham—the promos, the flamboyance. It's funny because I can kind of tell where people come from by the wrestler they mention to me from their youth. If they grew up in the Pacific Northwest, it might be Dutch Savage or Moondog Mayne. In Minnesota, it would be Verne Gagne. In Indiana, Dick the Bruiser. For me, it's Bruno, of course, and Billy Graham.

In 2003, I wrote a novel called Tietam Brown. *It was not a wrestling book, but I worked Billy's name into the story. There's one line where someone says that her husband is out of town meeting with Billy Graham. To which the main character replies, "The wrestler?"*

She says, "No, the preacher."

As I researched my book, a talented Web master named Steve Slagle helped create a Superstar Billy Graham Web site (www.superstarbilly graham.com). Now that I had a public forum, I wanted to resolve something else I'd done publicly: lying about Pat Patterson on *The Phil Donahue Show* in 1992. With the evil words I used that day, I told readers, I "descended to a level lower than a beast. . . . And, Pat, I'm directing this to you right now. I do apologize to you, right here, right now. I pray that you will accept my apology, and I ask for your forgiveness."

I also sent several letters to Pat. "I have absolutely no excuse for my behavior," I wrote in 2004. "I made a huge mistake, one that I deeply regret. You have never been anything but good to me. You were my mentor in Frisco, you loaned me money, taught me how to work, and were a tremendous friend. You certainly didn't deserve my wrath."

Pat has never responded. And who could blame him?

Vince McMahon: I've forgiven Superstar. Pat Patterson, to this day, can't forgive him. He would never forgive him.

By this point, my health was rapidly declining. I was becoming too weak to go to the gym, and became winded after just walking a few feet. My appetite was gone. After one apple, I felt full. Yet I was gaining weight, and couldn't understand why. What I didn't know was that my liver could not properly process toxins in my body, so there was an overflow of liquid— known as edema—into my legs, hands, and stomach. As if I was a pregnant woman, the spillover pushed against my diaphragm, inhibiting my breathing.

The increased pressure in my vascular system made the veins in my esophagus balloon dangerously outward. Having no idea that this was occurring, I assumed that I had a terrible case of heartburn, and tried correcting it by swallowing antacids. In December 2001 I felt sick to my stomach, and was tossing from side to side in bed. Suddenly I coughed and ruptured one of the veins, splashing a gusher of dark, chunky fluid all over Valerie. It was my own blood—mixed with mucus and every other vile thing in my stomach.

Valerie rushed me to John C. Lincoln Hospital, where I continued to vomit, filling literal buckets with blood. I'd get finished with one container, put it down, and start with another. From the loss of blood and the release of ammonia into my brain, I was overcome with confusion. Yet I knew that I was ebbing away.

Tears were flowing down Valerie's cheeks as she held her Bible and prayed openly.

"Father, in the name of your son Jesus Christ, I claim your promises for my husband, Wayne."

It took three hours before we even saw a doctor, who immediately turned me on my side to stick a scope down my throat to explore the source of the bleeding. Before inserting the device, though, he sprayed my mouth with a numbing medication. The moment he did, I vomited blood again, covering the wall and coating the doctor, who hadn't had time to put on his scrubs.

Valerie Coleman: *As unbelievable as it sounds, the doctor was actually angry at Wayne for ruining his suit. It was 6:00 A.M., and I was alone in the ICU waiting room when this idiot came in to tell me, "Your husband is bleeding from his entire stomach. We can't stop the bleeding. There's nothing we can do." He went on to say that Wayne would be gone in less than an hour. At that moment all I had was the Lord, and as I've done throughout my life, I placed my hope in Him.*

Within the hour, not only was Wayne still alive, but the bleeding had miraculously stopped without any medical intervention. Having spent way too much time in hospitals, I've learned a few things, so when I was allowed back into his room in ICU, the first thing I did was check his vital signs on the monitor. His blood pressure was extremely low, and his heart rate was very fast. I knew he was failing. In the doctor's rush to go home and change his clothes, he neglected to order a blood transfusion for my husband. I immediately got the nurse, who called for another doctor without hesitation. As soon as Wayne received the first unit of blood, he began to stabilize.

As soon as I began to stabilize, I had a team of doctors around me—kidney and liver specialists, a cardiologist, and a gastroenterologist. The problem was that they were all treating me separately, oblivious to how one medication was affecting another. Once again, I was starting to wane—until Dr. Deborah Michael stormed into the room and made the save, forcing the various "experts" to coordinate my care, and rescuing me from death.

Nonetheless, she concluded that my liver was losing its ability to function. At some point, I was going to need a transplant.

Two weeks later, I had my second bleed.

The difference was that now I knew what to expect when I became sick to my stomach. This time we drove to the Mayo Clinic in Scottsdale. I was a little bit dazed, but as I lay in the emergency room, I counted seven different people working on me at once. I was fearful; this was not a hopeful scene.

The plan was to place a scope down my throat again, and find the source of the bleeding and stop it there. I was wheeled upstairs to a hospital room where—yet another time—a doctor sprayed the inside of my mouth.

On this occasion, the wave of hepatitis-contaminated blood traveled some five feet and hit the wall—like a can of red paint flung against a canvas. As the doctors treated me, I was sure that I would not survive.

> **Steve Strong:** *Valerie called and—these are her exact words—she said, "If you want to see Wayne alive, you've got to get here right now."*
>
> *My girlfriend, Susan, and I ran to the hospital as fast as we could. Valerie was hunched over, crying. Our feet were sticking to the blood on the floor. I was looking at Superstar, and he was white, so white that I said, "Oh, Valerie, we're so glad that we were able to be here to say our good-byes."*
>
> *A couple of people from the church were there, and we all joined hands. We lock in, and we're all in a circle. We're all sending our light to Billy. I'm coming from an absolutely spiritual direction—I don't care what we're mumbling. I'm talking to Allah, Buddha, Isis, Krishna. At that point, Jesus was just one of the boys on the card.*
>
> *The nurse is looking at us, thinking, "Gosh, it's beautiful what you guys are doing. But I've been there, done that, and it's not going to happen." Then she tells us that we have to leave the room.*
>
> *My girlfriend and I go down to the cafeteria, and we're sitting there, just looking at each other. And we're saying, "At least we're a part of it. At least we got to see history pass before our eyes." We're*

down there an hour, an hour and a half, and the nurse says, "You guys can go back into the room now."

This is not a thing that I contrived. I watched Superstar Billy Graham come back from the dead. I saw him get the color back on his face. I saw him sit up on the bed. I heard him joke and smile and start talking to me in carny: "Where's the ne-iz-urse around here?"

While Steve was downstairs, the doctor, Dr. V. J. Balan, transfused me, went down my throat with an endoscope and banded seven varices, or burst veins. He was astonished that the doctor at the first hospital hadn't done the same. Because of the blood loss, Dr. Balan told me that it was very possible that I could experience heart or kidney failure, or lose some digits. As it turned out, I suffered none of these residual effects.

But I needed to get on the list for a liver transplant right away.

As cold as it sounds, doctors want to make sure that you're salvageable before performing a transplant. There are so few livers around that they can't waste one on somebody who's destined to die. The natural progression from hepatitis C is cirrhosis of the liver, then cancer. If the cancer is contained in the liver, you can still qualify for the list. If it's spread, you cannot. Anyone with serious heart disease would also be barred.

I was told that I might have a window of five years before my liver shut down. That certainly seemed manageable. Even with other people ahead of me, five years was a relatively long time.

Valerie Coleman: I was trying to think of what I could do to bring some joy to Wayne, to cheer him, to give him something to look forward to. So, without Wayne knowing, I called Vince McMahon and told him what the doctors had said about a liver transplant. I could hear the concern and emotion in his voice. He asked if there was anything he could do. I said, "Yes, could you please call Wayne personally?"

I picked up the receiver and heard Vince's unmistakable voice, "How you doing, Superstar?"

"Pretty good, Vince. This is a great phone call."

Although Vince and I never socialized or trained together in the gym, there had always been a strong bond between us. World Wrestling Entertainment business was through the roof, and he invited me to attend a live event in Phoenix.

"I'd love to come down and give you a hug," I answered, "but I'm just too sick."

"Well, Superstar," Vince replied, "if you change your mind, I'll have to put you in the main event."

I was elated. And, in recent months, there had been an even more satisfying development in my life: my son, Joey, and I were starting to become friends.

> *Joe Miluso: When I finally fell in love with somebody—Sarah, the girl who became my wife—I began thinking about the rest of my life. Sarah and I were talking about starting a family, and I didn't want my children not to know their grandfather. I thought, "Maybe it's time to give my dad a chance to be my dad again."*
>
> *I'd never known that my dad had been there for my surgeries. With all the animosity between my mom and my dad, it's not something she would have told me. I was so young that the only things I remembered were the operations. Everything else kind of blacked out. When my dad told me that he was at the hospital, too, it changed my perception.*

Meanwhile, the fluid was still continuing to accumulate in my body, expanding my stomach to the point that it popped my belly button outward, with a crease down the middle. As a result, I'd have to visit the Mayo every two weeks or more and have five to seven liters of the liquid—called ascites—drained. The buildup also caused two hernias—in my abdominal area and groin—that nullified any notion of working out. Incredibly, I still *wanted* to train. Sometimes the inability to do so seemed as unbearable as my physical pain.

In June 2002, Shawn Michaels was a guest at the Athletes International Ministries (AIM) annual conference in Phoenix. The two of us had never spoken—he was just starting in the World Wrestling Federation when I was on my way out—and he had recently become a Christian. Perhaps believing that I would not be around for the next meeting, the group dedicated the conference to me. During the banquet, I was so weak that I had to be helped onto the stage. When Shawn came up to pay his respects, we made eye contact in front of the podium. The Heartbreak Kid studied my sickly appearance—my gaunt features, my hollow eyes—broke into tears, and embraced me.

There were 1,000 people in the audience, and they all joined Shawn in crying for the real walking dead man.

The highlight of my evening came when Larry Kerychuk began reading a letter from Arnold. I have this letter framed and hanging on my wall at home. It's one of my most prized possessions.

This totally caught me by surprise. Taking time out from his busy schedule to write to a friend in need of encouragement speaks volumes about the man's character. He hasn't forgotten his friends.

The first person who offered to become a living donor was Don Chandler, a Christian waiter I knew from one of my favorite restaurants, and a National Guard reservist later dispatched to Afghanistan. In an adult-to-adult transplant, doctors generally remove 60 percent of the liver mass, on the right side of the donor's body. Within two or three weeks, that person's liver grows back to its normal size. Don prepared himself for this procedure by undergoing a battery of tests. When doctors discovered that he had a fatty liver, he was disqualified.

After the AIM conference another two guys also stepped forward as candidates—Terry Taylor, who'd been "The Red Rooster" in the World Wrestling Federation, and Michael Hegstrand, better known as Road Warrior Hawk. Doctors determined that Terry had the wrong blood type. And, like me, Hawk was afflicted with hepatitis C.

In a disturbing twist of irony, a year later—after cleaning up his life,

ARNOLD SCHWARZENEGGER

June 28, 2002

Mr. Wayne Coleman
VIA FACSIMILE
Radisson Resort: (480) 948-1381
Attn: Wendy Kerychuk / Guest with Athletes International

Dear Wayne,

I truly wish I could be there with you tonight to celebrate this fantastic occasion to honor you and your incredible career as "The Superstar Billy Graham". I am currently filming "Terminator 3" and am required to be on set this evening. However, we have shared so many terrific memories together and I want to express to you how thrilled I am that you are receiving this honor.

I will never forget all of the fun we had back then, such as the long photo shoots you would come along on, making me laugh the whole time, taking your mother to the wrestling matches and watching along with her as you entertained the audience with your dynamic moves, as well as many other memorable times.

I also remember very early in my career observing your professionalism and how considerate you were to all of your fans. I had and still have a tremendous amount of respect for you.

Now as you are encountering the incredible health challenges before you, I know you will tackle them with the grace, dignity and positive attitude you have always had in every situation you have faced.

My thoughts and prayers are with you, my friend. Enjoy your evening. This is your night and you deserve it!

Stay strong!

Warmest Regards,

It was great to talk to you on the phone the other day. :)

Arnold Schwarzenegger

following years of substance abuse—the forty-five-year-old Hegstrand died himself, from an apparent heart attack.

> **Larry Kerychuk, director, AIM:** *I felt that I was the perfect liver donor. My blood pressure was perfect. I had a good liver. I never drank or smoked my entire life. I passed the psychological exam. All I had to do was lose a few pounds before the operation, so I began climbing mountains and getting into shape. I lost between fifteen and twenty pounds.*

Wayne began coming to my home and connecting with my family. They were all supportive. We believed that this was what God wanted me to do.

Then they dropped the bomb on us. Someone had made a mistake in the lab. The blood types didn't match. I couldn't go any further.

Fans called the Mayo, volunteering to become donors. One seventy-nine-year-old woman claimed that she'd had a full life, and didn't need her liver anymore. The Mayo had a policy in place, forbidding "Good Samaritan" volunteers from off the street. But the hospital staff was mystified. Why would a person whom I'd never met let doctors sever a piece of a vital organ on my behalf?

I also found these offers amazing. Years ago, I'd abandoned the hardcore stance against so-called marks. A generation later, these fans were willing to risk their lives to save mine.

Other fans called and e-mailed, raising my morale. Andrew DiCiacco, a mechanical engineer, had grown up in Boston, stuffing Nerf footballs under his sleeves and cutting promos to his mother: *"I am the reflection of perfection. The number-one selection."* Now he became one of my primary sources of support.

Andrew DiCiacco: *I have Crohn's disease and multiple sclerosis, so I know what it's like to be very ill, and unsure of your future. Wayne and I sent each other books about positive thinking, and laughed over the phone about his old promos and matches. I was hoping and praying that everything would be all right. But I wasn't praying for Superstar Billy Graham. I was praying for Wayne Coleman, the man who'd become my friend.*

At age fifty-five, Ron Pritchard—my Navajo Indian reservation opponent—just met the eligibility requirement as a living donor. But he was in fantastic shape, and wanted to volunteer. While preparing for surgery, he took a requisite MRI—never suspecting that doctors would find a cancerous tumor on his kidney the size of a quarter. Through Ron's selfless act for an old friend, his own life was spared.

He was also eliminated as a donor.

Valerie and I were, naturally, relieved for Ron. But we'd run out of donors. Now we were really scared.

I was becoming even more disoriented too. While walking out of the kitchen one night, I tried stepping over the dog, but scared him. As he jumped up, I slipped and crashed my head against the kitchen tiles. When your body is so fragile, there's always a fear of massive bleeding in the brain. But a CAT scan revealed nothing.

> *Valerie Coleman: We were both very despondent. One morning, I was standing in the kitchen window, looking at Wayne sitting by himself, next to the pool in our apartment complex. His back was to me, so I couldn't figure out what he was doing. But when I saw his hand going back and forth in a violent motion, I knew. He was mutilating himself with his keys.*

I knew the statistics. There are approximately 20,000 Americans on the waiting list for liver transplants. And only about 3,000 receive the liver they need to stay alive. Now I was at the back of the line. I felt hopeless.

I didn't want to scare Valerie any further, but told my sister Joyce about the type of funeral that I wanted. Pastor Tommy would conduct the service. Vince McMahon would deliver part of the eulogy. The ceremony couldn't be on a Monday or Tuesday; those were days when WWE was busy producing its *Raw* and *SmackDown!* TV shows. I wanted a time convenient to my wrestling friends who'd want to attend.

I instructed Joyce not to have me cremated; it gave me chills just to think of that. I wanted to be buried on the north side of Phoenix, near Scottsdale, close to Valerie. And there couldn't be too many trees around the tombstone. I loved being in the sun my entire life, and wanted to stay there.

These plans came shockingly close to being realized. After Ron Pritchard was disqualified, doctors revised their analysis of my condition. I no longer had five years. I needed a transplant *now*. I later found out that more than 90 percent of my liver cells were dead. The prognosis was that I would die within thirty days. But then, Katie Gillroy entered my life.

> *Rita Gillroy: My daughter, Katie, loved animals—cats, dogs, horses, cows, whatever. Through the years, we've had parakeets and hamsters. Katie volunteered at the Humane Society, and once tried to talk me into taking in a dog with three legs. I said, "Honey, we've already got frogs and fish. I work all day. We've got enough to do." She went around to all of her friends until she found one who would take it.*
>
> *Katie's son, Jason, was born in 1998. She adored him. He was the love of her life. It was hard because she was a single mother, working as a waitress and in child care, and going to school to be an X-ray*

Katie Gillroy.

technician. I worked days. She worked evenings. But we made sure that one of us was always home with Jason.

Katie appreciated my help. She knew I loved cheesecake, so, I'd say at least once a month, she'd drive to my job—I'm a security guard at a high school—and drop off a few slices for me.

I guess that one of the most important things she ever did was signing her donor card. No one told her to. She did it on her own when she got her driver's license at sixteen. She told us, "If something happens to me, if I'm dead and gone, my organs are of no use to me anymore. Give them to people who can use them."

That's why, when Katie died, my husband, Dan, and I knew what she wanted us to do. We donated her heart, her kidneys, and her liver, out of respect for her wishes.

Valerie and I were about to go out to lunch when we received the crucial phone call, "Mr. Coleman, get to the Mayo immediately. We have your liver."

The two of us looked at each other, paralyzed in time for a moment. "Do we have time to shower?" I asked, walking in a circle. "Do we have time to brush our teeth?"

"Wayne," Valerie emphasized, "they said *now*. Let's go!"

"My God, Valerie," I told her. "This is it."

Valerie Coleman: *It was only after Wayne's surgery that his sister Joyce told me that she and the rest of his family believed that Wayne was going to die and, if he had, that they'd be planning* two *funerals—his and mine. My family and some of our closest friends were also worried about this. This may sound ridiculous to some people, but I have absolutely no desire to remain on this planet, not even for a single second, if Wayne isn't on it with me. In spite of everything, or maybe because of those very things, I am* still *crazy about my husband! As Ivan Koloff once told Wayne, "Valerie only has eyes for you, Star."*

Dusty Rhodes: *I believe that there are angels out there. They come on the scene at unbelievable times and take care. And at the bleakest moments, certain things happen for a reason. There was something else for Superstar Billy Graham out there. He hasn't reached his pinnacle yet.*

Even a man on death row knows when he's going to be executed. This came out of nowhere. Katie had been declared brain-dead several hours earlier, but the doctors kept her heart beating and blood pumping while they harvested the liver. Now it was waiting at the hospital—to become *my* liver.

There was something ethereal about the short ride over to the hospital. In other cars, people were driving to McDonald's or going shopping. I was either going to extend my life for years, or die when my body rejected the liver on the operating table.

I walked into the hospital like I was coming in for a checkup. But here's the strangest part of the day: as I was entering the building, former AWA champion Nick Bockwinkle's ex-wife was leaving. She'd just had a liver transplant herself.

The hospital staff had filled out the paperwork in advance. There was no time to waste; the liver would be viable only for a set number of hours. I signed my signature in a few places (I had already signed papers giving Valerie my power of attorney, just in case I wasn't capable of making medical decisions for myself), then started the preoperation procedure.

Joe Miluso: My sister called me and said, "Dad's going in for his liver transplant." So I told her, "You know what? I'm going to call him and wish him well." We spoke about ten minutes before he went into surgery. Then I talked to Valerie. She told me that he lit up.

World-renowned transplant surgeon Dr. David Mulligan and his team were ready for their mission. Everyone exuded total confidence. To relax me, some of the nurses pulled up my Web site on the computer, just before the anesthesia was administered. People were asking me wrestling questions and joking around. I noticed that the anesthesiologist was a body-builder.

"Man," I said, "you look incredible."

He smiled.

"Now," I instructed, "when you give me that stuff, please compare it to my body weight and height. I don't want too little, but I don't want to OD."

"You're a little hyper," he cracked. "You want some right now?"

"Yes," I said, my pulse racing. "I think I could use it."

Valerie told Dr. Mulligan that she wanted to say a prayer for her husband. Dr. Mulligan took her hand, and the entire transplant team formed a circle around my gurney, praying with her. Despite my surgeon's eminent qualifications, he still called on God to guide his hands. Dr. Mulligan later described himself as "just an instrument" of some larger plan.

"Who's the donor?" I asked.

"A twenty-six-year-old woman who died in a car crash."

"Twenty-six?" I repeated. From the beginning, I'd expected a living donor. Now I was struck by the reality that a young woman had paid the ultimate price in order for me to receive the gift of life.

Earlier in the day, Valerie had left a message for Vince, fulfilling a promise to keep him informed. As I was being wheeled toward the operating room, he called back.

"Well, Superstar," he said, in a strong and positive voice, "this is the main event. Hang in there. You'll make it through."

"Thank you, Vince," I replied, feeling a little bit woozy from the tranquilizer.

Valerie kissed me good-bye, telling me she loved me and would see me when I woke up. I told her just how much I loved her, then fell off to sleep.

I woke up with a tightness in my abdomen, which only made sense, since I'd been gutted and stapled back together. But I'd survived. I opened my eyes and shot my arms into the air. "Thank you, *Jesus!*" I shouted with an evangelist's cadence.

I had my life back.

Valerie Coleman: I'd been told that the surgery would last anywhere from four to six hours, maybe longer. And they said not to be frightened when I saw him after surgery because, for the first twenty-four hours, he'd be on a respirator and basically unconscious. Well, in just under three hours, Dr. Mulligan walked up to me in the waiting room and said that everything had gone flawlessly—beautifully, with no complications.

When they finally let me see Wayne in the intensive care unit, he was wide awake, without a respirator, telling nurses and everyone else who walked in that Jesus saved his life—in an incredibly strong voice I hadn't heard in a very long time. The nurses were going crazy because he refused to sleep.

I stayed up for thirty-six hours, savoring the sensation of life surging through my body. Arnold called. Jesse called. Vince called back. I'd lost seventy-five pounds of fluid. Valerie looked at my catheter and noticed that my urine was no longer the dark, rusted color of a man with a failing liver. It was a life-affirming pale yellow. And we both rejoiced.

Still, I couldn't shake the thought that another person had died to give me life. As I recovered from surgery, I read about Katie Gillroy in the

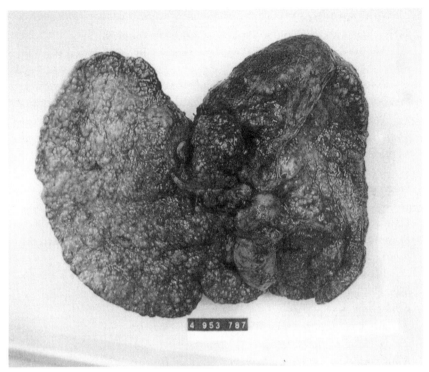

What my liver had become.

Arizona Republic. "Look at this," I said to Valerie. "She was twenty-six years old. She was killed in a car accident. This has to be our girl."

Valerie agreed.

There are rules about tracking down a donor family, but I didn't want to wait. Valerie and I were compelled to contact this woman's family and thank them.

> ***Rita Gillroy:*** *Katie died on a Friday. On, I think, Sunday morning, I was in the bathroom, getting dressed, and my husband, Dan, was in the kitchen. "Rita! Rita!" he yelled. "Come in here quick!" He was crying, and reading an article about a wrestler who received the liver of a twenty-six-year-old female who died in an auto accident. "That's got to be Katie's liver!"*
>
> *The writer, Pedro Gomez, also figured it out. He called my son, Jimmy, and told him that Wayne wanted to get together. But it was too soon. It was hard enough getting through the first month or two, and then the holidays came. I wasn't ready to discuss it. Even now, it's just so hard to talk about.*

After a while, I spoke to the woman at the donor network and asked, "How do we go about communicating with the recipient?"

She said, "You go through us. You write a letter, and we'll mail it to him."

It just so happened that Wayne had written a letter, too. And our letters both got to the donor network on the same day.

We spoke that night, and finally met in March 2003, five months after Katie died. I was never into wrestling, but when he pulled up and stepped out of the car, I said, "He looks like Hulk Hogan."

Of all the people to get her liver! The whole family was there, and we laughed and said, "Leave it to Katie!"

As soon as Wayne and Valerie walked in, there was hugging and kissing and crying all at the same time. I was worried that it was going to be tense, but it wasn't. It was a very comfortable feeling. It was an instant bond.

We have our grandson Jason, thank God, and we see Katie through him. But Wayne is like walking proof that she did something so nice for somebody.

After getting to know Wayne and Valerie, I tried to find out more about Katie's other recipients. A thirty-year-old lady who got one of Katie's kidneys, unfortunately, died three or four months later. The kidney was working fine. She just had too many other things wrong. I have a vase in my home from the other kidney recipient, a twenty-four-year-old Navajo girl. I never heard from the heart recipient.

I would really love to hear from her. She's the keeper of my daughter's heart. I don't know. Maybe she wants to put it behind her. All I want to do is talk to her, see if she's healthy, and wish her well.

Everybody's different.

During one of my checkups at the Mayo Clinic, another transplant recipient recognized me and introduced himself.

"Have you contacted the donor family yet?" I asked.

"No," he casually replied. "I haven't thought about it."

"Well, maybe you should," I stressed. "If it wasn't for that donor, you'd be dead."

I've repeatedly told the Gillroys how conflicted I feel about my new liver. I'd spent nearly sixty years on this earth, while Katie was just starting her run. I don't understand how God could have allowed her to die in a car accident. Why didn't he protect Katie Gillroy? Why did he watch out for me?

When I returned to church after the transplant, people came up to me and said, "God answered our prayers." I don't buy that for one second. It's very confusing. And I'll always feel guilty about it.

> *Rita Gillroy: I've told Wayne not to worry. When he gets to heaven, Katie's gonna kick his butt.*
>
> *The reason I'm able to joke like this is that Wayne and Valerie have been so honest about their feelings. I've seen Valerie break down and tell us, "I'm so happy for my husband, but I feel so bad for you."*
>
> *I was really touched by that. It put everybody's real feelings out in the open. It sort of made it better in a way.*
>
> *I would give anything to have Katie back, but I can't look at Wayne and say, "I wish she was here, and he wasn't." I can't do that.*

Valerie and I keep a photo of Katie on our mantel, her finger looped through her belt before her high school graduation as she smiles sweetly into the lens. With her long brown hair flowing down her shoulders, she kind of looks like Capella at the same age. For the rest of our lives, the picture of Katie will remain there, alongside photos of Joey and Capella and their children, as well as Valerie's family. I feel the presence of Katie inside me every day, and bless the Gillroys for both their daughter and their friendship.

CHAPTER TWENTY-TWO

"TOO SWEET TO BE SOUR"

The unexamined life is not worth living.

—Socrates

In 2002, following a court battle with the World Wildlife Fund over the company's initials, Vince McMahon was forced to change the name of his organization to World Wrestling Entertainment (WWE). Dr. Tom Prichard, an excellent worker in his day, was the developmental talent manager, and became my main liaison to WWE over the phone. Initially, I asked him to help arrange for a package of wrestling merchandise to be sent to Katie's son, Jason. But we were soon talking almost weekly.

> ***Dr. Tom Prichard:*** *This was an icon who wasn't sure about how he'd be accepted again. He wasn't sure about his own legacy with the boys. Sometimes I felt like he was calling me for reassurance. If he gets a positive feeling from me, everything's cool. Maybe the door would open a little bit more for him.*

With the Dudleys and Tommy Dreamer.

After I sent his donor's kid the package, he sent me a photo of his diseased liver, following his surgery. I thought that was, well, not really weird, but unique.

I saved the picture. Superstar Billy Graham sent it to me. How many people have a picture of Superstar Billy Graham's liver?

On August 24, 2003—Vince McMahon's fifty-eighth birthday—my long sojourn out of the Promised Land officially ended when I attended *SummerSlam* at the America West Arena in Phoenix. I wasn't sure if the boys would be cold to me—or if some of the younger ones even knew about the role I'd once played in the business. But as soon as I set foot in the dressing room, my fears were put to rest. Ric Flair, of course, was one of the first to embrace me. So did Sergeant Slaughter, now a road agent. Then, Eddie Guerrero, Bill Goldberg, Kurt Angle, Kevin Nash, and Triple H all filed over. I felt like Willie Mays being welcomed at the All-Star Game. I was back in the fold.

Bubba Ray Dudley: *I think Tommy Dreamer came up to me and said, "Guess who's here?" At first, I thought it was Terry Funk because Tommy knows what a big Terry Funk fan I am. He said, "No.*

Superstar Billy Graham." I was like a little kid all over again. I'm going to finally get to meet wrestling royalty.

The Superstar knew my name. He knew my Tag Team partners' names. He told us he liked watching us on TV. It was surreal. It was like having a concussion and being on my feet.

I could see that all three of the Dudleys—Bubba, D-Von, and Spike— were thrilled to meet me. And I was equally thrilled to meet them. They're fantastic, no-nonsense performers who take quality bumps. In 2003, they were among my favorites, along with Guerrero—who's so fluid and in control of his body that it sometimes seems like he's taking his time in the air—Chris Benoit, a kindred spirit from the bloody walls of Stu Hart's Dungeon, Triple H, Angle, Chris Jericho, Undertaker, Shawn Michaels, and— naturally—Flair, whose consistency and durability distinguish him from everyone else who's ever laced up their boots.

George Napolitano: *I wasn't sure if I'd ever see Superstar at a WWE show again. We hadn't spoken through the whole steroid scandal. He had to know that I knew what I knew. I had no number on him. I had nothing. But he called me out of the blue to tell me to meet him at SummerSlam. Just hearing the way his voice sounded on the phone, I said, "That's Superstar." It was like the seventies all over again. That was the guy I remembered.*

Linda McMahon was extremely warm, especially considering what I'd done to her husband and the company. With that beautiful North Carolina accent, she noted, "Well, Billy, you sure don't look like a man who's had a liver transplant." Her children, Stephanie and Shane, were equally as friendly, with Shane remembering how Vince used to sit him on a bench backstage in Boston Gardens while I gave the kid a bicep shot.

Suddenly a ripple swept through the dressing room area, like Paul Revere warning of a British invasion. Vince was on his way. I straightened my shoulders and waited for the man I hadn't seen since that day of infamy on *The Phil Donahue Show* in 1992. He swaggered into the back, locked eyes with me, and broke into a huge smile. I smiled back as he rushed forward, hugged me, and squeezed my cheeks.

"Look at that face," he said. "Look at that face."

We both had tears in our eyes.

Vince McMahon: *In 2004, we decided to induct Superstar Billy Graham into the WWE Hall of Fame. It's wound up that we're caretakers* *of the entire business now, and it's our responsibility to acknowledge everyone who has made an enormous contribution. Billy had enemies in the business, and a lot of people would say, "Vince, you shouldn't be doing this. It's wrong." I don't look at it that way. I look at it in terms of what somebody like Billy Graham meant to the audience more than what his dealings were with me.*

I first found out about the ceremony from Jesse Ventura, who called me and asked, "Superstar, are you going to be in the Hall of Fame?"

"What are you talking about, Hall of Fame?"

"Vince is having a Hall of Fame at *WrestleMania.* You mean, he hasn't asked you?" Jesse was stirring stuff up, as usual. "Hey, man, I'm not going unless they invite you."

I have to admit that Jesse made me feel a little insecure. Why *would* he be inducted before me, especially when I inspired his career? But sure enough, Vince called a short time later to invite me. Jesse and I would share the stage with Greg "The Hammer" Valentine, Tito Santana, Harley Race, Slaughter, Don Muraco, and Bobby "The Brain" Heenan. Big John Studd and the Junkyard Dog were going to be honored posthumously.

To garner some media attention, Vince was also inducting Pete Rose, baseball's all-time hit leader, restricted from his own Hall of Fame because of an alleged gambling offense. Some people complained that Rose's inclusion tarnished the event. But, let's not forget, this is wrestling.

"This is going to be fantastic," I told Vince. The circle had truly been completed.

But once I arrived in New York for the Hall of Fame ceremony, there were complications. The night before the event, as I attempted to move a heavy chair in our room at the Hilton, I felt the area behind my belly button swell up. Since my hernias, the region had been so weak that my intestines were pressing against the abdominal wall. Now, because of the strain I'd placed on the area, my intestines were trying to escape from my body, pushing my belly button out an extra two inches and becoming painfully trapped in the hole. I looked like an alien.

My liver doctor, David Mulligan, had prepared me for this type of crisis. I already knew the name of a hospital that specialized in liver emergencies, and the name of a surgeon who'd studied with Mulligan. Valerie picked up the phone and called Tom Prichard for help.

Dr. Tom Prichard: *I went up to Billy's room, and the door was slightly ajar. He was throwing up in a garbage can. He showed me* *his puffed-out belly button, and I arranged for a limo to take him to the hospital. This was a guy who'd cheated death already. How tragic would it be if something happened to him while he was in New York? He wasn't saying much when I walked him out to the car. Just, "Oh, brother. I've got to get this fixed. I can't miss tomorrow. I can't miss this deal for anything."*

I didn't want any kind of surgery. That would have kept me in the hospital through the Hall of Fame ceremony and *WrestleMania XX* the next night. At the hospital, the doctor administered muscle relaxers through an IV, then gently, with his fingers, kneaded the rise of the intestines, pushing them slowly into place.

About thirty minutes later, as I lay recuperating on the surgeon's table, the intestines popped out a second time. I screamed in agony, while the doctor manipulated them back again.

"It doesn't look like you're going to the Hall of Fame," he said.

My heart dropped. "Please, just call Dr. Mulligan," I pleaded.

The surgeon respected my wish. And Dr. Mulligan told him, "You get him to the Hall of Fame, no matter what."

So the surgeon gave me some muscle relaxers and wrapped a binder around my midsection. He told me that he wasn't as concerned about the Hall of Fame as he was about my five-hour flight home to Phoenix. If my intestines dislodged in the air, there would be no way to save me.

Vince's limo driver was waiting when I exited the hospital; he'd been circling the block for eight hours. We returned to the hotel, ate dinner, and tried to remain calm. When I woke up the next morning, my guts were still inside me.

Triple H was chosen to induct me. I was honored. There were parallels between both of our careers: he's renowned for his physique, and knows how to talk. And he's Vince's son-in-law—the husband of Stephanie McMahon. I couldn't help but feel that his selection was a message from the entire McMahon family.

Triple H: That's true. For Vince to have his son-in-law do the induction was the same as saying, "I'm giving you this award myself." Superstar Billy Graham had been trying to make amends for a long time. I knew how strongly Vince felt about this induction. I was going to display the same passion.

"Sometimes, in our quest for stardom in this business, a lot of controversy can be created," a tuxedo-clad Triple H began his speech, in front of a

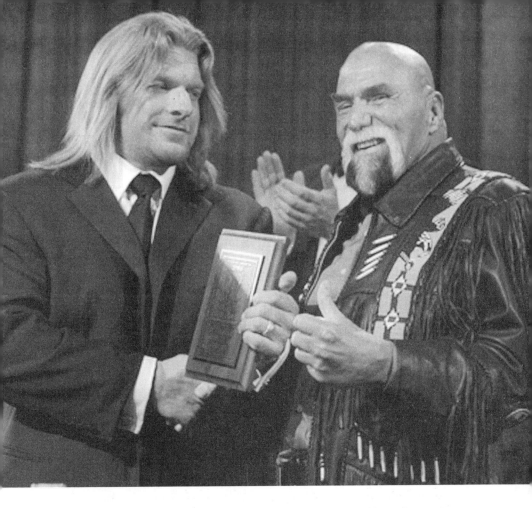

ballroom filled with wrestlers, friends, and fans. "Sometimes, that controversy and stardom go hand in hand. Sometimes, one can overshadow the
other. But if controversy indicates stardom, then our first inductee might be
the biggest star of them all."

> **Triple H:** *I wanted to include some of the rap that Superstar used in
> my speech. I put all of his rhymes down on paper. Then I thought,
> "What if Billy wants to use those same rhymes when he accepts the
> award? That's not a really good way to put him over." I had to go up
> to him the day of the Hall of Fame and ask, "Is it cool if I do your
> stuff?" And he told me, "I'd love for you to do my stuff." So I went
> full-tilt with it.*

    "If you indulge me"—Triple H turned to me on the podium and
smirked—"I've always wanted to do this."
    Then he launched into a vintage Billy Graham promo: "He eats T-bone
steaks. He lifts barbell plates. He's sweeter than a German chocolate cake.

He's the reflection of perfection. The number one selection. The women's pet, the men's regret. What you see is what you get. And what you don't see is better yet. He's the man of the hour, the man with the power. He's too sweet to be sour. And believe me, baby, he is bad to the bone. He is Superstar Billy Graham!"

I rose from my seat on the multitiered dais, absorbing the New York ovation I'd missed for so many years.

"This is a night of celebration," I told the crowd. "Fifteen months ago, the Grim Reaper was knocking heavily on my door." But on October 18, 2002, I added, my life was saved by Katie Gillroy. "There needs to be an asterisk at the bottom of my name in the Hall of Fame," I said, "because without her, I would have been long gone. So I love you, Katie."

As the attendees cheered, I accentuated my point even more: "I love her."

Vince and I had privately worked out our differences. But our clash had been a public one with public ramifications. Now it was time for a public display of my true sentiments.

"Some years ago," I revealed, "I sent Vince a letter and apologized and asked for forgiveness for some of the things I'd done. And I was trying to clean up my life. . . . With all my drug problems and all my problems of envy, jealousy, and bitterness, I put them all behind me and finally became a man, and asked that man, Vince McMahon, to accept my apology and forgive me of my transgressions. And Vince McMahon, with nothing to gain . . . accepted my apology, and accepted me back into the family of WWE."

Jerry McDevitt: *I stood up in the balcony and applauded with everybody else. It was great to see that time, distance, and reflection had done all it was supposed to do. The charisma still came through. I couldn't help but like Billy Graham.*

I continued my speech, looking into the audience and across the dais— at Flair, who'd inducted Harley, and Pat, who'd inducted Slaughter. "I'm so honored," I pronounced, "to be with these great men of wrestling . . . these classy men." My eyes shifted to the crowd again. "I love you."

I saw Valerie, standing next to Harley's wife, cheering wildly—and Jesse, the former governor of Minnesota whose loyalty to his mentor never vacillated, despite the vast divide between our political and religious views. For all the trials, so much of my life had been worthwhile. And the adulation that I felt reaffirmed my commitment to writing this book—and telling my story of struggle, disappointment, perseverance, and redemption.

Diamond Dallas Page: In February 2005, I got together with Super-star and Dusty in Tucson and just sat there, listening to them go back and forth about their bullrope matches and Bob Dylan. As a kid, you dream about just meeting these guys, never mind hanging out with them. People say it's amazing that Superstar's even alive. But not me. He's immortal!

Where do all the years go? Sometimes it seems like the world's changed around me, yet so many simple images and words are encoded in my memory forever.

I flash back to all those crackerbox buildings where I used to wrestle: the Long Beach Auditorium, Sacramento City Center, and that ice rink in Coney Island where, in the middle of winter, I once caught a group of fans leaping up and down on my vehicle with both feet. Now the boys park underground, the arenas are sleek and modern, and the people rush forward with their camera phones instead of switchblades and swinging knuckles.

I watch Batista and remember Dave Draper, who was also soft-spoken in private, but looked like he could punch an F-16 out of the air.

I've been backstage many times since *WrestleMania XX,* and can't believe that some of the younger wrestlers complain about the quality of the food in catering. The first time that I heard that, I made it a point to really look at the buffet provided for the boys before TV broadcasts, and saw an enormous selection of fresh fruit—already sliced and peeled—various assortments of cheese, meat, pasta, and chicken, bread and rolls, ice cream, cookies, an abundance of iced-down bottled water, and energy drinks. In 1977, when I was champion, Gorilla Monsoon was our caterer for tapings at the old Philadelphia Arena, hauling in a few dozen doughnuts that he'd purchased near his town in New Jersey. If you wanted real food, you'd pay some fan—like Paul Heyman when he was a kid—to run out for a hamburger. When we were thirsty, we stuck our mouths up to the shower nozzle. This was sometimes impossible on the road, particularly in the summer, when we'd find ourselves wrestling in high school gyms that had shut off the water for the season.

There is a lesson for the newer talent to learn here: you better count your blessings, guys. In late 2004 I had hernia surgery, and have since returned to the gym, where I'm trying to bring my body up to the potential of my age. Still, when I hug one of the boys and note his wideness and muscle density, I battle feelings of inferiority. Everyone knows that I've had a liver transplant and can't look anything like the Superstar Billy Graham of the 1970s, but I visualize myself differently. After nearly dying, I understand that old age is a gift; being wrinkled is better than being dead. Nonetheless, will I ever get back to being acceptable in my own eyes?

While I used to look at my life in terms of squandered probabilities, I now see boundless opportunities. Valerie and I are very active politically. Maybe I'll write books on different subjects. I'm going to paint more. Because of bodybuilding, wrestling, and other factors, I never reached my full potential as an artist. But I don't think a person ever does. First and foremost, I want to give back to the donor network, encouraging people to sign their donor cards. That's my calling today.

Or at least one of them . . .

While I was working on this book, Valerie and I went out to a restaurant with my co-author Keith, Capella, and a group of her friends. As we sat around the table, I realized that it was the first time that I'd done something like this with her when I wasn't drugged, or didn't have to run off to the arena. It was very sobering to think about how many of these small activities I'd missed in my children's lives.

Up until recently, Valerie held out hope that one day we'd have our own children. But in January 2005, a checkup revealed a mass in her left ovary. The doctors suspected it was cancerous and removed her entire reproductive system. Thankfully, she was free of the disease that had already claimed her left breast. Although we were both exhilarated by the news, Valerie is still struggling with the harsh reality that she will never know what it is to be pregnant and give birth. She's sometimes said that she'd rather have had a baby at twenty and died at forty than live a long life without ever knowing the experience of carrying a child and giving birth. She feels a tremendous sense of loss and mourns for our children who will never be born. At the same time, she's incredibly happy about the positive changes in our lives, and for the first time in many years, she's actually looking forward to each new day.

Valerie Coleman: When Wayne was ill, he was too weak to even carry on a conversation. There was no talking, no laughter, nothing. He would sometimes sleep twenty hours a day without the aid of sleeping pills. Since it's always been just the two of us, I was more alone than ever. We were existing, but we weren't living. And it had been that way for years.

As soon as I walked into Wayne's room in the ICU, I knew that I had my husband back. There he was, just out of surgery with his beautiful new liver, talking a mile a minute, laughing, crying, and rejoicing, all at the same time. He kept saying, "We have our liver, we have our liver. I love you so much, Val."

My walk with God continues, most of the time down a rocky path. Who will ever understand the mind of God? Not me. Despite my redemption, I rarely pray. When I do, I think the prayer instead of speaking it. There are times when I feel disconnected from my creator. Sometimes it's as if my soul has turned into steel. You will never hear me preach a sermon; I'll let people work out their own salvation with fear and trembling. Yet, through it all, I know that God is near. I press on, not looking back but looking forward, determined to finish the race that is set before me.

Even in my weakest, most abandoned state while living on Van Buren Street, I still had willpower. I just didn't tap into it. God's grace is always near, but sometimes you simply must help yourself. I am healthier now than I have been in a decade, no longer bound by the enslavement of drug addiction or haunted by demonic thoughts of suicide. My system is pure, and I am sharper of mind and wit. I have been restored. Redemption is mine. My new liver has invigorated me. I feel like I have a whole new lifetime to live.

Not long ago, I was talking with Triple H about my many troubles and setbacks I have suffered. "Yeah, you had a hell of a ride," he countered, "but look where you landed."

I see his point. I have indeed landed on solid ground.

My story shows the power of the human spirit to triumph and rise like the Phoenix bird, out of the ashes and above the obstacles of life. The towering peaks and the hellish troughs of my life are proof that "whatever a man sows, he will also reap." In fact, the story of Wayne Coleman, and the story of Superstar Billy Graham, are each testaments to the mysteries of life.

ACKNOWLEDGMENTS

This is a crucial part of my book because it's where I get to say very special thanks to everyone who was involved in making this idea a reality. To thank everyone who has given me encouragement and support throughout my life would take a volume of pages far exceeding these.

My co-author, Keith Elliot Greenberg, could have easily been cast as Jesus in Mel Gibson's movie *The Passion of the Christ*. With his long hair, beard, and countenance, he looks as if he has walked out of Nazareth from the not-too-distant past. In reality, he may have walked out of the famed hippie community of Greenwich Village. My kind of guy. When speaking with Vince about finishing my autobiography, he said, "I am going to assign Keith Greenberg to help you wrap up your book. Keith is a third-generation wrestling fan and was raised on Bruno Sammartino." Vince ended by saying, "He's one of the finest writers the WWE has ever had."

There was an instant bond for Valerie and me with Keith. We opened up our home to him, and he became like a member of the family. His enthusiasm and commitment were inspiring. We watched untold hours of wrestling videotapes and he wanted to know every story behind every photo I have. Keith Greenberg was a man on a mission, and my co-author more than succeeded. We had many laughs together over Benny Hinn's healing crusades, and tears were shed over the onslaught of life-and-death health issues. Through it all he was able to weave the many emotions of my journey on this earth into an impressive narrative. Valerie and I thank him.

There would never have been a *Tangled Ropes* without Vince McMahon. Words cannot do justice to the gratitude I have toward this man and the entire McMahon family. My liver transplant has given me a new life, and because of Vince's generosity, endless opportunities now await me in the WWE. Much has been given me by this man, and much I will give back. Thank you, sir.

On the *Tom Synder Show* (right) with Vince.

My dear friend Dr. Geoffrey Hull of the University of West Sydney has been endowed with many gifts. An amazing imagination and creativeness are among them. He is a true artist. Geoff offered his professional advice about writing my story and encouraged me to persist despite illness, despondency, dependency, and hard times. Enough can't be said.

Jack Carey, a friend in the truest sense of the word, is a former very important member of my church and was the chairman of the board of our fifteen-thousand-member congregation. A *real* Godly man who believed in me and my book from the very beginning. He read many of my early chapters as I wrote them, and gave me nothing but positive feedback. He urged me to press on and complete the manuscript. His financial and spiritual support never waivered, things which I can never say thank you enough for.

My longtime friend Dave Meltzer, of the *Wrestling Observer Newsletter,* has always been a source of uncanny insight and analysis in this unique business of professional sports entertainment. Dave was the first wrestling historian to bring to my attention that I have the highest percentage of sellouts in the history of Madison Square Garden, 19 out of 20. No one else has even come close. Thanks.

Special thanks to Randy Bodell for loaning me at least 100 pristine wrestling magazines and programs from the 70's for research; Eric of the Hollywood Book and Poster shop for finding early 1970's programs from the L.A. territory; James Melby for the issue of *San Francisco Wrestling Facts* that gave me exact dates and other info during my stint in the San Francisco territory in 1971; and Ronald Witmer, for researching an unbelievable amount of dates, locations, and results from my career. I must mention and give thanks to photographers George Napolitano and Bill Apter for the thousands of photos chronicling my career and all of the fun we had taking those shots.

Thanks to Dean Miller of WWE for his insight—and a very special thanks, too. Of course a big thank you to all the folks who took the time and effort to give quotes for me. You guys really made this book special.

Thank you to the incredibly gifted artist Jerry "The King" Lawler for his creepy illustration capturing my encounter with "thousands of snakes." And a special thanks to the legendary Jim Ross for his intellect and ability to peer into and interpret the sometimes bizarre world of this industry. But more importantly to me, a role model on how to overcome adversity with dignity. J.R., it was an honor for me having you write the foreword to my book.

And last but far from least, my co-author has said that Valerie is an editor unto herself. She has combed through every word of this book, doing spell-checks and correcting my typos along the way. It wasn't her job, it's just the way she is. She invested many hours trying to make stories and thought of many descriptions to events and, along with me, examined every photo for its merits before sending it along. Valerie created checklists of names that had to be included, and critiqued my writing constantly. And it goes without saying she suffered through all of my delays while trying to finish this project. From the very beginning we wanted to take the high road and still have a thought-provoking and entertaining book. Together, as always, we did it.

—Superstar Billy Graham

The Cadillac turning into my hotel parking lot had probably seen better days, but it was classic nonetheless. I live in New York and travel mostly by subway—oblivious to American car culture—but there was something about this vehicle that pulled my eye to it. Even before I recognized Wayne Coleman's two-toned goatee through the windshield, I knew that the Cadillac had to belong to Superstar Billy Graham.

Once I remember going to Convention Hall in Miami Beach during a visit to my grandparents, to see Superstar defend his WWWF title against Dusty Rhodes—a pretty novel event, since Miami Beach was in the heart of NWA country. When Graham left the dressing room, everybody stood, and it took me a while to find an opening between the animated bodies and grab an unobstructed view of the champ. But when I finally caught that glimpse of the cherished championship belt around the bronzed, rippled abdomen of the Superstar, my heart raced.

I thought about my friends up in New York, and how they were missing what announcer Vince McMahon would have termed "a most auspicious occasion." I couldn't imagine being anywhere else in the world that night but there, watching the self-professed Reflection of Perfection.

Now, so many years later, I was about to begin writing Superstar Billy Graham's autobiography. In the hotel parking lot, the Cadillac came to a stop, and Wayne popped out of the passenger seat, smiling, and embraced me. His wife, Valerie, came around from the driver's side and hugged me, as well.

The tone never changed from that day forward. Through the interviewing, writing, and rewriting process, Wayne and Valerie treated me like a best friend. We worked on the book, ate Mexican food, and watched movies together. When either battled a health crisis—unfortunately, a few came up over the course of this project—I spent my hours preoccupied with the challenge of the moment, relaxing only when I heard Wayne or Valerie on the other end of the phone, reassuring me that everything was better.

Needless to say, I want to thank both of them for making this such a pleasant experience, trusting me with a story that, as we all know by now, was often quite painful.

The beginning of this project coincided with the birth of my daughter, Summer Berton Esther Greenberg, on July 15, 2004. As she developed a personality and awareness of her surroundings, the story of Superstar Billy Graham also came to life. And through it all, my wife, Jennifer, and son, Dylan—whose hand-drawn jacket designs hang in my home office be-side copies of Wayne's own paintings—encouraged me to give the Super-star not just a readable autobiography, but the book a man of his depth, versatility, and history merits.

Obviously, I'm grateful to everyone who allowed their anecdotes to be included in this autobiography. Nonetheless, a number of individuals war-rant special mention.

Former WWE publisher Barry Werner and Pocket Books's Margaret Clark—who edited all three of the WWE autobiographies I co-authored—were the core of my professional support network. I also want to thank Stacey Pascarella, Dr. Aaron Feigenbaum—whose autobiography with Shawn Michaels will probably precede this one to the best-seller list—Brian "King" Solomon, Cage Nakayama, "Big" Bill Anderson, Anthony Cali, Bill Apter, "The Golden Greek" George Germanakos, Dr. Mike Lano, Glen Jones, Karin Cravotta, Jessica Dymczyk, and David Kumin.

Ronald Witmer deserves a paragraph all to himself. It's because of his meticulous record-keeping of the Superstar's career that both Wayne and myself were able to figure out exactly when certain events occurred.

As with all my wrestling autobiographies, Dave Meltzer's *Wrestling Observer Newsletter* was an important resource.

Also, a few folks I didn't get a chance to thank the last time around: Elliot Olshansky, Chuck Mazzone, Jerry Carita, Frank Mentesana, Nick Kostos, Lois Allen, Emily Johnson, Phil Speer, and Dick Bourne and David Chappell from *Mid-Atlantic Gateway.*

—Keith Elliot Greenberg